The Innocence Commission

The Innocence Commission

Preventing Wrongful Convictions and Restoring the Criminal Justice System

Jon B. Gould

NEW YORK UNIVERSITY PRESS
New York and London

NEW YORK UNIVERSITY PRESS
New York and London
www.nyupress.org

Library of Congress Cataloging-in-Publication Data
Gould, Jon B.
The Innocence Commission : preventing wrongful convictions and
restoring the criminal justice system / Jon B. Gould.
p.   cm.
Includes bibliographical references and index.
ISBN-13: 978-0-8147-3179-6 (cloth : acid-free paper)
ISBN-10: 0-8147-3179-1 (cloth : acid-free paper)
1. Judicial error—Virginia. 2. Judicial error—Virginia—Cases.
3. Innocence Commission for Virginia. 4. Criminal justice,
Administration of—Virginia.   I. Title.
KFV2987.G68 2007
347.755'012—dc22   2007023846

New York University Press books are printed on acid-free paper,
and their binding materials are chosen for strength and durability.

Manufactured in the United States of America
10 9 8 7 6 5 4 3 2 1

For Ann, my better angel. And to the memory of my father, whose commitment to civil liberty has had a lifelong influence.

Contents

Acknowledgments

To say that this book owes to a team of collaborators hardly does justice to the process that spawned its subject. Without the Innocence Commission for Virginia (ICVA), there would have been no book, and without a dedicated steering committee, advisory board, and strong team of pro bono lawyers, the ICVA would not have succeeded. My thanks goes, first, to the cofounders of the ICVA: Don Salzman, Ginny Sloan, Julia Sullivan, and Misty Thomas. I cannot say enough good things about the four. Not only are they incredibly talented and dedicated, but they are delightful to work with as well. Each is especially patient and good-humored, having put up with me as chair of the ICVA. Misty's replacement, Shawn Armbrust, has been a terrific addition, bringing energy, clear thinking, and a wonderfully wry sense of humor that helps brighten what otherwise might be a somber subject.

The ICVA's advisory board members—Joan Anderson, Steve Benjamin, Rodney Leffler, William Sessions, Frank Stokes, John Tucker, and John Whitehead—provided invaluable guidance, direction, and support as the ICVA pursued the investigations and published the report. They deserve special thanks for agreeing to associate with a fledging organization at a time when all we could show them was a blueprint for action. I only hope that the ICVA's work, some of it described here, justifies their support.

Most important, the ICVA's work could not have been done without the tremendous contribution of attorneys from eleven terrific law firms, who helped conduct the case investigations, completed legal research projects, and prepared recommendations for the ICVA's report. Some of these lawyers have since switched positions, but the firms deserve great credit for putting their money where their mouths are in supporting pro bono work. They make law a respectable profession and give lawyers a deservedly good name. Thanks go to the following law firms:

Alston & Bird
Arnold & Porter
Collier, Shannon Scott
Covington & Burling
DLA, Piper, Rudnick, Gray & Cary
Hogan & Hartson
King & Spalding
Morrison & Foerster
Skadden, Arps, Slate, Meagher & Flom
Steptoe & Johnson
Troutman Sanders

I first became interested in the subject of wrongful convictions while teaching an undergraduate honors clinical course on the death penalty in the fall of 2001. Little did those students know that their class would later help lead to the ICVA and this book, and for their interest and enthusiasm I am grateful. I also appreciate the influence of the many lawyers, justice officials, and scholars who have broadened my understanding of the criminal justice system and the process of reform. Among this group are Mark Agrast, Christopher Amolsch, Bill Dressel, Betsy Edwards, Keith Findley, Steve Hanlon, Robert Humphreys, Richard Leo, Michael Lieberman, Peter Loge, Barry Mahoney, Edwin Meese III, Christine Mumma, Janet Reno, Laurie Robinson, Frank Salvato, Dan Simon, Tom Sullivan, Rob Warden, and the anonymous reviewers for New York University Press. Similarly, I have had the good fortune to interact with several excellent journalists, who, perhaps without knowing it, have shown me how the subject of criminal justice reform can best reach an audience. For these lessons—and their able and pointed questions that keep me on my toes—I thank Margaret Edds, Frank Green, Laurence Hammack, Tom Jackman, Tim McGlone, and Candace Rondeaux.

The ICVA was supported by three organizations: the Innocence Project of the National Capitol Region (now the Mid-Atlantic Innocence Project), the Constitution Project, and George Mason University's Administration of Justice Program. I am grateful to each organization, although most so to George Mason University, where I am a faculty member. My colleagues at GMU have been supportive along the way, from my initial idea of the honors clinical course to the many hours I have devoted to the ICVA. Steve Mastrofski, chair of the Department of

Administration of Justice, deserves special thanks for his constant encouragement and pride throughout this project. I also am grateful to Jim Eaglin and the staff at the Federal Judicial Center, who allowed me time to complete the book while serving for a year as a Supreme Court Fellow.

Although this book is based to a large extent on the ICVA's work, it is not a duplicate of its report. When I quote from the ICVA's report, I generally include a citation, especially in chapter 3, where some of the case summaries quote research reports conducted by the ICVA's pro bono attorneys. The portions of chapters 3 and 4 that closely track sections of the ICVA's report are not cited, largely because I was one of the three authors and the final editor of the ICVA report. That said, I would be remiss if I did not credit and offer special thanks to Don Salzman and Julia Sullivan, who were coauthors of the ICVA's report and who have graciously allowed me to use their contributions to the ICVA report as the starting point for this book.

The reader may note that like the ICVA's report, this book does not identify any victims affected by the crimes chronicled here. This is done to protect their and their families' privacy, as they most certainly did not deserve these tragedies.

In a few places, this book uses material that I published earlier in different outlets. A short excerpt on Virginia's history, which appears in chapter 1, was included in a 2002 report I wrote for the Century Foundation.[1] Chapter 2 cites a passage I published earlier in the *Journal of Legal Education*,[2] and chapters 1 and 5 are based on an article I published in *Judicature*.[3] I am appreciative to these sources for allowing me to use my earlier work. Needless to say, any mistakes or omissions in the book are mine.

I have had considerable help in moving the manuscript from proposal to publication. My primary thanks goes to Ilene Kalish, my editor at NYU Press, who has been a joy to work with on this project. She is a testament to the power of an effective editor. I remember first meeting her at a professional gathering and casually talking to her about a possible book project. A couple of years later this book is being published, in large part because Ilene saw promise in the subject. That journey was greatly aided by Ilene's capable assistant, Salwa Jabado, who has kept the book moving even while Ilene and I were distracted by other responsibilities at times. I also wish to thank Despina Papazoglou Gimbel and Margaret Barrows Yamashita for excellent copy editing.

It is customary in most books to save family and friends for the end of the acknowledgments, when in fact we all know they should go at the start. No matter what help and support our professional colleagues and friends offer, book projects are virtually impossible without cheerleaders at home who believe in the project (and the author) and help see the project through. In my case I've been blessed by a wife, Ann, who not only trusts in me but also is a lawyer herself and was able to toss around ideas for the book as I was writing it. She did all of this while enduring painful medical treatments, and there is no greater testament to her love and support than this book's publication. I know of no one more committed to justice and equal treatment than Ann, and in many ways this book and my work with the ICVA are dedicated to her vision and example. I thank my lucky stars every day that I have Ann in my corner.

Our children, too, Michael and Emily, helped in the book's writing, although at nine and six, respectively, they may not recognize their influence. At many a dinner both kids would ask me about the ICVA and, later, about this book project. Having to explain to children what one does is often an eye-opener in justifying one's professional life. As I listened to their questions, and my answers, around the dinner table, I began to see how the book should be structured and what its ultimate message should be. In time, I hope both children will come to appreciate the issues raised here, although as even Emily can report now, laws should be fair.

It is difficult to single out particular friends for thanks, since so many have expressed interest in the project and offered regular support. Nonetheless, three warrant a special mention. Seth Tucker, my longtime friend and now counsel to the ICVA, continues to provide superb advice and good humor. His regular calls buoyed me while writing this book. Sharon Goodie and Peter Mandaville actually watched the book being written, although in their defense, they also were completing their own projects at the time. Among the three of us, we have sampled many coffee houses in the Washington, D.C., area. For their moral support and (more than) occasional break from writing, I am thankful.

My father became ill and died as this book was being finished. Anyone who has lost a parent knows how such a loss can shake one's foundation, and in my case all the more, since my dad was a lawyer himself and a strong defender of civil liberties. That our family has rallied around one another, from my mother to my brothers, sisters-in-law, and in-laws, is a fitting testament to Dad. He was interested in the topic of this book and looked forward to its release. As delighted I am that the project is completed, the book's publication is, nonetheless, bittersweet.

Finally, we cannot forget the very people affected by wrongful convictions—those erroneously convicted as well as the victims of crime who otherwise might have been spared. They warrant more than our sympathy; their plight demands action. To those justice officials who have taken the lead in understanding and preventing wrongful convictions, we all owe a debt of thanks. They are the true heroes of the American justice system.

Introduction

In December 2005, the ABC television network issued a press release announcing a new project to "to overturn wrongful convictions, liberate the falsely accused and discover the identity of those really to blame."[1] Rather than heralding an advocacy organization, however, ABC's release concerned a new television series it would air, called *In Justice*. According to Stephen McPherson, president of ABC entertainment, the show represented

> a completely new take on the procedural drama. Focusing on cases of justice run amok—sloppy police work, false testimony and biased juries—the show would feature the fictitious National Justice Project, a high-profile, non-profit organization made up of hungry young associates who approach their work like a puzzle, a puzzle that's been put together wrong."[2]

In Justice lasted for only thirteen episodes, earning such pans as "cutesy," "drab," and "not-so-amazing" from television critics.[3] Yet the show's airing marked an important milestone, for its creation reflected a growing recognition in popular culture that the criminal justice system was capable of serious errors. Gone was the presumption found in other shows that police officers, prosecutors, and judges wear white hats. ABC's new offering not only showed a criminal justice system that could imprison the innocent, but it also trumpeted the effort of advocates working against the odds to free convicted defendants.

How did American society reach the point that a writer would feel confident pitching a series like *In Justice* to a television executive and that one of the nation's major networks would crow about "modern-day heroes" who represent the convicted?[4] To be sure, no reasonable person doubts that the American criminal justice system is more accurate than not, but American society seems to have moved past the "get tough" period of the 1980s, in which public support for punitive policies ran high and trust in the justice process was vast, to reach the present point at which people are at least receptive to evidence of error.

Social scientists have identified several sources for the shift in public opinion. By the 1990s, the rising crime wave of the 1960s and early 1970s had dropped substantially; conservative politicians, who rode the public's fear of disorder to victory in the 1980s and 1990s, had reached ascendance by 2000 and had no higher political hill to climb; and sentencing policy had become so strict that it was difficult to consider even more severe policies. Yet as important as these sources might be, there is no question that the arrival of DNA testing and the commensurate jump in factually indisputable exonerations engineered a stunning drop in public confidence about the criminal justice system. Over the span of a few years at the turn of the new century, more than one hundred innocent individuals were identified and freed from the nation's prisons, many because of the advent of DNA testing that conclusively excluded them as suspects.

Much of the credit for these exonerations goes to teams of reporters, professors, students, and pro bono attorneys who were willing to listen to the claims of innocence from imprisoned defendants and who dedicated hundreds of hours of uncompensated time to proving these men innocent. Journalism professor David Protess and his students at Northwestern University were some of the first advocates to successfully free innocent defendants. They were soon followed by Barry Scheck, Peter Neufeld, and their colleagues at the now-famous Innocence Project in New York, who effectively set the standard for postconviction representation. Indeed, ABC's fictional National Justice Project undoubtedly had as its model the Innocence Project or Northwestern University's Center on Wrongful Convictions.

These groups have been frighteningly successful in their investigations, frightening only in the number of innocent defendants found to be sentenced to prison or worse. As of 2005, there were more than 340 known exonerations nationwide.[5] Over a twenty-year span in Illinois, more capital convicts were released from death row because of questions about their guilt than were actually executed.[6] This disquieting finding, along with shocking details of police deception reported by the *Chicago Tribune*,[7] convinced former Illinois governor George Ryan to impose a moratorium on executions in 2000. Three years later, Ryan "emptied Illinois' death row" by pardoning four defendants and commuting the sentences of 167 others to life in prison.[8]

Governor Ryan's decision necessarily raises the question of what it means for a convicted defendant to be considered innocent. Joshua Marquis, a district attorney from Oregon and a frequent spokesman for the National District Attorneys' Association, has decried the improper usage of "innocence" when describing defendants who have been released from prison on what some might consider a "legal technicality." Says Marquis, "To call a man with blood on his hands innocent stains not only the truth, but calls into question the actual innocence of the fewer number who are truly exonerated."[9]

Marquis's is not an inconsequential point, but the vast majority of defendants freed by the Innocence Project, the Center on Wrongful Conviction, and other affiliated groups have won their release upon a showing of *factual innocence,* meaning that someone else committed the crime. Instead, what Marquis refers to here is a system of constitutional jurisprudence that penalizes the state for violating a defendant's fundamental rights by overturning the ensuing conviction and ordering a new trial or excluding particular evidence from subsequent proceedings. In these cases of *legal innocence,* the defendant is released, regardless of who committed the crime. A finding of legal innocence does not necessarily mean that a "guilty man will walk," for prosecutors may retry the suspect as long as they avoid evidence tainted by unconstitutional procedures. Still, Marquis is correct that legal innocence is not synonymous with blamelessness. Whereas the former seeks a criminal justice process that protects constitutional rights, the latter aims to acquit or exonerate those who did not commit the crime.

In several cases, factual innocence and legal innocence coincide, when, for example, the constitutional violations that produce legal innocence also lead to the conviction of a factually innocent person. A good example is the case of Earl Washington Jr. in Virginia. By now, many people are familiar with the plight of Washington, an African American man with an IQ of 69 who came within nine days of execution before he finally received capable, pro bono counsel who helped clear him and eventually win his freedom.[10] Washington was convicted of rape and murder based largely on a "confession" that he gave to police more than a year after the crime. However, it was not until much later that the true nature of that interrogation emerged. Washington had been heavily coached by law enforcement officers, who, a civil jury concluded, had "deliberately fabricated" the evidence against Washington and ignored other inconsistencies between his coached confession and the facts of the crime.[11] Nonetheless, it took seventeen years from Washington's original conviction before he was finally released from prison. In 2006, Washington won the largest civil rights judgment in Virginia history for the state's mishandling of his case.[12]

Washington's case and those like it became a cause célèbre at the turn of the new century, in part because several involved the death penalty and also because DNA technology left little doubt about the factual innocence of many defendants eventually released from prison. That these exonerations would contradict the portrayal of a fair, accurate, and equal justice system and that the contrast would come on the heels of a conservative period in American politics and criminal justice only led to more media reports of systemic errors that could convict innocent individuals.

In addition, the exonerated had powerful advocates in the pro bono attorneys, investigators, and professors and students who worked on their cases. The creation of organizations like the Innocence Project and the Center on Wrongful Convictions reflect the rise of a national network of advocates who not only are tied together as a cohesive community but also act collectively. Together, they have fought wrongful convictions in court, advanced the subject of wrongful convictions in media reports, and sought to remedy the sources and address the consequences of wrongful convictions in the political arena.

What may have started as a limited legal question—whether a particular defendant was correctly convicted—has evolved into a larger political and policy debate. The uncovering of DNA exonerations and the public's increasing awareness of flaws in the criminal justice system have placed a number of questions on the national agenda. How prevalent are these errors? What reforms, if any, are necessary? Is the death penalty acceptable under these circumstances? These are only a smattering of the issues now raised by the revelation of wrongful convictions. At present, it is unclear how those questions will eventually play out. Indeed, it is possible that in time, wrongful convictions will fade from public view, the issue and potential reforms swept from the national agenda as pretrial DNA testing reduces the number of factual exonerations and, with them, the considerable media coverage that has sustained the issue. Still, the fact that these questions are now being asked and that the criminal justice process is attracting considerable public attention and debate are proof that advocates have successfully moved criminal justice reform from the province of police officers, lawyers, and judges to encompass a wider audience.

In 2003, a fledgling group stepped into this debate. Organized by a small band of lawyers, academicians, and activists, the Innocence Commission for Virginia (ICVA) was created to investigate the causes of factual exonerations and to recommend measures to prevent such errors in the future. In many ways the ICVA was formed in response to a challenge from Scheck and Neufeld. Writing in the journal *Judicature,* the two lawyers-cum-activists urged the creation of state-sponsored innocence commissions "to review the causes of any officially acknowledged case of wrongful conviction . . . [and] recommend remedies to prevent such miscarriages of justice from happening again."[13] Given Scheck and Neufeld's reputation for exonerating the innocent, their call to understand the sources of wrongful convictions attracted considerable attention, not the least for the strong message they were sending to states: Stop wasting resources opposing exoneration claims and invest that time and money to prevent wrongful convictions in the first place.

At first, the response to Scheck and Neufeld's charge was tepid. In 2002, North Carolina's chief justice convened a roundtable of justice leaders that eventually turned into the North Carolina Actual Innocence Commission. Then in 2003, the ICVA was formed. Today, California and Wisconsin have innocence review bodies, and several states have sponsored committees or boards to evaluate the fairness of their criminal justice processes.[14] Although the ICVA is but one of many fine organizations, its work has been remarkable in several respects. First, the ICVA is a private entity, staffed and funded by more than $500,000 in pro bono contributions from eleven nationally known law firms. The ICVA had to construct an advisory board, reflecting a variety of professional experiences and ideological perspectives; recruit law firms to participate in the project; supervise the work of volunteer investigators; compile case findings and reach consensus on recommendations; and draft and publish a report that others would consider legitimate. That report, entitled *A Vision for Justice,* was released in March 2005, the product of fifteen months of work.

The ICVA's efforts also concerned Virginia, a state with a mixed history of criminal justice, especially when the subject had racial connotations. The Virginia of the new millennium, however, was little like the

"Old Dominion" of the antebellum years, and in fact the Commonwealth's criminal justice system was undergoing serious reform at the time of the ICVA's work. The combination offered a remarkable field lab for criminal justice policymakers and practitioners. With the ICVA investigating the sources of erroneous convictions and the General Assembly and State Crime Commission considering new practices for criminal cases, Virginia in many ways has become a national leader in criminal justice research and reform.

The experience of the ICVA is instructive on a number of levels. At the most practical, it offers insights into the sources of wrongful convictions and recommendations for reforms in order to prevent future tragic errors. As the number of postconviction exonerations continues to rise, it makes sense to study how wrongful convictions occur and to take action only when the measures are feasible and efficient. This is not to say that Virginia's experience is universal or that the ICVA's recommendations are suited to all contexts, but as one of the first and most thorough innocence commissions, the ICVA holds valuable lessons for policymakers, activists, and criminal justice professionals.

On a larger level, the ICVA also tells a tale of legal activism and policy change. The fact that the problem of wrongful convictions is now on the national agenda is nothing short of remarkable, following, as it does, an era in politics when being "tough on crime" dominated the electoral discourse. The transition to reform—and the work of those lawyers, investigators, and advocates who pushed the specter of wrongful convictions—illustrates the finest qualities of social movement activism and interest-group politics. The ICVA was only one part of this larger process, but the commission's background and activities, and the response to its report, exemplify many of these principles—concepts that go beyond the province of law to combine elements from criminal justice, media coverage, social activism, electoral politics, and policymaking.

The ICVA, then, is a useful basis for examining the law, politics, and policy of wrongful convictions and criminal justice reform. This book, *The Innocence Commission: Preventing Wrongful Convictions and Restoring the Criminal Justice System,* tells that story, linking Virginia's experience to developments in other states and across the nation. The first decade of the twenty-first century is proving to be a remarkable period in criminal justice reform, which this book helps summarize and synthesize. It explains what has happened and why, and it also offers an agenda and strategy for further attention. *The Innocence Commission* is intended for a general audience, including lawyers, students, journalists, and the interested public, and avoids "legalese" or other legal formalities that might discourage the lay reader. The book offers an insider's perspective on a process that few people get to see and a clear and accurate assessment of the American criminal justice system.

Chapter 1 begins the story, describing the history of wrongful conviction and attendant criminal justice reform. The chapter is divided into several sections, exploring past findings on wrongful convictions, explaining the response of political leaders and justice officials to criminal justice reform, and offering a brief primer on the experience of both in Virginia, a state whose move from pariah to emerging leader in the field has been impressive.

Chapter 2 explains the development and activities of the ICVA. Rising from the collective efforts of five motivated individuals, this organization spearheaded a thorough, sober investigation into Virginia's criminal justice system. The ICVA's successes, challenges, and failings offer lessons for other individuals or groups considering their own review bodies, as well as anyone interested in the process of strategic action. A half decade after Scheck and Neufeld's call for state innocence commissions, the United States still lags behind two of its closest allies, Canada and the United Kingdom, which have institutionalized postexoneration review. There is a definite need and opportunity for other jurisdictions to establish their own innocence commissions. Indeed, as this book argues, states should assume these responsibilities themselves instead of relying on private initiatives.

Chapters 3 and 4 provide the bulk of information on the sources and potential responses to wrongful convictions. These chapters detail case findings from Virginia and elsewhere and make recommendations addressing the known contributors to wrongful convictions. Although these sections build on the ICVA's work, they do not replicate its earlier report. Instead, they synthesize past research from several jurisdictions, highlighting those issues that remain contentious and others where consensus has been achieved, and steer debate to those reforms that could and should be instituted most efficiently and effectively.

Finally, chapter 5 updates the research, describing contemporary efforts to address erroneous convictions—both in Virginia and nationwide—and outlining an agenda and strategy for future criminal justice reform.

The book tries to avoid two shortcomings, whether merely chronicling the ICVA's experience or offering a definitive "how to" list for other interested reformers. Indeed, the ICVA has already written its report, with recommendations that may or may not work for other jurisdictions. This book instead situates the ICVA in the research of legal activism and social movements and examines both the law and wrongful convictions through social science and criminal justice policy.

On one issue, though, this book pleads guilty. I have an agenda. I want to see the criminal justice system live up to the lofty standards of a field that should now rightly be seen as a profession, not merely a vocation. Contrary to some perspectives, this is neither an ideological nor a partisan bias. I am well aware that some critics instinctively label reformers as liberals and those that seek change in the criminal justice system as prodefense. Regardless of whether these presumptions have merit, they do not apply to me or this book. I teach in a justice studies program and at a law school. I routinely work with judges, police officers, and prosecutors. I *want* to see them succeed. We all should wish the same. Criminals should be caught, prosecuted, convicted, and punished.

Implicit in that wish is the presumption that the criminal justice system should accurately distinguish between the innocent and guilty. The conviction of an innocent person has serious implications, not only for the defendant who suffers a severe loss of freedom and civil rights, but also for society at large. As the ICVA explained,

> Every time a crime occurs and the justice system convicts the wrong person, the truly guilty person remains at large, free to inflict more damage on the community. Victims, who have a right to see their victimizers punished, suffer when the criminal justice system convicts the innocent, and suffer again if the true perpetrator is apprehended and the victims must relive the crime through another trial.[15]

Taxpayers must foot the bill for incarcerating and then compensating the innocent suspect, not to mention the costs of reopening a case to seek the actual perpetrator. In the process, the public may come to doubt the legitimacy of the justice process.

Apart from concerns of innocence, we should seek a criminal justice system that meets the high standards of an important profession. That must merit the review of errors to learn from them, address the frailties involved, and try to prevent mistakes in the future. These lessons learned, and the best practices that will follow, will improve criminal justice management, whether protecting the innocent or more efficiently capturing and punishing the guilty.

Other professions in America, most notably transportation and medicine, routinely convene review bodies to learn from errors. It is embarrassing, and should be unacceptable, that the legal and criminal justice fields largely do not. Some say that our criminal justice system already is fair, that the costs of review and recommendation are too high. They likely are correct about the first point but dead wrong about the latter. There is considerable disagreement about how often the criminal justice system convicts a factually innocent suspect, but even a small estimate would leave thousands of wrongful convictions each year in the United States. Each year that a wrongly convicted person is in prison costs $20,000, added to which are the considerable expenditures necessary to rectify the error.

Perhaps as a society, we should be willing to accept these costs as the charge for a criminal justice system run by human beings who inevitably make mistakes. It is not an unreasonable point, but it ignores the fact that criminal justice officials have little idea whether the errors could be prevented, what the costs of review would be, and what the benefits of a systematic review might be. Consider the problem of false or coerced confessions. Some law officials reflexively refuse to consider new technologies, most notably videotaped interrogations, that could significantly reduce the risk. Video machines currently cost an average of $4,500 per interrogation room,[16] yet they accomplish several important goals. Judges and jurors can properly evaluate the full context of a confession, allowing them to weigh the knowledge and certainty of the subject, as well as to appraise the credibility of any later claims that the admission was coerced. Electronic recording encourages shorter proceedings because defendants are more likely to plead guilty, and it protects police officers from false accusations of impropriety. The experience of Minnesota bears this out, where law enforcement agencies are now required to record felony interrogations.[17] Although some police departments had to be brought "kicking and screaming" to the new technology,[18] most agencies now acknowledge that electronically recording interrogations has made their jobs easier, and many officers now "enthusiastically support [the] practice."[19]

Kicking and screaming is an apt metaphor to describe the reaction of politicians and criminal justice officials to the call for review commissions. Why is this so? Chapter 1 suggests political fears as a likely source, officials worried about being labeled soft on crime by their opponents. But we have moved into a new period of realism in criminal justice in which the general public recognizes that errors occur and applauds when the mistakes are rectified. We also are in a period in which the next shoe might drop at any time as researchers continue to seek conclusive proof that an executed defendant was innocent. Although previous work has sown doubts about the guilt of some individuals put to death, the research still lacks unequivocal evidence of factual innocence. Were a factual exoneration to be conclusively proven and a state to acknowledge that it had executed an innocent man, the call for swift and immediate reform—perhaps including the abolition of the death penalty in some jurisdictions—would be loud indeed.

It is time for leaders in law and criminal justice to follow the example of their peers in transportation and medicine and undertake a systematic review of errors, much as groups like the ICVA have done. If the ICVA's experience stands for anything, it is that people of goodwill from a variety of perspectives can come together to investigate errors, identify the likely sources, and suggest a variety of responses. We will not always agree on the appropriate recommendations, but we must be willing to investigate and learn from the system's errors. To refuse or stonewall, to blindly defend the criminal justice process without being open to new, best practices, is to dishonor the oath that many of us took as officers of the court, the law, or the state. Criminal justice is a profession. It is time that we started treating it like one.

1

History and Background

Twenty years ago, the claim that innocent people had been wrongly convicted of serious crimes would have been "treated with general incredulity." By 2001, however, a "Harris Poll found 94 percent of Americans believed that innocent defendants are sometimes executed."[1] How did we get to this point? Many observers point their fingers at DNA testing, saying the exonerations that came to light in the late 1990s made it impossible to deny that the criminal justice system makes mistakes. But this was hardly the first evidence of erroneous convictions; that line of research goes back more than eighty years now and possibly much longer, depending on whom you believe.

There sometimes is a tendency to see wrongful convictions as a legal issue. That is, the causes of wrongful convictions rest with officers and agents of a legal process; the existence of such errors represents the denial of important legal protections; and the response to mistaken convictions is legal reforms pressed by legal activists and adopted by lawmakers or jurists. Such a view, however, misses the broader, political context in which policy issues are identified, advanced, and resolved in America. Erroneous convictions have become a cause célèbre, not simply because there now is incontrovertible evidence of innocence, but also because changes in political and social life have raised the salience of the issue. In turn, a legal and political constituency arose to demand the resolution of this problem, and people from across the political spectrum—most notably, traditional conservatives—came to support reform.

Nor can we ignore the issue's connection to the death penalty, where the stakes of error are much higher than for other felonies. Indeed, the fact that many of the first erroneous convictions were found in capital cases propelled the issue ahead at a sometimes breakneck pace in the late 1990s and early 2000s. But no one should be fooled into believing that wrongful convictions exist only in capital matters; in fact, the research by the Innocence Commission for Virginia suggests that the problems are just as great in other cases. Nonetheless, the heightened stakes of error in capital cases served to launch reform once DNA testing provided the kind of irrefutable evidence that mistakes had been made.

Virginia provides a remarkable laboratory in which to observe the changing political and legal cultures that have made wrongful convictions a subject worthy not only of serious political consideration but also reform. A state that had rightfully earned its reputation as the cradle of the confederacy and whose criminal justice system was lambasted as one of the most needlessly severe in the country, Virginia has remade itself in the first decade of the new millennium as a leader in criminal justice reform. To be sure, Virginia's transformation may reflect just how far it had to come—and as will be detailed in later chapters, the Commonwealth still has much further to go—but if meaningful reform can take place in Virginia, the same is certainly true elsewhere. Virginia's change also illustrates one of the central themes of this book: that the discovery and reform of problems in the criminal justice system do not happen by chance, nor do they occur by some rational, legalistic formula by which activists identify a problem, propose a reform, and advance their proposal to legal policymakers who adopt the measure. Wrongful convictions have been with us for decades, if not centuries. That the issue reached the national policy agenda and has engendered reform over the last decade is a reflection of political processes and social pressures at work on a legal issue. This is not to say that lawyers or legal processes are irrelevant to the resolution of problems in the criminal justice system. Rather, observers and activists for legal change must understand that the process is about much more than law.

In this chapter, I outline the history of wrongful convictions and explain how the issue began its rise to the national policy agenda, especially in Virginia. Both the legal and political worlds found it convenient to downplay the probability of wrongful convictions until scientific evidence made it impossible to ignore them. As the rest of the book argues, though, it would be a tragedy if policymakers came to believe that the modest reforms adopted in the last few years have "solved" the problem of wrongful convictions. There are many forces behind these errors, and they are likely to continue in the criminal justice system without serious reform. The challenge for policymakers and judicial officers, then, is to continue to watch for sources of error and to address them immediately rather than blindly hoping that everything will be all right.

Early Evidence of Wrongful Convictions

In his article "The History of Wrongful Execution," law professor Bruce Smith traces wrongful convictions—specifically, wrongful executions—back to seventeenth-century England. As he notes, the execution "of innocent persons for crimes that had never even occurred generated widespread anxiety among Anglo-American legal commentators from the seventeenth through early nineteenth centuries," with many "influential treatise writers and public officials . . . urg[ing] the courts [to] adopt stricter evidentiary safeguards in capital cases."[2]

In America, by contrast, Smith observes, "Criminal justice administrators" largely "sought to preserve the legitimacy of the death penalty by denying the existence of a 'wrongful conviction problem.'"[3] Although Smith's conclusion concerned nineteenth-century America, he could just as easily have been describing the nation's experience a century later. "As a prosecutor in Worcester County, Massachusetts, put it [more recently], 'Innocent men are never convicted. Don't worry about it, it never happens in the world. It is a physical impossibility.'"[4]

According to many observers, wrongful convictions were first probed in the United States by Yale law professor Edwin Borchard, who in 1932 published *Convicting the Innocent: Sixty-Five Actual Errors of Criminal Justice*. Closely examining cases in America and England, Borchard not only identified sixty-five in which an innocent defendant had been convicted, but he also classified the likely "sources of error, including erroneous eyewitness testimony, false confessions, faulty circumstantial evidence, and prosecutorial excesses."[5] Interestingly, Borchard did not limit his inquiry to capital cases but looked at a wide range of cases in the criminal justice system.

From the release of Borchard's book until the early 1990s, "there was typically one big-picture book or major article published every decade or so on the subject of miscarriages of justice," many of which "followed a familiar structure."[6] Writers would assert the premise of the American criminal justice system, that it was better to release more than one hundred guilty men than to convict one innocent person. They would then describe cases in which innocent suspects had been wrongly convicted, and they would finish by proposing reforms to address the scourge of wrongful convictions.[7] For example, in the late 1940s Erle Gardner, the author of fictional defense lawyer Perry Mason, created the "Court of Last Resort," an unofficial body to investigate suspected cases of wrongful conviction. "Gardner's efforts caught the public's imagination, but not even an author with Gardner's reach succeeded in reforming the systemic problems that led to unfair trials."[8]

Gardner was not the only writer of renown to find his work falling on the deaf ears of lawmakers and justice officials. The famous judge Jerome Frank collaborated with his daughter Barbara in their 1957 book *Not Guilty*. As in works to come, the Franks documented suspected cases of wrongful conviction and offered recommendations for reform.[9] In the 1960s, the journalist Edward Radin "carried on [a] public education campaign, turning up unfair trials and cases of actual innocence by tirelessly reading newspapers and magazines."[10] Still, the American political and legal processes slumbered, content to permit the wheels of justice to continue to grind even in the face of evidence of errors.

Bedau and Radelet and the New Era of Research

The first indication that change might be afoot came in November 1985 when philosophy professor Hugo Bedau and sociologist Michael Radelet presented a paper at the annual meeting of the American Society of Criminology (ASC) reporting that many death row defendants, including some already executed, were, in fact, innocent. The American Civil Liberties Union (ACLU) helped arrange publicity for Bedau and Radelet's conclusions, which found their way into major publications, including the *New York Times*.[11]

Following the ASC meeting, Bedau and Radelet completed their research and published their conclusions in a landmark article, "Miscarriages of Justice in Potentially Capital Cases," in a 1987 issue of *Stanford Law Review*.[12] Their article reported on

> 350 cases of defendants erroneously convicted of capital—or potentially capital—crimes in the United States in the interval 1900–1985. Of those convictions, 139 resulted in actual death sentences and ulti-

mately 23 executions. An additional 8 died in prison and 22 were re-
prieved within 72 hours of execution. Of those cases in which the inmate was ultimately released, 40% of releases came more than 5 years
after conviction; 20% of releases arrived after more than 10 years.[13]

Bedau and Radelet's research found its way to President Ronald
Reagan's Justice Department, where Assistant Attorney General Stephen
Markman responded to the findings in an internal memorandum to Attorney General Edwin Meese.[14] Markman drew on this report when he
and Associate Deputy Attorney General (now a federal judge) Paul Cassell challenged Bedau and Radelet in 1988 with a separate piece in the
Stanford Law Review. Labeling Bedau and Radelet's work "severely
flawed in critical respects," Markman and Cassell criticized their research methodology, their evaluations of the defendants' innocence, and
their conclusions about the efficacy and accuracy of the death penalty.[15]
Bedau and Radelet were given an opportunity to respond,[16] but
rather than continuing a largely intralegal debate, the two teamed up
with Bedau's wife, the professional journalist Constance Putnam, to
publish their famous book *In Spite of Innocence*.[17] Released in 1992,
the book "extended their research to mid-1991 and added 66 new cases
to their list."[18] Of particular note, the authors claimed that more than
90 percent of the cases they had identified involved "official judgments
of error."[19]
By itself, Bedau, Radelet, and Putnam's work did not lead to a change
in policy, but their research began to chip away at a legal and political
culture that presumed wrongful convictions were rare and virtually
nonexistent in capital cases. The fact that Markham and Cassell felt
compelled to respond to Bedau and Radelet—not to mention that a
publication as prestigious as Stanford's law journal would publish the
research and sponsor the dialogue—was a signal that the findings were
significant and that the possibility of wrongful convictions was more
than speculative. Indeed, Bedau and Radelet's research seemed to usher
in a new period in research on wrongful convictions in general and the
death penalty in particular.
In 1996, the trio of Ronald Huff, Arye Rattner, and Edward Sagarin
published their book *Convicted but Innocent: Wrongful Conviction and
Public Policy*, which provided a historical analysis of cases of wrongful conviction.[20] In 1998, Richard Leo and Richard Ofshe released
their groundbreaking research, which analyzed sixty cases of police-

induced false confessions.[21] Martin Yant[22] and others also published works on wrongful conviction, the collection of which "signaled a new and deepening interest in the study of miscarriages of justice by journalists and scholars unlike any time since Borchard's founding work in the 1930s."[23]

DNA Changes Everything

The renewed interest in wrongful convictions was catapulted forward by the introduction of DNA testing in the late 1990s. DNA, short for deoxyribonucleic acid, is the genetic building blocks of living cells. With the exception of identical twins, each person's DNA is unique, thereby making it a better marker for an individual's identity than blood type or fingerprints. DNA is found in bodily secretions, including blood, saliva, sweat, and semen, and also in sloughed-off skin cells and hair. In criminal cases, then, DNA evidence represents a potential gold mine, permitting investigators to identify an individual's presence at a crime scene. In particular crimes, primarily rape and murder, DNA evidence can identify the likely perpetrator when, for example, the suspect's semen is found inside the victim or his skin cells are located under the victim's fingernails.[24]

By the same token, DNA evidence can help clear innocent defendants who are erroneously linked to, or even convicted of, a crime. When semen is collected from a rape victim and properly retained in a physical evidence recovery kit (PERK), the evidence can later be tested for the DNA profile of the perpetrator who deposited the semen. If the genetic markers do not match those of the suspect being held, he can petition the courts for release. Now, as DNA evidence is more routinely collected from suspects at arrest, DNA testing holds the prospect of additional "cold hits," in which genetic evidence left at a crime scene is tested and matched with DNA profiles already on file to identify the actual perpetrators.

DNA can be tested in several ways. "The current standard for forensic DNA testing is the Short Tandem Repeat (STR) test . . . which allows for very small and degraded samples to be tested successfully."[25] Mitochondrial DNA testing is available as well. Similar to that done in genealogical research, mitochondrial DNA testing looks for individual profiles found in the mitochondria, or "power centers," of cells. [26] Mitochondrial DNA is passed through matrilineal lines, meaning that siblings with the same mother have similar DNA. Finally, a relatively new form of DNA testing, Y-Chromosome STR testing, "allows scientists to target only the DNA left by male contributors." Among other advantages, "Y-STR results can . . . help determine how many male contributors there are in any given sample."[27] This is particularly useful where more than one defendant is suspected in a rape.

In 1988, DNA testing was first allowed into court as evidence in the New York case of *People v. Wesley*.[28] Since then, as testing methods have been verified as reliable, many states have accepted DNA evidence. Virginia has permitted DNA evidence for almost as long.[29] Recognizing the promise of DNA evidence, Congress passed the DNA Identification Act in 1994, which authorized the FBI to "establish a national DNA index for law enforcement purposes."[30] That database, known as the Combined DNA Index System (CODIS), became operational in 1998 and collects DNA profiles from state and other law enforcement databases. The evidence usually is obtained when a suspect is arrested, and CODIS "enables federal, state, and local crime labs to exchange and compare DNA profiles electronically, thereby linking crimes to each other and to convicted offenders."[31] Cold hits have been much easier to obtain with the emergence of a national database of DNA profiles.

Exonerating the Innocent

From the perspective of wrongful convictions, the "forensic DNA age dawned . . . on August 14, 1989, when the emerging technology exonerated a hapless high school dropout from a working-class suburb of Chicago of a rape that in fact had not occurred." Gary Dotson, who had been convicted twelve years earlier "based on a story fabricated by his presumed victim," and whose ordeal to clear himself had been hampered by government misconduct, finally won his freedom when DNA testing showed that he could not have been the perpetrator of a crime that the victim had by then disavowed.[32]

DNA testing was further legitimized in 1996 when the National Institute of Justice (NIJ), the research and development agency of the U.S. Department of Justice, released a report, *Convicted by Juries, Exonerated by Science: Case Studies in the Use of DNA Evidence to Establish Innocence after Trial*.[33] In this comprehensive study, independent researchers for NIJ examined twenty-eight cases of wrongful conviction in which DNA testing had established innocence. Of the many important findings identified in the report, one particularly stood out: "Every year since 1989, in about 25 percent of the sexual assault cases referred to the FBI . . . the primary suspect has been excluded by DNA testing."[34] Put another way, of those rape cases referred to the FBI, law enforcement officers initially named the wrong suspect one-quarter of the time, their errors caught only with the advent of DNA testing.

The NIJ report included commentary by Peter Neufeld and Barry Scheck, two former Legal Aid attorneys who in 1992 founded the Innocence Project at Benjamin N. Cardozo School of Law. The Innocence Project (IP) is a nonprofit legal clinic that "handles cases where postconviction DNA testing of evidence can yield conclusive proof of innocence. As a clinic, students handle the case work while supervised by a team of attorneys and clinic staff."[35] The IP has now gained an international reputation as a leader in the investigation and reversal of wrongful convictions; today, a national innocence network of activists is working on wrongful convictions, and forty-two states are covered by an innocence project. Largely through the IP's work, there have been more than 180 postconviction DNA exonerations in the United States. Exonerations have been won in thirty-one states, with eighteen DNA exonerations in 2005. Of the total number of defendants exonerated through DNA, fourteen of them were at one time sentenced to death or served time on death row.[36]

How Large a Problem?

There may be a tendency to see the DNA exonerations as a special circumstance in criminal law, in which law enforcement officers or prosecutors make tragic but rare errors. To be sure, the number of known wrongful convictions is still quite modest compared with the number of criminal cases heard each year by American trial courts. In 2005, Professor Samuel Gross and his colleagues released a report chronicling 340 exonerations that took place between 1989 and 2003.[37] U.S. Supreme Court Justice Antonin Scalia has dismissed this number as "fairly modest," even considering his view that the study used a "distorted concept of what constitutes 'exoneration.'"[38] Joshua Marquis, a district attorney in Oregon and a leader of the National District Attorneys' Association, extrapolated from Gross and his colleagues' figures, claiming that even if they understated the results by a factor of 10, the data would still represent an error rate of just 0.027 percent in felony convictions.[39]

The difficulty with Marquis's figures and Scalia's conclusion, says University of Southern California law professor Dan Simon, is that the "overall rate of error in the criminal justice system is unknown, and unknowable." According to Simon, the 0.027 percent figure is "flat wrong and badly misleading. In fact, it's much higher."[40] The "Scalia–Marquis ratio," as Simon calls it, divides the number of exonerations by the total number of felonies. However, the numerator is likely many times larger than Marquis's estimates, and the denominator is probably several times smaller than he suggests. For example, most of the known wrongful convictions come from rape and murder cases, which constitute just 1.9 percent of all felonies. This fact alone should expand Marquis's estimate of error by a factor of 50. Furthermore, almost all exonerations for rape cases were committed by strangers, even though stranger rape constitutes less than 30 percent of rape convictions.[41] These figures should further shrink the denominator and in turn raise the error rate.

With respect to the numerator, most of the exonerations to date have been based on DNA testing, yet fewer than 20 percent of violent crimes involve biological evidence, and in the vast majority of past cases, the biological evidence was not properly collected and held for future testing.[42] There is no reason to believe that erroneous convictions are limited to cases in which biological evidence is available, meaning the number of known exonerations is likely a serious underestimation of the actual number of exonerations.

Moreover, these figures do not even take into account the practice of plea bargaining. Presuming that most defendants who plead are truly guilty of the crime for which they are convicted, the defendants who actually go to trial likely include a higher percentage of innocent suspects than Marquis's estimate acknowledges.[43] If these errors exist in the most serious cases—and, indeed, most of the exonerations to date come from crimes of rape and murder—it is possible that the error rate would be higher for "minor" crimes that do not receive the same time and attention of law enforcement officers and prosecutors.

The result of these machinations is, by turns, both simple and complex. As Simon suggests, the "true" rate of error in the criminal justice system is unknown and likely unknowable. It is, nonetheless, assuredly several times higher than that offered by Marquis and cited by Scalia. Few observers would place the error rate higher than 5 percent, but even a rate as low as 1 or 2 percent would mean ten thousand to twenty thousand erroneous felony convictions across the country in a single year.[44]

For that matter, other empirical evidence shows that the criminal justice system has been failing to meet its promise. Most notably, research on "racial profiling" has uncovered bias in which minorities, irrespective of criminal behavior, are more likely to be stopped and arrested by law enforcement officers than whites are. Verifiable research on profiling stretches back several decades, with a 1978 study finding that "nonwhites were more likely than whites to be arrested under circumstances that would not constitute sufficient grounds for prosecution."[45] Racial profiling attracted greater attention in the early 1990s, even as casual observers came to see that African Americans were disproportionately subject to arrest. In 1992, for example, blacks represented 12 percent of the U.S. population but 30 percent of all arrests, a disparity that could not be explained by criminality patterns.[46] Perhaps the seminal evidence came in a 1993 study of traffic stops in New Jersey, which found "the rate at which blacks were stopped was greatly disproportionate to their numbers on the road and to their propensity to violate traffic laws."[47] These results, among others, led to *New Jersey v. Soto*, in which the Superior Court of New Jersey concluded that the New Jersey State Police was "targeting blacks for investigation and arrest."[48] Maryland, too, agreed to a consent decree in 2003 to settle charges that state troopers were engaged in racial profiling when stopping motorists.[49]

A Gradual Shift in Opinion

Whether racial profiling or wrongful convictions were any worse in the late twentieth and early twenty-first centuries than at other times is doubtful, but news reports of such failings grew as empirical evidence became available and known to reporters. The combined result of these findings and the "exposés" of wrongful convictions that followed planted doubts in the minds of the public about the accuracy and fairness of the American criminal justice system. If Illinois could exonerate more people from death row than it would execute, and if evidence arose that police officers were stopping motorists on the basis of race, there was reason to question the trust generally placed in many institutions of criminal justice. The effects are seen in reports like those I received in 2002 while conducting research on federal prosecutors. Given news coverage of the Rodney King incident, in which police officers were caught on videotape beating a suspect, and criticism of the FBI's tactics during the siege in Waco and the standoff at Ruby Ridge, several assistant U.S. attorneys told me they were finding it harder to obtain convictions because jurors were no longer as willing to credit the testimony of federal agents, whose motives and behavior they seemed to be scrutinizing more closely.

At the same time, the public's support for the death penalty has dropped dramatically. Whereas in 1994 nearly 80 percent of the American public supported the death penalty (itself a rise from 42 percent in 1966), today only about two-thirds of those surveyed support capital punishment.[50] Furthermore, when respondents are asked to compare the death penalty against life without parole, support for capital punishment drops again, to nearly 50 percent.[51] The connection between wrongful convictions and changing public opinion is necessarily indirect (there being no surveys that link the two), but it is not difficult to trace the link. With a steady drumbeat of news stories chronicling errors in the criminal justice process—from mistaken eyewitness identification to false confessions, and forensic and scientific errors—"most Americans [today] believe that persons convicted of crimes have, indeed, been wrongly executed."[52] It should hardly be a surprise, then, that support for the death penalty should fall and, with it, public trust in the criminal justice system.

Virginia: A Slow Convert

Virginia, too, saw a series of exonerations beginning in the late 1980s, but it took more than a decade before Virginians and their elected leaders seriously considered the issue of criminal justice reform.[53] Part of the reason for Virginia's intransigence is its contradictory political and cultural history. On one hand, American democracy was born in Virginia. The Commonwealth is justly proud of its native sons, including George Washington, Thomas Jefferson, James Madison, and George Mason who, respectively, won the Revolutionary War and drafted the Declaration of Independence, the U.S. Constitution, and the Bill of Rights. But

Virginia also was the "Cradle of the Confederacy" during the Civil War and actively resisted civil rights reform until late into the twentieth century. Now, in the new millennium, Virginia is in the midst of a heady, vibrant, and transforming time, moving a socially and culturally conservative "Old Dominion" into the mainstream of American politics. Though still more conservative than liberal in its politics, Virginia is home to an increasingly diverse economic and social climate.[54]

A Quick History of Virginia

Most American schoolchildren are familiar with Patrick Henry's rallying cry of "Give me liberty or give me death," and in fact, Virginia was one of the earliest states in the union to create its own government and establish democratic voting. On June 29, 1776, Virginia adopted its first constitution, establishing both legislative and executive functions for the representation of freeholding white men. Since that time, Virginia has created five other constitutions, most of which struggled at some level with the question of who should have the right to vote. Indeed, nine years after the first constitution was adopted, Virginia's favorite son, Thomas Jefferson, published a critique of it, concluding that "the majority of men in the state, who pay and fight for its support, are [*sic*] under represented in the legislature."

Of course, many more populations than men—and white men at that —were underrepresented in eighteenth-century Virginia, but it took almost two hundred years to fully open the Commonwealth's political process. The central intervening event was the Civil War, during which Richmond became the new capital of the Confederacy. With the fall of the South, Virginia again created a new constitution. The Fifteenth Amendment to the U.S. Constitution had already extended the vote to African American men, and the new Virginia constitution reorganized the state government by permitting a larger number of citizens to participate in governing localities. But Virginia's traditional political leaders strenuously fought Reconstruction, trying to turn back the clock on political and electoral reform. Their efforts culminated in the Constitutional Convention of 1901/1902, which, Professor Dick Howard noted, "is most often characterized, and rightly so, in terms of its disenfranchisement of blacks."[55]

V. O. Key aptly described Virginia in the first half of the twentieth century as a "political museum piece," a "well-disciplined and ably managed oligarchy."[56] Under the control of Harry Byrd's political machine, Virginia's political and legal processes were just the type of closed practices that civil rights activists fought in the 1960s. Some forty years later, Virginia has changed remarkably in several respects. The number of voters who participate in the political process is many times larger than the relatively few who were permitted suffrage earlier. Both the Voting Rights Act and the end of the poll tax have contributed substantially to these changes, as has the Twenty-sixth Amendment to the U.S. Constitution. In addition, there have been the legal, political, economic, and cultural changes afoot in Virginia that have altered the Commonwealth's character. The 1968 Commission on Constitutional Revision reflected many of these developments, taking nearly three years to create Virginia's sixth and latest constitution of 1971. Among its many protections, the current constitution shields Virginians "against any governmental discrimination upon the basis of religious conviction, race, color, sex, or national origin."

During the same period, the growth of northern Virginia and its suburbs began to shift the center of political life away from the Commonwealth's rural areas and an agricultural and mining economy to its new cities and suburbs and more hi-tech enterprises. In 1989, Virginia became the first state after Reconstruction to elect an African American as governor when L. Douglas Wilder won an extremely close contest, and four years before that, Mary Sue Terry became the first woman in Virginia to win a statewide election when she was elected attorney general. In addition, the Republican Party, which had been moribund while Harry Byrd held sway, became a keen competitor in the Commonwealth, to the point that Republicans currently control majorities in the Virginia House of Delegates and Senate. As the Virginia State Library acknowledges, these elections "reflect the many complicated changes taking place in Virginia's political life."[57]

Virginia's Criminal Justice System

Even though Virginia has been a leader in reforming and opening its political process, the Commonwealth's criminal justice system received much less critical attention through much of the twentieth century. If asked to describe Virginia's approach to criminal justice, many observers would likely respond, "strict, stern, and severe." In his book *The History of Corrections in Virginia,*[58] Paul Keve "maintains that

Virginia's penal institutions" through the early twentieth century reflected "isolated, fragmented, and generally racist, sexist and repressive forms of social control."[59] Only in the 1970s and 1980s did the "state's system generally provide [humane treatment]."[60]

The situation was little better for defendants charged with a crime who lacked adequate resources to defend themselves. A 2004 report by the Spangenberg Group for the American Bar Association found that Virginia ranked among the worst states in providing quality legal representation to indigent defendants.[61] The Commonwealth came in for special criticism for its system of fee caps, which at this writing remain the lowest in the country. Appointed counsel are limited to payments of $112 for the defense of each misdemeanor charge, $395 for a felony charge carrying a penalty of up to twenty years' imprisonment, and $1,096 for a felony punishable by twenty years or more in prison.[62] Even figuring an attorney's time at the maximum rate permitted under Virginia's rules of $90 an hour (and recognizing that many partners in large law firms charge more than $400 an hour), an indigent defendant charged with manslaughter could be limited to little more than four hours of attorney time.

Virginia also has been criticized for its infamous "21-day rule," which until 2002 prevented a convicted defendant from introducing newly discovered evidence of innocence more than twenty-one days after sentencing. Virginia modeled its law after a Texas statute that "provided automatic review of death sentences and a stipulation that a convicted person had 30 days to sway the judge or jury from imposing death." Virginia and Texas were "long known as the most restrictive states in the country as far as allowing new evidence." Then, in April 1994 the Texas appeals court eased its rule for death row appeals, leaving Virginia as "the most restrictive" in the nation.[63]

Interestingly, "the establishment of Virginia's 21-day rule resulted more from an oversight than any conscious policy-making," explains former Delegate Samuel Glasscock, a foe of the death penalty. "I don't think there was any conscious consideration for the 21 days. . . . I don't recall any real discussion on . . . the 21-day rule until recent years."[64] Miles Godwin Jr., a proponent of capital punishment and the governor at the time that the statute was drafted, said as late as 1994 that he didn't feel "any urgency on the part of the people of Virginia to do anything about it. I thought it was good legislation at the time."[65] In the mid-1990s Virginia came close to changing the 21-day rule when

Delegate Clifton Woodrum sponsored a bill to permit death row prisoners to petition for a hearing at any time if new evidence of innocence
were discovered, but at the last minute, the Virginia Senate derailed the
legislation.[66]

Virginia has also been known for its enthusiastic endorsement of the
death penalty. From 1608 to 1972, when executions were temporarily
halted by the U.S. Supreme Court,[67] Virginia executed 1,277 people,
the most of any state in the union. Virginia reclaimed its place once
the death penalty resumed, [68] executing ninety-five people from 1976
through the spring of 2006 and ranking second only to Texas in the
number of persons executed by the states.[69]

The combination of these features earned Virginia the ignominious
label in legal circles as "the worst state in the nation for both unfair
trials and a lack of due process protection—even when considerable
doubt concerning an inmate's guilt is found."[70] The personification of
this view was former Attorney General Mary Sue Terry, a Democrat,
who in defending the Commonwealth against a claim of postconviction
relief said of Virginia law, "After conviction, innocence is irrelevant."[71]
Even though Terry came in for considerable criticism from the defense
bar and others in the legal reform community, her comment correctly
summarized the state of Virginia's justice system at the time.

In 1993, the U.S. Supreme Court ruled that there was no independent
claim for "actual innocence" in federal habeas corpus petitions, meaning that erroneously convicted defendants had to rely on state processes
to prove their innocence. [72] But coupling Virginia's 21-day rule with
its woeful system of indigent defense left many defendants in a "legal
Catch-22"[73] that both increased the likelihood of an inadequate defense
and prevented them from introducing new exculpatory evidence if a
postconviction investigation proved more fruitful. As a 1994 investigation by one of Virginia's largest newspapers concluded, "Though the
Supreme Court ruled in 1986 that capital cases warrant extra scrutiny,
court records show only a pretense of such scrutiny in Virginia. The appeals court looks at procedure, not evidence."[74]

The Politics and Culture of Criminal Justice

In some sense, it should not be surprising that Virginia or its sister states
would be slow to change, for from the 1970s until just recently America

has been in a "conservative era" of criminal justice.[75] In his controversial book *The Rich Get Richer and the Poor Get Prison,* Jeffrey Reiman argues that "the goal of our criminal justice system is not to eliminate crime or to achieve justice, but to project to the American public a visible image of the threat of crime as a threat from the poor."[76] He claims that whereas malfeasance of the rich is not classified as a crime, bad acts by the poor are considered dangerous, which serves only to justify further punitive policies against society's "have-nots."

Reinman's is perhaps an extreme position, but other scholars and observers have noted the increasingly punitive nature of American criminal justice over the last thirty years, as conservative politicians found that being "tough on crime" both paid electoral dividends and fueled the attack on social welfare policies.[77] In her 1997 book *Making Crime Pay,* sociologist Katherine Beckett analyzes news coverage of crime and drugs over twenty-five years in the late twentieth century, finding that the media's coverage of crime has increasingly reflected conservative explanations, including such rhetoric as "liberal permissiveness, leniency in the criminal justice system, and provision of welfare to those who do not want to work[, which has] nurtured a criminal 'underclass.' "[78]

Duke law professor Sara Sun Beale went a step further, pointing a finger at Republicans who "used the crime issue to gain national political strength, particularly in the South where the Democratic Party's support of civil rights legislation left it vulnerable."[79] According to Beal, "the most significant criminal justice initiatives in the 1980s—mandatory minimums, three strikes, and expanding the federal death penalty —are 'contrary to what almost everyone with close knowledge of the topic thinks makes much sense.' "[80] Yet the "coincidence of an increase in the postwar crime rates at a time of antiwar and civil rights disturbances [has set] the stage for opportunistic political behavior."[81]

There is no doubt that the politicians, particularly conservatives who reached ascendance in the 1990s, have taken greater interest in crime over the last several decades. Beginning in the early 1960s, criminal justice became a prominent issue in national politics when from 1960 to 1975 the murder rate doubled, and robbery more than tripled.[82] At the same time, the Supreme Court issued a series of seminal civil liberties rulings, including *Mapp v. Ohio,*[83] *Miranda v. Arizona,*[84] and *Gideon v. Wainwright,*[85] which seemed to restrict law enforcement by offering additional rights to the accused. Concurrently, the civil rights movement began and, with it, concern for the racially differential effects of the criminal justice process. In many ways, criminal justice became a Rorschach test for politicians during this period. Liberals saw a biased system that required reform,[86] but conservatives, including most notably Barry Goldwater and Ronald Reagan, argued for greater "law and order" to address a breakdown in American society that had led to an epidemic of serious crime.[87]

That the conservatives' approach would take precedence from 1975 to 2000 is interesting considering that the crime rate was falling during this period, though public hysteria was not.[88] But most research on public opinion has found that support for greater punitive measures is not tied directly to past victimization. The work of noted researchers Robert Langworthy and John Whitehead in the 1980s, for example, tied punitiveness to Americans' fear of crime and conservative attitudes but not to their past experience with crime.[89] Nor is this fear evenly felt. In 1991, Steven Cohn, Steven Barkan, and William Halteman published their analysis of national polling, concluding that "the punitive attitudes of whites toward criminals are based partly on racial prejudice, while those of blacks are associated with their fear of crime." These results, said the authors, suggest that consensus "on punitiveness toward criminals may be apparent rather than real, and that . . . attitudes toward punitiveness reflect the[] disparate positions [of whites and blacks] in the social and economic orders."[90]

Perhaps the most interesting work comes from Tom Tyler and Robert Boeckmann, who analyzed support for "three strikes" legislation in California.[91] According to the two researchers, support for this measure was tied not to fear of crime, as widely believed, but to people's "evaluation of social conditions, including the decline in morality and discipline within the family and increases in the diversity of society. These concerns are about issues of moral cohesion—with people feeling that the quality and extent of social bonds and social consensus has deteriorated in American society."[92] In effect, Tyler and Boeckmann said, the fear of loss—of moral values, of social order, of control over popular culture—encouraged support for increasingly punitive measures to enforce moral norms.

If we examine criminal justice policy through the lens of Tyler and Boeckmann's findings, it is easier to understand how politicians could foment support for punitive measures at a time when the crime rate was falling. In this context, the call for "law and order" flows not from the fear of crime but from the fear of disorder, of finding one's self on the declining end of the culture curve with a loosening grip over dominant traditions. As immigration rises, as minorities and women take more important positions in society, as gays and lesbians gain rights, as the number of "broken homes" skyrockets and pornography and coarser communication become more commonplace, and as society becomes more secularized, those who fear the erosion of traditional mores in civil society push back by seeking to tighten social control. Criminal justice "reform," then, is as much a means to this end as the goal itself. As Beckett might say, the goal of the "conservative era"[93] in American criminal justice was to "replace social welfare with social control as the principle of state policy."[94]

The result of the conservative era in American criminal justice was an American public that by the early 1990s strongly supported the death penalty and harsher penalties for most serious crimes and that seemed unmoved by (or perhaps unaware of) a "get tough" approach in sentencing that removed significant discretion from judges and led to an explosion in the U.S. prison population. Not coincidentally, the jump was felt disproportionately by African Americans and Hispanics, as the federal government's "war on drugs" and its disparate treatment of crack and powder cocaine locked up more young minority men under "mandatory minimum" sentences.[95] For politicians, crime paid, or at least the appearance of being "tough on crime" brought electoral dividends, as the presidential campaigns of 1988 and 1996 and countless "down ticket" races showcased candidates who seemed to propel themselves to victory by emphasizing their willingness to "get tough" on criminals.[96] Without significant evidence to the contrary, there was little reason to doubt that the criminal justice system was accurately convicting the guilty and acquitting the innocent, and if fears of crime or a desire for order led to increasingly punitive policies, few protests proved persuasive in the larger political process.

An Impetus for Change in Virginia

In 1985, Earl Washington Jr. sat on death row in Virginia, just nine days away from his scheduled execution. Washington, who has an IQ of 69, had been convicted of the 1982 murder of a Culpeper, Virginia, mother who was raped and stabbed in front of her two young children. According to sheriff's deputies, Washington confessed to the crime, but a later investigation showed him to be wildly off the mark and the "confession" to be as much deputies putting words in Washington's mouth as Washington actually understanding the nature of the case. Without a right to counsel in state habeas corpus proceedings,[97] Washington was moved to death row, where he remained, without representation, until nine days before his scheduled execution date of September 5, 1985.

Although it took fifteen years, Earl Washington was eventually exonerated of the Culpeper murder through the advent of DNA testing. Washington's case, and the plight of several other exonerated defendants in Virginia, began to direct attention in Virginia to the failings of its criminal justice system. In June 1994, shortly after Governor Douglas Wilder commuted Washington's sentence from death to life in prison but before Governor James Gilmore eventually pardoned Washington, the *Virginian-Pilot,* one of the state's most respected newspapers, released the report of its own investigation into Virginia's system of criminal justice. The results were shocking. According to the paper:

> Nine men sentenced to death by Virginia juries did not receive fair trials. . . . For three of these men, questions about the quality of the evidence led the governor to grant clemency [which meant a life term]. Three others were executed with questions left unanswered. The other three men remain on death row, trying to get the courts to listen before time runs out. . . . The nine represent 12 percent of the 75 men sentenced to die in Virginia since the U.S. Supreme Court allowed states to resume the death penalty in 1976.[98]

For an editor of the *Virginian-Pilot,* these injustices were unacceptable, and almost single-handedly, she refused to let the issue be swept under the rug. During a five-year period beginning in the late 1990s, the *Virginian-Pilot* repeatedly issued editorials urging the state's elected officials to reform a criminal justice system that not only paid scant attention to the needs of indigent defendants but also made it virtually impossible for an innocent defendant to win release after a wrongful conviction. That editor, Margaret Edds, published a book in 2003 recounting the disturbing facts of the Earl Washington case. As Edds announced, "Anyone who doubts the existence of such wrongful convictions should remember what it took to save Earl Washington from such a fate. He was freed not because of a system designed to excise error, but in spite of one committed to affirming its own judgments." Quoting British psychologist Gisli Gudjonsson, Edds declared the criminal justice system to be deficient in "discovering, admitting to, and doing something about, errors which they make."[99]

In May 2000, as it was becoming increasingly apparent that DNA testing would exonerate Earl Washington, Virginia State Senator Ken Stolle convened a task force of the Virginia State Crime Commission to consider an exception to the 21-day rule. Stolle, a former police officer and prosecutor, might have been an odd choice to take up criminal justice reform, although he is respected across the aisle in the General Assembly for being tough, fair, and shrewd. As chair of the crime commission, he was interested in legislative options to permit postconviction DNA testing. Five months later, shortly after Washington was pardoned, the Virginia Supreme Court joined the fray, announcing that it was considering a change in the 21-day rule, which had been codified as Rule 1:1 of the court, to "allow death-row inmates to present newly discovered evidence of innocence to the Virginia Supreme Court at any time after conviction."[100]

Stolle was successful in getting the court to stop and wait for the General Assembly to address the problem, although in the 2000 session, legislators were unable to agree on a bill. In January 2001, however, Stolle introduced a resolution to amend the state constitution to give the Virginia Supreme Court authority to consider postconviction appeals by defendants who present biological evidence of innocence. The bill also ordered the preservation of human biological evidence in capital cases and, upon motion by the defendant, in other felony cases as well.[101] The initiative raced through the General Assembly but faced a recalcitrant Governor Gilmore, who opposed the initiative's application to defendants who pleaded guilty as well as the lack of a time limit for the defendant's appeal.[102] Eventually, however, Gilmore was persuaded to sign the legislation, and that fall Virginia voters passed the constitutional amendment by a percent margin of 73 to 27.[103] Dubbed a writ of actual innocence, the amendment was the first crack in the 21-day rule, permitting convicted defendants an opportunity to present biological evidence to the Virginia Supreme Court as a means of obtaining a new trial.

Explaining his interest in the legislation, Stolle said he sensed a concern among Virginians that the 21-day rule blocked innocent defendants from exonerating themselves. "How do you tell people a guy is innocent and has no forum to get out of jail?" Stolle asked.[104] "You just can't sell that product, and if we of the crime commission and legislators don't fix this I'm afraid we're going to lose the confidence of our citizens."[105] Stolle's efforts were aided by the plethora of more "extreme" bills that were introduced at the same time, calling for the abolition of the death penalty or at least a moratorium on executions, as well as new jury instructions that would caution jurors that "Virginia convicted and nearly executed someone who was eventually determined to be innocent."[106] Against these measures, which did not pass, Stolle's proposal appeared modest.

Stolle, however, was hesitant to extend the new writ of actual innocence to nonbiological evidence. In early 2002, as the General Assembly was drafting legislation to expand the writ, Stolle persuaded his senate colleagues to reconsider, much to the disdain of Senator Henry Marsh and Delegate Jim Almand, Democratic legislators who had pushed the extension. That November, though, the Virginia Supreme Court released a proposal to eliminate the 21-day rule completely.[107] The court's action provided the ammunition to propel new legislation forward, especially when Virginia's governor, Mark Warner, promoted the issue. In his January 2003 state of the state address, Warner declared:

> Just as we work to promote economic security, we remain vigilant in protecting our communities from crime and terrorism. Preserving public safety is among government's most basic functions. . . .
>
> But on rare occasions, the system does fail. Last summer, due to DNA evidence, I pardoned Marvin Lamont Anderson, who had served 15 years in prison for a crime he did not commit.
>
> Nevertheless, our state continues to cling to the outdated "21-day rule" that can actually prevent evidence of innocence from coming to light. No other state has such a restrictive rule. The Judicial Council and the Crime Commission are working on important reforms to the rule. I believe the rule should be changed.[108]

After considerable haggling, the General Assembly passed a bill to extend the 21-day rule to 90 days for defendants presenting nonbiological evidence of innocence, although they would have just one crack at the writ of actual innocence. Governor Warner and the General Assembly negotiated over these terms, the governor rejecting the 90-day limit and urging legislators to permit defendants more than one "bite at the apple." Eventually, the two agreed on compromise legislation, which the governor signed in May 2004. The new law expanded the writ of actual innocence, permitting a convicted felon to petition the court of appeals with newly discovered nonbiological evidence of innocence. An individual may file for the writ at any time but is limited to one opportunity and may not use this procedure after pleading guilty.[109]

To veterans of Virginia's criminal justice and political processes, the first few years of the twenty-first century appeared to be an unprecedented period of reform. The pace was only hastened by the U.S. Supreme Court, which in 2000 and 2002 ruled on two Virginia cases and broadened the Sixth and Eighth Amendment rights of defendants convicted in the Commonwealth. In *Williams v. Taylor,* the High Court overruled decisions of the Virginia Supreme Court and the U.S. Court of Appeals for the Fourth Circuit, concluding that the defendant's Sixth Amendment right to effective assistance of counsel was denied "when his trial lawyers failed to investigate and to present substantial mitigating evidence to the sentencing jury."[110] Two years later in the watershed case of *Atkins v. Smith,* the Supreme Court ruled that the execution of mentally retarded criminals violated the Eighth Amendment's prohibition against cruel and unusual punishment.[111] The Commonwealth seemed to get the message. As of April 1, 2006, Virginia had only twenty-two inmates on death row, now ranking twenty-first among the states in the number of defendants sentenced to death.[112]

Virginia also has tried to amend its system of indigent defense. Shortly after the American Bar Association's scathing report on the state of indigent defense in Virginia,[113] the General Assembly in 2004 established the Indigent Defense Commission to provide oversight and certification of attorneys representing indigent defendants in the Commonwealth. Among other duties, the commission maintains a list of Virginia attorneys certified to represent indigents.[114]

Why Virginia?

If Virginia has done so much over the last decade, it is only because it had so far to come. Undoubtedly, the Commonwealth's reform owes much to the goodwill of leaders like State Senators Ken Stolle and Henry Marsh, Delegate Jim Almand, the justices of the Virginia Supreme Court, and former Governor Mark Warner, who refused to stand idly by as new exonerations and other independent reports highlighted problems with the state's system of criminal justice. But Virginia's efforts did not exist in a vacuum. The steady beat of DNA exonerations in the late 1990s and early 2000s kept the issue in the public eye, and the political will of leaders in other states to acknowledge their own problems and tackle these deficiencies provided both an impetus and a "cover" for Virginia leaders to resolve the issue themselves.

We also must give credit to the many activists and reformers in Virginia who kept the pressure on legislators and other justice leaders, urging them to test newly found biological evidence and to reform the system when results showed that innocent men had been convicted and, in one case, almost executed. Special recognition here goes to a loosely organized collection of lawyers, social activists, religious leaders, reporters, and progressive legislators who kept the heat on their more reluctant colleagues. But they also had a strong issue on their side: innocence. No reasonable person is in favor of imprisoning or executing the innocent. When DNA testing proved that the Commonwealth had convicted the truly innocent, there was little cover for opponents to claim that suspects had been released on "legal technicalities." So when the ABA and other reform groups came calling, arguing that Virginia had to change its 21-day rule and improve its provision of indigent defense to prevent wrongful convictions, legislators felt compelled to do something. And when confronted with more "extreme" proposals to eliminate the death penalty or institute a moratorium, legislators reached for more modest measures that still represented real reform. Without DNA testing and a series of publicized exonerations, the train of reform might never have left the station.

Nor can we ignore the issue of race, one of the most important but least often addressed issues in criminal justice. Certainly, Virginia has had a dubious history in protecting racial equality, but there is considerable evidence showing that racial discrimination continues to exist throughout the American criminal justice system.[115] Consider the work of David Baldus, who found that race was a predictor for capital sentencing in Georgia and Philadelphia;[116] Michigan law professor Samuel Gross has reported similar findings.[117]

When combining these national findings with Virginia's history on race, it is easier to understand how the Commonwealth's political establishment might have mobilized in the new millennium, since many of the first exonerated defendants turned out to be minorities. Indeed, eight of the eleven cases investigated by the Innocence Commission for Virginia were of minorities who had been wrongly convicted. The fact that several of these cases were rapes, with white women inaccurately accusing black men of assault, only rekindled odious images from the Commonwealth's past in which similar charges would have been met by a lynch mob. The Virginia of 2000 was a much more diverse state, particularly as its northern suburbs welcomed immigrants from a host of nations and ethnicities. To uncover evidence, then, that the state's criminal justice system still was treating minorities worse than whites and, most troubling, that these disparities were connected to wrongful convictions might very well have spurred the state's leadership to correct an impression that did not fit the Commonwealth's more modern claim to be among the best governed in the nation.[118]

Innocence Review

Still, for all of Virginia's recent efforts at criminal justice reform, the state has resisted a review of wrongful convictions or a comprehensive analysis of the deficits in its criminal justice system. Not that Virginia is alone. Few states have taken the lead of America's closest allies, the United Kingdom and Canada, to institutionalize innocence review. In 1997, the United Kingdom established an independent public body, the Criminal Cases Review Commission (CCRC), "to review suspected miscarriages of justice and decide if they should be referred to an appeal court."[119] The CCRC was a product of the Royal Commission on Criminal Justice, established in 1991 in response to the release of the "Birmingham Six," whose convictions sixteen years earlier for terrorist murder had been overturned.[120]

By 1993, the Royal Commission had returned "352 recommendations covering a range of activities, including police investigations, safeguards for suspects, the prosecution process, pretrial procedures, the trial process, forensic science, and other expert evidence and the appeals process." Indeed, its report was entitled "Corrections of Miscarriages of Justice."[121] Among its recommendations was the establishment of a body like the CCRC. Today, the CCRC has jurisdiction over criminal cases from any magistrate's or crown court in England, Wales, and Northern Ireland. According to the CCRC:

Our main job is to review the cases of those that feel they have been wrongly convicted of criminal offences, or unfairly sentenced. We do not consider innocence or guilt, but whether there is new evidence or argument that may cast doubt on the safety of an original decision. Once we have completed our investigations into a case, we can refer it back to the appropriate appeal court for re-consideration. We have wide-ranging investigative powers and can obtain and preserve documentation held by any public body. We can also appoint an Investigating Officer from another public body to carry out inquiries on our behalf.[122]

According to a member of the CCRC, 67 percent of the commission's referrals to an appellate court have led to the reversal of a conviction.[123]

Canada uses a different mechanism to review suspected cases of wrongful conviction. More than a century ago Canada created royal commissions of inquiry to permit national and provincial governments to "conduct independent, nongovernment-affiliated investigations regarding the conduct of public businesses or the fair administration of justice."[124] These commissions formed the basis for public inquiries into two celebrated postconviction exonerations involving Guy Paul Morin and Thomas Sophonow. In both inquiries the commissions "held hearings, recruited, when necessary, government laboratories or independent experts, and issued reports that dealt with the specific causes of these wrongful convictions and made policy recommendations about remedies to prevent wrongful convictions in the future."[125] According to Canadian lawyers familiar with these commissions, the public inquiry process has as its primary goal

to determine the particular errors that contributed to the wrongful conviction in the instant case. This backward-looking process is essential to determine the specific causes that contributed to a particular wrongful conviction, and it may inform the compensatory aspect of any inquiry. It is the forward-looking application, however, that has broader social policy impacts, because the publication of the findings and, more importantly, recommendations, while not carrying any binding precedential value, provides stakeholders with a weighty reminder of the pitfalls that must be avoided.[126]

Efforts in the United States

Closer to home, Martin Yant's 1991 book *Presumed Guilty: When Innocent People Are Wrongly Convicted* called for the creation of a "quasi-judicial 'Court of Last Resort'" to consider claims of factual innocence. Such courts would have authority to investigate cases when necessary, rather than being limited to questions of legal error.[127] Yant's call was echoed in 2000 in an article in the *Northern Illinois University Law Review,* in which Yale law student David Horan strongly urged the "state governments of the United States . . . to follow Great Britain's lead in establishing an independent review commission to investigate suspected wrongful convictions."[128] As Horan explained,

> Such an extra-legal or "quasi-judicial" review commission would offer convicted defendants with viable claims of actual innocence a state-funded mechanism to consider and investigate their claims after convictions and unsuccessful appeals, instead of relegating such defendants to attempts to make a disfavored and often restricted or even procedurally prohibited successive petition for postconviction relief. The commission should be equipped with full investigative and subpoena power, including free and full access to police and prosecutors' files and court records. The commission should also have the power to discuss cases with the applicant and should maintain an internal staff of "experienced criminal lawyers, forensic scientists, and other experts to give it independence from any of the institutions and individuals it may have to investigate and criticize."[129]

The drumbeat for postconviction review in the United States grew stronger in the next year. Lissa Griffin, a professor of law at Pace University, seconded Horan's Anglophilic recommendation, urging the "U.S. criminal justice system [to] look to its English counterpart for new approaches," most notably an independent commission to investigate and consider "claims of innocence where new evidence strongly supports the claim."[130] Then, in their best-selling book, *Actual Innocence,* Barry Scheck and Peter Neufeld, along with journalist Jim Dwyer, called for "state and federal institutions modeled after the Criminal Case Review Commission in the United Kingdom to investigate wrongful convictions."[131] Scheck and Neufeld continued to hammer home this recommendation, writing a year later in *Judicature* that the federal and state governments should create independent "innocence commissions . . . to review the causes of any officially acknowledged case of wrongful conviction." These commissions, Scheck and Neufeld maintained, should "recommend remedies to prevent such miscarriages of justice from happening again."[132]

In making their case, Scheck and Neufeld have compared innocence commissions with the work of the National Transportation Safety Board. Known by the acronym NTSB, the safety board is an independent federal agency responsible for investigating transportation accidents in the United States and offering recommendations to prevent future mishaps and tragedies. The NTSB was created by Congress in 1967, and since that time the agency has investigated more than 130,000 transportation accidents and has issued more than 12,000 safety recommendations.[133]

If the accident of an aircraft involves a substantial question of public safety, the NTSB has statutory authority to hold a public hearing at which board members hear evidence of the cause of the tragedy and consider remedies to prevent similar errors.[134] Although the NTSB does not initiate enforcement action, more than 80 percent "of its recommendations have been adopted by those in a position to effect change. Many safety features currently incorporated into airplanes, automobiles, trains, pipelines and marine vessels had their genesis in NTSB recommendations."[135]

The NTSB's approach has been adopted by the American medical profession, whose interest in preventing serious harm has led it to institutionalize postmortem reviews of error. Known as "morbidity and mortality conferences," or simply M&M, doctors in the early twentieth century established a standardized case report system to investigate the reasons and responsibility for adverse outcomes of care.[136] Mandated in 1983 by the Accreditation Council for Graduate Medical Education, "M&M is a weekly conference at which, under the moderation of a faculty member, medical and surgical residents and attending [physicians] present cases of all complications and deaths."[137] M&M conferences are not intended to address systemic issues; rather, they are case-by-case reviews to help physicians learn what "might have been done differently in a given case" and train doctors to anticipate similar problems in the future.[138] A regional survey of 1,100 doctors in the last decade found that 43 percent of residents and 47 percent of surgical faculty believed that M&M conferences were an important educational tool.[139]

Like transportation and medicine, the legal profession would seem to be a good candidate for post-error review. Although the mistakes made in criminal investigations and prosecutions may not threaten as many lives as do the errors that cause an airplane crash or a patient's untimely death,[140] the Constitution charges justice officials with protecting the liberty and lives of suspects, especially those who are innocent. For that matter, erroneous convictions do harm to other "innocent bystanders" —from victims who must relive the crime a second time if the actual perpetrator is caught and a new trial is pursued, to members of the public who are at risk while dangerous criminals are free, to taxpayers who must foot the bill for fixing the errors, to the police and courts whose reputation for fairness and professional may suffer. Wrongful convictions are a tragedy all around, a misfortune that should be avoided when possible.

Nonetheless, only a handful of states have undertaken a serious and systematic review of wrongful convictions or related errors in order to prevent these mistakes from occurring in the future. At the time the Innocence Commission for Virginia was created, just two states, Illinois and North Carolina, had established formal commissions to investigate erroneous convictions. Several others maintained official bodies to improve the administration of justice in their states,[141] but these committees had various, and sometimes vague, charges, and in any case numbered many fewer than a majority of jurisdictions. Compared with its sister profession, medicine, law has shown an unwillingness to understand, let alone admit, its most tragic mistakes and to try to prevent these errors in the future. In Illinois, the so-called Ryan Commission lasted for two years, and in North Carolina the Actual Innocence Commission investigates likely sources of errors without examining particular cases. Both bodies are a significant step forward for the American criminal justice system, yet even they have limitations. More important, they have had too few takers from other states.

The Ryan Commission

If one had to choose a single state as the impetus for justice reform in the new millennium, it would have to be Illinois. But Illinois's badge of honor flows from a discomfiting discovery. Between 1977 and 1999, of the more than 250 murder cases in which a defendant was sentenced to death in Illinois, fewer persons were actually executed (12) than were later released from prison upon questions of their guilt (13).[142]

Much of the postconviction investigation in Illinois was done by former, current, and future journalists. Professor David Protess and his students in Northwestern University's journalism program took on a number of cases as clinical projects. They were supplemented by crusading journalist Rob Warden of the *Chicago Lawyer*, now the executive director of the Center on Wrongful Conviction at Northwestern, and their efforts were propelled forward by reporters at the *Chicago Tribune*, who conducted two in-depth investigations of homicide prosecutions in Illinois. Collectively, the results were shocking. The *Tribune*'s investigation alone found "nearly 400 cases where prosecutors obtained homicide convictions by committing the most unforgivable kinds of deception. They hid evidence that could have set defendants free. They allowed witnesses to lie. All in defiance of the law."[143]

The findings were too shocking to ignore, and in January 2000 Governor George Ryan imposed a moratorium on further executions in Illinois "pending an investigation into why more executions [had] been overturned than carried out since 1977, when Illinois reinstated capital punishment."[144] Five months later, Governor Ryan created the Commission on Capital Punishment to study the system of capital investigations and prosecutions in Illinois. Chaired by the former chief judge of the U.S. District Court in Chicago, the commission had fourteen members, including such luminaries as former U.S. Senator Paul Simon; Thomas Sullivan, a partner at the international law firm of Jenner & Block and a former U.S. attorney for Chicago; and Scott Turow, a former prosecutor, best-selling author, and partner at a Chicago law firm. Twelve of the fourteen members were lawyers, and nine were former or current prosecutors.

The board, later known popularly as the Ryan Commission, was Illinois's equivalent of a royal commission of inquiry. With a staff, state budget, and gubernatorial license, the Ryan Commission spent two years studying the capital punishment system in Illinois, eventually releasing a report in April 2002 enumerating eighty-five recommendations for reform. That report formed the basis of Governor Ryan's unprecedented decision in January 2003 to pardon four men sentenced to death and to commute the sentences of the other 167 defendants on Illinois's death row. In one fell swoop, the outgoing governor had "emptied Illinois' death row."[145] In issuing his decision, Ryan observed,

> Because our three-year study has found only more questions about the fairness of the sentencing, and because of the spectacular failure to reform the system, because we have seen justice delayed for countless death row inmates with potentially meritorious claims, and because the Illinois death penalty system is arbitrary and capricious and therefore immoral, I no longer shall tinker with the machinery of death.[146]

The North Carolina Actual Innocence Commission

As important as the Ryan Commission was, its work was a one-time inquiry into the state's criminal justice system. By contrast, North Carolina is the first state in the United States to create and maintain an innocence commission. As in Illinois, the North Carolina effort owes to the interest of a leading figure in state government. In October 2002, North Carolina's chief justice, I. Beverly Lake, invited representatives from law enforcement, criminal justice, and academia to join him at a roundtable discussion of wrongful convictions and to consider establishing the North Carolina Actual Innocence Commission.[147] In issuing the invitations, Chief Justice Lake offered a personal appeal:

> During my years of public service, I have often spoken of my concerns regarding needed reform in our justice system, including the need for increased accessibility to justice for our less fortunate, the need for increased funding to improve court efficiency and service, and the need for increased professionalism in our court operations. An additional growing concern, which partly results from those above mentioned, is the prospect of conviction and incarceration of innocent persons, as evidenced by the recent exonerations of the innocent from our nation's and state's prisons. . . . These exonerations challenge us to further review our criminal justice system for potential changes, which can minimize future convictions of the innocent, without jeopardizing the conviction of the guilty, and also establish a mechanism for objective review of credible innocence claims.[148]

The North Carolina Actual Innocence Commission, which followed from Justice Lake's initial discussion, accomplishes many of the aims he outlined in the invitation. The commission has thirty-one members; in addition to the chief justice, they include the state attorney general, the director of the state bureau of investigation, the secretary of crime control and public safety, an associate supreme court justice, superior court judges, legislators, prosecutors, sheriffs, police chiefs, deputies in law enforcement, defense attorneys, victim advocates, law professors, and private attorneys. All serve as volunteers. But whereas Lake urged a mechanism for reviewing postconviction claims of innocence, the North Carolina Actual Innocence Commission does not investigate individual cases. Rather, it considers the general sources of erroneous convictions and issues reports and best practices to prevent such errors.[149]

In October 2003 the commission released its first report, which focused on the deficiencies of eyewitness identification. As Christine Mumma, the commission's executive director, explained, "The synthesis of the Commission's work on the topic of eyewitness identification was a document, unanimously adopted by Commission members, outlining recommended procedures for conducting eyewitness identification through the use of photos, live lineups, or showups."[150] Today, "North Carolina's law enforcement agencies are increasingly implementing the Commission's eyewitness recommendations."[151]

Illinois and North Carolina have helped highlight the causes of wrongful convictions in the American criminal justice system and have challenged other states to follow their lead in addressing the problems that can lead to erroneous cases. As the following chapters illustrate, several states, particularly Virginia, are now making progress as well. The Innocence Commission for Virginia was a step in this direction. But as impressive as this progress has been, the future of reform and improved best practices is still very much up in the air. To understand where we should be going, it is crucial to appreciate how we have gotten here.

2

The Innocence Commission
for Virginia (ICVA)

It is sometimes said that we academicians live in an ivory tower, weighing philosophical issues under ideal conditions without having to get our hands dirty in "the real world." By the same token, lawyers in private practice, particularly those in large law firms, are sometimes accused of trading ideals for wealth and prestige. Who cares about justice, it's said, when you can attain the good life representing the highest bidder. Whether these adages have any truth to them—and I, for one, would challenge their general application—the Innocence Commission for Virginia is proof that representatives of academia, private law firms, and public-interest organizations can come together to advance an issue of reform that speaks not only to the real world but also to the common good.

The story starts for me in the spring of 2000, when I was teaching a large undergraduate course on constitutional procedure. We were just beginning to discuss the Sixth Amendment and its guarantee of a right to counsel when a student blurted out, "I don't think the Sixth Amendment protects anything." Taken aback a step, I asked him to explain what he meant. The student mentioned a case from the news in which a defense attorney had slept throughout the trial. On appeal from a habeas corpus petition, the U.S. Court of Appeals for the Fifth Circuit had affirmed the conviction, concluding that an "unconscious counsel" is not in itself prejudicial.[1] "Come on," the student told me, "if the courts consider a sleeping lawyer 'effective,' then what protection does any defendant really have that his rights will be protected in a case?"

The student's outburst set in motion a lively discussion about the Sixth Amendment and the bounds of its protections, but the student's message resonated in my gut. Not only did I share his concern, but having once practiced law, I also was aware that a client's fate can often turn on the skill and interest of his or her attorney. Now an academician with appointments in justice and law, I also recognize that the courts are hesitant to find ineffective assistance of counsel.[2] For the defendant who must accept an appointed attorney, his case may become the ultimate game of chance.

At about the same time as the student's eruption, Barry Scheck and Peter Neufeld were beginning to gain fame for their work at the Innocence Project.[3] I have great respect for the work of the Innocence Project and for those other academicians and journalists who have devoted countless hours to ensuring that innocent individuals are not executed or otherwise punished for crimes they did not commit. In Illinois, Northwestern University Professors David Protess, Rob Warden, Larry Marshall, and their students, as well as several reporters for the *Chicago Tribune,* were largely responsible for amassing the data necessary to convince Governor George Ryan to stay executions in the state pending a systematic investigation.[4] But if Scheck, Protess, Warden, Marshall, and others can raise enough doubts to have exonerated more than one hundred individuals from death row,[5] what has been done to ensure that innocent individuals are acquitted in the first place?

Many public-interest groups have concentrated on this issue for several years. The National Association of Criminal Defense Lawyers, the Capital Defense Network, the Southern Center for Human Rights, and the ABA's Death Penalty Representation Project, among others, have helped provide adequate representation to defendants at trial. But even they recognize that the need is greater than the available resources. In 1996, "Congress ended funding for the nation's 20 death penalty resources centers, eliminating major resources for indigent defendants,"[6] and as a result, many capital defendants have been left with "appointed attorneys who lack the training, experience or resources to provide effective representation."[7] In a study of U.S. capital cases from 1973 to 1995, "the single most common cause of reversible error was incompetent defense lawyering, which accounted for 37 percent of all state post-conviction reversals."[8] The situation is even worse for defendants accused of "lesser" crimes. Virginia's fee caps are a prime example of the limited resources available to indigent defendants in most criminal matters.

In some instances, academics have mobilized to fill this breach. At a number of law schools, legal clinics place students on criminal cases, and a few even allow students to work alongside counsel on capital trials. At New York University, law students have assisted on capital cases in Alabama and New York.[9] In Chicago, the Death Penalty Clinic at DePaul University offers law students an opportunity to research cases, locate and interview witnesses, and write motions on active capital cases.[10] And at the University of Georgia, the law school's Legal Aid and Defender Clinic serves as public defender in two counties, with faculty and students working together on death penalty cases.[11] Many more law schools have legal clinics that permit third-year students to represent indigent defendants in court on misdemeanor charges. In the nation's capital, the law schools of Georgetown University and American University have some of the most extensive clinical programs, placing students with defense attorneys and prosecutors to serve in court.[12]

Rare has been the undergraduate program, however, that involves students on criminal cases, whether investigating cases postconviction or assisting at trial. Professor Protess's journalism students at Northwestern are perhaps the most famous undergraduates to have examined capital cases—albeit once the defendants are on death row—but the more common approach has been to study the issue from afar, from the relative comfort of the classroom.[13]

I certainly do not mean to disparage the many faculty members who have offered classes that examine the criminal justice process or the death penalty. Assuredly, few issues are more important or controversial in law and justice than the state's execution of its citizens, and it is admirable that academicians would seek to expose their students to the many philosophical, legal, ethical, and equitable issues surrounding capital punishment and due process. The topic cuts across many disciplines, and its study may warrant a number of approaches.

In my own case, I was interested in exposing undergraduates to the "real" workings of the criminal justice process, but I also felt compelled to answer my student's charge that participants in that process—and even more, the public at large—were content to sit back and accept failings in the system that would permit defendants, most problematically the innocent, to receive substandard representation. In the fall of 2001, I offered an honors clinical course on the death penalty to a group of fifteen highly qualified undergraduates. One-third of the class worked on the defense of a pending capital case. Under the direction of two capable defense attorneys and with my additional supervision, five students assisted in reviewing case documents, constructing a time line of the crime, and canvassing the area of the crime scene to locate potential witnesses.

The other ten students took a step back from the day-to-day operations of the criminal justice process to understand how mistakes might occur in capital prosecutions. Pulling a page from the Innocence Project, these students investigated cases in which a defendant on death row was later exonerated. But rather than trying to prove the defendant's innocence, the students chronicled the investigation and prosecution of capital defendants to determine what had gone wrong in these cases. Beginning with a wide net of cases in which a defendant on death row had been exonerated of the crime, the students eventually whittled their way down to three cases: *Florida v. Smith,* in which a questionable detective and faulty eyewitness testimony convicted a suspect who was guilty of theft but not murder; *Idaho v. Fain,* in which primitive forensic methods fingered the wrong person; and *Louisiana v. Graham,* a case that can only be described as a soap opera, with cheating spouses, lying neighbors, an insane snitch, inexperienced lawyers, inept investigators, and a small-town sheriff on the take.

The students used a variety of methods to conduct their research, from reading news stories; reviewing case files; interviewing attorneys, observers, and family members; and, in one case, traveling to Louisiana to obtain additional information. When their research was finished, they spent several months drafting a report of their findings, which identified several common problems in the cases, including poorly trained investigators, inaccurate eyewitnesses, compromised informants, and inadequate representation. The students then proposed reforms that would address several of these issues. Their report, entitled "Dead Wrong: An Examination of Capital Prosecutions and Recommendations for Change," was released in April 2002, laying out what they considered to be the likely causes of the erroneous convictions and offering recommendations to address the flaws in these cases.[14] The students had a chance to brief a panel of justice officials on their findings, including a former U.S. attorney general. George Mason University released their report publicly in June 2002.

The students' work had piqued my interest, and I began to delve more extensively into the literature of wrongful convictions for my own research. In the process, I came across Christopher Amolsch, a criminal defense attorney in Northern Virginia, who had been recommended to me when I was originally searching for an active case for the clinical seminar.[15] As it turned out, Chris didn't have a suitable case in the pipeline, but he proved invaluable in an unexpected way. He was just leaving the board of the Innocence Project for the National Capital Region (IPNCR) and happened to introduce me to Julia Sullivan, a litigator with the firm of Sidley, Austin, Brown & Wood, who was just starting her own practice. Julia also served as president of the IPNCR and had a great deal of experience in criminal justice reform, particularly the emerging area of "life after exoneration."

The IPNCR—now the Mid Atlantic Innocence Project (MAIP)—is an offshoot of the Innocence Project created by Scheck and Neufeld and takes cases from prisoners convicted in Maryland, Virginia, or the District of Columbia who claim they have been wrongly convicted. Through teams of volunteer law students and pro bono attorneys, the MAIP investigates credible claims of innocence to exonerate those who have been erroneously convicted. Today, there are several innocence projects around the country, all dedicated to "seek[ing] the exoneration and release from incarceration of persons who have been convicted of crimes they did not commit."[16]

Julia suggested that we meet to discuss wrongful convictions in Virginia. The IPNCR had just won the case of Marvin Anderson, in which members of the national and regional innocence projects had managed to clear Anderson of rape and had earned him a pardon by Governor James Gilmore. As Julia noted, the IPNCR's work had uncovered many problems with criminal cases in Virginia—most notably, the Commonwealth's notorious "21-day rule"—and she believed the IPNCR or some other collective should take a hard look at the conditions that gave rise to erroneous convictions in Virginia.

Somehow our discussion got sidetracked, but in the spring of 2003 Don Salzman, the new president of the IPNCR, brought us together for a meeting at Skadden Arps, where Don practices law and serves as the firm's pro bono counsel. In addition to Julia and Don, we were joined by Misty Thomas, project director for the IPNCR; Ginny Sloan, president and founder of the Constitution Project, a bipartisan organization dedicated to commonsense solutions to issues of justice and law; and Steve Hanlon, a partner with the law firm of Holland and Knight and the "gray eminence" at the table whose many years of experience in practice and pro bono service brought a welcome perspective. The six of us had three things in common: we had experience in cases of erroneous convictions; we were concerned about the sources of these mistakes; and we believed the "ball needed to be moved forward" on the subject.

As we sat down in Skadden's conference room, we weren't sure what we could or should do. Some of us sought greater advocacy to publicize wrongful convictions; others pushed for additional research. After much discussion, we explored the possibility of an innocence commission. Less than a year earlier, North Carolina had created its Actual Innocence Commission, and several of us were intrigued by the possibility of constructing a similar organization for Virginia. Maybe if we were able to investigate the cases of exoneration, we could shine a light on the problems that underlay wrongful convictions in the first place. With a report in hand, it might be possible to build on the growing wave of criminal justice reform in the Commonwealth.

A Model for Social Change?

I add these details not to bore the reader or flatter myself or the other founders of the ICVA. Rather, it is to illustrate how an organization or project can be generated from a simple idea or single meeting. How absurd it was for six people to think that they could advance criminal justice reform. But from that first meeting tucked away in a small conference room, we eventually built an organization that completed an eighteen-month investigation at a price tag of more than a half-million dollars in pro bono attorney time. Nor is this story unusual. Anyone who is familiar with the founding of the National Abortion and Reproductive Rights Action League (NARAL) knows that it originated from a doctor, a minister, a rabbi, and a suburban housewife near Chicago who cared deeply about birth control and decided to try to convince the Illinois General Assembly to make contraceptives more widely available.[17]

The ICVA, of course, is nothing like NARAL, nor do we have plans to expand its reach considerably. Still, the story of much social reform over the last fifty years involves public-interest organizations whose members took it upon themselves to push for social change. The National Association for the Advancement of Colored People (NAACP) was instrumental in the civil rights movement; NARAL and the National Right to Life Coalition are active in the debate over abortion; and Mothers Against Drunk Driving (MADD) has advanced sobriety legislation. Most recently, several immigrant groups were active in leading protests against legislation to limit immigration and punish illegal immigrants already in the country.

These stories are familiar to academicians who study social movements and social change. Sociologists John McCarthy and Mayer Zald, for example, have examined the influence of social movement organizations, or coordinating groups, that organize movement members and keep them networked. According to McCarthy and Zald, social movements begin when people who see themselves as connected create ideas for social change and are willing to voice those ideas in order to change public attitudes.[18]

The work of academics like McCarthy and Zald examine collective action that occurs in the shadow of formal political institutions and processes. Familiar to most lay readers as social movements, collective protests, or mass gatherings, this research addresses the processes by which activists use popular protest to pressure lawmaking institutions into adopting their agendas. By contrast, political scientist John Kingdon looks at policy change through more formal political processes. In his book *Agendas, Alternatives and Public Policies,* Kingdon argues that policy change occurs when an actor, an initiative, and a policy window all converge at the same time.[19] To outsiders, the process may appear as "an idea whose time has come," but to Kingdon, policy change does not happen by chance.[20] Actors must still offer decision makers a plausible proposal when that agenda is ripe for consideration.

I do not mean to press too fine a point, for the ICVA is only one of the recent initiatives in the realm of criminal justice to advance reform. But the growing collective of similar groups needs to be seen in the light of social change literature and not simply as isolated, one-time initiatives that receive a little press coverage and then recede from view. Indeed, the more I think back over our initial meetings in forming the ICVA, the more I see elements of the social movement literature peaking through. Each member of the ICVA's steering committee was concerned about the issue of erroneous convictions (actors); we wanted to shine more light on the problem to initiate legislative changes and advance best practices in the field (proposals); and we were acting because the rise of DNA exonerations had given the issue greater salience (window of opportunity). Moreover, we wanted to create an organization that would offer a vehicle for pressing this cause.

This is not to say that our efforts were destined for success; indeed, the odds were—and still are—stacked against innocence commissions making significant headway, or at least the kind that observers would later rate as "social change." In our minds we had a vision of a classic

Big Ten grudge match in football, in which an off-tackle play and a cloud of dust would move the ball forward three yards. In reality, I believe that we have made at least a first down, but to continue this analogy a little further, the growing number of innocence commissions and similar such advocacy groups likely means that we're seeing a sustained drive toward the goal line of criminal justice reform.

This is how social change happens, when people who care about an issue take the seemingly illogical step of believing they can do something about it and organize collectively to advance a cause. Mancur Olson, who famously wrote about the process of collective action, claimed that an individual's decision to engage in such behavior may be irrational when it will not have direct, personal benefits for the participants.[21] What, then, moves people to reform? Is it unfounded altruism, moral righteousness, an overly inflated ego? Is this a luxury for the "haves," who, unlike the "have-nots," are freed from some daily struggles of subsistence to consider larger societal needs? Certainly, the topic has been debated for years in academic literature, the consensus being that organizing people is difficult, particularly when there are not immediate and personal payoffs for those who must take time and effort away from their other activities to join a quixotic movement for "change."

Perhaps, then, the way to look at the ICVA and similar such groups is not through the prism of McCarthy and Zald, who would call them social movement organizations on a journey for social change. A different approach would see justice reform as a two-step process based on John Kingdon's model of agenda setting. According to Kingdon, actors with "agency" (or a sense of self-confidence in their abilities and resources) advance proposals for policy change, trying to take advantage of a window of opportunity in political debate to accomplish their goals. It is only when a critical mass of such groups succeeds—when their proposals begin to become accepted thinking in informal or formal policy agendas—that we can speak of social change in the works.

Even then, it's difficult to say whether broader change requires specific policy initiatives to be enacted or, instead, whether a shift in public opinion or national consensus is sufficient. For example, public support for the death penalty dropped significantly in the last decade, from a high of 80 percent in 1994 to a slimmer majority in 2004.[22] Most states, however, still have the death penalty on their books and regularly convict and sentence capital defendants to death. Has social change, then, occurred because the needle of public support has been pushed back toward the middle? Should abolitionists declare victory, especially since some states have enacted moratoriums or tempered their enthusiasm for charging murders as capital cases? Or would social change require a declaration that capital punishment is unconstitutional, that its practice would be halted by at least a majority of the states?

This, too, is a question in the academic literature, the lessons from which suggest that social change is on a continuum. In some cases, changes in public opinion drive changes in policy. An example is MADD's success in convincing Americans that alcohol and vehicles don't mix, a move that has led to new statutes that continue to lower the acceptable blood alcohol level for drivers. In other cases, policy change precedes or moves in parallel with attitudinal change. The desegregation of the nation's schools may be an example, when the first iteration of *Brown v. Board of Education* came before much of white America was willing to countenance black children in its classrooms.[23]

In some cases, attitudinal change is enough to say that social change has occurred without any statute or policy initiative having been passed. The number of cohabiting American heterosexual couples reflects a loosening from 1950s mores that regarded "shacking up" as a sin. Few states, though, grant rights to opposite-sex unions if the couple is not married. Indeed, the current debate over gay marriage is a prime example of the tension over the definition of social change. Certainly, homosexuality is much more accepted in American society today than it was even ten years ago. Public opinion polls continue to show a drop in prejudice against gays and lesbians and a greater acceptance of employment protection against discrimination on the basis of sexual orientation. To many observers, these shifts reflect social change. Attitudes have moderated, bringing with them private initiatives like same-sex partner benefits and other measures that reflect the increased acceptance of gays and lesbians in American society. But the federal government has yet to enshrine legal protection for gays and lesbians by prohibiting discrimination on the basis of sexual orientation, offering employment benefits to a gay employee's partner, or, most notably, permitting homosexuals to marry. Attitudinal change may be nice, gays and lesbians might say, but until legal discrimination is abandoned, social change has not yet occurred.

There still is a great deal of debate about whether social change is best achieved by gradually building public support and then petitioning the government, or by quickly seeking to vault popular opinion to seek the protection of government agencies or the courts when a policy problem is identified. In either case, though, social change begins with actors who are willing to take the highly irrational step of believing that they can advance some proposal for change. Their action may be only protest, the proverbial howling at the wind, but history provides many examples in which heedless protest has accomplished social change. Consider the protesters of the Vietnam War, who were responsible in part for bringing down the Johnson administration. In other cases, the opposition is more strategic, with activists sensing their "moment" to advance an initiative that can help set the policy agenda.

The ICVA was somewhere in the middle. Certainly, no one expected that our initial efforts would immediately alter criminal justice policy, whether in Virginia or elsewhere, but neither did we envision our initiative as some sort of collective catharsis for frustrated reformers. We each had considerable experience in the justice system; we believed that changes were necessary to improve the way that criminal cases were handled; and we felt compelled to do more than simply get together and complain about the status quo. For that matter, we were more than quixotic actors with few powers to call upon. True, none of us was exceptionally wealthy, nor did we have the ability to move policy with a single decision, but we did have other resources on which to draw—our networks. Three of us were connected to well-known law firms; several of us had good relations and reputations with criminal justice officials and legal policymakers; and more than one of us had what I came to call the "golden Rolodex."

My intention here is not to puff up myself or my colleagues. By this point, I am quite well aware of our collective flaws. Rather, this description is intended to locate the ICVA's development in the collective action and social movement literature. McCarthy and Zald, for example, emphasize the importance of resources when an organization seeks to advance social change. Their model is called *resource mobilization theory*, through which actors cultivate a variety of resources to create a central movement organization and then organize others for change. Resources can—and, in many cases, must—encompass money, but there are other assets that permit actors to advance their cause. The ICVA's initial core leadership represented many of these resources, including expertise in the issue area, good professional reputations, and networks of influential individuals. Indeed, the organization's success turned on these very resources.

A Window of Opportunity

The first meeting of the ICVA's founders reflected two of Kingdon's three requisites for policy change. We had willing actors, and we sensed a window of opportunity to address wrongful convictions. The rise of DNA testing and the commensurate jump in postconviction exonerations had made it increasingly difficult for officials to claim that the criminal justice system was working effectively and that an examination of its process was unneeded. Governor Ryan's commission in Illinois and the subsequent commutation of the death row population there had really turned the tides politically, as even traditional "law and order" types were beginning to countenance reform. In many ways, it was difficult for anyone to avoid the issue. After all, who among us is in favor of erroneous convictions? But until the DNA exonerations and the Illinois commission, it was possible, perhaps even reasonable, for politicians and other policymakers to claim that a thorough examination of the criminal justice system was unwarranted. Why spend the time and resources, not to mention risk public support for the system, if there was not clear evidence that serious errors had been made? When, however, that evidence began to trickle—then gush—forth, it was virtually impossible for policymakers to claim that all was well.

In Virginia, the political climate was more hospitable to reform at that time than any of us could remember. The Earl Washington and Marvin Anderson cases had shocked many observers, who believed that Virginia's strict approach to criminal justice was effective, efficient, and accurate. Whether or not Washington or Anderson were typical of other defendants' cases, the facts of their wrongful convictions became fodder for many press reports questioning the legitimacy of Virginia's criminal justice system. Washington's story was particularly compelling, since almost any account of his case noted that he had come within nine days of execution before receiving effective legal representation.

The Virginia General Assembly and the State Crime Commission also had shown their willingness to undertake modest, prudent reform of the criminal justice system. Postconviction testing had just been approved for human biological evidence, and the Commonwealth's notorious 21-day rule seemed as though it might be headed on a one-way trip toward extinction. "This is the time," I remember one of the ICVA's steering committee members saying. Not only had problems been noted at the national level, but one of the states most notorious for its antipathy to criminal defendants—the Old Dominion—was even opening a window to consider criminal justice reform.

In fact, the calls for reform had been so ratcheted up—with state newspapers editorializing against the 21-day rule, the ABA and ACLU criticizing the state's system of indigent defense, and local organizations calling for the abolition of, or at least a moratorium on, the death penalty—that we saw a real opportunity to move the debate forward if we took a moderate, sober approach. The irony was not lost on us: here we were, a group that might otherwise have been dismissed as a bunch of liberal reformers, whose efforts and message could be politically palatable simply by taking a more temperate approach to the issue than had others who were already involved. To be sure, none of us was—or is—a "wide-eyed liberal," and several of us had had considerable experience "working across the aisle" on a variety of political issues. But any word game that would link "criminal justice" and "reform" in the same sentence would undoubtedly connote political liberalism. Whereas this issue and our potential efforts might have been ignored at an earlier time, recent developments had opened the door to justice reform, and a real opportunity awaited a group that could portray itself as competent, sober, and moderate.

The ICVA's Mission and Structure

If we sensed a window of opportunity and had the actors interested in reform, we were less clear about our proposed initiative. We knew we wanted to do something to improve the system of criminal justice, an effort that might help reduce wrongful convictions, but we did not start with a clear vision of what that work would entail. If anything, we sensed the tension between specificity and effectiveness. The more generic and amorphous our proposal was—for example, preventing the imprisonment of the innocent—the more likely it would find broad support but accomplish little. But if we narrowed our efforts to a particular problem—raising fee caps for indigent attorneys, for example—we would likely encounter greater opposition from policymakers who disagreed with the proposed remedy

As we surveyed the landscape of wrongful convictions, we were relieved to see the rise of organizations assisting the wrongly convicted to prove their innocence; in fact, several of us were already involved in such a group, the Innocence Project of the National Capital Region (IPNCR). But what was being done to prevent these errors in the first place? The Virginia Crime Commission had begun a study of eyewitness identification, but most of the legislative action had been to rectify individual cases. It was important for Virginia—and other states—to address the deficiencies that led to wrongful convictions in the first place.

Many of us were familiar with these problems from our own legal representation or research, but we also recognized the limits of our influence if we were to show up in Richmond or call a news conference to announce that the six of us "had the answers" for Virginia's criminal justice system. Influence would require data, the kind of "findings" that, if based on serious research, could attract the media's attention and, with it, additional resources to reach policymakers.

A Nongovernmental Innocence Commission

It was here that we paused to consider a structure. Our discussions were painting the outlines of an innocence commission, a notion with which we were familiar from several sources. To our south, North Carolina's chief justice had just created that state's Actual Innocence Commission; Scheck and Neufeld had called for the creation of state innocence commissions in their 2002 *Judicature* article;[24] and of course, some of the United States' closest allies, most notably Canada and the United Kingdom, had maintained state-sponsored innocence commissions for years.

In his article "Cautionary Notes on Commission Recommendations: A Public Policy Approach to Wrongful Convictions," Marvin Zalman effectively summarizes, as follows, most of the models of innocence commissions in existence at the time we considered the creation of the ICVA:[25]

1. A permanent governmental body that reviews and investigates prisoners' claims of actual innocence and forwards positive claims

to appellate courts, much like the British Criminal Case Review Commission.

2. Occasional commissions set up to investigate specific wrongful conviction cases, not unlike the Royal Commissions of Inquiry in Canada.

3. A permanent, governmental body that performs "postmortem" investigations of proven wrongful convictions, and reports on justice system failures that caused a particular miscarriage of justice.

4. One-time "blue-ribbon" study commissions established by a branch of government, similar to the Ryan Commission.

The North Carolina Actual Innocence Commission was more of a hybrid. Although it shares much with study commissions, the North Carolina body has become a permanent structure. Its structure and membership mirror the advice of Wisconsin law professor Keith Findley, who in 2002 recommended the formation of study commissions to bring together "prosecution and defense attorneys, members of the judiciary, representatives of police groups, victims rights groups, academics, and importantly, non-lawyers and individuals outside the criminal justice system" in a process that is "credible, respected, and above politics."[26]

As we contemplated the work of the ICVA, we envisioned ourselves as being in the mold of the North Carolina commission. We wanted to conduct a study of wrongful convictions, but rather than choosing a specific issue for reform and then looking at the cases for lessons on improving its practice, we were planning to begin with the cases and see where the findings took us. Ultimately, our goal was to bring a series of recommendations to light, and as much as we may have expected particular issues to arise, we were committed to conducting a serious, thorough review of the cases in order to understand what mistakes had occurred and why.

Unlike the North Carolina commission, we knew that our efforts had to come from a private entity, not the state. Some people might see this independence as offering us greater latitude to "speak our minds," but in truth we were deeply disappointed that the Commonwealth of Virginia had failed to take on the task itself. Not that we were surprised. Only North Carolina had initiated an innocence commission, and while a few more states were beginning to make noise about reviewing weaknesses in their criminal justice systems, it would have been folly to expect a state with a history like Virginia's to be among the first to commit public resources and acknowledge that the errors uncovered might go beyond the facts of a few cases. We were, of course, gratified to see some state leaders reconsider the 21-day rule, but none of us harbored any illusions that the Republican-controlled General Assembly or Virginia's new governor, Democrat Mark Warner, would make the issue of wrongful convictions a priority. To this day, I still am disappointed that we had to pursue the ICVA as a private exercise, for I deeply believe that it is the state's responsibility to provide oversight of the punitive system it employs. But if a private group was needed to address an issue that might otherwise have gone unexamined, then I'm glad the ICVA was able to undertake its research.

In his article calling for "a criminal justice commission to study wrongful convictions," Professor Findley urges participants to avoid "the temptation . . . to call these commissions 'Innocence Commissions.'" To Findley, such titles are "too narrow, too likely to marginalize the effort as a criminal defense movement when it really is much more."[27] We took Findley's advice seriously, but we still felt compelled to call our body an innocence commission, for innocence was what had made this venture possible. Policymakers had begun to take notice, and the public was starting to show interest, because Virginia had indisputable proof that innocent defendants had been wrongly convicted. If it were not for the exoneration of innocent men, one of whom had come dangerously close to execution, justice reform would not even have been on the public agenda. Although we agreed with Findley that the measures we ultimately recommended would likely go beyond the problems of wrongful conviction, we felt we had to call our body an innocence commission in order to maintain the political momentum. Criminal justice reform may be a difficult case to sell, but protecting the innocent—both current defendants and future victims—is an easier argument to advance. That said, I did insist on one tweak to our project's name. It was the Innocence Commission *for* Virginia, not *of* Virginia. Not only did I want to avoid any misconceptions about our private status, but I also could not help using another reminder (admittedly oblique) that this should have been the state's responsibility.

In many ways, the ICVA's private nature hamstrung us as much as it aided our deliberations. To be sure, we were not answerable to elected officials and did not have to temper our findings or conclusions to comport with a political sponsor's perspective. But at the same time our political currency was our ability to appear measured and reasonable. If we had wished, we could have taken a strident approach, conducting a cursory review of the cases to justify preconceptions of the criminal justice process and then used the findings as the basis of a shrill media campaign that the criminal justice system was broken and needed major repair. This would have been a mistake. First, we would have alienated policymakers and criminal justice officials, whose support or open ear we needed to make any headway in improving prosecutions or criminal investigations. Second, none of us believed that Virginia's criminal justice process was in shambles. We saw strengths and weaknesses in the system as we began our project, and we are even more committed to that conclusion today with the research and report completed. The causes of erroneous convictions are nuanced, occurring in many more cases than most people realize but leading to wrongful convictions in only a few. To convey the seriousness of this issue would require an approach that eschewed puerile flamethrowing. This is not to say that we would fail to make our eventual case clearly and directly—as veterans of Capitol Hill and several presidential campaigns, we knew the importance of explaining a complicated issue in simple terms—but we wanted to be taken seriously. Because we could be seen as self-appointed experts on the issue, we knew that our approach had to be sober and careful. This realization led to one of our first principles for the ICVA: it would be nonpartisan, an ethic I have assiduously enforced whenever there have been questions about the direction in which the commission might turn.

As we continued planning, one of the original six conveners, Steve Hanlon, had to drop out. He was embroiled in a complex case with the state of Florida over its handling of indigent defense, and we all agreed that his efforts were better spent on that. So now we were down to a steering committee of five, who became the guiding force behind the ICVA. Eventually, we agreed on a three-part structure. The five of us would serve as the directors of the ICVA. Don Salzman graciously agreed to become the legal director and to supervise the case investigations and legal research that formed the backbone of the ICVA's report. I became the chair of the commission and was responsible for coordinating the steering committee and leading our efforts to build a larger, more formal structure.

Outside the steering committee would be an advisory board, a collection of noted experts and other interested persons to whom we could turn for advice and guidance and whose fine and varied reputations would help provide "political cover" for the ICVA should anyone ever challenge its work. We recruited seven superb people for the advisory board: Joan Anderson, whose son Marvin had been wrongly convicted and then exonerated in Virginia; Steve Benjamin, the talented dean of the criminal defense bar in Richmond; Rodney Leffler, a former police officer and prosecutor in Virginia who is now a top criminal defense attorney in Fairfax County, Virginia; William Sessions, a former federal judge and director of the FBI under President Ronald Reagan and now an attorney at the law firm of Holland and Knight; Frank Stokes, a retired FBI agent whose independent efforts in Virginia helped exonerate Jeffrey Cox; John Tucker, a protégé of Tom Sullivan in the U.S. Attorney's Office in Chicago and a former partner at the law firm of Jenner & Block, who moved to Virginia and began to write books about the Commonwealth's criminal justice system; and John Whitehead, president of the Rutherford Institute, a libertarian civil liberties organization that had sponsored Paula Jones's lawsuit against President Bill Clinton.

We had few resources to support the ICVA and were not interested in taking time to write grant applications or raise funds to jumpstart our work. Instead, we agreed that the three organizations represented by our steering committee members—the Innocence Project of the National Capital Region (IPNCR), the Administration of Justice Program at George Mason University, and the Constitution Project—would become the ICVA's sponsors. In reality, the IPNCR was the lead partner in the ICVA, offering the commission staff time and the occasional student intern, as well as using its connections to obtain preferential printing rates and other benefits for the ICVA. Still, even these modest contributions were not enough to propel the commission forward.

Our saving grace came in the form of pro bono contributions from eleven superb law firms. When we considered the resources available to the ICVA, we realized that the work itself was potential capital. Our first meeting took place at a law firm in Washington, D.C., a legal market that not only encourages pro bono activity but whose bar probably consists of a disproportionately high number of attorneys interested in public policy or public service. Most of us had worked in large law firms at some point, and we remembered the recruiting literature emphasizing the interesting opportunities for young associates to participate in meaningful pro bono projects. Perhaps the ICVA also could provide such an opportunity. Idealistic attorneys who wanted to "do something" while still remaining with their corporate firms might jump at the chance to conduct a case investigation for the ICVA or pursue legal research that would help inform the eventual conclusions. Given our connections to a variety of law firms, we pitched the idea to the partners and found that we were correct: there was considerable interest. The following eleven law firms became our greatest resource:

Alston & Bird
Arnold & Porter
Collier, Shannon Scott
Covington & Burling
DLA, Piper, Rudnick, Gray & Cary
Hogan & Hartson
King & Spalding
Morrison & Foerster
Skadden, Arps, Slate, Meagher & Flom
Steptoe & Johnson
Troutman Sanders

Over eighteen months of investigation and research, these firms provided nearly $500,000 in free attorney time, offering more than thirty talented lawyers who conducted case investigations and undertook additional research projects to help the commission uncover its findings and reach its conclusions. The firms helped in other ways as well. As we neared the end of our investigation, two of them lent us their public relations specialists to offer guidance on the release of the ICVA's report. Several more made contributions to the IPNCR, which used a portion of the proceeds to fund the ICVA's activities. Although I am hesitant to single out any firms above the others, it's impossible to ignore the extraordinary contribution of Skadden Arps, Don's law firm. Skadden offered the ICVA considerable assistance, from the work of its graphic artists who created the logo for the ICVA and designed the final report, to photocopying and postage costs. Skadden, like the other ten law firms involved with the ICVA, puts its money where its mouth is in regard to pro bono service. We hear a lot in the popular media about the avarice of attorneys, but many forget that law is fundamentally a profession of service. These eleven law firms deserve great credit for their dedication to such ideals.

Case Criteria

With the three pieces of the ICVA in place—the steering committee, the advisory committee, and the law firms—our method began to take shape as well. We had decided to investigate known cases of wrongful conviction in Virginia, identify common problems from those cases that had led to the mistaken convictions, and then make recommendations based on additional research to address these deficiencies. In effect, we had another three-part structure: case investigations and identification of common problems. research into best practices to address these problems, and recommendations for improvement.

Before turning over the case research to the pro bono law firms, we needed to decide on the scope of our inquiry by defining the criteria for case selection. Although we already knew of several recent exonerations in Virginia, we wanted our approach to be thorough while ensuring that the scope of work was reasonable and that the findings were valid. We eventually settled on three standards. First, we focused on serious felonies, generally rape and murder. Of note, we did not limit our efforts to capital cases; in fact, we made *very* clear that the project would not be exclusively about capital cases. The death penalty remains a divisive issue nationwide and particularly in Virginia, and although doubts about capital convictions had softened support for the death penalty, we did not sense an opportunity in Virginia to address capital punishment as much as we saw a chance to improve the general practice of criminal investigations and prosecutions. For that matter, the five of us did not share the same view of capital punishment.

By leaving out "lesser" crimes, from other felonies down to simple misdemeanors, we were aware that we were significantly limiting our sample. Although wrongful convictions are likely in many kinds of cases, the stakes are highest for serious crimes, and we believed that these would receive the most attention if investigated.

Our second criterion limited our cases to those in which the defendant had been convicted after 1980. Because available case information dissipates over time (especially since much of the information collected before the 1990s is on paper and may have been thrown out), we were concerned about the reliability of the data if we were to push the investigation much further into the past.

Finally, we looked only at official exonerations, meaning cases in which a defendant's conviction was later overturned by a governor's pardon or a court's order, or when prosecutors conceded that the wrong person had been convicted. These are not matters of legal error—in which procedural shortcomings command a new trial or release—but cases of factual mistakes, in which the wrong person was convicted of a serious crime and later was cleared. We chose this criterion for two reasons. Since we were a nongovernmental group, one whose leadership came primarily from the reform community, we did not want to risk any charges that we had biased the selection of cases to include defendants who were not really innocent. Official exonerations rested these judgments on the Commonwealth itself. In addition, although we were concerned about cases in which a defendant's rights were ignored, we recognized that "legal technicalities" were less likely to generate public concern than were factual exonerations.

With research assistance from lawyers at a few of the volunteer firms, the ICVA's steering committee identified the cases of official exoneration for our thorough review. The ICVA's researchers combed news accounts and legal archives. We also mailed a survey to law enforcement agencies, Commonwealth's attorneys' offices, and nongovernmental organizations throughout Virginia to ferret out these cases. Our initial inquiry yielded ten that met each of the criteria as well as another case that teetered on the borderline.

The ambiguous case involved Beverly Monroe, who had been convicted of murdering her lover, an eccentric millionaire. Monroe's case ended in her release from prison on the order of a federal judge and the affirmation of the U.S. Circuit Court of Appeals for the Fourth Circuit. However, while the postconviction proceedings brought to light many facts that cast considerable doubt on her guilt, the basis for the court's decision was a procedural failure by the prosecution to disclose important and potentially exculpatory evidence to the defense.[28] Monroe was assured of her freedom only when the Commonwealth's attorney for Powhatan County decided in June 2003 not to retry her for the charge prosecuted by his predecessor. Even then, however, the prosecutor did not base his decision on her innocence but on the desire of the victim's family to avoid additional pain and the unavailability of some witnesses eleven years after the original case.[29] Hence, as much as the newly un-covered evidence seemed to exonerate Monroe—and while the Fourth Circuit's language criticizing the prosecution for poor dealing seemed both rare and worthy of further investigation—the case did not fit our narrow criteria for the ICVA. After much debate, we decided to assign the case to an interested firm for investigation with the goal of better understanding how and why the prosecution would fail to disclose exculpatory evidence. Given how unusual it is for a court to overturn a conviction on a *Brady* violation[30] (especially the so-called rocket docket of the Fourth Circuit), we wanted additional information about this case. In making its conclusions and recommendations in the final report, however, the ICVA limited itself to the cases that met the three criteria.[31]

During our investigation, an eleventh defendant was exonerated of a serious crime in Virginia. Arthur Lee Whitfield had been convicted in 1981 of raping two women, but by 2004 DNA evidence not only cleared Whitfield of the crimes but also identified a different man as the likely perpetrator. Although at least one of the victims continues to believe that Whitfield was her attacker, the Commonwealth's attorney for Norfolk—where the crimes occurred and were originally tried—"stands by" his conclusion that Whitfield is factually innocent, a view that Dr. Paul Ferrara, then the director of the Virginia Department of Forensic Science, supports.[32] Accordingly, the ICVA added the case for our inquiry and assigned the Whitfield case to a law firm for further investigation.

In the end, the ICVA investigated eleven cases that met each of our three criteria and supplemented this work with additional research into the Monroe case. The eleven cases, which are discussed in detail in the next chapter, were those of

Marvin Anderson
Craig Bell
Jeffrey Cox
Russell Gray
Edward Honaker
Julius Ruffin
Walter Snyder
David Vasquez
Earl Washington
Troy Webb
Arthur Lee Whitfield

ICVA Research and Report

With the three pillars of the ICVA in place—the steering committee, the advisory board, and the pro bono law firms—and having agreed to a research protocol, we crafted a mission statement for the ICVA. Our purpose was not so much to generate press coverage for the ICVA, and in fact I cannot recall a single news story that came from the statement's dissemination. Rather, we wanted to put others on notice that the case review was under way and that they could expect a series of findings and recommendations in the months ahead. This approach proved to be important in three respects. First, it helped facilitate dialogue with groups in other states who were concerned about similar issues, which helped us identify useful existing research on the issues we later identified as sources of the wrongful convictions. Second, it began to put us on the radar screens of reporters, who started calling us for commentary on issues of criminal justice in Virginia. We were careful not to preempt our own report, but the relationships we established with reporters in these early months helped us considerably when it was time to release our report. Finally, if nothing else, the mission statement convinced us that the ICVA really existed, that we now had an obligation to produce a report or end up looking like fools in the process. The mission statement, accompanied by our new logo, was distributed largely by e-mail and was posted on the website—www.icva.us—that we registered for the ICVA.

We had hoped to begin the case research in the summer of 2003, in order to take advantage of the arrival of summer law clerks at the participating law firms. In reality, most of the investigation had to wait until the fall to start, and even then we conducted the case investigations in waves, adding more firms and cases as we became more accustomed to the issues entailed in research and supervision. That fall we convened a meeting of the firms that had signed on, introducing a group of twenty or so lawyers to the ICVA and discussing the process of the case investigations we hoped they would undertake. In opening up the investigations, we had two main goals: (1) to understand and be able to explain what forces led to each erroneous conviction and (2) to offer any recommendations that, in their evaluation of their cases, might have prevented the mistake. Although the ICVA's steering committee and advisory board later conducted their own evaluation of recommended reforms, we were guided by the case findings and, to a lesser

The Innocence Commission for Virginia

*Jointly sponsored by the Innocence Project of the National Capital Region,
the Administration of Justice Program at George Mason University,
and the Constitution Project*

Mission Statement

Since 1973, over 100 people have been exonerated and released from death row. Wrongful convictions are not limited to capital cases, where the heightened attention and greater available resources may ensure more careful consideration of the charges and evidence. Innocent defendants charged with other crimes may face worse odds.

When an airplane crashes, the National Transportation Safety Board has responsibility to examine what went wrong and how such a disaster can be prevented in the future. Similarly, when the criminal justice system fails in its most critical functions—convicting the guilty and exonerating the innocent—the government should step in to determine the causes of the failure and identify appropriate reforms. For this reason, experts in the criminal justice system have advocated the establishment of "innocence commissions" in jurisdictions where wrongful convictions have occurred. All citizens have an interest in such examinations. When an innocent person is convicted, many people suffer. The innocent person is wrongly incarcerated and perhaps put to death. The real perpetrator often remains free to prey on society. And, if an exoneration occurs and the real perpetrator is identified, the victims and their families must relive the crime through any retrial.

Canada has long had formal processes to investigate wrongful convictions. In the United States, jurisdictions have begun to establish innocence commissions to investigate erroneous convictions and recommend policy reforms to address systemic problems. Virginia, in particular, has instituted some laudable reforms. Both the Governor and General Assembly have proposed extending the 21-day rule, and in the last year the Virginia State Crime Commission has established a task force to continue to review the rule. A 2002 referendum provided death row defendants an avenue to introduce DNA evidence post-conviction. Yet, despite the good faith and hard work of the Commonwealth's prosecutors and police, there is more work to be done to ensure that Virginia's criminal justice system is accurately identifying the perpetrators of serious crimes and protecting its citizens.

To assist in examining the problems that may lead to wrongful convictions, a coalition of three organizations has created the Innocence Commission for Virginia (ICVA). Led by the Innocence Project of the National Capital Region, the Administration of Justice Program at George Mason University, and the Constitution Project, researchers will canvas the state to identify cases in which defendants have been erroneously convicted of serious crimes. After reviewing these cases to understand the mistakes that led to conviction, the Commission will release a report of its findings. That report will chronicle the common errors in these cases, propose policy reforms to address the sources of those errors, and offer a series of best practices to improve the investigation and prosecution of serious criminal cases in Virginia.

ICVA is a non-profit, non-partisan organization, dedicated to improving the administration of justice in Virginia. ICVA's advisory board includes former prosecutors and defense counsel, notable public officials, and members of law enforcement and public interest groups, among others. ICVA's work will take it across the Commonwealth, seeking input and feedback from the many individuals and offices involved in criminal investigations and prosecutions.

For more information on the Innocence Commission for Virginia, please contact:

Professor Jon Gould
Administration of Justice Program
George Mason University
(703) 993-8481
jbgould@gmu.edu

Misty Thomas
Innocence Project of the National Capital Region
American University, Washington College of Law
(202) 274-4199
innocenceproject@wcl.american.edu

extent, by the recommendations of the lawyers involved in the case research.

We prepared a series of instructions for the volunteer lawyers (shown in appendix 1), encouraging them to be expansive and creative in their case investigations. The attorneys read the case files, reviewed the court transcripts, and interviewed the participants, including law enforcement personnel, prosecutors, defendants, their families, their defense counsel, and reporters. In a few cases, the information was fairly limited, when, for example, case documents remained under seal, but in most cases the researchers were able to draw up an expansive and in-depth description of the investigations and prosecutions that had led to the erroneous convictions.

As the case investigations progressed, certain themes began to recur in the wrongful convictions. Witnesses who misidentified perpetrators, defense lawyers who offered inadequate representation, and postconviction proceedings that made it difficult to rectify errors were among the common problems that we were beginning to see in the cases. In response, Don Salzman, the ICVA's legal director, commissioned legal research projects from additional firms to investigate similar practices in other jurisdictions as well as the federal and state legal norms governing these matters. These reports on law and practice helped inform the ICVA's eventual recommendations.

At the same time, the ICVA conducted its own confidential survey of law enforcement agencies and prosecutors' offices in the Commonwealth. Researchers contacted 276 law enforcement agencies, surveying staff on their practices for eyewitness identification and custodial questioning. In addition, researchers sought information from 120 Commonwealth's attorneys' offices about their discovery practices. The surveys were confidential, meaning that no agency or office was identified in the report. Appendix 2 provides copies of the surveys, which used a combination of structured and open-ended questions to discover how often and under what circumstances law enforcement agencies conducted eyewitness identifications, what their practices for custodial interrogations were, and the extent to which prosecutors shared information from their investigations with defendants and defense counsel.

After each stage of research was completed—case investigations, traditional legal research, and surveys of justice agencies—the ICVA convened first its steering committee and then its advisory board to consider the many findings and their ramifications. Weighing a variety of responses and suggestions, both groups were again called on to complete the report and the commission's conclusions and recommendations. Three members of the steering committee, Don Salzman, Julia Sullivan, and myself, took primary responsibility for drafting the report, which was vetted countless times by our advisory board and public relations specialists, who helped us with word choice and design. Once again, Skadden's graphics design team came through with the layout and an impressive and creative cover.

The report was finally released in the last week of March 2005, timed to coincide with a meeting of the national Innocence Network in Washington, D.C. Ironically, this was our third choice for a release date, our previous plans having passed by as the process of editing and preparation took longer than expected. At one point we had hoped to release the report in November 2004, shortly after press attention to the presidential election subsided and before the Virginia General Assembly reconvened in January. However, we finally recognized that little was likely to occur in an abbreviated legislative session during a state election year.[33] So rather than rush the report into print, we decided to take extra time to prepare it properly and complete the website that would include the report and all the case investigations. To conserve our limited resources—and to spare readers an imposing document—we chose to summarize the case reports in the printed document while making the full investigations available on our website.

A day before the national release of the report, we held a luncheon at the Richmond office of Troutman, Sanders, one of our pro bono firms, to brief a select group of Virginia reporters on the report's contents. We were gratified by the turnout, which included reporters from three of the top four circulating newspapers in Virginia. We brought several of our advisory board members to the meeting, having briefed them on our talking points ahead of time, and helped reporters understand the extent of our investigation and the key points in our findings and conclusions. We were rewarded the next day and for weeks to come with favorable coverage in Virginia.

The ICVA's eighteen-month investigation culminated on March 30, 2005, when we released our report nationally at the Innocence Network conference, providing a copy of the report on CD-ROM to the participants and blanketing the national news media with our press releases. The IPNCR also held a reception that week to thank the ICVA's many pro bono lawyers. Although the event was closed to the press, the evening's main attraction was Bill Kurtis, host of A&E's popular show *American Justice,* and we expected that our report would continue to generate news coverage. Here we were not as successful, since a number of news media saw the report as a regional or even a local story. Over time, however, as other states have toyed with innocence reviews, we have gained more attention from reporters, reformers, justice officials, and even state legislators, who are interested in our comparative perspective.

Chapters 3 and 4 of this book describe many of the ICVA's findings and recommendations. It is important to appreciate the tenor of our discussions at the ICVA, for we often were balancing two considerations. That is, many people on the steering committee and the advisory board believed that that the problems identified in the case investigations were evidence of serious problems that necessitated broad reform. Others, however, pushed for a more incremental approach, arguing that successful change rarely comes from systemic reforms, which often are viewed as too radical, particularly when advocated by people outside formal political or policy processes. Politicians are generally timid, this line of argument went, fearing substantial change unless they sense a momentous swing in public opinion. Justice officials, too, are often attached to the status quo and may interpret change as a threat to their own positions, power, or prestige.

Balancing the two sides was difficult but was one that members of the steering committee and advisory board took seriously. In general, we erred on the side of caution and conservatism, trying to temper any inflammatory rhetoric or unnecessarily provocative conclusions in the case reports to ensure that our report and recommendations would have the greatest chance to reach legislators and justice officials in Virginia. Indeed, Virginia remains a fundamentally conservative state. If we wanted to preach to the converted on justice reform, then we would not have to worry about the breadth or militancy of our conclusions. But from the beginning of our work, we saw our audience as made up of four constituencies: elected policymakers, prosecutors and law enforcement officers, media opinion leaders, and the general public. If we wished to reach them, if we expected them to accept our findings and consider our conclusions, then we needed to couch our work in the rhetoric and values that undergird Virginia politics. For this reason, we paid less attention to the rights of innocent suspects in the ICVA report and put greater emphasis on the tax savings and greater security that come with preventing wrongful convictions.

These are not specious arguments; on the contrary, they are real reasons to tackle the problems behind erroneous convictions. But to "work" as a political issue, we believed that criminal justice reform had to be separated from its usual connotations with civil liberties, liberalism, or even the dreaded "criminals' rights"—none of which speaks to the self-interest of elected officials or the general public—and repositioned to address matters that people care about in their everyday lives, like protecting their families and saving tax dollars. To be sure, we all can agree in principle that the criminal justice system should protect the innocent and convict the guilty, but it's difficult to move wrongful convictions from this generic ethos that fails to mobilize action to a more pressing concern that would spur reform.

Lessons from the ICVA

Chapter 5 discusses the future of the ICVA and other state innocence commissions and proposes broader legal and political strategies to advance reform of the criminal justice system. In addition, the ICVA's work offers more immediate lessons that may guide other postconviction efforts as well as illuminate the ability of nongovernmental actors to make headway on an issue of state public policy.

Advantages

Innocence commissions, even those convened by nongovernmental actors, offer several important advantages and few drawbacks. Rather than pointing fingers or affixing blame, these bodies represent an effective and constructive mechanism to evaluate errors objectively. They help identify weaknesses in the criminal justice system and propose reasonable and workable improvements. Most important, they may help protect society by enhancing the accuracy of criminal investigations and prosecutions, thereby ensuring that the actual perpetrators are caught—and quickly—in similar cases.

From the ICVA's perspective, a nongovernmental commission can get the ball rolling, whereas a state might be reluctant to address the problem of erroneous convictions for fear of raising public doubts about the accuracy and effectiveness of the state's criminal justice system. Because postconviction review has often been associated with a "pro-defendant agenda," other state actors may be hesitant to embrace the issue for fear of appearing soft on crime or unsympathetic to victims. Of course, neither needs be the case—and, indeed, victims have a strong interest in ensuring that convictions are accurate—but, politically, wrongful convictions have not often been the kind of issue that attracts serious attention from lawmakers or justice officials. Too often, policymakers try to discount the problem, undoubtedly fearful that if serious errors have occurred on their watch, a postexoneration review may end up assigning blame.

This is where a nongovernmental body can help propel the issue forward, gathering facts and data that cannot be discounted. Innocence commissions need not even succeed in achieving legislative change. Simply putting the issue on the public's radar screen and having it reach the policy agenda may itself generate interest in new, best practices for law enforcement officers and prosecutors. For that matter, nongovernmental review can provide political "cover" for governmental officials, in some cases allowing important or even provocative points to be made—and the arguments to be introduced into policy debate—without politicians or particular officials worrying about being tagged with the perspective. For example, a district attorney who believes that detectives fail to disclose exculpatory evidence to his office but who also worries about publicly accusing the local sheriff's office of misconduct might welcome an impartial inquiry that reaches this conclusion as well. (The ICVA encountered this situation.) The same might be true for a sympathetic legislator in a vulnerable district, who might feel freer to "vote his conscience" if known and respected individuals are involved in a commission's investigation. Call it the equivalent of political protection, but if a commission is serious, thorough, and sober, its conclusions may induce political leaders and policymakers to respond to the report's findings. What's more, government gains the benefit of the investigation without having to spend tax dollars on the effort.

Challenges

These advantages aside, innocence review should be the obligation of the state. As a matter of philosophy, the same state that uses its power to punish the guilty should be required to use its own resources to ensure that its processes of justice accurately accomplish those aims. Yet few states seem willing to admit that their systems of law enforcement and prosecution have systemic flaws, and fewer still have made efforts to evaluate those errors and respond with appropriate reforms.

More practically, a state has the powers to compel evidence and enact reform that nongovernmental actors lack. Without subpoena power, innocence commissions like the ICVA have only their own powers of persuasion and cajolement to convince potential witnesses to offer evidence. The ICVA tried to work around these limitations through extensive interviews and intensive document reviews, but our findings would have been even more detailed if we had had the state's powers to compel evidence.

Nongovernmental bodies also must generate their own resources. In Virginia, we patched together support from a variety of sources. Every member of the ICVA served without compensation, with each of the sponsoring organizations providing a measure of logistical support. We also relied on extensive pro bono assistance from several law firms, which gave us thousands of hours of attorney time and covered research expenses. We could not have done this work without their support, but these contributions probably will not continue. That is, all of us involved with the ICVA have "day jobs" that command our regular attention. The fact that we could attract such devoted volunteers was explained in no small measure by the project's limited duration. Were we to ask our steering committee or pro bono attorneys to continue to devote hundreds of hours a year to a similar, ongoing project, I doubt that we would be so successful.

Therein lies an unpleasant reality for nongovernmental institutions, which must secure more permanent institutional support—much of it likely from foundations—if they wish to "keep up the heat" on these issues, whether by conducting additional investigations or offering training or technical assistance. This also is an important lesson for the policymaking process. If the states are allowed to rely on nongovernmental institutions as a check, if the impetus for reform comes from those outside the criminal justice system, then that attention will be subject to the waxing and waning of third-sector support. Some opponents of justice reform may choose simply to "wait out" the interest and resources of nongovernmental institutions in the hope that the issue of justice reform will recede from the policy agenda. But even those who support the work of private innocence commissions must recognize that relying on "outsiders" to do the work of government runs the risk that public attention and, with it, the prospects for reform will quickly recede if nongovernmental actors are unable to keep up their efforts.

Nongovernmental commissions also face a question of legitimacy. Without the state's imprimatur of authority, some people may doubt the commission's intentions or question its ability to accomplish a tangible result. In Virginia, we established our credibility by two means. First, we secured the backing of a prestigious and bipartisan group of volunteers and advisers. The ICVA's steering and advisory committees included people from multiple perspectives and positions, and this support from such a varied and estimable group provided us a baseline of respectability and legitimacy. The involvement of top law firms also helped, which by nature are seen as careful, cautious, and conservative institutions. Second, we consciously chose a sober, thorough investigation. Early on, we were warned about the folly of past "do-good exposés" in Virginia, and in turn, we were careful at every turn to include a variety of perspectives and to circumscribe the investigations and conclusions. In effect, we banked on the seriousness and intensiveness of our review to build our credibility.

We were also aided by the advice of several public relations specialists, who helped us draft press releases, attract reporters, and organize our press conference. The fact that we held our press briefing on the top-floor conference room of one of Richmond's most prestigious law firms undoubtedly helped, for the opulence of the setting seemed to suggest that the state's legal elite accepted and endorsed our work. We had invited our advisory board members to attend this event, and the presence of representatives from both poles of the political spectrum reinforced our claim that the case investigations and recommendations had been careful, nonpartisan, and worthy of consideration.

Positive articles and editorials in the Commonwealth's papers soon followed, with editorials in the *Virginian-Pilot* and *Roanoke Times* praising the ICVA's "in-depth study" and "exhaustive review."[34] We also were careful about how we described the report, seeking, as one story noted, not to "accuse [anyone] of corruption or evil in these cases" because our research had not found such evidence. We intentionally presented the conclusions to appeal to as broad a political audience in Virginia as possible, and fortunately the reporters printed many of the quotations we most wanted. "This [report] is as much about crime reduction as it is about how to protect the innocent," the *Richmond Times-Dispatch* quoted me saying, as it and other papers correctly summarized our recommendations. We could not have been more pleased, for we recognized that our legitimacy as a nongovernmental institution rested largely on our public profile.

Some observers may wonder whether we "watered down" our conclusions so that the report would not scare off Virginia's largely conservative political establishment. Did we fail to provide a complete diagnosis of Virginia's criminal justice system in order to be politically palatable? The short answer is no, for we went where the investigations took us, accurately reporting what the case research concluded and offering reasonable recommendations to address those problems. At the same time, there is no doubt that we were circumspect in some of the language we used, trying whenever possible not to needlessly inflame policymakers. In the editing process, for example, when the steering committee read the case reports compiled by enthusiastic young attorneys, it sometimes tempered the impassioned wording of their recommendations.

It is a fine line between grabbing the public's attention and alienating them with polemical rhetoric. We all had seen enough reports from earnest justice "activists" who passionately accused state officials of neglect or malfeasance, only to see their reports quickly dismissed as too strident. We had not engaged in an eighteen-month process and recruited several top law firms to the project to see it set aside for lack of good political judgment. It bears saying again: Virginia remains a conservative state, especially on issues of criminal justice, and anyone who seeks to make headway in reforming that process must recognize that legitimacy comes from appealing to values that policy leaders and the public embrace.

Nor was this a Machiavellian calculation on our part to find political consensus. Many members of the ICVA's steering committee and advisory board—not to mention several of the attorneys at the participating law firms—have considerable experience "working across the aisle" on issues of public concern. One of our tenets in starting the commission was a collective belief that people of goodwill from across the political spectrum share an interest in convicting the guilty and freeing the innocent. If our final report and outreach efforts could not mirror those fundamental values, then we did not deserve the legitimacy we sought.

Whether we succeeded in our ultimate aims is a question left to chapter 5 and future developments in Virginia and elsewhere. The next two chapters examine in detail the ICVA's findings and conclusions and link them to the efforts of other investigative commissions and activities. If the ICVA has done nothing else, its work has highlighted a disquieting discrepancy between the commonality of problems uncovered in wrongful convictions and the lack of systemic criminal justice reform across the states.

3

The Cases

Many of us tend to view wrongful convictions through a model of cause and effect. We know there was a grievous error; we presume there was a cause; and we seek to uncover the trigger in order to prevent its harmful effects in the future. Noted criminologist Richard Leo has labeled this the "familiar plot" of scholarship on wrongful conviction, in which the supposedly "well-known" causes of wrongful conviction appear to necessitate a series of "obvious" policy solutions.[1] It's not surprising that the research on erroneous convictions should appear that way, since most of the people who have investigated these cases are lawyers and are trained in the law's model of cause and effect.[2] Law school teaches us that wrongs have causes, that causes can be prevented, and that injuries from unacceptable causes warrant recompense to the victim and punishment to the wrongdoer. Indeed, that is the very basis of both criminal and tort law.

In many ways, the ICVA followed this model as well. But a better way to understand the ICVA's conclusions—and more broadly, a better model to comprehend the nature of wrongful convictions—is not through law but science. That may seem odd to many readers. After all, wrongful convictions occur in the justice system at the hands of people sworn to enforce, uphold, and defend the law. But wrongful convictions have no simple explanation of cause and effect. To be sure, the ICVA and other earlier research and commissions have identified likely factors behind wrongful convictions, but to call these factors *causes* is to miss the fact that many of these forces are found in other cases that do not end in erroneous conviction. Chapter 1 described the Spangenberg Report, a research project commissioned by the American Bar Association, which found that over the years, thousands of defendants received substandard lawyering in Virginia. Were all these clients wrongly convicted because they were innocent? Probably not, even if the problems they encountered with their lawyers were similar to those found in the wrongful convictions studied here or elsewhere. But it would be a grave error to dismiss the seriousness of these problems because they did not directly lead to wrongful convictions.

In a June 2006 op-ed in the *New York Times,* David Dow, a law professor at the University of Houston, argued that emphasis on the wrongful conviction of innocent suspects diverts attention from the "appalling violations of legal principles" found in many other cases.[3] If we worry only about those defendants who are convicted but are factually innocent, he suggested, we give carte blanche to the justice system to treat the guilty any way it wishes, even if the result is to violate legal and constitutional norms we claim to hold dear. Dow did not say so, but the linchpin in his argument is, again, this legal presumption of cause and effect. To focus exclusively on wrongful convictions is to suggest that they have discrete or specialized causes—sources that are problematic only because they convict innocent people. Wait a minute, Dow seems to say. These "causes" are perilous because they "violate [the very] legal principles" that purport to undergird the criminal justice system in the first place.

Dow's point is important, but he goes too far in recommending that we abandon our focus on cases of innocence. The exoneration of innocent people is what breathed life into the latest justice reform movement. To claim that innocence is irrelevant not only ignores political reality but also abandons one of our most fervent hopes for the criminal justice system: that it convict the guilty and acquit the innocent. Nor should we call off the investigation of exonerations. Just as the NTSB investigates airplane accidents to identify their causes and recommend needed reforms, the justice system should be willing to address its unfortunate errors to learn from and help prevent such mistakes. If private entities must assume this function in place of the state, so be it.

Dow is correct, though, in suggesting that the errors found in wrongful convictions occur in other criminal cases, and he is right in urging reforms that go beyond the known exonerations. The analogy here is to cigarette smoking and lung cancer. How many reasonably educated people believe that cigarette smoking is good for them? After all, 90 percent of lung cancer deaths occur in smokers.[4] Yet as bad as we know smoking to be, only one in ten smokers gets lung cancer in his or her lifetime.[5] Does this mean that smoking causes cancer? Not if you ask the tobacco industry, which for years has argued that research lacks a cause-and-effect relationship between smoking and cancer. But the correlation is so strong between smoking and cancer (not to mention other maladies) that our society has taken many measures to prevent smoking. We have banned smoking in restaurants and on airplanes, required warning labels on cigarette packs, and funded litigation against the tobacco industry, even though cigarettes are not a direct cause of cancer.

A similar model applies when considering the factors that lead to wrongful convictions. The fact that they do not directly "cause" the conviction of innocent defendants—or more specifically, the fact that they are not limited to wrongful convictions—does not mean that they should go unaddressed. Instead, they warrant our attention and energy precisely because they apply to other cases. Our challenge, then, is to identify errors that occur in wrongful convictions and to do so in a manner that leaves observers confident that the research was done fairly, competently, and thoroughly. When possible, we also must identify those factors that specifically lead to erroneous convictions, but in reality we are likely dealing with a "perfect storm" of errors that together have convicted an innocent suspect.

Defenders of the status quo use this postulate to claim that the criminal justice system is fair and accurate, or at least that few people are ever wrongly convicted. They may ultimately be correct, but their defense would be more credible if the criminal justice system opened itself for review. As chapter 1 indicated, wrongful convictions may run as high as 1 or 2 percent of all cases, but we'll never know until the various constituencies of the criminal justice system come together to examine the system's errors with an eye on improving it. These reforms need not be limited to preventing wrongful convictions. Just as a recommendation by the NTSB may improve airline efficiency as well as safety, a procedural reform for the police may not only prevent mistaken convictions but also encourage guilty pleas. *That* should be the ultimate goal of both "reformers" and "defenders" of the criminal justice system: a regular process of review that seeks to improve the professionalism of police, prosecutors, defense attorneys, and judges, and in so doing helps prevent errors that lead to wrongful convictions.

The ICVA's Findings

The Virginia State Crime Commission has undertaken several credible research projects to identify and improve potential frailties in the Commonwealth's criminal justice process. But Virginia still lacks a public body to review wrongful convictions and other serious errors in criminal investigations and prosecutions. For this reason, the ICVA pursued its own eighteen-month investigation of erroneous convictions in Virginia, examining eleven known exonerations of rapes and murders since 1980. Recognizing, of course, that each case presents unique facts, the ICVA identified nine primary factors that have been linked to erroneous convictions in Virginia:

- The honest, mistaken identification of defendants by victims or other eyewitnesses, particularly in cases involving cross-racial identifications. This problem is exacerbated by the heavy emphasis placed on, and great credibility given to, eyewitness identification in criminal prosecutions. The shortcomings of eyewitness identifications are most pronounced when a prosecution proceeds in the face of little corroborating evidence, or even when the available evidence points to the defendant's innocence, such as when a victim's initial description of the perpetrator does not match the suspect's characteristics.
- Suggestive identification procedures, including photo arrays and lineups that unduly highlight a particular suspect. These problems are most pronounced when they reinforce an initial, incorrect identification, such as when a victim picks the one color picture out of an array of otherwise black-and-white photos and then is shown that suspect in a lineup shortly afterward.
- "Tunnel vision" by police officers and detectives. Many of the crimes were high profile, generating considerable press coverage and a public demand for quick resolution. In some cases, law enforcement became convinced that a particular suspect was the actual perpetrator even when other factors suggested innocence or alternative suspects.
- Antiquated forensic testing methods of biological evidence that was later shown to be exculpatory. With the availability of DNA testing and the Commonwealth's recent initiative to examine and test biological evidence from old cases, many of these problems have now been alleviated. Stricter evidentiary rules, better preservation of biological evidence, and effective use of the adversarial process to challenge the opinions of those who claim to be experts would enhance DNA technology and other scientific evidence in preventing wrongful convictions.

- Inadequate, if not ineffective, assistance of defense counsel. In none of the cases did a reviewing court later find ineffective assistance, but in several matters the defendants had to rely on inexperienced or inattentive attorneys, proving their innocence only later when skilled counsel took over and devoted considerably more time to the cases after conviction.
- Failure to disclose exculpatory reports or other evidence to the defense. In some cases, prosecutors were unaware that detectives or forensic specialists had relevant exculpatory evidence.
- Interrogations involving suspects with mental incapacities. Mentally impaired defendants often are confused and can be more easily convinced to "confess" to a crime, even when they do not understand the circumstances of the case.
- Inconsistent statements by defendants. Under the pressures of a criminal investigation, some suspects gave the police contradictory information, thereby turning suspicion on themselves. Officers understandably targeted these defendants when their stories changed or their alibis were contradictory.
- The unavailability of adequate postconviction remedies to address wrongful convictions once they occurred. Virginia has made significant progress in this area in the last few years. Even today, however, many of Virginia's exonerees would have to rely on the clemency process and would have no remedy available to them in the Commonwealth's courts.

It is one thing to recognize these problems in a list of deficiencies in the criminal justice process and another thing to understand how the inherent weaknesses in criminal investigations and prosecutions erroneously convict innocent suspects. Unlike some televised "movies of the week," wrongful convictions are not usually the result of intentional bad actions by police officers or deliberate bias by prosecutors. Instead, many of the causes of erroneous convictions are built into the criminal justice system, reflecting traditional practices that need to be updated or improved or a standard operating procedure that has been tolerated and allowed to fester.

In a sense, then, any individual who becomes a criminal suspect is subject to these problems, including such questionable processes as suggestive identification procedures, tunnel vision, and inadequate representation. Certainly, the cases investigated by the ICVA show how an innocent person can be mistakenly caught up in a criminal investigation and unwittingly convicted and sentenced for a crime he or she did not commit.

The Cases

ICVA researchers investigated eleven cases that fit the commission's case selection criteria, plus a twelfth in which the defendant, though not officially exonerated, had been released from prison under circumstances suggesting serious errors during the case's investigatory phase. The following section explains how these wrongful convictions occurred.[6]

Earl Washington Jr.

Perhaps the most notorious case is that of Earl Washington Jr., an African American man with an IQ of 69 who came within nine days of execution before he finally received capable, pro bono counsel who helped clear him and eventually win his freedom.[7]

On June 4, 1982, a nineteen-year-old white woman was raped and fatally stabbed in front of her two children in Culpeper, Virginia. As the victim lay dying, she told police officers and her husband that her assailant had been a lone black man. This was a horrific crime, and one all the worse because there were no other obvious leads.

Nearly a year later, on May 21, 1983, Earl Washington Jr. was arrested in Warrenton, Virginia, after a night of heavy drinking. Washington was charged with entering an elderly neighbor's house, taking her gun, and hitting her with a chair. After several hours in police custody, an investigator with the Fauquier County Sheriff's Department began to interrogate Washington. Over the course of two hours, Washington allegedly confessed to four unrelated crimes in Fauquier County, including two rapes, an attempted rape, and one case of breaking and entering. The only problem was that in each case a victim refuted Washington's involvement or his confession was determined to be wildly at odds with the facts known to law enforcement officers.

Then the investigator asked Washington about the unsolved murder of a young woman one year earlier in Culpeper County. Again, Washington confessed, admitting to killing the victim but not mentioning the rape. He had difficulty explaining other details of the crime as well.

When investigators drove him to Culpeper to identify the victim's apartment building, Washington directed them to the wrong building and, when taken to the correct building, identified the wrong apartment.

Washington's "confession" had many other serious inconsistencies as well. Under further questioning, Washington identified the victim as black when she was white; he said that he had stabbed her "once or twice," when the actual crime involved thirty-eight separate wounds; he said he hadn't seen anyone else in the apartment, even though the victim's two small children were present during the attack; and he claimed that he had "kicked the door open" when there was no evidence of forced entry at the victim's home. About the only thing he got "right" was saying that he had left a shirt behind at the crime scene. Even here, though, investigators held the shirt in front of Washington while he described it in an official statement. As it was, Washington required three rehearsals before authorities accepted a written statement of confession from him. They apparently refused to consider that Washington might not be the perpetrator.

The prosecution's case hinged on Washington's statements as well as his identification of the shirt given to the police by the victim's family six weeks after the crime. The defense failed to point out the inconsistencies of the prosecution's case, including three especially serious weaknesses. Only after Washington secured postconviction counsel did attorneys scour the Commonwealth's lab reports and discover that the seminal fluid found at the crime scene did not match Washington's blood type. Whether prosecutors were aware of this inconsistency is not known, but the Commonwealth had turned over the evidence to Washington's trial counsel, where it sat unappreciated in the case file. The trial counsel also failed to take appropriate issue with the prosecution's use of the T-shirt left at the crime scene. Washington already had confessed to leaving a shirt behind and described it clearly when making his confession, but the defense counsel did not note for the jury that Washington had known to do this only because the investigators held the shirt out for him during the interrogation and asked him to describe it. Finally, the defense did not present competing witnesses for the prosecution's claim that Washington was competent to stand trial or make his confession. When asked why he failed to ask the court for funds to hire an independent mental health expert, the attorney said he thought that the judge would deny his request.

A jury of ten whites and two blacks deliberated for fifty minutes before returning a verdict of guilt. After a short penalty phase, during which Washington's inexperienced counsel was unable to offer a meaningful counterargument to the testimony of the victim's mother, the jury recommended a sentence of death. The trial judge concurred and imposed the death verdict on March 20, 1984. In a separate case, Washington pleaded guilty in May of that year to a case of burglary and malicious wounding and was sentenced to two consecutive fifteen-year sentences.

Washington's direct appeal failed. Without a right of counsel for a state habeas corpus appeal,[8] Washington was moved to death row, where he sat unrepresented until nine days before his scheduled execution date of September 5, 1985. Without the intercession of a fellow inmate to his own pro bono lawyer, Washington might very well have been executed. The attorney persuaded her large New York City law firm to draft a state habeas corpus petition for Washington and to investigate his case. The firm assigned a senior associate to the case who enlisted a new local counsel, a lawyer who had just been elected president of the Virginia Trial Lawyers' Association. Together they uncovered the evidence that Washington's earlier counsel had missed at trial and that prosecutors and law enforcement officials had either ignored or dismissed previously.

The legal process, however, did not turn in their favor. At the time, Virginia's 21-day rule prevented the introduction of new exculpatory evidence, and both state and federal appeals courts refused to overturn Washington's conviction on the grounds that his trial counsel should have introduced the lab reports showing that Washington was not the source of the semen stain found at the crime scene. Although the U.S. Court of Appeals for the Fourth Circuit agreed that Washington's trial counsel had been inadequate, it concluded that the attorney's failings were not prejudicial to Washington's case, largely because of his "confessions" to the crime. What no one seemed willing to acknowledge was Washington's mental inability to knowingly confess.

Washington's legal team pursued other alternatives. They persuaded the Virginia Attorney General's Office to conduct additional testing of the semen stain, which found that the sperm in and around the victim's body contained a genetic marker that did not belong to Washington. With this new evidence, Washington's lawyers petitioned Virginia's governor, L. Douglas Wilder, to pardon Washington. Governor Wilder sought additional DNA testing, the results of which were kept secret from Washington's legal team. With his gubernatorial term coming to a close, Wilder denied Washington's request for a pardon but offered him commutation to life in prison with the possibility of parole.[9] Given just two hours to consider the offer, Washington accepted in January 1994.

Governor Wilder's offer of commutation was based in part on the theory that there may have been an "unindicted co-ejaculator"[10] who participated in the crime with Washington. However, neither the Commonwealth nor Washington had ever suggested that he had been joined in the crime by a co-conspirator who raped the victim before Washington killed her. Wilder further supported his decision by Washington's "knowledge of evidence relating to the crime which . . . only the perpetrator would have known,"[11] even though Washington's only "knowledge" was his description of a shirt left at the crime scene, which detectives had held up for Washington to describe at his interrogation. Once again, no one seemed willing to consider the case's central weakness: that as a man with an IQ of 69, Washington hardly seemed able to confess to the initial crime without serious coaching from sheriff's deputies.

Wilder's offer of commutation did hold out an additional hope for Washington. In his official declaration, the governor urged the General Assembly to reconsider the Commonwealth's 21-day rule and offer Washington and others the opportunity to present new evidence of innocence in a court of law. With that, Wilder left office at the end of his term, and Washington's supporters took their efforts to the General Assembly. Although the Virginia House of Delegates passed a bill in 1994 to permit the presentation of new evidence in cases in which a death sentence has been commuted to life in prison, the Virginia Senate never voted on the bill. Washington continued to serve his sentence.

Then in 1999, a reporter for the PBS series *Frontline* requested copies of the DNA tests on Washington's case from the Virginia Division of Forensic Science.[12] These were the results that Governor Wilder had seen on his last day in office five years earlier but did not share with Washington or his legal team. The results concluded that Earl Washington Jr. was "eliminated" as the donor of the semen stains found at the crime scene. Between pressure from the media and Washington's legal team, Virginia's new governor, James Gilmore, ordered additional testing of the evidence in Washington's case, using more advanced DNA technology. A year later, Gilmore offered Washington a complete pardon, the testing having once again excluded Washington. This time, the results even generated a "cold hit." According to a final report in the case, the DNA found in the semen at the crime scene matched that of Kenneth Tinsley, a convicted felon who remains incarcerated in Virginia on a separate charge.[13]

Washington, however, was not immediately released. Although he would have been paroled years earlier for the unrelated burglary sentence if he had not also been convicted of the rape and murder, Washington was held in prison until his mandatory release date of February 12, 2001. Now a free man, Earl Washington Jr. filed a civil suit against the Commonwealth of Virginia alleging that police and prosecutors coerced him into confessing to a crime he did not commit and ignored details that proved his innocence. On May 5, 2006, Washington won the largest civil rights judgment in Virginia history, which was settled in lieu of appeal for $1.9 million.[14]

Marvin Anderson

The case of Marvin Anderson also has received considerable attention. PBS's *Frontline* program and other news media have reported on the case of an otherwise innocent young man from central Virginia who was convicted of a rape that he did not commit on the basis of the victim's testimony, which itself was based on a tainted identification procedure.[15]

On July 17, 1982, a young white woman was raped twice, sodomized, robbed, and beaten while she was walking home to her apartment after picking up dinner at a nearby shopping center. During the two-hour ordeal, her assailant told her that he had a gun and threatened to shoot her if she "gave him any problems." During both of the rapes, he ordered her to undress herself, telling her that by taking her own clothes off, she was consenting to whatever happened next. Frustrated by his inability to ejaculate during the second rape, her assailant sodomized the victim, ordered her to defecate, and then forced her to ingest her own feces, again threatening to shoot her if she did not comply. Twice, the assailant severely beat the victim, the young woman testifying that she tried to fight back by scratching him.

Throughout the episode, the man spoke to the victim, once telling her that he was assaulting her to "get back for what happened to [his] people in 'Roots.'" Perhaps the most significant thing he said during the attack was that she reminded him of his white girlfriend. This statement would be the source of Marvin Anderson's involvement in the case.

After abandoning the victim in the woods, the assailant left. The victim returned to the shopping center to seek help. Police arrived and took her to a local hospital, where she was treated and a physical evidence recovery kit ("PERK") was obtained. The victim described her attacker to officers as a black man of medium complexion, five feet, four inches, to five feet, seven inches in height, with short, kinky hair and a thin mustache. Based on this description, one of the officers constructed a composite photo of the assailant. Upon viewing the picture, the victim told officers, "That is the individual that attacked me. That face will haunt me as long as I live."

During her interview with police, the victim reiterated that her attacker said he was "living with a white girl" and that "he was either married or staying with a white girl or he had a white wife." According to one of the responding officers, there "wasn't [sic] too many [black] people in that area at that time that were staying or were married to a white girl." However, Marin Anderson was one of these men, whom the officer "had observed . . . around with [his] white wife or girlfriend." For this reason, Anderson was added to the list of initial suspects.

That summer Marvin Anderson was eighteen years old. Unlike the victim's description of her attacker, Anderson was clean shaven, had no scratches on his face, and had a dark complexion, especially after having worked outdoors that summer at King's Dominion Amusement Park. Nonetheless, an investigator with the Hanover County Sheriff's Office traveled to King's Dominion and obtained a color photograph of Anderson from his employer. The investigator also searched the apartment that Anderson was sharing with his girlfriend. The sheriff's office subsequently seized a pair of Anderson's shoes and work pants that belonged to his girlfriend, but neither was introduced at trial.

Despite the differences between Anderson's appearance and that of the composite photo, officers included Anderson's photo in an array of six to ten suspects shown to the victim at her house. All the photographs, which the victim was asked to view one at a time, were black-and-white "mug shots," except for Marvin Anderson's color King's Dominion employee photograph. When she got to Anderson's photo, she became upset and threw the photograph at her boyfriend, saying, "Take it away, I don't want to see it." She had positively identified Marvin Anderson as her attacker.

Less than thirty minutes later, the victim identified him twice in a lineup at the Hanover County Jail. Marvin Anderson had not objected to being included in the lineup. Seven men were assembled for the identification procedure (five inmates from the county jail, one police officer, and Marvin Anderson), each wearing a green Hanover County prison uniform. The victim was brought to the Hanover County Jail in a police car and ushered into a holding area. Two officers accompanied her into the lineup room. At trial, an officer from the Ashland Police Department stated that he asked her to "go in and look at the people in the line up to see if she could pick out the suspect." The victim looked at the seven men and identified Anderson as her assailant. She told the police that she "didn't want to make any mistakes, and after seeing the lineup, [she was] quite sure. There [was] no doubt in [her] mind."

After identifying Marvin Anderson once, the two officers asked the victim to go back into the lineup room and make sure. She identified Anderson again, telling a deputy from the Hanover County Sheriff's Office, "That's him; I don't care what you say." After being identified, Marvin Anderson broke down, "said 'My God, she picked me,' and started to cry."

It is unclear if officers included a photograph of Otis Lincoln, the man who actually attacked the victim, in the photo identification or if he was included in the lineup at the county jail, even though Lincoln had been identified by the investigators as another potential suspect. A Hanover County deputy initially testified at trial that Anderson and Lincoln were the only two individuals in the lineup whose photographs also were in the photo identification. However, on cross-examination, the deputy testified that he could not be certain if Lincoln had been included because the police did not keep track of the names of individuals used in lineups. Furthermore, an Ashland officer testified at Otis Lincoln's later rape trial that he was not sure if Lincoln's photo had been included in the original photo spread.

Marvin Anderson's trial for rape, sodomy, kidnapping, and robbery began on December 14, 1982. The trial lasted less than five hours. After deliberating for only three hours, an all-white jury recommended a total sentence of 210 years, the maximum for each of the five counts charged. The jury reached this verdict despite the total absence of physical evidence linking Marvin Anderson to the crime. DNA testing was not available in 1982, but Mary Jane Burton, a supervisor of serology and forensic laboratories for Virginia's Bureau of Forensic Sciences, had performed blood-typing tests on portions of swabs containing sperm and semen recovered from the victim's body. After reviewing the results of the test, Burton was unable to identify Marvin Anderson as the source of these fluids.

As was Burton's personal practice, she taped the remaining swab materials to her case folder and filed the folder in her office's records. Had Burton returned these swabs to the Ashland Police Department, as she was supposed to do under the then-existing protocol, the police would have destroyed them. Instead, the folder was kept in an unlocked file cabinet at the Division of Forensic Sciences building in Hanover, Virginia. On November 30, 1990, the file was transferred to the State Records Center in Richmond, where it remained until December 7, 1993. The file was then recalled to the Division of Forensic Science in Hanover by Deanne Dabbs, the DNA program manager, who later returned it to the State Records Center. Establishing the validity of the chain of custody regarding these swabs became crucial when Marvin Anderson later petitioned to have new scientific testing done as part of his exoneration. Unfortunately, this constant shifting of these materials, coupled with the evidence-handling policies in place at the time of Anderson's conviction, led state officials to believe for years that the physical evidence from Marvin Anderson's trial had been either lost or destroyed.

At trial, the Commonwealth relied primarily on the testimony of the victim and the two investigating officers. In the words of then assistant Commonwealth's attorney, Ramon Chalkley, "It was purely a question of do you want to believe . . . the victim in this case." Indeed, until Anderson's subsequent exoneration by DNA, Chalkley believed that Marvin Anderson was "the clearest case [he] had ever had." Not only was the victim certain of her identification of Anderson, but she also was unassailable as a witness because she had had such extensive exposure to her attacker.

Anderson, by contrast, relied on an alibi defense. But unknown to him, his defense attorney, Donald White, had represented one of the other suspects, Otis Lincoln, on an earlier attempted rape charge. White did not divulge this conflict until after Anderson's trial.

Marvin Anderson ended up serving fifteen years of his sentence, eventually being paroled in 1997 for good behavior, although he still had the conviction around his neck. As DNA testing became increasingly widespread, Anderson sought to prove his innocence by subjecting the various sperm and semen samples collected in the rape kit to a more sophisticated scientific analysis than what had been available at his trial.

Anderson and his counsel were repeatedly advised that biological evidence from his case could not be located. Then in the winter of 2001, Dr. Paul Ferrara, director of the Virginia Division of Forensic Science, notified Anderson's pro bono co-counsel that certain physical evidence from Anderson's case, including sperm and semen samples from the victim's body, had been located. Despite this breakthrough, the Virginia Department of Criminal Justice Services denied Anderson's request for DNA testing because of "the current number of cases pending in the Division and the potential for establishing an unwelcome precedent." The department stated that it would permit postconviction testing only "upon a defendant's showing ample cause to the court or the Governor's Office to order such testing."

This procedural roadblock to Anderson's exoneration was removed later that year with the passage of Virginia Code §19.2-327.1. This statute permits individuals convicted of a felony to move the circuit court that entered their original conviction to order a new scientific analysis of previously untested scientific material. Two months later, Anderson's lawyers filed a motion under the statute requesting DNA analysis of previously untested swabs taken from the victim's PERK. In October of that year, the Circuit Court for Hanover County authorized the DNA testing despite the objection of the Commonwealth's attorney that Anderson could not establish the chain of custody for these swabs. The DNA testing conclusively excluded Marvin Anderson as the source of the semen found on the victim and confirmed what he had said for years —that he was innocent of the crime. In December 2001, Marvin Anderson was officially exonerated by the Hanover circuit court, and the original rape case was reopened by the Commonwealth Attorneys' office.

Since his exoneration, Anderson has succeeded at restoring some semblance of normalcy to his life. He filed a petition for an absolute gubernatorial pardon from Governor Mark Warner on April 3, 2002, which was granted on August 21, 2002. On June 4, 2003, Anderson filed a motion to expunge the conviction from his record. The Commonwealth did not oppose this motion, and the conviction has been expunged from Anderson's records. In February 2003, the General Assembly approved a relief package for Anderson worth approximately $750,000 in compensation for spending fifteen years in prison and five years on parole for a crime he did not commit. Marvin Anderson, now a father, still lives in Hanover County, Virginia, and works as a truck driver.

In 2003, Otis Lincoln was convicted of the rape for which Marvin Anderson had unfortunately served time. Not only did the DNA evidence match Lincoln's profile, but Lincoln had already confessed to the crime at Anderson's 1988 hearing for a writ of habeas corpus. Until the DNA testing in 2001, however, neither prosecutors nor the courts were willing to acknowledge that Lincoln was the actual perpetrator. Subsequent investigations have shown that police had good cause to inquire about Lincoln at the time of the 1982 rape. Indeed, a new Commonwealth's attorney for Hanover County acknowledges that police and prosecutors mistakenly latched on to Anderson after the victim's identification of him, even in the face of serious contradictory evidence.

Shortly after Anderson's arrest, two witnesses came forward to say that they had seen Lincoln outside near the site of the attack on the day in question making sexually suggestive comments to young white girls. When the two confronted Lincoln and told him to leave the girls alone because they were young, Lincoln responded that "if he wanted pussy he asked for it and if they didn't give it to him, he would just take it." Hanover residents also reported that Lincoln drove by the house of Anderson's mother because he wanted to see "the young boy who was taking his rap." None of these claims was investigated by police officers, a surprising fact given that Lincoln already had a lengthy record as a sex offender. He had served jail time for a different attack committed the year before the rape. Upon his release in the spring of 1982, Lincoln committed a second sexual assault on a female student at Randolph Macon College. He was awaiting trial for this attack during the summer that he raped the woman who erroneously identified Marvin Anderson. Today, Otis Lincoln is serving three life sentences plus forty years.

Craig Bell

On October 5, 1986, a young woman was murdered in her apartment in Virginia Beach. She was living there with her fiancé, Craig Bell, a petty officer in the U.S. Navy. Bell, who had been out to dinner and drinking with two friends, returned home after 2 A.M. to find his fiancée on the couch watching television. He left her there and headed off to bed. Some time in the early morning, Bell was awakened by her yelling for him to "get a tourniquet" because she had been stabbed. Bell asked her who had stabbed her, but she went into shock and could not answer. Bell put on his jeans and called 911 for help.

An officer responded to Bell's call shortly before 4 A.M. Upon arriving at the scene, he found Bell covered in blood, as well as blood spattered across the living room and all the way up the stairway. He also noticed a lamp partially hanging out the window and a removed window screen. When he took the victim's pulse, she was dead. Downstairs in the living room officers found a butcher knife, shorts, and a tank top, the clothing belonging to neither Mr. Bell nor his fiancée.

Bell was quickly questioned at the scene, and although officers reported there was a strong odor of alcohol on Mr. Bell's breath, they stated that "his speech and coordination did not indicate that he was intoxicated." Bell told officers he had been awakened by his fiancée, who stated she had been outside the apartment and was attacked by a group of black men. Seeking more information, a detective asked Bell to accompany him to police headquarters to answer questions about his relationship with his fiancée. Mr. Bell agreed and drove to police headquarters with the detective who then interviewed him. The detective attempted to videotape the interrogation, but it was discovered later that the audio portion of the recording failed to function. This proved to be important, since the detective's recollection of—and subsequent testimony about—the interrogation was different from Mr. Bell's.

At the police station, Mr. Bell signed a voluntary search request and gave blood, head hair, pubic hair, and saliva samples. The detective requested and received permission to search Mr. Bell's residence without a search warrant. The following day, Mr. Bell was asked whether he was willing to take a polygraph test, and after conferring with his attorney he declined.

Meanwhile, the police began to build a case against Mr. Bell based largely on inconsistencies in his statements to investigators. According to the detectives, Mr. Bell gave two accounts of how he was awakened by the victim. One detective testified that Mr. Bell stated that "he was awakened by [his fiancée] standing at the bedroom door calling out his name and stating 'I have been stabbed.'" But a different officer testified that Mr. Bell said the victim "grabbed him by the arm and was shaking him, waking him up, saying she had been stabbed." No blood was found in or around the bed, which called into question both Bell's and the detectives' accounts of the events. Another alleged inconsistency was Mr. Bell's account of his fiancée's last statements. For example, an officer testified that Mr. Bell stated "somebody must of [*sic*] broke into his house." But an emergency medical technician (EMT) reported that Mr.

Bell claimed the victim had stated that a group of black men attacked her outside the house. In an interview several years after his exoneration, Mr. Bell said that both the detective and the EMT lied about these facts.[16]

Police also became suspicious of Mr. Bell because he claimed that he did not wear the type of bikini underwear left behind by the perpetrator. But during the search of Mr. Bell's apartment, police found underwear similar to the bikini underwear left at the scene. Other inconsistencies in Mr. Bell's story included the location of a fan in the apartment and the location of the clothes he wore on the night of the murder.

In addition, a number of coincidences were consistent with Mr. Bell's guilt. For example, the clothing found at the crime scene matched both the size and style of Mr. Bell's own clothing. Mr. Bell smoked Newport cigarettes, which were the brand of cigarettes in the pocket of the shorts left behind by the perpetrator. Mr. Bell's blood type also matched that of the assailant, which was determined by an analysis of a semen stain in the shorts found at the crime scene. Both the assailant and Bell had blood type O. Finally, Mr. Bell's presence in the apartment when the murder took place, the couple's quarrel the previous day, Mr. Bell's alcohol consumption, and the use of a knife from the couple's kitchen as the murder weapon all led the police to focus on Mr. Bell.

The case against Bell, however, was at best circumstantial, and the police ignored a number of inconsistencies, none of which was more important than the evidence that someone had broken into Bell's house immediately before his fiancée was murdered. The window screen was ajar, having been pried open from the outside; police found fingerprints adjacent to the crime scene that failed to match those of Bell, the victim, their acquaintances, or any officers involved in the investigation; pubic hairs were recovered from the mysterious shorts and underwear in the couple's living room that did not belong to Bell or his fiancée; and neighbors reported hearing a woman screaming and a man yelling at her in surprise around the time of the murder. Nor did police follow up leads that a black man had been seen running without clothes through the neighborhood on the night of the murder. This fact later proved crucial when the actual assailant, Jesse Smith, an African American, stated that he had indeed fled naked from the apartment after killing Mr. Bell's fiancée.

Police arrested Mr. Bell ten days after the murder and took him to trial ten months later in a five-day proceeding. In its opening statement the prosecution admitted that the case was based largely on circumstantial evidence, with the prosecutor telling the jury: "The case that is going to be presented to you by the Commonwealth of Virginia in proving the Defendant is guilty is a circumstantial case. There's nothing wrong with that. . . . [Y]ou are going to receive evidence that is like building blocks."

The prosecution, however, did not address physical evidence like the unidentified fingerprints, clothing, and hair samples that could not be linked to Mr. Bell. Commonwealth's Attorney Robert Humphreys later stated, "We didn't try to explain them because we couldn't."

Defense counsel introduced very little character evidence, concerned that emphasizing Mr. Bell's character "would deflect juror's attention from the strong physical evidence." Although this may have been a reasonable strategic decision at the time, the defense's tactic proved to be problematic with the jurors. Mr. Bell took the stand in his defense, but jurors were put off by his "unusually inexpressive demeanor." Indeed, three jurors interviewed by the *Virginian-Pilot* after the trial stated that Mr. Bell's testimony did more harm than good, as they viewed him as "unemotional and inconsistent." One juror stated that if Mr. Bell "wouldn't have been put on the stand [*sic*], I believe he would have been found innocent." Jurors also sought additional character evidence about Bell, telling a reporter that "there were several things missing on the defense of the young man. Things that would have swayed the jury. For example, no individual came forward to testify what kind of young man this was. No one ever knew what kind of guy he was."

By contrast, the prosecution managed to plant doubts in the jurors' minds about Bell, at one point suggesting that he was bisexual. Apparently, the prosecution had received an anonymous phone call accusing Mr. Bell of being bisexual. Mr. Bell recalled, "When I got on the stand, [the prosecutor] said, 'Isn't it true, Mr. Bell, that you are bisexual?' I said, 'No ma'am, I am not bisexual.'" This exchange occurred during the prosecution's cross-examination of Mr. Bell. According to defense counsel, this accusation was the turning point in the case: "It was just like in the movies. When [the prosecutor] asked that, there was dead silence in the courtroom, and then you could hear people shuffling around and stuff. . . . It was like a bomb dropped. [The words] couldn't have had a more dramatic effect on the jury. Their jaws dropped."

Defense counsel hypothesized that the question about Mr. Bell's sexuality suggested a motive for killing his fiancée so that she would not reveal his sexual orientation.

The twelve jurors deliberated for approximately six hours. On August 7, 1987, the jury returned a guilty verdict on the count of second-degree murder. On October 6, 1987, one day after the anniversary of his fiancée's death, Mr. Bell was sentenced to serve twenty years in the Virginia State Penitentiary.

For Mr. Bell, the process of exoneration moved much faster than it did for the other defendants examined by the ICVA, although in his case the impetus came from the real perpetrator, who continued his crime spree. During the fall of 1987, several women in the vicinity of Craig Bell's apartment complex became targets of a sexual predator. On September 5, 1987, a twelve-year-old girl was raped after the perpetrator entered through her window and threatened her with a kitchen utensil. On September 16, a twenty-one-year-old woman was raped and her residence was burglarized after the perpetrator entered through a window. Finally, on September 26, two undercover police officers spotted a "Peeping Tom" looking in the window of a woman who lived in the same apartment complex as the other rape victims. The suspect was Jesse Calvin Smith, an eighteen-year-old junior at a local high school. The twelve-year-old victim identified Smith in a police lineup, and his blood and hair samples matched evidence recovered from the crime scenes. Mr. Smith was arrested on October 14, 1987, and brought in for questioning, during which he confessed to raping two women in September.

Detective Raymond Greenwood was in the bureau on the day of Smith's questioning. Greenwood had become interested in Smith's story because he recognized similarities between the two rape cases and the Bell murder. All three attacks had occurred in the same apartment complex; all the victims were white women; and in each case, the intruder threatened the victims with a kitchen utensil, at night, as the victims were sleeping. Greenwood asked investigators to show Smith a few of the photographs of the Bell crime scene. Smith immediately identified the clothing in one of the pictures as his. Specifically, he told police that the safety pin found in the underpants had been placed there by his grandmother. The police found this statement particularly important because the information about the safety pin had never been released to the public, and it was something only the real murderer would know.

Detective Greenwood later questioned Smith, who at first stated that he could not remember what happened the night of the Bell murder. After further interrogation, however, Smith confessed to the killing. He told police that he had left a party shortly after 1 A.M. and that the light in Bell's apartment had caught his eye. Smith then noticed the victim lying asleep on the couch; he removed the window screen, pushed the window open, and climbed into the apartment. He took a serrated knife from the kitchen, returned to the living room, took off his blue jogging shorts and blue underwear, and approached the victim. When she awoke to find Smith standing over her, she screamed and the two began to struggle. Smith stabbed her in the chest and then became frightened, dropped the knife, jumped out of the window (noting that his foot had caught something on the way out), and ran home naked.

Detective Greenwood reported Smith's confession to the Commonwealth Attorney's Office. That evening, Commonwealth's Attorney Robert Humphreys called Bell's defense counsel, Phillip Barr, to tell him that a suspect in other cases had confessed to the murder of Bell's fiancée. The following morning, October 15, 1987, Mr. Humphreys asked the circuit court to set aside Mr. Bell's conviction. Mr. Bell was released the next day after spending two months in jail.

Jesse Calvin Smith was eventually tried and convicted of the murder of Mr. Bell's fiancée and was sentenced to life imprisonment for the murder and five years for the burglary. He received an additional life sentence for the other crimes and is currently incarcerated in Virginia.

Upon his release, Bell commented on the investigation and trial. When asked about the police investigation he stated, "They did a crummy job of investigating. I honestly feel that when the police accused me, they believed it. But as the investigation went along and the stuff did not come together, they said, 'Sorry, it is too late to turn back now.'" Mr. Bell also stated that he had always believed in the justice system, "but this really makes me wonder. I can't say [I believe] in it anymore. But I don't know how the jury came up with the verdict with other evidence indicat[ing] that there was a third party there."

Mr. Bell's prosecutor, Commonwealth's Attorney Robert Humphreys, has said that his office would not have done anything differently in the prosecution of Craig Bell: "There was enough evidence to charge Mr. Bell. . . . There was enough evidence to convict Mr. Bell. . . . Twelve jurors agreed unanimously that he was guilty beyond a reasonable doubt." Humphreys, who is now a judge on the Virginia Court of Appeals, believes that if he were faced with the same suspect and the same set of circumstances, he would again authorize prosecution.

Although Humphreys deserves praise for rectifying Bell's conviction as soon as new evidence was uncovered, a public apology was left to Humphreys's successor as Commonwealth's attorney, Paul A. Sciortino. As Sciortino publicly stated, Bell

> deserves the apology because [his conviction] was wrong. . . . The criminal justice system is basically designed to try and protect the innocent, [but] we are human beings and we have human frailties. At best, the system is going to have its imperfections. . . . I felt that he has suffered a wrong at the hands of the Commonwealth, the criminal justice system and he deserved an apology.

Mr. Sciortino's view, however, has failed to attract a majority of the Virginia General Assembly, which twice voted down legislation to compensate Mr. Bell for the erroneous conviction. To date, Craig Bell has received no compensation—monetary or otherwise. He has since moved back to Michigan and gotten married, but according to Bell, the memory of his wrongful conviction continues to haunt him.[17]

Jeffrey Cox

In August 1990, Jeffrey Cox was a twenty-two-year-old air conditioner installer who lived just outside Richmond. Less than six months later he was a convicted felon sentenced to life plus fifty years for the kidnap and murder of a sixty-three-year-old Richmond woman whose brutally stabbed body was found dumped along a dirt road. The chain of events that led from the crime to his conviction and his ultimate exoneration reveals a case that relied heavily on flawed eyewitness evidence and a criminal justice system that took too little interest in the plight of a young man who was fighting to prove his innocence.

On the night of August 31, 1990, an older African American woman was snatched from her home in Richmond. The victim's husband reported that a stranger banged on their door late at night, identified himself as a narcotics detective from a nearby county, and when the victim opened the door, the perpetrator grabbed her and dragged her to a car driven by a waiting accomplice. Two neighbors reported seeing the crime, and at least one called the police. They described the abductor as a drunk white man carrying a knife, accompanied by a second white man driving a small red car that was stopped on the wrong side of the street with the engine running.

Later that evening, the victim's partially clothed body was found on an isolated road elsewhere in Richmond. She had been stabbed to death. The chief medical examiner collected blood and hair samples from the crime scene and the victim's body.

> According to the autopsy report, the items of recovered physical evidence included "[h]air on the [victim's] left index finger and base of the left middle finger" and a "fiber caught in" a broken fingernail on the victim's right hand. The report indicate[s] that the hairs and fingers, along with the victim's clothing and wrappings were sent to the serology lab, and that a serology report would follow.[18]

Early on, Richmond police detectives theorized that the crime was a case of mistaken revenge. Their theory was that a known suspect, Billy Madison, had sold drugs to a man who had then beaten up Madison and stolen money from him. On the night in question, authorities believed that Madison and a friend were looking for this person or his relatives, who, they believed, lived on the same street as the victim. In their drunken state, Madison and his accomplice did not realize that they had abducted the wrong person. Detectives brought Madison and his friend, Steven Hood, in for questioning. Neither was arrested, but Hood did tell officers that Madison sometimes associated with Jeffrey Cox.

Detectives visited Cox at his place of employment and asked if they could take Cox's picture; he agreed. Detectives placed his photograph among those they showed to the two witnesses who purported to have watched their neighbor abducted from her home. It is unclear whether one or both witnesses singled out Cox's photograph before his arrest, but eventually each neighbor "identified Cox's picture as resembling the knife-wielding man they had seen the morning of August 31, 1990. However, both . . . told police that they would have to see the man in person to be sure of the identification."[19]

On this basis, Virginia state police officers, accompanied by members of the Richmond Police Department, arrested Jeffrey Cox and began to interrogate him about his whereabouts on the night of the murder. Unfortunately for Cox, his mind began to race, trying to remember where he had been and what he had been doing that night. The police asked whether he had been at a party at Billy Madison's, who, unbeknownst to Cox, was the prime suspect in the crime. Cox recalled having attended a party at Billy Madison's around that time. Trying to be cooperative, Cox told the police he had been at Billy Madison's party that night. Unfortunately, Cox was mistaken about the day of the party; Billy Madison's party actually had taken place on the night of Saturday, September 1.[20]

Cox's explanation only got worse at trial, where his alibi seemed more convoluted and confused. His defense attorney introduced other witnesses to verify his whereabouts, but the prosecution tried to discredit these people by noting that they had not immediately come to the police on their own to clear Cox.

For its part, the prosecution relied almost exclusively on the testimony of the two neighbors who purported to have seen Cox as the abductor. But many facts raised questions about their veracity and accuracy. Their in-person identification of Cox was at his preliminary hearing, an "atmosphere [that was] highly suggestive of Cox's guilt."[21] Moreover, both witnesses had ample reason to stretch their testimony in the prosecution's favor. One witness had three prior felony convictions and was a fugitive from Alabama. The other witness "had criminal charges pending with the same office that was prosecuting Cox at the time she testified at Cox's preliminary hearing."[22] Although the defense originally sought all these facts in a pretrial motion, most were not disclosed. The prosecutor in the case "has sworn that he disclosed [the first witness's] full history but that 'defense counsel and I agreed that, for impeachment purposes, [the witness] had only one felony conviction, a robbery, and one misdemeanor larceny conviction.'"[23] Such a decision by defense counsel seems odd, but more troubling was the government's statement at summation when the prosecutor told jurors:

> Now, what did we produce to convince you beyond a reasonable doubt? We took two eyewitnesses, not one, but two people who have absolutely no ax to grind, and no reason to come in here and misidentify anybody. They are simply citizens in the City of Richmond that happen to be living in the community on the night this occurred.[24]

Prosecutors offered no motive for Cox's involvement in the kidnapping and murder, nor did they introduce any forensic evidence. In fact, during their deliberations, jurors noted that the autopsy report seemed to indicate relevant forensic facts—the hair on the victim's finger and the fiber caught under her fingernail—but none of this evidence was introduced at trial. Instead, the case turned on the word of the neighbors versus that of Cox and his friends. The jury sided with the prosecution and convicted Cox after a one-day trial. They recommended a sentence of life plus fifty years, which the judge imposed.

Three months after Cox's conviction and before any appeals had been filed, the Richmond Police Department destroyed physical evidence from Cox's case. This was common practice at the time, but it seemed to fly in the face of the neighbors' reports that two men had been involved in the crime. Why destroy evidence when an accomplice to murder was still at large?

Cox's family retained an attorney for his appeal, a lawyer who, interestingly, had previously represented Billy Madison. The attorney included only two issues on appeal, which the Court of Appeals summarily rejected. He then missed a deadline for a direct appeal to Virginia's Supreme Court and began to prepare Cox's habeas corpus petition on very bare ground. Worried that he would lose his "one bite at the apple," Cox fired the attorney and took on his own representation. In a pro se filing, Cox sought a writ of mandamus for the prosecution to disclose all forensic evidence in his case. This writ went unanswered for almost a year, and then at a short hearing, a Richmond circuit judge declared that the items Cox sought were not in the possession of the Commonwealth's attorney. Cox did not know whether the evidence might still be at the Richmond Police Department.

Finally, in February 1997 Cox was able to interest one of Virginia's preeminent defense firms, Benjamin and DesPortes, in his case. As Cox's new attorneys conducted more research, they uncovered the criminal backgrounds of the two witnesses offered by the prosecution, including the charges pending against the two at the time of trial. Whether the prosecution was aware of their witnesses' records, each certainly had motivation to tell prosecutors what they believed the Commonwealth wanted to hear. Benjamin and DesPortes also discovered that potentially critical forensic evidence had been lost before it could be tested. Together, Cox's new defense attorneys began the process of filing an amended habeas corpus petition on his behalf. The Virginia Attorney General's Office opposed them right up to the last minute.

Two years later, a private investigator working with Benjamin and

DesPortes contacted the FBI's Richmond office to determine whether the federal agency was aware of any forensic evidence still in existence in the Cox case. Agent Frank Stokes took the inquiry. Although the FBI had not been involved in the investigation, Stokes remembered the murder and recalled "rumors in the law enforcement community about the possibility that an innocent man had been convicted."[25] Stokes failed to locate old evidence, but he and his partner, Donald Lacey, opened their own investigation into the kidnapping and murder. Because the case was technically classified as a drug murder, the FBI had jurisdiction, and although their superiors were opposed to the FBI's involvement, Stokes and Lacey began to uncover new evidence not previously presented in court or reported to Cox.

Under further questioning, the stories of the prosecution's two witnesses began to wilt under the weight of their inconsistencies. Stokes and Lacey also checked the files of the Richmond Police Department, where they found a composite sketch of the abductor different from any previously turned over to the defense. Benjamin and DesPortes also came to learn informally of other evidence still in possession of the Richmond Police Department, evidence that would have helped the defense at trial. None of this had been shared with Cox or his defense team, even after Cox filed a writ of mandamus for evidence in possession of the Commonwealth's attorney.

On May 8, 2000, the FBI issued a "Crime Stoppers" report asking for the public's help in solving the abduction and murder for which Cox had been convicted. "The description in the report contained details [about the abductor] that had not appeared in any prior releases or testimony . . . causing Benjamin to deduce that the FBI had uncovered even more exculpatory evidence that had not been disclosed to Cox."[26] Cox's attorneys continued to press their habeas claim in the Richmond Circuit Court, all the while opposed by the Virginia attorney general. On January 11, 2001, the circuit court finally denied Cox's writ.

Before the defense team could appeal the circuit court's decision, the FBI arrested Stephen Hood and charged him with the abduction and murder of the victim in Cox's case. "The most incriminating evidence against Hood was his own admission . . . that he was the driver of the red car and Billy Madison was the abductor and murderer."[27] Notwithstanding Hood's admission, the attorney general's office contended that his arrest was irrelevant to Cox's case because two men had committed the crime—Cox and Hood. However, on September 12, 2001, the Virginia Supreme Court signaled that it was prepared to reconsider the circuit court's dismissal of Cox's habeas corpus claim.

The court's action seemed to take the attorney general's office by surprise, which agreed to settlement discussions with Cox's defense team. Finally on November 13, 2001, both sides reached an agreement in which the circuit court granted Cox a writ of habeas corpus and vacated his convictions. After serving eleven years in prison, Jeffrey Cox was finally a free—and innocent—man.

In reaching this agreement, the Virginia Attorney General's Office declared that " 'reliable information has been developed . . . that the interest of justice requires" that Cox's appeal be granted."[28] The Richmond Commonwealth's attorney, David Hicks, went even further, saying, "We have reliable and compelling evidence that it was not Mr. Cox. An innocent man spent 11 years in jail." Others, however, questioned the Commonwealth's motives. According to University of Virginia law professor George Rutherglen, the attorney general caved in "to settle a case that [was] a clear loser rather than go down in flames and have the constitutional principle established that you have a right to be free if you are innocent." Although by the time of Cox's exoneration, Virginia's 21-day law had changed to permit the introduction of biological evidence, there still was no mechanism to consider factual evidence of innocence on appeal.

In 2002, the Virginia General Assembly awarded Cox $750,000 for his eleven years of wrongful incarceration. The same year, a Virginia jury convicted Hood of abduction and murder and sentenced him to sixty-five years in prison. Billy Madison, however, has never been charged.

Russell Gray

On June 30, 1986, a fight broke out in a Richmond neighborhood among several men, eventually leading to the shooting death of an African American man. The confrontation had its roots in an altercation more than a week earlier between the victim's stepson and a group of nine others on a local basketball court, the larger group having been harassing the stepson for nearly six weeks. A day before the murder, the group confronted the stepson at the victim's home, retreating only when the victim fired a shotgun into the air and threatened the group's leader,

Charles Gray, saying, "If you come one stop closer, I will shoot you." The police soon arrived, and although no arrests were made, the crowd dispersed.

The next evening Charles Gray again confronted the stepson at the victim's home. Charles Gray retreated for a short time, but he eventually returned with his brother Russell, and the two hid behind some shrubs near the corner of the building. Charles Gray pulled out a stick or bat, and three shots were fired. One shot hit the victim in his neck, immediately paralyzing him. Eight days later, the man died.

In interviews with police detectives on the night of the shooting, both the victim's wife and the stepson named Russell Gray as the assailant. By this time, Gray was well known to the Richmond police, having been involved with car theft and other less serious crimes, but neither witness had seen Russell Gray before the shooting. The stepson was able to give police officers a description of the perpetrator's clothing on the night of the murder—black and yellow "Jamm-type" shorts— and picked Russell Gray out of a photo book, saying that he had seen him pull the trigger. The decedent's wife, while not an eyewitness to the crime, identified Gray from a mug shot, eventually placing him at the scene of the crime moments before shots were fired and approximately fifteen minutes afterward. But she contradicted her son, saying that it was dark at the time of the shooting and that Gray had been wearing sweatpants.

Russell Gray was twenty-one years old at the time of his arrest, which took place nearly four months after the crime. Prosecutors charged him with murder, and his trial lasted less than a day. Gray's attorney, Carey Bowen, called several witnesses who placed the defendant at a different location at the time of the murder. Gray also testified in his own defense, telling the jury that he never wore shorts because of a disfiguring scar on his leg, which he showed to jurors. Ultimately, the defense argued that Gray had little motive to commit the crime and that the only eyewitness to the crime, the victim's stepson, may have mistaken another man for Gray.

During deliberation, jurors seemed skeptical of the stepson's testimony and asked the judge for a copy of the transcript for review. The judge denied their request, telling jurors to use their own best judgment. They then returned for another hour of deliberation and convicted Gray. The judge sentenced Russell Gray to fifty-two years in prison.

Gray's lawyer, however, continued to believe in his client's innocence and effectively took on the role of detective, interviewing more witnesses to the crime. All pointed to a third man, Michael Harvey, as the shooter. Attorney Bowen confronted Harvey, who denied his involvement, but Bowen eventually convinced Detective L. B. Quick of the Richmond Police Department—the detective who had originally investigated the murder—to speak with Harvey. Harvey had testified for the defense at Gray's trail, claiming he was nowhere near the scene of the crime. Now, speaking with Detective Quick, he confessed to the crime, claiming that he had shot in defense of a friend, presumably Russell Gray's brother, Charles.

Harvey's confession, however, could not free Gray. Under Virginia's then 21-day rule, exculpatory evidence uncovered more than twenty-one days after sentencing could not be presented to the courts. Bowen therefore sought Gray's release through a habeas corpus action, which was denied. He also filed a motion to vacate Gray's conviction and order a new trial, arguing that the courts had been defrauded. The trial court held a hearing at which Harvey and a new witness, Linda Connors, testified. Harvey admitted that he had perjured himself at Gray's trial, saying that he, in fact, was the shooter. But Harvey could not produce the handgun in question, saying he had thrown it in the river shortly after the crime. Connors said that she had heard gunshots after dark on the night in question. When she looked out her window, she saw Harvey running down the street and away from the crime scene dressed in a black shirt and "black magic shorts." Since Connors knew Harvey well, she said she was sure she had seen him. Connors also testified that she went to the crime scene shortly after the shooting, where she saw Russell Gray walking *toward* the scene. She recalled that he was not wearing shorts, nor had she ever seen him wear shorts in the twelve years she had known him.

Judge Wilkinson, sitting in for the sentencing judge, William Spain, who had since retired, declined to find fraud against the court. If anything, he said, it was a fraud on the defense, since Gray's team had originally called Harvey as a witness at trial. If "every convicted criminal could bring a perjury suit against [his] own witnesses subsequent to [his] conviction, the court system would be in chaos."[29]

Left without judicial options, Gray wrote to Learned Barry of the Commonwealth's Attorney's Office, pleading his innocence. Barry was impressed with Gray's letters and agreed to meet with him. Reviewing the case file and Bowen's postconviction investigations, Barry became convinced that Gray was innocent. Indeed, Barry later observed, "There were a ton of people who could have testified that didn't. . . . We ended up trying a case with half the evidence and convicted the wrong man."[30]

Barry took the case to the Virginia Parole Board, which, after additional review, recommended a pardon to the governor's office. In April 1990, three years after Russell Gray was erroneously convicted, Governor L. Douglas Wilder pardoned Gray and released him from prison.

When Gray wrote to Learned Barry, he seemed sincere, saying that he was not upset by the mistaken conviction, figuring that it was punishment for all the bad things he had done in his past. However, after his release from prison, Gray soon became involved in the criminal justice system again. On August 29, 1990, he was convicted of an unrelated murder in Richmond. He is currently serving time in Virginia. For his part, Harvey pleaded guilty to manslaughter and was sentenced to eight years in prison.

Edward Honaker

On June 22, 1984, a young woman and her boyfriend traveled to Virginia's Blue Ridge Parkway to camp. Late at night they became lost and pulled over to the side of the road to sleep in their car. At some point in the evening they were awakened by someone knocking on the window of their car and shining a flashlight into the passenger compartment. The individual, who identified himself as a police officer, ordered the two out of the car and demanded the car keys. Dressed in camouflage with a large crucifix and brandishing a handgun, the individual directed the boyfriend to begin running, saying he would be shot if he did not comply. The young man did so and ran into the nearby woods.

The assailant then ordered the young woman into his vehicle at gunpoint. He drove her about two miles down the parkway into an uninhabited area, where he sodomized and raped her on the tailgate of his truck and on a brown sleeping bag. All the while the perpetrator spoke to the victim, recounting his experience as a soldier in Vietnam. After two hours, he let her go, telling her how to find her vehicle on the Blue Ridge Parkway.

As soon as the victim was abducted, her boyfriend began walking down the parkway looking for assistance. He flagged down a car and was taken to a pay phone where he called the local sheriff's office. By the time a deputy reached him and they returned to the scene of the abduction, the victim had returned on foot. The deputy immediately took her to a local hospital, where a PERK was administered. Local authorities also recovered a strip of cloth, two cigarette butts, and a match at the scene of the rape. The victim and her boyfriend helped create a composite sketch of the attacker, whom they described as a white man of about thirty-four or thirty-five years old with a mustache, double chin, and brown hair.

Approximately four months later, the Nelson County Police showed the victim and her boyfriend a photo array of possible suspects, which included a picture of Edward Honaker. Honaker had come to the attention of authorities because of a different rape that had occurred about one hundred miles away, near Honaker's home around Roanoke. The victim in that case said the perpetrator resembled her neighbor, Edward Honaker.

Both the victim and her boyfriend identified Honaker as the assailant, at which point police obtained and executed a search warrant of Honaker's truck, his mother's home, and a storage facility used by his brother. Police impounded the truck and seized a blue sleeping bag, a camouflage suit and jacket, a bullet, a crucifix, and a police identification badge of Honaker's father. Honaker subsequently was arrested and charged with rape, abduction, and a firearms offense. During a preliminary hearing, Honaker was seated in a courtroom along with twenty-four other individuals, at which point the victim and her boyfriend were brought into the room. They picked out Honaker as the attacker.

The prosecution's case turned largely on the testimony of the victim and her boyfriend, who identified Honaker as the attacker. In addition, the prosecution presented testimony from a forensic hair expert, who maintained that Honaker's hair was a definitive match with hair found on the victim's shorts. Prosecutors introduced evidence that Honaker drove a truck that resembled the attacker's and that they had found camouflage clothes in Honaker's residence. In addition, the prosecution was able to include the testimony of an officer that the Roanoke Police had suspected Honaker in a separate rape case.

Honaker's defense consisted of a series of alibi witnesses, who placed Honaker at his brother's and mother's homes on the night of the attack. In response, the prosecution, however, labeled these as a "put-up job."[31] Honaker took the stand in his defense and denied any involvement. Significantly, he testified that as a result of a vasectomy, he was unable to produce sperm. His attorney, however, did not present any medical evidence to corroborate his claim, a potentially serious omission considering that the Commonwealth's forensic witnesses had testified that semen samples taken from the victim included sperm.

After two hours of deliberation, the jury convicted Honaker of the charges, and on April 10, 1985, he was sentenced to three life sentences plus thirty-four years on seven felony counts. After his conviction, Honaker sought the assistance of Centurion Ministries, an organization that works to free the wrongfully convicted. Centurion conducted an initial investigation and then contacted attorneys from the faculty of Cardozo Law School's Innocence Project, which took an interest in the case and intervened on Honaker's behalf. The new defense team uncovered startling evidence that had not been disclosed by the Commonwealth at or before trial. Apparently one week after the attack, police had taken both the victim and her boyfriend to a hypnotist to help them construct the composite sketch of her attacker. Until this session the victim had been unable to recollect the face of the assailant, telling officers that she hadn't been able to "see her attacker clearly throughout the entire ordeal."[32]

When defense investigators scoured the trial record, they also came across Honaker's testimony that he had previously undergone a vasectomy. This information had been unknown to the prosecution's witnesses and would seemingly have excluded him as the source of the semen found on the victim. The defense team contacted the prosecution to retest the biological evidence in Honaker's case using more advanced DNA technology.

The prosecution agreed to release the evidence, which an independent scientist tested. The expert's report excluded both Honaker and the victim's boyfriend as the source of the semen. Since the victim indicated that she hadn't had sex with anyone other than her boyfriend in the six weeks before the attack, it seemed that the semen could have come only from the rapist. During additional interviews with the Virginia State Police, however, the victim admitted for the first time that she had had a "secret lover" at the time of the attack. This revelation left open the possibility that the semen belonged to the secret lover and that Honaker, unable to produce sperm, could still have perpetrated the rape.

A DNA sample was obtained from the secret lover, which was compared with the biological evidence in the PERK. After several rounds of testing, including examinations by a private laboratory and the Virginia Division of Forensic Science, Honaker and both of the victim's boyfriends were excluded as possible sources of the biological evidence from the crime. Based on the DNA exclusion, Honaker filed for clemency, a petition that was joined by the Commonwealth. On October 22, 1994, Governor George Allen granted Honaker clemency. Honaker was released from prison after ten years of incarceration. He had long since been cleared as a suspect in the Roanoke rape as well.

A subsequent review of Honaker's case revealed a number of other facts that poked holes in the prosecution's original case against him—and that did not reach Honaker or his attorneys until the Innocence Project took over his defense. Apart from the hypnosis, which should have raised doubts about the witnesses' identification, investigators and prosecutors seem to have ignored several inconsistencies in their desire to build a case against Honaker. Among these were that:

- The rapist extensively discussed his service in Vietnam. Honaker never served in Vietnam.
- Fingerprints recovered from the hood of the boyfriend's car were compared with Honaker's prints. They did not match.
- The perpetrator of the offense appeared to have been left-handed. He took the car keys from the victim's boyfriend with his left hand and drew his weapon on his left side with his left hand. Honaker is right-handed.
- In the initial police report, both the victim and her boyfriend described the assailant's vehicle as yellow or light colored. At trial, the two identified Honaker's vehicle as that of the assailant. Honaker's vehicle was blue.
- The victim said she was raped on a brown sleeping bag. The sleeping bag recovered from Honaker's residence was blue with a red plaid liner.
- Elmer Gist, an analyst with the Virginia Division of Forensic Science (VDFS), testified at trial that it was "unlikely that the hair [found on the victim's shorts] would match anyone other than the defendant, but it is possible." However, Dr. Paul Ferrara, director of the VDFS, has said that the strongest statement that can be made about hair comparison is that two hairs are "consistent."

As of today, no perpetrator has been caught in the original attack. Honaker, who received a phone call and an apology from Governor Allen upon his release from prison, has been rebuffed at receiving reparations. Allen stated that reparations are unwarranted because the prosecution, judge, and jury "all acted in complete accordance with the law."[33]

Julius Ruffin

On December 6, 1981, a black man with a knife broke into a Norfolk woman's apartment and sodomized and raped her. Over a forty-five-minute period, the intruder would attack her, leave, and return, pretending to be someone else, saying, "I am the crazy one." After the attack, he forced the victim to wash herself.

The victim, a white woman, waited another forty-five minutes to call police, who took her to a hospital, where a PERK yielded a sperm specimen. After the examination, officers took her to the police station and showed her a binder of five hundred black offenders, none of whom resembled her attacker. A few weeks later, the police showed her a smaller photo array of five or six men. She identified one, a dark-skinned black man, as having the "same shaped body," but officers did not bring in the suspect for further inquiry.

The victim was working as a technician at Eastern Virginia Medical School, and she testified that after the attack she would scan crowds for African American men, looking for her attacker. In January 1982, about six weeks after the attack, she was in a hallway at the medical school and spotted an African American man in an elevator wearing a maintenance uniform. She thought that he might be her attacker and quickly called school officials. They arranged for him to come to her office under the guise of making a repair. After observing him in her office, she felt sure that he had been her attacker.

The man she identified was Julius Ruffin, a twenty-eight-year-old, light-skinned black man, who worked in maintenance at the medical school. Ruffin was called to the security office of the medical school, where he found two Norfolk police officers who wanted to ask him questions. He agreed to accompany them to the police station, presuming that the questions concerned a mistake that would be clarified quickly if he cooperated. He had a previous criminal history and was a known former drug user, but he had no record of violence or crimes against women.

At the police station Ruffin was briefly locked up and then interrogated about the crime. He expressed surprise that he was a suspect, vehemently denied any charges, and asked officers how the victim had initially identified her attacker. The investigating officer said the description was an African American man between five feet, six inches, and five feet, eight inches, 150 pounds, with dark skin. At the time Ruffin was six feet, one inch, 170 pounds, fair-skinned, with two prominent gold teeth and facial hair. Later that evening, Ruffin was put into a lineup with four or five other men who already were incarcerated, had dark skin, and were ungroomed. Ruffin was asked to wear hospital scrubs. From a place he could not see, the victim identified him as her attacker.

Ruffin was arrested and given a "perp test" that involved an oral swab and hair and pubic hair samples. Later, officers obtained a shoe print from Ruffin. His trial commenced a few months later, and the prosecution's first witness was the victim herself, who was compelling in identifying Ruffin as her attacker. Also testifying was a forensic scientist, who said that based on serological evidence, both Ruffin and the attacker were type-B secretors, matching roughly 8 percent of the male population.

By the time of the trial, Ruffin's family had helped him hire private counsel, who called Ruffin's brother and the brother's girlfriend as witnesses, who testified that they all were together on the night of the rape. The attorney also sought to sow doubt about the victim's identification of Ruffin.

The first trial deadlocked, with nine white jurors favoring conviction and three black jurors prepared to acquit. The case was declared a mistrial. A second trial ended in the same way, with jurors split along racial lines. Ruffin's counsel tried to get the case dismissed based on the jurors' doubt in the first two trials, but the case proceeded to trial a third time. During voir dire at the third trial, the prosecutor used four peremptory challenges to remove four black members of the jury pool and empanel an all-white jury. (This was before the U.S. Supreme Court's decision in *Batson v. Kentucky,* which required prosecutors to provide a race-neutral reason for striking jurors.)[34] The prosecution's basis for excluding the four African Americans from the jury is not known.

At the third trial the testimony varied somewhat from the first two. This time the witness testified that the attacker was a foot or more taller than her four-foot, eleven-inch, frame, rather than the five-foot, eight-inch, figure she originally gave police. In addition, the prosecution called Ruffin's supervisor from work, who testified that Ruffin's appearance at work matched the victim's description of Ruffin on the day she identified him, even though the supervisor had told Ruffin's attorney privately that he had no memory of what Ruffin looked like on the day in question. Although Ruffin's counsel did a good job of planting doubts about the certainty of the victim's identification of Ruffin, he did not introduce evidence of the problems in eyewitness identification, especially cross-racial identification—largely because such research was not available at the time.

In contrast to the first two trials, the third, all-white jury deliberated for seven minutes before convicting Ruffin of rape and related charges, the punishment for which was life in prison. The foreman of the third jury told journalists years later that the evidence was "overwhelming," but another juror wrote Ruffin anonymously after his release from prison to say that jurors had relied entirely on the victim's testimony in convicting. Her testimony must have been persuasive, because Ruffin looked so unlike her original description of the attacker. More troubling, the police and prosecutors seem to have ignored these inconsistencies as soon as the victim named Ruffin as her attacker.

Ruffin's attempts at appeal failed, and he was denied parole on four separate occasions, mainly because he would not admit his guilt. With the rise of DNA testing, Ruffin began a letter-writing campaign to the Norfolk Commonwealth's attorney, the Norfolk police, and the Virginia Division of Forensic Science to have the Commonwealth retest the evidence in his case. The Circuit Court of Norfolk responded that all evidence from his case had been destroyed in 1986. VDFS in Richmond and its lab in Norfolk also responded that they could not comply with his request. In fact, the evidence was available, but no one had checked thoroughly to find this out.

In 2002, Ruffin filed a request under Virginia's new statute for post-conviction DNA testing. The Commonwealth's attorney had a prosecutor contact the state lab to see whether any evidence still existed. There, in Mary Anne Burton's files, was biological evidence from Ruffin's case. The court appointed counsel for Ruffin, and six months after the discovery of the old evidence, new DNA testing was ordered. Ruffin was cleared as the source of the semen found on the victim, with the results identifying another convicted rapist as the likely suspect. That man, Aaron Doxie III, proved to be a troubling discovery for the Commonwealth, as he was later identified as the perpetrator in another two rapes from 1981, for which an innocent man, Arthur Lee Whitfield, served twenty years in prison. By 2003, when Ruffin was cleared, Doxie was already serving three life sentences for a rape conviction in 1984. Had Doxie been caught at the time of the first rapes, the victim in Ruffin's case might have been spared.

In March 2003, Virginia Governor Mark Warner issued Ruffin a pardon, and the Commonwealth released Ruffin twenty-one years after his original arrest. The victim wrote Ruffin to express her "sorrow and devastation" at his conviction, but in issuing a pardon, Governor Warner said, "I find no fault with the verdict of the jury based upon the evidence available to it at the time of trial, nor with the actions of the attorneys for the Commonwealth or the court at trial." Since then, Mr. Ruffin has succeeded in having all remaining police and court records in his case expunged.

Walter Snyder

On October 28, 1985, an Alexandria woman was raped and sodomized by an assailant, whom she described as a black man wearing red shorts, a gray hooded sweatshirt, and white tennis shorts. Although she did not get a good look at the attacker's face, she said he smelled of alcohol and body odor and that his hands were soft and smooth.

The next day, an Alexandria detective canvassed the victim's neighborhood, including the mother of Walter Snyder, who lived across the street from the victim. For reasons still not clear, the detective visited Snyder at work the next day and asked him to accompany the police officer to the station. Snyder agreed to go and permitted police to fingerprint and photograph him. The detective asked Snyder whether he owned red shorts and white tennis shoes, which Snyder said he did.

Almost two weeks after the crime, the Alexandria detective met with the victim and showed her photographs of seven men. Included in this array was the photo of Snyder taken at the police station. But unlike the other six photos, Snyder's was a head-and-face shot, whereas the others were full-body photographs. The victim initially indicated that four of the suspects—but not Snyder—looked familiar but then decided that none of them was the rapist. After examining the photos again, she picked up Snyder's picture and said there was something familiar about his eyebrows, but she was not prepared to identify him as the rapist.

On the same day, the detective obtained a warrant to search Snyder's home. In the supporting affidavit, the detective said that neighbors had seen Snyder wearing a gray hooded sweatshirt on the night of the rape and that Snyder had admitted he owed such a sweatshirt. But the neighbors testified at trial that they had seen Snyder without a shirt on, and Snyder denied ever making a statement about a sweatshirt. Nonetheless, the detective obtained a search warrant and found red boxing shorts and white tennis shoes in Snyder's home.

Over the next months the victim observed Snyder wearing shorts and washing his car in his driveway across the street from her. She called the detective to say that Snyder looked familiar. According to the detective's testimony at trial, the witness had not been told to watch Snyder and that, unprompted, she called to positively identify Snyder. Subsequent fact-finding in Snyder's civil suit against the city of Alexandria suggested that the detective had already given the victim Snyder's name and told her that he was a suspect. Moreover, there is reason to believe that the victim mentioned only that Snyder's thighs looked familiar, not that she recognized his face.

In January 1986, Snyder approached the Alexandria police to return his shorts and tennis shoes. He was refused, the original detective telling Snyder that the clothes had been sent to a laboratory for testing. Snyder returned the next day, again seeking his clothes. He was escorted to the building's lobby and asked to wait. Meanwhile, the detective phoned the victim and asked her to come to the police station. When she arrived, she saw Snyder in the waiting room of the station and identified him as her rapist.

The detective and two police officers began to question Snyder about the rape, the three claiming that Snyder confessed to the crime. Snyder, however, contends that he consistently maintained his innocence. Shortly after this time, Snyder was told he was under arrest, and he was handcuffed to the chair in the interrogation room. The exact events that followed remain in contention. The detective removed a number of hairs from Snyder's head. Snyder either blew the hairs off the table or attempted to leap from the chair and lunge for the door. Snyder's mother says that the detective then attacked her son, striking his face; a court report says that officers merely restrained Snyder as he struggled for the door. In either event, Snyder's nose was broken in the melee. The detective then pulled down Snyder's pants and removed a pubic hair. With Snyder's pants still down around his ankles, officers moved him to a different part of the station.

Snyder pleaded not guilty to all charges. His family helped him obtain counsel, who filed several motions to exclude Snyder's alleged confession and suppress the victim's "showup" identification, the shorts and tennis shoes, and Snyder's hairs seized at the police station. The state trial judge ruled against Snyder on all points. Snyder's trial was held over three days in late June 1986. The defense called a few alibi witnesses, who claimed that Snyder had been in bed sleeping at the time of the attack. Conventional serology failed to exclude Snyder as the perpetrator because he had the same blood type as the attacker. But the strongest evidence at trial was that of the victim, who pointed at Snyder and identified him as her assailant. Snyder was convicted on all charges and sentenced to forty-five years in prison.

At some point early in his incarceration, Snyder read an article in *Newsweek* about DNA testing and told his mother about the technology. Snyder and his mother went through eleven attorneys after his conviction to secure DNA testing of the biological evidence in the case. At one point, in 1989 or 1990, a form of DNA testing was performed on the victim's underwear containing traces of semen from the rape, but there was not enough biological material to draw a conclusion about its connection to Snyder.

In 1992, a friend and colleague of Snyder's mother told her about a new form of DNA testing that could be performed on even small fragments of evidence. After hiring yet another attorney, the Snyders were able to get the prosecution to release the evidence to an independent lab that successfully completed the tests. A few weeks later, the lab reported that Snyder was excluded as a suspect.

Snyder and his family presumed that he would be released immediately, based on the test results, but Snyder's attorney did not know how to proceed. The independent lab then put Snyder's mother in touch with Cardozo Law School's Innocence Project, which accepted Snyder's case pro bono and petitioned the Alexandria Commonwealth's attorney to seek Snyder's release. After three more DNA tests—two conducted by the state and one by the FBI—the Commonwealth's attorney agreed that Snyder was innocent of the rape and appealed to Virginia Governor L. Douglas Wilder for Snyder's clemency. Governor Wilder signed an executive order on April 23, 1993, releasing Snyder after seven years in prison.

After his exoneration and release, Snyder successfully petitioned the court to expunge his criminal record and seal all records of the case. He then filed a civil suit against the city of Alexandria and the detective and two officers involved in his case. That case has since settled, with the terms of settlement sealed and confidential.

Without an official declaration on Snyder's civil suit, it is difficult to know whether his allegations of police misconduct are true and to what extent any suspected misdeeds led to his wrongful conviction. Snyder claims that officers lied to obtain a search warrant, perjured themselves at trial, beat him while in custody, and knowingly steered the victim to misidentify him. An audiotape or videotape of the interrogation could certainly have resolved the discrepancies. At the very least, suggestive identification methods may have contributed to the victim's mistaken identification. This factor—and the victim's subsequent in-court identification of Snyder—may have had the largest influence on the jury when it errantly convicted Walter Snyder.

David Vasquez

On the night of January 23, 1984, a young lawyer was raped and strangled in her Arlington home. The murder scene suggested an especially dangerous perpetrator, one who was strong enough to lift the victim, cunning enough to construct bindings and a noose from Venetian blinds and a rope in the victim's home, and frighteningly deranged to both rape and hang the young woman.

Neighbors found the woman's body the next day and called police, who began to canvass the neighborhood. Two neighbors, including one whose brother was a potential suspect, placed David Vasquez at or near the crime scene. Vasquez, who was described by two neighbors as "creepy," a "peeping Tom," and "weird . . . due to his attitude towards women," used to live in the victim's neighborhood.[35] He was known to have a low intellect and had moved to Manassas, about thirty miles away, where he worked at a McDonald's restaurant and lived with his mother. Still, the witnesses claimed that he had been in the neighborhood.

Almost three weeks after the murder, two Arlington detectives visited Vasquez at the McDonald's in Manassas where he worked and asked him whether he would accompany them to the Prince William County Police Department to talk. Despite Vasquez's repeated questions, the detectives did not tell him the reason for their query, only that they did not want to question him in front of his coworkers. Vasquez left with the detectives. At the Prince William police station, Vasquez asked for his mother and was repeatedly put off as he was questioned for several hours about the rape and murder. Detectives did not read him his *Miranda* rights. Vasquez initially told officers that he had gone bowling and then returned home to his mother's house on the night in question. Believing that Vasquez was lying, the Arlington detectives falsely told Vasquez that they had found his fingerprints inside the victim's house. For the first time Vasquez admitted to being present that evening, "albeit only obliquely: 'Maybe I might have gone there for a visit.'"[36]

As the ICVA's report indicates, Vasquez was unable to answer the questions that inevitably followed:[37]

> When asked how he got to Arlington, for example, Vasquez stated: "I want to know. Because if my mom was working and she can't drive [me] and I don't drive." Nevertheless, Vasquez slowly admitted that on the night of the murder he had been in Arlington and had gone to [the victim's] home, ostensibly for the purpose of helping her move some furniture. Still, Vasquez could not quite settle on an answer: "It was my imagination that was there, [but] how my body would get there if I didn't."
>
> As the interview lengthened, Vasquez's "ability to communicate became progressively worse. At times his statements were virtually incomprehensible." Eventually, Vasquez admitted that he had sexual intercourse with the victim.

[*Detective 1*]: David, did you have sex with her?
Vasquez: No.
[*Detective 1*]: David, we'll be able to find that out very easily.
Vasquez: If I did I . . .
[*Detective 2*]: Where did you have sex with her? On the second floor? Or was it in the basement that you had sex with her?
Vasquez: Uh, no.
[*Detective 2*]: So, it wasn't on the second floor. OK. So we're down to the first floor. The living room, is that where you had sex with her?
Vasquez: Yeah.
[*Detective 2*]: Where?
Vasquez: Right in the middle of the living room . . .
[*Detective 2*]: Was she naked when you had sex with her?
Vasquez: Maybe.

Following the exchange, Vasquez explained to the detectives that "[the victim] had *asked* him to tie her up because she was into bondage, something David himself didn't like." But, until prompted by [the] detectives . . . , Vasquez could not explain what he had used to tie [the victim's] hands.

[*Detective 2*]: Whatcha [*sic*] use?

Vasquez: The ropes?

[*Detective 2*]: No, not the ropes. Whatcha [*sic*] use?

Vasquez: Ah, my belt?

[*Detective 2*]: No. Not your belt.

[*Detective 1*]: Come on, David, think about what you used now!

Vasquez: I just don't . . .

[*Detective 1*]: Remember being out in the sun room, the room that sits out to the back of the house?

Vasquez: Yeah, I know—

[*Detective 1*]: The new addition, you remember being out there?

Vasquez: I think so.

[*Detective 1*]: And what did you cut down?

Vasquez: A coat hanger?

[*Detective 1*]: No, it wasn't a coat hanger, it was something like a coat hanger. What was it? By the window? . . . Think about the Venetian blinds David. Remember cutting the Venetian blind cord?

Vasquez: Ah, it was a thin rope.

[*Detective 1*]: Yeah!

Shortly thereafter, Vasquez told the detectives that [the victim] had actually asked him to kill her: "I told her no, I didn't want to do it and she said, 'Do it!'" Once again, though, detectives . . . provided the details, not Vasquez.

[*Detective 2*]: Okay now tell us how . . . you did it.

Vasquez: I grabbed the knife and just stabbed her, that's all.

[Detective 1]: Oh David! No David! Now if you would have told us the way it happened, we could believe you a little bit better.

Vasquez: I only say that it did happen and I did it, and my fingerprints were on it . . .

[*Detective 1*]: You hung her!

Vasquez: What?

[*Detective 1*]: You hung her!
Vasquez: Okay so I hung her.

These "admissions" notwithstanding, Vasquez remained equivocal—and above all confused—about his role in the murder. Towards the end of the near[ly] two-hour interview, Vasquez took off his glasses, rubbed his eyes, and in a manner that seemed to indicate that he was talking to himself said, "I know I did it, but I don't know how my fingerprints got there. I wasn't there. I know I wasn't there. I know I wasn't . . . I know I didn't do it. How would I get there if I didn't drive and I didn't hitch-hike?"

Rather than arresting Vasquez at this point, the detectives asked him to accompany them to Arlington. He reluctantly agreed, again asking for his mother, which detectives deflected. At the Arlington police station, detectives began to question Vasquez a second time, again without advising him of his *Miranda* rights. As the ICVA report found,

The second interrogation went much like the first, with Vasquez vacillating between admitting he was in [the victim's] home on the night of the murder and protesting that "I don't even know how I got to that place." Once again, Vasquez provided "a rather disjointed rendition" of his involvement in the murder and burglary. Vasquez "only appeared sure of one thing: that he hadn't been in Arlington in six months. Yet, in a rambling and inconsistent account, he continued to repeat the detail of how he had bound [the victim], had sex with her, and hung her."

Approximately fifty minutes into the interrogation, [one of the detectives] left the room to discuss the next step with his superiors, taking the tape recorder with him. [The other detective] stayed behind and began shooting the breeze with Vasquez, chatting with him about his favorite bars and deep-sea fishing. Suddenly, Vasquez stopped speaking in mid-sentence. He dropped his head and said in a low, rumbling tone, "I have horrible dreams." Vasquez was not addressing [the detective], though, but "just talking at the air." According to the detectives, "Vasquez was completely transformed. He seemed clear, certain. The vacancy was gone." By the time [one of the detectives] retrieved the tape recorder, Vasquez was five minutes into his "dream" statement:

Girl was in my dream, it's a horrible dream, it's a horrible dream, too horrible, I got myself in hell by breaking the glass. The dryer was hooked up, cut my hand in glass. I need help, then I went upstairs, she kept coming out, she startled me. I startled her. We both kinda screamed a little bit, she told me what was I doing. I said I came over to see you. My dream's too horrible to go back in it again. . . .

She wanted to make love. She said yes and no and then she said OK and we went upstairs to her bedroom. Kissed a little and then took each other's clothes off. Bit her, I guess hard, then she told me would I tie her hands. . . . She said there's a knife in the kitchen, cut string off the blinds, just tie me. Then I asked her while I was tying her hands if it's too tight. She said no. . . . Walk downstairs . . . took her pictures, she's nice. . . . She said tie me some more. . . . I brought . . . some big rope and . . . she told me the other way. I says what way is that? She says, by hanging. I says no, don't have to hang, no, no, no, no. She said yes and called me a chicken. So I did it.

I tied it to the car and threw it over the beam and then I put the rope around her. I was gonna pull and then I says I can't do it. She call me a chicken again, a couple of times. I says I can't. She call me man or mouse. And I says neither but I'm not . . . I was like I said in that dream, dream was so dreamable, that dream. And she says do it. So I did it. I tried to hold on to rope, she was off the ground already. Try to hold rope as tight as I could but . . . . I couldn't. The rope burned my hands, God it hurt. I let her down. I couldn't tell if she was dead or alive. I went back upstairs, got the camera, took some pictures of her. Put her on her belly. God. See her face 'cause I didn't know if she was dead or alive. I was in my underclothes. . . . That dream, dream, dream, dream. That dream trying to get dream to go away but I couldn't.

Vasquez's "dream" statement, which lasted nearly thirty minutes, left him emotionally spent: "I don't want my dream anymore. That dream, too much."

After this interrogation, Arlington detectives arrested Vasquez, booked him for murder, and took him before a magistrate before placing him in the county jail. The next day, one of the detectives again brought Vasquez in for some questioning to clear up "some confusion . . . with respect to certain aspects of the case."[38] During questioning, the detective succeeded in getting Vasquez to repeat his "dream" statement, this time, however, after police had obtained a written waiver from Vasquez of his *Miranda* rights.

Vasquez's defense attorneys, Matthew Bangs and Richard McCue, soon moved to suppress all three statements by Vasquez on the grounds that his admissions were the fruits of custodial interrogations in which Vasquez was not advised of his rights. The Arlington circuit court agreed with the defense team on the first two statements, but the judge permitted prosecutors to introduce Vasquez's third statement made after his arrest and following the waiver of his *Miranda* rights. According to the court, the " 'taint of illegality' of the earlier statement[s] had been removed by the subsequent *Miranda* warnings, the passage of time, and Vasquez's court appearance."[39]

Vasquez was looking at a tough case against him. The prosecution had his confession, complete with the "correct" details of the crime by the time that detectives had led Vasquez to his third telling of the story. Investigators had uncovered two neighbors of the victim, who fingered Vasquez as a possible suspect, one even putting him near the scene on the night of the crime. A search of Vasquez's room had discovered a number of pornographic magazines, some with pictures of women bound and gagged. Finally, the Commonwealth's forensic scientists were prepared to testify that the pubic hairs found on the victim were consistent with those of Vasquez.

The Commonwealth's case, however, was not completely airtight. Even prosecutors acknowledged that Vasquez's confession was "oblique" and at other times "disjointed."[40] None of the footprints found at the crime scene matched those of Vasquez's shoes. One of the neighbors who was certain that Vasquez had been in the area on the night of the murder did not come forward until after her brother had been named a suspect. Perhaps most troubling for the Commonwealth's case, Vasquez's blood type did not match that of the semen found on the victim's body. If Vasquez had been involved in the crime—as his "admission" would seem to indicate—he must have worked with someone else who actually committed the rape. Vasquez's story, however, did not include an accomplice.

As trial approached, Vasquez's lawyers became concerned that a jury would convict him of the rape and murder, a crime that was considered a capital offense. They were having trouble establishing Vasquez's alibi, and psychologists who examined him testified that he was competent to stand trial. On the eve of the trial's start, Vasquez's attorneys hammered out a plea deal with prosecutors under which Vasquez would enter an "Alford plea" to second-degree murder and burglary. Named for the Supreme Court case *North Carolina v. Alford*,[41] a defendant may steadfastly maintain his innocence under an Alford plea while still agreeing to plead guilty. Vasquez was sentenced to thirty-five years in prison.

Throughout their investigation, the Arlington police had been convinced that Vasquez had acted with an accomplice. How else, they figured, could a man of such low intelligence have raped, bound, hoisted, and strangled a woman? Plus his blood type did not match that of the semen found on the victim. Yet their investigation for the "unindicted co-ejaculator" ended with Vasquez's plea and incarceration.

About three years following the first rape and murder, Arlington experienced a similar crime. On December 1, 1987, police responded to a call in the same neighborhood as the first murder and found a young woman who had been raped and strangled. The facts were eerily similar to the crime for which Vasquez had been sentenced. The victim was young and white; she lived alone; the perpetrator had entered her home through a small basement window; her hands had been tied behind her back before she was hanged; the home was ransacked, and the crime scene was wiped down for fingerprints.

The detective assigned to the case, Joe Horgas, recalled Vasquez's case and the fact that detectives believed at the time that Vasquez had not acted alone. Horgas also was aware of a string of other burglaries, rapes, and murders that had occurred on the Richmond–Arlington corridor over the previous four years. The crime spree began in "June 1983, continued through the Vasquez murder, and then recommenced, after an odd three-year lapse in time, with the murder by strangulation of a Richmond woman on September 18, 1987."[42]

Detective Horgas went to visit David Vasquez in prison. Accompanied by Vasquez's attorney Richard McCue, Horgas sought any clues from Vasquez about the identity of the new murderer. Vasquez had no answers for Horgas, instead continuing to raise questions about his own involvement in the 1984 murder.

> Horgas distinctly recalls that Vasquez kept asking how, on the evening of January 23, 1984, he could have gotten from Manassas to Arlington to commit the crime, since he owned no car and in fact did not even have a driver's license. [Indeed,] Horgas remembers leaving the penitentiary with the feeling that Vasquez was an innocent man.[43]

Horgas concluded that the string of murders must have been committed by a single perpetrator, and he began to cull a list of potential suspects. His attention was soon drawn to Timothy Spencer, an ex-convict who was living at a halfway house between Richmond and Arlington. Spencer had ties to the South Arlington neighborhood of the two rapes and murders, and the three-year gap in the attacks could be explained by Spencer's incarceration during that period. Gradually, Horgas began to build a case against Spencer.

Needless to say, Horgas's conclusion met with many doubts. His methods were novel, and until he convinced the FBI of Spencer's guilt, several of his colleagues remained skeptical. But the head of the FBI's Behavioral Science Unit replied that the so-called South Side Strangler was responsible for both of the Arlington murders and that he had acted alone. This seemed to rule out Vasquez, who was in prison at the time of the second murder.

In response to the FBI's report, as well as the results of its own internal investigation, the Arlington Commonwealth's attorney, Helen Fahey, became convinced of Vasquez's innocence and contacted the defendant's attorney to prepare a pardon application for Virginia's governor. Together, the prosecution and defense filed the request for pardon, which the Virginia governor, Gerald Baliles, granted on January 4, 1989. David Vasquez was released from prison that evening, almost five years after the original rape and murder. After his release, details of Vasquez's time in prison were revealed. Despite an agreement in his plea deal, Vasquez had not been assigned to a psychiatric unit in prison, instead remaining in the general population where he was repeatedly raped and abused. The General Assembly eventually passed a $117,000 annuity that provides Vasquez a $1,000 monthly payment. Vasquez's mother, however, has sharply criticized the award, saying, "No amount of money is going to pay for this, to make us forget it."[44]

Timothy Spencer, the true "Southside Strangler," was ultimately convicted of murdering four women, including the two from Arlington. He was sentenced to death and executed on April 27, 1994.

Troy Webb

On January 23, 1988, a white twenty-five-year-old Virginia Beach woman was robbed and raped in the parking lot of her apartment complex. The assailant stood about two and a half feet in front of her and pointed a gun directly at her face, but after the initial confrontation the victim had her back to him throughout the rest of the crime.

The victim immediately reported the crime to police, who took her to the hospital where a PERK was collected. The next day the victim met with detectives to try to construct a composite of the man who attacked her. Unfortunately, she was unable to provide enough information about the perpetrator to design the composite. Nor was she able to identify her attacker by looking through books of mug shots.

Almost a week later, while working at her waitressing job, the victim saw an African American man who, she thought, was acting suspiciously. She asked her manager to call the police because she thought the man was her assailant, but before police arrived the victim got a closer look at the man and realized he was not the perpetrator. As she later testified at trial, "I was still upset to where any black man I seen [*sic*] I was going to think it was him."[45]

Nearly three weeks after the incident a Virginia Beach detective went to the victim's house and presented her with a photographic lineup of six individuals. This time, she was able to make an identification: she named one of the men in the photographic lineup, Troy Webb, an African American, as the perpetrator, saying she was "99 percent" sure. The detective returned to her house the next day and presented her with a second photographic lineup. Again, she identified Webb.

The police also conducted serology tests of the evidence obtained in the PERK, concluding that the semen in the kit and on the victim's underwear was from a secretor. Although Webb was a nonsecretor, the victim's live-in boyfriend was a secretor. If there were mixed semen in the sample, officers theorized, the boyfriend's semen could have masked that of a nonsecretor like Webb.

Based on the victim's identification of Webb and the inconclusive serology tests, police officers arrested Webb. He was indicted by a grand jury in June 1988 and went to trial seven months later on the charges of rape, abduction with intent to defile, robbery, and use of a firearm during the commission of a robbery. Webb was represented by a public defender who, although zealous in the defense, may have appeared insensitive to the victim at trial. During cross-examination, the attorney questioned the victim's decision to leave her infant in the care of her thirteen-year-old nephew:

Q: This place where you lived—I mean, it's not for me to judge living conditions. You worked as a cocktail waitress. Did you have your own apartment?

A: I was living with my boyfriend and my child.

Q: And your thirteen-year-old nephew was living there, too?

A: He was spending the night.

Q: He was spending the night?

A: He watched my baby.

Q: Here's a thirteen-year-old staying in your apartment and you're staying with your boyfriend and . . . And this thirteen-year-old babysits for your child while you work as a cocktail waitress until 3:00 in the morning? Not your mother, but this thirteen-year-old child was babysitting?

During his closing argument, the defense attorney acknowledged that he may have been "obnoxious" during his cross-examination of the victim. As he explained to the jury, "It's kind of hard to talk about the case without being disgusting. You may think I have a somewhat obnoxious personality, anyway. Most people gain that impression of me after watching me cross-examine witnesses in trials." Yet he continued with comments that may have appeared insensitive to the victim. For instance, when describing her appearance to the jury, he remarked:

[The victim] had told us she had a black mini skirt on. It was part of the outfit of a waitress. Some weird—you know—whoever designed the thing. Buttoned up to the collar. Right? Prim and proper like Mary Poppins, but a mini skirt on with black hose. You tell me. Is that weird or what? That must appeal to somebody's sexual interest. That's why they dress the waitresses that way.

Moreover, he seemed to disparage the victim's intelligence and personal life and perhaps those of jury members as well. Describing her testimony, the attorney warned about

the word of a tenth-grade dropout. Why did I go into her education? I don't know what educational level you people have. I could be insulting half the jury. I don't think so, but what difference does that make? That doesn't mean that we remember or we don't remember; but what I went into is, I didn't know the answers to the questions that I asked her. I didn't know when she dropped out of school. Tenth grade. She ran a bunch of unsuccessful businesses. She's had, obviously, an unsuccessful love life. Do you hold that against her? There are people on the jury that I am sure have had similar problems, and some of us obviously either business failures or love life failures.

To some people, the attorney's behavior may resemble a strategy used at an earlier time by defense teams: disparage the reputation of a rape victim. Indeed, the very reason that "rape shield laws" were created in the 1970s was to protect victims of rape, whose personal lives and sexual histories often were paraded into court to question their morals and thus their veracity as complaining witnesses.[46] Although there is no reason to believe that Webb's counsel adopted this strategy, behavior that evoked such arguments might well have fallen on deaf ears. Or even worse, it may have portrayed the defense as unfairly attacking the victim, particularly in a case of a black defendant and a white woman. Especially in the South, the vision of black-on-white rape may have had more emotional power than the accusation of a wayward woman.

After a two-day trial, Webb was convicted, and on March 9, 1989, he was sentenced to forty-seven years in prison. His attorneys appealed the conviction, arguing, among other things, that the judge has been wrong not to strike a juror who, like the victim, had been both a cocktail waitress and raped. Although the Virginia Court of Appeals allowed Webb to appeal on this ground, a divided court eventually rejected his claim, concluding that the matter raised an issue of fact, not law, which it would not overturn because the trial judge had acted within his discretion.

While continuing to maintain his innocence, Webb began to serve his sentence. In 1996, lawyers from Cardozo Law School's Innocence Project became involved in Webb's case and contacted the Virginia Beach Commonwealth's Attorneys' Office asking to retest the evidence in the case using DNA. Deputy Commonwealth's Attorney Pamela Albert, the same lawyer who had prosecuted Webb, agreed to petition the circuit court to order the testing of evidence from the victim, her boyfriend at the time, and Webb. Subsequent DNA tests by the Virginia Department of Forensic Science excluded both the boyfriend and Webb as possible rapists in the case. The Innocence Project then petitioned Governor George Allen for Webb's clemency. Webb was joined in the petition by the Commonwealth's Attorney for Virginia Beach, Robert Humphreys, who announced, "The DNA results in this case, available in 1996 [and not at the time of trial], conclusively prove that Troy Webb could not have contributed the sperm found in the samples taken from the victim." On October 16, 1996—more than eight years after the original crime—Governor Allen granted Troy Webb clemency.

Arthur Lee Whitfield

On August 14, 1981, two women were raped within forty-five minutes of each other in the same neighborhood in Norfolk, Virginia. Both women were accosted at knifepoint by a black man as they got out of their cars near their homes. Both women were forced by their attacker to go to a nearby secluded spot where they were sodomized, raped, and robbed. Coincidentally, the two victims were friends, but there was no sign that the women were specifically targeted.

Both victims described their attacker in similar terms. The first woman said her assailant was a black man, approximately thirty years old, about six feet tall, and wearing a black or blue T-shirt and nylon running shorts. The second woman described the assailant as a black man between five feet, ten inches, and six feet tall. She was certain that her attacker was clean shaven, whereas the first victim was uncertain. Both were sure, though, that the assailant was uncircumcised and that he had distinctive, light eyes.

The police investigation of the two rapes focused on Arthur Whitfield because police suspected him of having committed a burglary two miles away from the rapes on the same night. The burglar matched the same general description of the rapist, and like the rapist, the burglar carried a knife. The police put Whitfield's color photograph in an array containing color photographs of five other people and showed the array to the first rape victim. She selected Whitfield's photograph and said that she was 95 percent sure he was the man who raped her.

The next day detectives arranged an in-person lineup at the police station and asked both victims to come in to view Whitfield. The two women drove to the station together, and as the second victim admitted at trial, "compared notes" about the descriptions of the assailants they had given police. At the station the women were separated and viewed the lineups independently. Each identified Whitfield as the assailant, and the first victim was asked to view photos of Whifield's chest and genitals to determine whether they matched those of her assailant. She confirmed the match. At this point, the second victim was asked to make a similar identification of Whitfield's anatomy, which she did in the company of the first victim, who was visibly upset because she had just made her identification. Indeed, at trial the second victim admitted that she had known at the time of her identification that the first victim had just identified the photos of Whitfield's genitals as those belonging to the rapist.

Whitfield was charged with sexually assaulting the two women and with attempting to break into a third woman's home. The trial judge later severed the three cases and set them for separate trials. In January 1982, Whitfield stood trial for the rape, sodomy, and robbery of the first victim. In an unusual legal decision, however, the judge permitted both rape victims to testify at the first trial, concluding that the testimony of the second victim was relevant to challenge the defense's alibi that Whitfield had been attending a birthday party that evening. Each victim identified Arthur Whitfield as her attacker.

Whitfield did not testify in his own defense, but four defense alibi witnesses testified that Whitfield had attended a birthday party on the night of the incident and was present at the party at the time of the crime. Whitfield's attorney put on evidence that the defendant did not match the description of the victims. A photograph of Whitfield taken a week after the attacks showed him with a heavy mustache, which contradicted the second victim's initial description of her attacker as clean shaven. Defense counsel also had a detective read a portion of the lab report concluding there was no physical evidence connecting Whitfield to the rapes. As the defense recognized, the prosecution's case turned almost exclusively on the testimony of the two victims.

The jury convicted Whitfield on all three counts and sentenced him to a total of forty-five years in prison. Fearing that another jury would convict him in his upcoming trial for the rape of the second woman and sentence him to a long prison term, Whitfield pleaded guilty to the second offense. Pursuant to the plea agreement, the judge sentenced Whitfield to an additional eighteen-year sentence, and the Commonwealth dropped the attempted burglary charges in the third case. Whitfield, then twenty-seven years old, was looking at a total sentence of sixty-three years.

Although Whitfield pleaded guilty to the second offense, he always maintained he was innocent of all the charges. The Virginia Supreme Court rejected his appeal from his trial in the first rape case and affirmed his conviction, finding no reversible error. Whitfield later asked the Circuit Court for the City of Norfolk for a copy of his trial transcript so that he could prepare a petition for habeas corpus relief, but his request was rejected and he never filed a habeas petition.

In 2002, twenty years after Whitfield was convicted, Virginia enacted a writ of actual innocence. Whitfield seized this opportunity and, on his own, filed a petition to have the forensic evidence from both rapes tested for a DNA match. The court appointed a lawyer, Michael Fasanaro, to assist him, and the two asked the Virginia Department of Criminal Justice Services to see whether any physical evidence from the original crimes remained.

Once again, Mary Jane Burton came to the rescue. Although by then she had died, Burton had defied the policy of the Virginia Division of Forensic Science during the 1970s and 1980s by routinely attaching biological evidence to her case files instead of destroying them. Whitfield and Fasanaro were delighted to learn that swabs still remained from the PERK in his cases, and Fasanaro promptly filed a motion to have the evidence tested using DNA technology. In June 2004 the court ordered VDFS to conduct the testing. The results were startling. Not only was Whitfield cleared as the source of semen in both rapes, but the assailant's DNA matched that of another defendant in custody—Aaron Doxie III—who had been identified also as the assailant in the Julius Ruffin case and was serving three life sentences for a 1984 rape conviction. Virginia apparently had a mass rapist on its hands, whose horrid acts had terrorized several women and wrongly imprisoned two men for more than four decades.

The Norfolk Commonwealth's attorney received word on Friday August 20, 2004, that the DNA evidence had eliminated Whitfield as a source of semen in both rapes. Because Whitfield was eligible for parole, the Commonwealth's Attorneys' Office decided that the parole board was the quickest means of securing Whitfield's release. That Friday, Commonwealth's Attorney John Doyle phoned Helen Fahey, chair of the Virginia Parole Board, and requested that the board release Whitfield on parole. Over the weekend, Fahey got the approval of the entire board, and on Monday August 23, 2004, Whitfield was paroled. As Whitfield noted, his release came almost twenty-three years to the day from the original rapes.

The story, however, did not end there. Whitfield petitioned the Virginia Supreme Court to clear his name, but in an odd procedural decision in 2005, the justices said they were authorized to declare writs of actual innocence only for defendants who were still incarcerated.[47] Whitfield thus filed a petition with Virginia's governor, Mark Warner, for a pardon, at which time he was challenged by one of the victims in the 1981 rapes. Still certain that Whitfield was her attacker, the victim wrote a fifteen-page letter to Warner saying she "believes the state lab inadvertently 'commingled and misidentified' evidence from her case with that of the other victim. She said there are discrepancies in the blood types from the testing and believes that she and the other woman were raped by different men."[48] Apart from the victim's contention, there is another unusual circumstance to the case. Both victims claimed that their attacker was uncircumcised. Whitfield is uncircumcised, whereas the suspect identified by DNA testing, Doxie, is circumcised.[49]

In response to the first victim's letter, the VDFS director, Dr. Paul Ferrara, declared that "the possibility of a mix-up in the two cases was 'checked and double-checked,' and discounted."[50] Norfolk Commonwealth's Attorney John Doyle "stands by" his decision to recommend Whitfield's release.

> "I have nothing but empathy" for the victim, Doyle said. "My heart goes out to her. She is 1,000 percent sincere in what she's said then and now." However, he said, evidence that came from samples taken from the woman and her clothing [that] night excludes Whitfield and points to Doxie. "Based on the evidence before me, the case would not now come to trial."[51]

That said, Doyle has no plans to charge Doxie with the 1981 rapes. Because Mary Anne Burton has died, there is no way of proving the chain of custody from the original PERK to the biological evidence taped to Burton's files.

In January 2006, Virginia's governor, Mark Warner, left office, not having acted on Whitfield's pardon request. The matter was left for the incoming governor, Tim Kaine, who at the time of this book's writing had not yet made a decision.

Making Sense of the "Causes" of Erroneous Convictions

How should we understand the forces behind wrongful convictions? When examining the Virginia cases, it is clear that few of the errors that

TABLE 3.1
Factors Found in Virginia's Erroneous Convictions

Case	Eyewitness Identification	Interrogation Methods	Forensic Science	Defense Counsel	Discovery	Tunnel Vision	Post-conviction
Marvin Anderson	X		X	X		X	X
Craig Bell		X	X			X	
Jeffrey Cox	X		X	X	X	X	X
Russell Gray	X					X	X
Edward Honaker	X		X	X	X	X	
Julius Ruffin	X		X			X	
Walter Snyder	X	X	X		X		X
David Vasquez		X	X			X	X
Earl Washington Jr.		X	X	X		X	X
Troy Webb	X		X	X			
Arthur Whitfield	X		X			X	X

led to mistaken convictions were deliberate or malicious. These were not the cases of a different time, or a different state,[52] in which law enforcement officers or prosecutors intentionally turned a blind eye to errors or investigated or prosecuted someone they thought was innocent. Rather, the wrongful convictions identified by the ICVA largely resulted from honest people making honest mistakes, albeit with tragic consequences.

The ICVA's research also makes it difficult to speak of a "cause" of wrongful convictions. A number of forces were associated with the erroneous convictions, and in fact, the cases often displayed more than one problem. As table 3.1 indicates, the ICVA's investigation uncovered several discrete factors associated with the wrongful conviction and continued imprisonment of innocent persons. These factors include weak eyewitness identifications, through either the frailties of human perception or the influence of suggestive identification procedures; the use of interrogation methods that unduly lead innocent suspects to confess and that have no electronic record against which to weigh the veracity of their confessions; the use of substandard forensic science methods and the inability to obtain accurate postconviction testing of new exculpatory evidence; inadequate assistance from defense counsel; limited discovery procedures that prevent the parties from investigating and presenting potentially relevant evidence; the unfortunate presence of "tunnel vision" in criminal investigations and prosecutions; and inadequate postconviction legal procedures that prevented innocent defendants from proving their blamelessness.

The association of these factors with Virginia's wrongful convictions does not mean, however, that they are "causes," at least not in the way that a researcher would explain how social phenomena occur. Social scientists distinguish between correlation and causation, the former suggesting that two events are linked and the latter concluding that no other factor could "explain away" the ability of one event to lead to the other. This distinction has allowed the tobacco lobby to claim for years, apparently with a straight face, that cigarette smoking does not cause cancer.[53] To be sure, tobacco use may be correlated with lung and mouth cancers, the industry acknowledges, but other factors—including hereditary predispositions, other environmental exposures, and lifestyle choices—may explain why some smokers get cancer and others do not. Today the surgeon general and the Centers for Disease Control have discarded previous warnings, like the original disclaimer that "cigarette smoking may be dangerous to your health," and replaced it with "smoking causes lung cancer."[54] Although other factors may mute or exacerbate the connection between smoking and cancer in particular individuals, it is virtually impossible to deny the direct link between tobacco use and the development of cancer.

The courts have often struggled with the distinction between causation and correlation in criminal justice cases. Perhaps the most famous is *McCleskey v. Kemp,*[55] in which University of Iowa law professor David Baldus and colleagues presented the U.S. Supreme Court with compelling evidence concerning the death penalty. Baldus's team conducted a comprehensive analysis of the administration of the death penalty in Georgia during the 1970s, finding that the killers of white victims were four times more likely to be sentenced to death than were the murderers of blacks. This evidence, however, did not convince a majority of the justices that Georgia's capital-sentencing scheme violated the Eighth or Fourteenth Amendments to the U.S. Constitution. Said Justice Lewis Powell for the Court, "Statistics cannot *prove* that race enters into any capital sentencing decisions, or that race was a factor in McCleskey's particular case [emphasis in the original]. . . . At most, the Baldus study indicates a discrepancy that appears to correlate with race."[56]

The Court has been roundly criticized for its inability to comprehend statistics in *McCleskey,*[57] but its distinction between correlation and causation is relevant to examining the nature of wrongful convictions. Applying this distinction to the Virginia cases, it is difficult to say that any single source is a cause of an erroneous conviction. For example, the fact that a defendant is represented by a substandard attorney does not mean that he will inevitably be convicted of a crime he did not commit. If the evidence against him is weak, if the case is simple, or perhaps if a prosecutor intervenes when she recognizes a defense attorney's incompetence, an innocent defendant may be spared jail time or worse. Nor is it guaranteed that a suspect will be convicted when a witness erroneously identifies him as the perpetrator. Again, the defendant may have an airtight alibi, his attorney may be skilled at cross-examination, or biological evidence may exist that clears him of the crime.

A better way to understand the influence of the shortcomings identified in the ICVA's research is through contingency or path analysis. Some readers may recognize this concept from the decision trees taught in business or public policy schools, for the exercise is the same. We begin with an initial condition regarding a case and then trace through the competing scenarios to identify the possible outcomes in a case. A true path analysis would stretch from one side of a blackboard to the other —if not down the hall to another room—but for our purposes, let's consider the possible scenarios concerning eyewitness identification in cases of stranger rape, as this was the most common crime found in the Virginia exonerations. Although the following example traces only a few paths of a possible scenario, there obviously are many potential outcomes from this tree, depending on the particular facts of each case.

Stranger Rape and Eyewitness Identification

Q_1: Did the victim see the perpetrator?

A_1: No. Unlikely that she will later be able to identify him.

A_2: Yes. Continue to next query.

Q_2: Does the victim remember the perpetrator's depiction and believe she can identify him?

A_1: No. Unlikely that she will later be able to identify him.

A_2: Yes. Continue to next query.

Q_3: Was a composite sketch drawn?

A_1: No. Potentially more difficult to catch a perpetrator or for the victim to identify a suspect later. Explore why the sketch was not made.

A_2: Yes. Potentially easier to catch perpetrator. Continue to next query.

Q_4: Did officers provide photos of potential suspects for the victim to observe?

A_1: No. Potentially more difficult to catch a perpetrator. Explore why no photos were provided.

A_2: Yes. Continue to next query.

Q_5: How were the photos presented?[58]

A_1: Simultaneously and/or with feedback. Identification may be more likely yet less accurate. Risk of wrongful conviction rises. Continue to next query.

A_2: Sequentially without feedback. Any identification is likely to be more accurate. Continue to next query.

Q_6: Did the victim identify a perpetrator from the photos?

A_1: No. More difficult to catch the perpetrator.

A_2: Yes. Continue to the next query.

Q_7: How certain was the victim in her identification?[59]

A_1: Certain. Continue to next query.

A_2: Doubtful. May continue to the next query depending on officers' judgment. Officers may discount the identification, search for additional evidence to corroborate the identification, or pursue the suspect identified. The risk of wrongful conviction rises if officers lock onto a suspect to the exclusion of others when identifications are weak or doubtful.

Q_8: Was a suspect stopped/seized?

A_1: No. Case remains unsolved.

A_2: Yes. Continue to next query.

Q_9: Do law enforcement officers believe the suspect matches the victim's earlier description, identification or composite sketch?

A_1: Yes. Arrest and charge are likely.

A_2: No. Move to next query.

Q_{10}: If law enforcement officers have doubts about the connection between the suspect and the prior depiction/sketch, do they act on those doubts?

A_1: No. Officers may arrest and charge the suspect, arrest and hold him while seeking corroborating evidence, or arrest the suspect and leave the charging decision to the prosecutor. The risk of wrongful conviction rises when officers arrest and charge suspects whose guilt they doubt.

A_2: Yes. Depending on the depths of the officers' doubts and their willingness to intercede, they may release the suspect and pursue other potential perpetrators or wait to charge the suspect while seeking corroborating evidence. In either case, the risk of wrongful conviction is ameliorated.

Again, this example is only one of the many possible paths a criminal investigation might take. Officers may stop and arrest a suspect before the victim is shown a book of mug shots or asked to create a sketch, and in some crimes detectives may have no reason to show the victim a series of photos of potential suspects. The point of this exercise is not to suggest that it applies to every case but to outline the kind of path analysis that can be performed on any criminal case. For that matter, many other parts of a case should be analyzed like this. The process of custodial interrogations, the work of a defense attorney, and even the willingness of prosecutors to open their case files all are suitable for path analysis, for together they show that few errors absolutely predict a wrongful conviction without the interplay of other factors. An uncertain identification, for example, need not provide the basis for a criminal prosecution if detectives or prosecutors wait to seek corroborating evidence. For that matter, a questionable identification might be challenged and discounted if an experienced and talented defense attorney were available to observe and object to particular lineup practices.

I am not prepared to offer here a new criminological theory of wrongful convictions, although I do take seriously Richard Leo's challenge to "systematically develop a more sophisticated, insightful, and generalizable criminology of wrongful conviction."[60] As Leo maintains, "Eyewitness misidentification, false confession, and police and prosecutorial misconduct are not actual root causes" of erroneous convictions,[61] but they are serious contributors to the problem that, in tandem and under the wrong circumstances, convict innocent suspects.

Leo's commentary should not be interpreted, however, as showing that the focus on cases of wrongful conviction is ill conceived or that an examination of the errors in these cases is unwise. Indeed, the mistakes uncovered are real and serious, and they undoubtedly extend to many more cases than those that end in a wrongful conviction. That the errors are uncovered, addressed, or fortuitously circumvented in other cases does not mean that we can ignore them or breathe easily, content in the belief that the justice system is self-correcting. Whether the goal is to prevent wrongful convictions, to reduce costs and increase efficiency in investigations and prosecutions, or, more broadly, to raise the standards of criminal justice, each deserves critical attention.

4

An Unmet Obligation

It is difficult to confront the deficiencies of the criminal justice process that can send innocent people to prison or allow the guilty to roam free without feeling compelled to prevent future errors from occurring. Whether we identify with the innocent suspect, who is convicted and left to serve time for a crime he did not commit; the helpless victim, who is attacked by a criminal who should have been locked up; the police officer or prosecutor, who errantly is convinced of a case he later comes to doubt; or the taxpayer, who must pay for the costs of convicting the innocent, it is both good public policy and common human decency to wish to eliminate wrongful convictions.

As the last chapter argued, however, it is virtually impossible to eradicate erroneous convictions, for these cases share many features with others in which errors are caught or offset by other convincing, exculpatory evidence. But it is possible to reduce the rate by which errors occur in the criminal justice system or the likelihood that questionable evidence will find its way into a criminal prosecution. In doing so, the justice system not only will further protect the civil liberties of suspects, but it also will bring the latest and best practices to justice professionals.

Everyone has an interest in adopting the most advanced practices to investigate and prosecute cases, and indeed a number of justice officials have taken the lead in investigating wrongful convictions and responding to their causes. As Samuel Walker noted in his book *A Critical History of Police Reform*, policing in the twentieth century embraced a new model of professionalism in which officers saw themselves not simply as crime fighters but also as upholders of the law. Prosecutors, too, are held to the professional and ethical canons of law, which consider attorneys to be officers of the court rather than mere pugilists seeking to win their cases. The impressive list of justice officials who have been involved in the investigation, consideration, and reversal of erroneous convictions, therefore, should not be surprising: Thomas Sullivan, a former U.S. attorney for the Northern District of Illinois, who cochaired Governor Ryan's Commission in Illinois; I. Beverly Lake, chief justice of the North Carolina Supreme Court, who inaugurated his state's Actual Innocence Commission; Robert Olson, the former police chief of Minneapolis, who has been a leader in reforming interrogation techniques; and Judge William S. Sessions, former director of the FBI, who, among other roles, has served as an advisory board member for the Innocence Commission for Virginia.

With the guidance of Judge Sessions and the other members of its diverse advisory board, the ICVA took aim at the principal sources for the erroneous convictions in Virginia that its investigation had uncovered. After considerable consultation and research, the ICVA issued a series of recommendations to address these factors and reduce the likelihood that such errors would lead to more mistaken convictions. Although each of the sources is itself problematic, the ICVA concentrated much of its energy on three leading reforms: increasing the accuracy of eyewitness identification, improving the reliability of interrogation proceedings, and providing postconviction remedies for erroneous convictions.

Eyewitness Identification

There is little doubt that an eyewitness's identification is one of the most powerful tools available to police officers and prosecutors. In fact, a "positive id" can often seal the fate of a suspect long before going to trial. As the ICVA report stated:

> A defendant who chooses to go to trial despite being identified as the perpetrator faces an uphill and daunting battle, for judges, juries, and the public place overwhelming weight on the testimony of eyewitnesses and victims of crime when they point to a defendant in court and state: "That is the person who committed this crime."

Nonetheless, eyewitness identification can be problematic. Nationwide, nearly 75 percent of the more than one hundred DNA exonerations have involved mistaken eyewitness identification.[1] In Virginia, nine of the eleven cases investigated by the ICVA revealed problems with eyewitness identification. Marvin Anderson, for example, was convicted largely on the testimony of the victim, who had initially identified him in a suggestive photo array in which his was the only color photograph. Jeffrey Cox, too, was imprisoned in a case that relied heavily on two questionable witnesses who claimed to have seen him from a distance late at night.

The Law of Eyewitness Identification

Many forces explain the heavy reliance on questionable eyewitness testimony in criminal cases, but the greatest contributor is the courts themselves. More than thirty years ago, in the case of *Neil v. Biggers,* the U.S. Supreme Court declared that an eyewitness's identification of a suspect may be used at trial unless the identification procedures are "so impermissibly suggestive as to give rise to a very substantial likelihood of irreparable misidentification."[2] Virginia's courts, like those in most of the other states, have applied a "totality of the circumstances" approach in interpreting this standard.[3] Virginia courts consider five factors: (1) the witness's opportunity to view the criminal at the time the crime was committed, (2) the witness's degree of attention during the incident, (3) the accuracy of the witness's prior description of the perpetrator, (4) the level of certainty demonstrated by the witness during the identification procedure, and (5) the length of time between the crime and the identification.[4]

In practice, however, Virginia courts permit the introduction of most eyewitness identifications and reject challenges by defendants alleging suggestive and unreliable identification procedures. Even overly suggestive identification procedures have been admitted in court when the identifications were deemed otherwise reliable. For example, identifications in which the accused stood out as distinctive among the array,[5] when the accused was viewed alone rather than in a group,[6] and even procedures conducted after eyewitnesses were told that a specific suspect was the perpetrator all have been admitted at trial against defendants when the judge concluded that the witnesses' identifications of the accused were reliable.

Virginia law leaves the decision about whether to allow expert testimony regarding eyewitness identification to the discretion of the trial judge. However, the courts have sanctioned expert eyewitness testimony in only narrow circumstances, such as cases involving "cross-racial identification, identification after a long delay, identification after observation under stress, and psychological phenomena [such] as the feedback factor and unconscious transference."[7] Virginia's courts also have consistently refused to permit special jury instructions about the reliability of eyewitness identifications, because judges reason that these instructions have the "effect of emphasizing the testimony of those witnesses who made identifications."[8]

Research on Eyewitness Identification

Nationally, there is now a growing recognition that police officers, lawyers, judges, and juries should be more skeptical about the accuracy and certainty of eyewitnesses' identification of potential suspects is growing. The leader on this issue is Gary Wells, a professor at Iowa State University and president of the American Psychology–Law Society. His research and that of several other social scientists have identified three primary flaws in the standards used by the courts to evaluate and admit eyewitness identifications.[9]

The first factor—an eyewitness's opportunity to view the assailant—has been shown to rely too heavily on the witness's "self-report,"[10] which itself is highly unreliable.[11] Eyewitnesses substantially overestimate the amount of time that they witnessed an event and focused on a suspect's face, especially when they are under a great deal of stress.[12] At the same time, witnesses typically underestimate the amount of time the perpetrator's face was out of view.[13]

These findings critically undermine the reliability of the second factor used by the courts: the eyewitness' degree of attention during the incident. Again, this factor relies on self-reporting, which can be extremely unreliable when the witness is under a great deal of stress.

The courts' third factor—prior, accurate descriptions of the perpetrator by eyewitnesses—also is based on a faulty assumption.[14] The presumption is that an eyewitness's subsequent description of a perpetrator will be accurate if her initial description, given soon after a crime has occurred, also is correct. In fact, however, a witness's description of the perpetrator and the accuracy of the witness's subsequent identification of a particular suspect in a lineup have no meaningful correlation.[15]

The courts' test also fails to account for the influence of suggestive identification procedures, including comments and feedback from law enforcement officers to eyewitnesses, on mistaken identifications.[16] In a 1998 study by Professor Wells, participants were shown a video of a suspect they were later told committed a crime. They then viewed a photo array that did not include the correct suspect and were asked to make an identification.[17] After making an identification, researchers gave the participants positive feedback, negative feedback, or no feedback at all and then interviewed them about their identification.[18] Those participants who received positive feedback gave not only much higher estimates of their certainty at the time they made their identification but also higher estimates of the quality of their view of the suspect, the speed with which they made the identification, the quality of their memory of the incident, and their degree of attention and the ease with which they made the identification—even though they all had identified the wrong photo.[19]

As Wells and his colleagues concluded, suggestion during an identification process "leads eyewitnesses to distort their reports of the witnessing experience across a broad array of questions."[20] Yet this type of inherently inaccurate self-reporting is a significant factor that courts in Virginia and elsewhere use to assess the reliability of eyewitness identifications. As a result, the very "existence of suggestiveness [in the identification process] serves to guarantee that the witness will pass" the reliability test, which is then used to justify the suggestive procedure.[21]

In practice, suggestion can enter the identification process in two ways. First, law enforcement personnel or other observers can confirm a witness's identification, whether at the time of the identification procedure or at any point before an in-court identification.[22] Law enforcement officers may also employ suggestive identification procedures, such as presenting the suspect in ways that make him stand out from other lineup participants. In either event, external suggestion can give witnesses false confidence in their identifications, even if they are mistaken. Moreover, witnesses whose confidence has been inflated often deny that a reinforcing comment or suggestive lineup in any way influenced their identification.[23]

A suggestive identification procedure may lead witnesses to make "relative judgments," subtly encouraging them to select the individual in an identification procedure who looks most like the offender, rather than ensuring an independent judgment that the individual identified is the actual perpetrator.[24] Under traditional police procedures, officers often ask witnesses to view a group of photographs displayed together or a group of individuals shown together in a lineup and ask them whether they can identify the perpetrator(s). Because there always is someone in the group who looks more like the actual offender than the others present, witnesses are apt to identify the individual that most resembles the offender, rather than not to make an identification if they are not sure or do not see the perpetrator.[25] Research shows that witnesses may then confuse or replace their memory of the true perpetrator with the image of the person who looked most like the offender in the identification procedure.[26]

To address these problems, researchers recommend that witnesses be shown photographs or individuals in a lineup sequentially—that is, one at a time—rather than all together as a group. Researchers recommend that when witnesses look at each photograph or individual, they be asked to determine whether they recognize the perpetrator. A recent, comprehensive analysis of twenty-five studies comparing simultaneous and sequential lineups and photo array procedures indicated that sequential procedures reduced the chances of a mistaken identification by nearly one half.[27] This study also suggested that sequential techniques might reduce the rate of accurate identifications when the culprit is present in the identification procedure, although the reduction is not nearly as pronounced as the reduction in mistaken identifications.

Eyewitness Identification Practices

As part of its investigation, the ICVA surveyed Virginia law enforcement agencies about their practices for eyewitness identification and received responses from 108 Virginia law enforcement agencies with general law enforcement functions. As table 4.1 indicates, about 6 percent of these agencies reported that they use the most suggestive identification procedure: showing a witness a single photograph of a suspect. Nearly two-thirds of the agencies reported using showup identifications. Twenty-eight percent of the agencies use in-person lineups as an

TABLE 4.1
Out-of-Court Identification Methods Used by
Virginia Agencies with Law Enforcement Duties

Identification Method	Percentage of Agencies Employing Method
Showups	63
Lineups	28
Photo arrays	98
Single photo	6

Note: N = 108.

identification tool, and 98 percent show multiple photographs to eye-witnesses in photo arrays or photo spreads.

A number of Virginia law enforcement agencies further weaken eye-witness identification because of the procedures they employ. In three-quarters of the cases reported to the ICVA in which identification procedures were used, the officer in charge "always" or "mostly" knows the identity of the suspect who is the subject of the procedure. Although 85 percent of law enforcement agencies reported that they never tell eye-witnesses that the suspect is included in a lineup or photo array, nearly a quarter fail to tell witnesses that they do not have to identify anyone in the identification procedure. When showing photos to eyewitnesses, 77 percent of responding agencies present the photographs together in a group, and fewer than 15 percent display the photographs one at a time. Similarly, 83 percent of agencies that use in-person lineups present the participants together in a group; just 2 percent show the participants one at a time. These findings are consistent with those obtained by the Virginia State Crime Commission, which in 2004 found that less than 5 percent of responding law enforcement agencies in the Common-wealth "solely us[e] the sequential method to conduct photographic line ups."[28] Nor do departments videotape eyewitness identifications so that jurors can observe the entire process. Seventy-eight percent of the agencies reported that they never videotape, while an additional 14 percent said that they rarely do so.

Several law enforcement agencies submitted comments along with their survey responses that reflect sensitivity to suggestive identification procedures. Some departments said that they asked witnesses to give a percentage of certainty for their identification or asked witnesses whether they were "100 hundred percent positive." One agency said it usually asks witnesses

> if they see [the] suspect. Witness[es] must indicate they are absolutely sure of identity, we do not [accept] maybes. . . . We absolutely require a very positive response on identification. However, NO pressure is put on witnesses and witnesses are NOT told to identify someone unless there is no doubt in their mind. (emphasis in original)

Another department explained that witnesses are told that they do not have to identify someone, "especially if there is any hesitation evi-dent," and a third department said that it uses a standard instruction sheet informing witnesses that they do not have to identify any of the photographs. One law enforcement agency said that it recently switched from showing photographs to witnesses simultaneously to showing them sequentially. Finally, in response to the survey question asking whether the officer administering the identification procedure knows the likely suspect, one agency said that its officers always do, "but we are considering getting an officer that is not familiar with the case."

Recommendations

The challenge in addressing the problems of eyewitness identification is that in most cases the errors and their sources are not intentional. Victims and other eyewitnesses do not set out to identify the wrong perpetrator, and the vast majority of law enforcement officers are dedicated to locating the actual suspect as quickly and as accurately as possible.

To improve eyewitness identification procedures, the three branches of government should work together: legislative bodies to set standards for accurate and fair procedures; law enforcement agencies and prosecutors to adopt and follow best practices; and courts to enforce these rules and allow appropriate testimony and instructions in court so that jurors are better informed about eyewitness identification when they are called upon to weigh the credibility of a particular identification.

The ICVA made several recommendations to improve eyewitness identifications, proposals that cut across all three branches of government responsible for this issue. First, the commission recommended using, whenever possible, multiple-person lineups or photo arrays instead of single-suspect identification procedures. This recommendation questions the validity of such procedures as "showup" identifications, in which an individual suspect is shown to an eyewitness in the vicinity of the crime shortly after the crime has occurred. Showups may be appropriate in exigent circumstances when no other method of identification is available, but they come with considerable risk of suggesting guilt when a suspect is innocent.

The risk becomes unacceptable when single-participant identification procedures are held even later after a crime. Sometimes these one-suspect identifications occur by chance and are not arranged by the police. Julius Ruffin's case is one example of a chance encounter between the victim and someone she perceived as her offender. But sometimes the police may arrange for eyewitnesses to view a single suspect days, weeks, or even longer after the crime occurred, under circumstances with no exigency, as in Walter Snyder's case. These showup identifications or single-witness photo identifications should be avoided when substantial time has passed since the crime. Not only are the resulting identifications suggestive, but research also has shown that the effects on witnesses' diminishing memories may taint the reliability of future proceedings.

One way to counteract this potential problem is to include enough participants in an identification procedure to fairly test an eyewitness's ability to identify the true perpetrator. Although there is no magic number, research and practice have found that six to eight participants, including the individual suspected by the police, is a good number. In addition, as the ICVA noted, only one witness at a time should be permitted to view the potential suspect(s), in order to avoid witnesses' influence on one another's decisions. In cases with more than one suspect, experts even recommend that only one suspect at a time be included in an identification procedure. Additional spots in a lineup, or more pictures in a photo array, should be reserved for similar-looking nonsuspects, who are commonly called *fillers*. Of course, the fillers should have features like those of the single suspect in the lineup or photo array. Marvin Anderson, Julius Ruffin, and Walter Snyder are examples of the tragic consequences of identification procedures in which innocent suspects inappropriately stand out from the other participants, whether from the quality of the photos used, the participants' attire, or their physical attributes.

APPROPRIATE INSTRUCTIONS

Because eyewitnesses naturally assume that a suspect will be included in the photo array or lineup, an instruction that the perpetrator may or may not be included in the procedure helps counter eyewitnesses' inclination to identify a participant, regardless of whether the actual offender is present. Research shows that witnesses who do not receive this instruction are more likely to identify a participant, even when the true offender is not included in the procedure.[29]

To counter a witness's natural but erroneous assumption, many experts recommend using uniform and standardized written instructions for witnesses viewing identification procedures. These instructions should be read to all witnesses looking at photo arrays and lineups, and the witnesses should be asked to sign the instructions acknowledging

that they have received and understood them. Law enforcement personnel should tell each witness that the person who committed the crime
may or may not be included in the identification procedures and that
the witness should not feel obligated to make an identification unless he
or she recognizes the perpetrator. Each witness should be instructed that
it is just as important to clear an innocent person of wrongdoing as it is
to identify the perpetrator.

To prevent witnesses from undue, and often unconscious, influence in
the identification process, the law enforcement officials who conduct
identification processes should be shielded from the identity of the actual suspects involved. Although it is rare for a law enforcement officer
to deliberately steer a witness's identification, unconscious body language, tone of voice, and questions or comments by the officials conducting an identification procedure can significantly influence the witnesses' selections and can have long-term and pervasive effects on their
memory. Indeed, in at least four of the cases investigated by the ICVA in
which misidentifications occurred, the investigating officers knew that
the eventual exonerees were suspects and these officers also participated
in the identification procedures with the eyewitnesses.

In keeping with the recommendations of other experts, including,
most notably, the National Institute of Justice,[30] the ICVA urged Virginia's law enforcement agencies to adopt "double-blind procedures" in
which the officers conducting photo arrays and lineups are shielded
from the suspicions of investigating officers. The fact that the former do
not know the identity of the suspect(s) should be shared with witnesses,
so they are not unduly influenced by the behavior of the officers conducting the identification procedure. Even if the law enforcement officer
conducting the identification procedure actually does know the identity
of the suspect, witnesses should still be instructed otherwise. For similar
reasons, law enforcement officers should avoid giving feedback to witnesses during or after identification procedures. Congratulating a witness on his identification, for example, can alter his or her perception,
memory, and later testimony in court.

SEQUENTIAL, NOT SIMULTANEOUS, IDENTIFICATION PROCEDURES

Historically, many law enforcement agencies used simultaneous identification procedures in which all the persons in a lineup are viewed at
the same time. However, as just mentioned, simultaneous procedures

encourage the use of "relative judgments," in which witnesses may be inclined to identify the individual who most resembles the suspect, even if this person is not actually the perpetrator.

To combat this unfortunate tendency, the ICVA recommended the use of sequential identification procedures, in which suspects or their photos are shown to witnesses one at a time. Each witness should be asked to state whether the person shown is the perpetrator, as well as any similarities or differences the witness observes between the photo and the perpetrator, before moving on to the next person or photo. Among other advantages, gathering information from a witness as she views each photograph or each individual in a live procedure permits the judge or jury at any subsequent trial to assess whether the witness's identification has been consistent or has changed over time.

ELECTRONIC RECORDING

A witness's independent assessment is even more useful if law enforcement agencies electronically record the identification procedures. Videotape is the superior method because it allows fact finders to evaluate verbal and nonverbal cues, but even audiotape is an improvement over a written transcript. Police and other law enforcement officers are already well trained in recording and preserving the observations and experiences of victims and witnesses immediately after a crime occurs. Officers should be able to apply these same skills to videotaping a witness's identification of a suspect, the witness's level of confidence in the identification, and any other comments the witness has about the identification procedure. This practice preserves the identification process for later review in court and also protect officers against unfounded claims of misconduct.

EXPERT TESTIMONY

Many jurors walk into court with misconceptions about the reliability and accuracy of identification evidence. For example, although common sense might suggest otherwise, research has shown that witnesses' self-reports about their opportunities to view assailants and their confidence in identifications often are inflated. Moreover, as explained earlier, witnesses who have made an identification tend to understate, minimize, or simply deny the impact of any subsequent influence or suggestions on their memory. Unfortunately, many courts compound these misconceptions by failing to admit expert testimony about human memory or best practices for identification procedures.

The courts must rethink their hesitance, for expert testimony can help counterbalance common misunderstandings and assumptions that jurors bring to the courtroom when evaluating eyewitness evidence. Since much of this information comes from psychological research, it is outside most jurors' realm of knowledge and thus is suitable for expert testimony to the extent the witness is qualified.[31] Similarly, a judge's cautionary instructions to juries concerning the reliability of eyewitness testimony can help them assess this type of evidence and better ensure that jurors rely on valid eyewitness evidence.

How These Recommendations Would Have Helped Exonerees

Nationally, nearly three-quarters of known wrongful convictions are partly based on mistaken identifications.[32] In the Commonwealth, nine of the eleven official exonerations investigated by the ICVA involved eyewitness errors. Wrongful convictions due to mistaken identifications seem to be particularly common in rape and sexual offenses cases. Nationwide, 88 percent of wrongful rape convictions were based in large part on misidentifications.[33] In Virginia, seven of the eight sexual offense cases studied by the ICVA included a mistaken identification by a witness or victim. These problems are compounded even further when perpetrators and victims are of different races, for cross-racial identifications are fraught with imprecision.[34]

Of course, it is one thing to say that questionable procedures play a role in wrongful convictions and another to conclude that reforming these methods would have prevented an innocent suspect from conviction and imprisonment. Nevertheless, there is reason to believe that several of the cases investigated by the ICVA would have had a different outcome had law enforcement officials used the kind of identification procedures recommended by the ICVA.

EDWARD HONAKER

In the case of Edward Honaker, police investigators relied on a highly unreliable identification procedure. The Commonwealth's case was based largely on the identification of Honaker by the victim and her boyfriend, and it was not until years after Honaker's conviction that the initial identification method came to light: both the victim and her boyfriend were under hypnosis when they picked Honaker from a photo array. Had this information been conveyed to a jury—and if the defense had been permitted an expert to testify on the shortcomings of these identification methods—the jurors might well have found reasonable doubt about Honaker's involvement.

MARVIN ANDERSON

The police had no reason to suspect Anderson other than his relationship with a white woman, which mirrored that of the actual perpetrator, a black man who told the victim that she reminded him of his white girlfriend. Police officers conducted a simultaneous photo array for the victim, and Anderson's picture stood out as the only one presented in color. Despite Anderson's dissimilarities from the victim's initial description of her attacker—Anderson was dark, not light skinned, and he did not have a mustache or scratches on his face—the police conducted an in-person lineup within thirty minutes of the victim's identification of Anderson. Anderson was the only suspect to appear in both the photo array and the lineup, and the victim's subsequent identification of Anderson only reinforced her earlier, erroneous statement.

ARTHUR WHITFIELD

Arthur Whitfield's case highlights two potential problems in identification procedures: suggestive lineups and concurrent discussion between witnesses when identifying a suspect. The first rape victim told police that her assailant had distinctive, light eyes, and both victims testified at trial about the rapist's unusual light eyes. But Whitfield was the only lineup participant with light eyes. In addition, the second rape victim testified at trial that none of the other lineup participants had the same complexion as Whitfield.

Whitfield did not match the second rape victim's description of her assailant in another important way. She told police on the day she was raped that the perpetrator was kissing her during the entire assault, and she specifically said he did not have facial hair. Photographs taken during Whitfield's lineup one week after the assaults showed he had a heavy moustache.

Much of this information was available at trial, and jurors presumably were aware of the inconsistencies when weighing the women's testimony. But they were not aware that the two victims had had significant contact with each other that could have unconsciously influenced their identifications of Whitfield. The women knew each other and even drove to the police station together to view the Whitfield lineup. They "compared notes" during the drive by discussing the descriptions they gave to the police of their assailant, and the second victim was aware at the time of her lineup that the first victim had already identified Whitfield and was certain of her judgment. Had this information been properly conveyed to jurors, and had the jury been able to watch a videotape of the actual lineups, jurors might have appreciated the serious inconsistencies between the victims' descriptions of their attackers and Whitfield's appearance at the time of the crimes.

Interrogation Procedures

Viewers of television shows like *NYPD Blue* or *Law and Order* are familiar with the climatic scene in which police detectives interrogate their main suspect and lay the trap for his confession. Apart from good drama, interrogation is an important tool in criminal investigations and subsequent prosecutions. The defendant who is willing to say "I did it" and even sign his name to a confession has effectively closed the case and secured his conviction.

Modern police interrogation methods often rely on psychological techniques. These techniques have proved to be extremely effective and have caused many truly guilty suspects to admit their responsibility for the crimes they have committed. Indeed, today's interrogation methods are so effective, so powerful, and so calculated to obtain incriminating admissions that they sometimes influence innocent people to falsely admit to crimes in which they had no involvement. Although the frequency of false confessions is difficult to quantify, research has demonstrated that false confessions are not isolated phenomena but instead occur in disturbing numbers.

Five studies of erroneous prosecutions conducted since 1987[35] have shown that from 14 to 25 percent of the cases reviewed involved false confessions.[36] These studies are further supported by media reports of false confessions. In 2001, the *Washington Post* ran a series describing the pressures that can cause innocent men and women to confess to crimes they did not commit. The series exposed numerous false confessions in Prince George's County, Maryland.[37] Then, on December 22,

2002, the *Miami Herald* published a story uncovering at least thirty-eight false confessions in Broward County, Florida, over a twelve-year period.[38] False confessions captured national headlines again in 2003 when DNA exonerated five teens who had been imprisoned for the notorious 1989 rape of the Central Park jogger in New York.

In the Virginia cases studied by the ICVA, two of the eleven official exonerations involved innocent men—both facing the death penalty—who confessed to crimes that evidence later proved they did not commit. In a third case, the police claimed that the exoneree confessed, but he adamantly denied making any admission.

It is difficult to understand that innocent people would confess to crimes that they did not commit.[39] Yet false confessions do occur, and their consequences extend beyond the injustice of accusing and incarcerating an innocent person. Unfortunately, false confessions have sidetracked police from pursuing the real perpetrators, dissuaded police and prosecutors from reversing course once they have mistakenly concluded that the confessor is guilty, and caused courts to confirm convictions long after compelling evidence surfaces that the system has prosecuted the wrong person.

Because modern interrogation techniques are effective in obtaining confessions from guilty suspects, wholesale changes are neither practical nor necessary. Indeed, for the most part we should welcome interrogations that lead to confessions. Instead, what we need is an appropriate check on the accuracy of confessions, a safeguard that not only will permit judges and juries to evaluate the veracity of a suspect's confession but also will aid in securing convictions of the guilty. That check is videotaping interrogations.

Videotaping an interrogation creates a permanent record that can become powerful evidence against the guilty, can conserve scarce prosecution and judicial resources by limiting meritless challenges to properly obtained confessions, and can limit frivolous claims of police misconduct during questioning. The videotape can be reviewed later by police, prosecutors, the defense, the courts, and juries so that the influence of police interrogation techniques and the capabilities and limitations of the suspect being questioned can be measured and weighed by the responsible parties in the criminal justice system.

In addition to videotaping interrogations, special measures can be taken when the suspects to be interrogated are children or adults known to have mental retardation or mental illness. These vulnerable suspects are particularly susceptible to manipulation and pressure and can more easily be led to an inaccurate confession they do not understand.

The Law of Interrogations

Many Americans are undoubtedly familiar with their right to remain silent if questioned by the police upon their arrest. What they likely do not know is that this right—articulated in the U.S. Supreme Court case of *Miranda v. Arizona*—comes from the Fifth, Sixth, and Fourteenth Amendments to the U.S. Constitution.[40] Under federal constitutional law, criminal defendants' statements may be used against them in court if the statements meet two separate standards. Under the due process clauses of the Fifth and Fourteenth Amendments, the statement must be voluntary and free of physical coercion, threats of violence, or improper promises or inducements.[41] In addition, according to *Miranda*, suspects subjected to custodial interrogation must be advised of their right to re-main silent and their right to counsel.[42] In this context, a person is "in custody" when arrested or "otherwise deprived of his freedom of action in any significant way."[43] Interrogation refers to "express questioning" as well as "any words or actions on the part of the police (other than those normally attendant to arrest and custody) that the police should know are reasonably likely to elicit an incriminating response" from the suspect.[44]

The courts apply a "totality of the circumstances" approach to deter-mine the voluntariness of confessions, considering both the nature of the interrogation and the characteristics of the suspect. Accordingly, the courts weigh the presence or absence of police coercion or inducement; the location, duration, and continuity of the interrogation; and whether the suspects were advised of their right to counsel and their right to re-main silent.[45] The courts also consider the suspects' age and level of ma-turity; their education level; any mental health problems or develop-mental disabilities; and their physical condition, including whether they were deprived of sleep or under the influence of drugs or alcohol.[46]

In practical terms, the question of whether a court admits a defen-dant's statement often hinges on a determination of credibility—does the court credit the officers' assertion that they did not unreasonably overcome the defendant's will, or does the court believe the defense that the statement was involuntary? Practice suggests that the courts regu-larly rule in favor of the prosecution,[47] which may be a sign that officers are generally doing a good job or that judges are inclined to believe law enforcement officers over defendants. Virginia's courts have allowed expert testimony to help explain false confessions by defendants with mental retardation or mental disorders,[48] but there appear to be no reported Virginia cases in which the courts have permitted expert testimony about such issues when defendants have a normal mental capacity.

False Confession Research

It is difficult to estimate the prevalence of false confessions. As mentioned earlier, research on erroneous convictions has fingered false confessions as a culprit, but much less is known about their prevalence in cases in which innocence is not later proved. Research on false confessions has concluded that many factors are relevant, including the suspect's fear of violence, coercive interrogation tactics, intoxication, diminished capacity, ignorance of the law, and mental impairment.[49] Although some innocent suspects who confess to the police are socially marginalized—including various combinations of poverty, poor education, mental incapacity, and young age[50]—the vast majority of reported false confessions come from cognitively and intellectually "normal" people.[51] For these individuals, false confession may be perceived as a logical response to their predicament, given the significant sentence reductions that can result from cooperating with the police.

Of these several factors in securing a confession, perhaps the most important is the effectiveness of police interrogation techniques, which rely on subtle (and sometimes even overt) forms of manipulation, deception, and coercion. These techniques have been repeatedly upheld by the courts. In the modern psychological form of interrogation, police often isolate a suspect; repeatedly and consistently accuse him of committing the crime; reject proffered alibis; confront the suspect with suspicious or incriminating facts; offer alternative scenarios that "recast the suspect's behavior so that he is no longer morally and/or legally culpable"; and offer inducements to confess.[52]

These methods are designed to persuade suspects that

> the evidence against them is overwhelming, that their fate is certain (whether or not they confess), and that there are advantages that follow if they confess. Investigators elicit the decision to confess from the innocent in one of two ways: either by leading them to believe that their sit-

uation, though unjust, is hopeless and will only be improved by confessing; or by persuading them that they probably committed a crime about
which they have no memory and that confessing is the proper and opti-
mal course of action.[53]

Even though many innocent suspects are able to resist these techniques
and maintain their innocence during questioning, some succumb to the
pressure and confess to crimes that they did not commit.

The developmental characteristics of mentally retarded persons make
them particularly susceptible to suggestive interrogation tactics. They
are slow thinkers; they tend to place greater weight on short-term than
on long-term consequences; and they have difficulty appreciating the seriousness of their situations. They often have short attention spans and
poor impulse control, are highly submissive, and are responsive to stress
and pressure.[54] Juveniles share with mentally retarded adults many of
the same developmental, cognitive, and social deficits and, until their
brains and reasoning powers mature, are equally susceptible to the pressures of interrogation.[55]

Interrogations with an Added Safeguard: Videotaping

The crux of the concern posed by police interrogation practices is
that interrogations almost always occur in private and under circumstances in which the police are in complete control.[56] Although the police sometimes make contemporaneous records of the course of interrogations—through notes, statements, or electronic recordings—suspects
almost never do, and the police always control what parts of the interrogations or subsequent confessions are preserved, documented, or recorded. Moreover, police interrogation tactics are specifically designed
to produce stress in suspects, which undermines the reliability of their
statements and actions during interrogations and purported confessions.

All these facts create significant challenges for the judicial system
when the reliability and truthfulness of confessions are considered in
court. Because of the imbalance of power in the interrogation process
and the tendency of juries and judges to believe the police's version over
that of the criminal suspect, the judge and jury are more inclined to accept the memories, perceptions, and assertions of the police over those
of the suspect when deciding whether the confession is voluntary and
genuine.[57]

The goal of reform should not be to curtail custodial interrogations but to shine a light into the interrogation room so that judges and juries can evaluate the reliability of a subsequent confession. The most effective way to do this is to require police and other law enforcement departments to videotape, whenever practical, all custodial interrogations in serious felony cases. When videotaping an interrogation is not possible, law enforcement should be required to use audiotape to record custodial interrogations in serious felony cases.

Uniform, thorough, and mandatory videotaping policies present many advantages to police and prosecutors as well, saving them and the courts resources that might otherwise be spent on unnecessary pretrial hearings and postconviction challenges to legitimate convictions. Videotape creates powerful evidence of guilt in the vast number of instances when suspects make reliable, genuine confessions to crimes they did commit. It also can reduce the number of frivolous challenges made against police officers. As long as it covers the entire interrogation, videotaping is an effective defense against allegations that police either failed to advise suspects of their rights or did so in an inadequate manner, that police used improper or high-pressure interrogation practices, or that suspects never made incriminating statements.

Interrogation Practices

As part of its research, the ICVA surveyed Virginia law enforcement departments about the methods they use to preserve statements made by suspects during custodial interrogation. Of the 108 responding agencies that interrogate suspects, 87 percent ask suspects to write statements; 64 percent have officers write out suspects' statements; 80 percent use audiotape to record suspects' statements; 50 percent use videotape to record suspects' statements; and 3 percent record the statements in other ways. More telling is how often agencies videotape interrogations. Fewer than 4 percent of departments said they always videotape custodial interrogations, and an additional 12 percent reported that they usually do so. In contrast, 84 percent of the responding departments that question suspects said that they never, rarely, or only occasionally use videotape to record interrogations. Although these numbers suggest that videotaping is far from routine among Virginia law enforcement agencies, a majority of departments have at some point vide-

TABLE 4.2
*Methods Used to Record Custodial
Interrogation by Virginia Law
Enforcement Departments*

Method	Percentage of Agencies
Suspect writes statement	87
Officer records statement	64
Audiotape statement	80
Videotape statement	50
Other	3

Note: N = 108.

TABLE 4.3
*How Often Virginia Law Enforcement
Departments Record Custodial
Interrogation by Videotape*

Frequency of Videotaping	Percentage of Agencies
Always	4
Mostly	12
Occasionally	30
Rarely	22
Never	32

Note: N = 108.

otaped custodial interrogations. Presumably, then, many departments have some access to recording equipment. Tables 4.2 and 4.3 summarize these data.

The ICVA's survey also solicited open-ended comments about electronically recording interrogations. Two departments indicated that their budgets limit the use of videotape, although both expressed a desire to use the technology if it were available. Another department reported intermittently using videotape because some interrogations take place in areas without video surveillance. A different respondent indicated that most small departments cannot afford video equipment or do not have space available to use it. But the department also indicated that "the greater number of law-enforcement agencies" should embrace videotape to protect "their officers' integrity and . . . credibility."

One law enforcement department indicated that it uses videotaping in serious felonies and "cases involving children," and another reported that it uses videotape in child molestation cases. One department said the decision to videotape interrogations is at its officers' discretion or "when the circumstances dictate it prudent." Finally, two departments said they do not use videotaping because "the Commonwealth's Attorney does not want it done" and the "prosecutor does not like video." A third law enforcement agency reported that the "Commonwealth's Attorney does not allow" videotaping.

Recommendations

The results from the ICVA's survey mirror the informal feedback from several departments in the state as well as the experience elsewhere: that law enforcement does not necessarily oppose electronic recording of interrogations and may see the value of having an indisputable record of a suspect's behavior and statements. The larger questions, then, are how to implement electronic recording, what type of recording is best, and how should it be used. Ideally, recording should be mandated by statewide legislation to ensure uniformity and underscore its importance, but if necessary, on a department-by-department basis as law enforcement agencies come to appreciate the value.

Videotaping is superior to audiotaping, as it records both the verbal and nonverbal communication between police and suspects during custodial questioning.[58] Audiotape, in contrast, fails to capture body language, facial expressions, and demeanor; the physical proximity of interrogators to the suspect; and many other factors that could contribute to or induce false confessions. But audiotaping is preferable to not electronically recording interrogations at all.

In the past, videotaping all police questioning has been impractical; after all, police frequently question potential suspects at crime scenes, in their homes, at work, or in other locations where videotape equipment is not generally available. Recent technological advances, including portable cameras and digital cameras, now make videotaping and storing recorded interrogations more practical and affordable, especially when police and other law enforcement agencies use specifically designated rooms for custodial interrogation in their station houses. These areas can be, and often are, outfitted with videotape equipment that should be used to record custodial interrogations. Although cameras come with fixed initial costs and modest expenses for upkeep, these can be offset by reductions in frivolous challenges to police conduct and by the greater speed with which defendants who confess to a crime are likely to plead guilty.[59]

Law enforcement officers are not required under Virginia law to obtain suspects' consent or even inform them that their interrogations are being electronically recorded.[60] In fact, the surreptitious recording of custodial interrogations is advantageous to law enforcement because it reduces the likelihood that suspects will measure their words, perform for the camera, or engage in other behavior that interferes with the interrogation process. But the full benefits of mandatory videotaping can be achieved only if the entire interrogation process is recorded. Historically, police have often documented custodial interrogations, through either written documents or electronic recordings, only after questioning has started and frequently only after suspects have begun to make incriminating statements. A Florida wrongful conviction is an extreme example of the problem posed by taping only part of an interrogation:

> What jurors in the Behan murder case saw: a bland muddled 14-page narrative in which a 15-year-old mentally retarded Timothy Brown implicates himself in the shooting of Broward sheriff's Deputy Patrick Behan. What jurors did not see: the almost three-hour interrogation that preceded that "confession," an off-the-record span during which Brown claims he was screamed at, smacked, and menaced with a detective's revolver.[61]

Videotaping should start as soon as the police begin questioning a suspect in the stationhouse and before the police first advise suspects of their *Miranda* rights. This will help eliminate many frivolous claims that suspects received either improper or no warnings and, in some cases, may verify that *Miranda* warnings were not properly administered. Every time the recording is interrupted, the police should be required to note the time and reason for the interruption and the time that the videotaping resumed. This will ensure that the complete interrogation has been recorded and will prevent allegations of gaps in recording the interrogations.

To ensure that law enforcement agents have an incentive to record custodial interrogations, either the courts or legislatures should make the failure to record an entire, complete custodial interrogation grounds for excluding a confession obtained from that interrogation. This is not to say that the confession *must* be excluded, but certainly substantial violations should lead to the suppression of any statements made by suspects during such interrogations. The Constitution Project, a bipartisan organization dedicated to prudent justice reform, has proposed rules delineating substantial violations.[62] These include the failure to use interrogation rooms outfitted with videotape technology when such facilities exist, as well as intentional efforts to induce suspects to waive their right to the complete recording of custodial interrogations.[63] By contrast, the Constitution Project would excuse such instances as unavoidable power or equipment failures and the refusal of suspects to speak on tape.[64] Even in these circumstances, trial courts may wish to caution juries to consider the lack of recording when deciding what was said and done and whether the purported statement was voluntary.

Videotaped interrogations can help judges and jurors access the mental or developmental capacity of the suspect being questioned. Even so, when police interrogate children or those they have reason to believe are mentally retarded or have other significant developmental disabilities, care should be taken to avoid high-pressure, suggestive interrogation techniques that may induce false confessions. Law enforcement officers have long been trained how to avoid leading, suggestive questions when interviewing child victims, and they also should apply these same techniques when questioning other vulnerable suspects, including those with developmental or mental disabilities. To help officers identify adults with intellectual deficits, further training is likely needed.

None of these measures will absolutely prevent an innocent suspect from confessing to a crime. Indeed, some innocent people simply want to confess, although such a scenario would likely be foreign to most jurors, who understandably have difficulty appreciating why anyone would confess to a crime he did not commit. Especially when electronic recording is unavailable or fails to work, jurors may have little reason to believe the testimony of a defendant who later claims he is innocent over a police officer who testifies that the defendant confessed to him. Some states resolve such situations by permitting expert testimony about the factors that can lead suspects suffering from mental retardation to falsely confess to crimes that they did not commit. However, Virginia is not one of these states, there being no reported appellate court decisions that address the admissibility of expert testimony in alleged false confessions when the defendant does not suffer from an intellectual deficit.

How Videotaped Interrogations Can Prevent Wrongful Convictions

In a study of the first seventy DNA-based exonerations nationwide, the defendants falsely confessed in fifteen, or 21 percent, of the cases examined.[65] A more recent study of 328 exonerations nationwide found false confessions in fifty-one cases, or 15 percent of those exonerations. Furthermore, it concluded that 69 percent of exonerated, mentally retarded, or mentally ill defendants falsely confessed and that 44 percent of juvenile exonerees falsely confessed.[66]

Virginia's experience mirrors the national data. Of the eleven cases investigated by the ICVA, two (or 18 percent) involved false confessions, but several more reflected problematic interrogation techniques.

Of course, there is no guarantee that the ICVA's recommendations would have avoided erroneous convictions in these cases, but it seems plausible that law enforcement officers using appropriate cautions when interrogating mentally diminished suspects would not have led two defendants into false confessions. Moreover, jurors who could have viewed the entire interrogation in these cases and not simply the nicely sealed written confession might very well have found a reasonable amount of doubt to halt a miscarriage of justice. Indeed, I have read the full transcript from one of these interrogations to an introductory class of undergraduate students, who routinely come away from the experience astonished that detectives believed the suspect, let alone that jurors would have convicted him had they seen the entire transcript. If a group of novice undergraduates can express such surprise, it does not seem unreasonable to expect at least as much from criminal justice professionals.

EARL WASHINGTON JR.

The wrongful conviction of Earl Washington Jr. turned on a heavily coached confession that never should have been believed. Washington has an IQ of 69 and had to be led through a confession that a civil jury later found incredible.[67] Among other things, law enforcement officers chose to discount Washington's confession to four other crimes but focused instead on a fifth crime—the brutal rape and murder of a young Culpeper woman—in which Washington had equal difficulty describing the facts accurately.

As part of the investigation, officers took Washington to Culpeper so he could show them where he committed the crime, but he was unable to locate the crime scene, even when police drove him directly by the apartment building where the victim was stabbed. He initially told the police that he had killed a black woman, although the victim was white, and he claimed that he had stabbed the victim only twice when the killer had actually stabbed her nearly forty times. Finally, Washington told the police that he had "kicked in the door" and found the victim alone. In actuality, the victim's two small children were in the home when she was attacked, and the door had not been kicked in.

The police did not use audio or videotape to record their interrogations of Washington but instead obtained a written confession from a man of low IQ who was nearly illiterate. Despite little physical evidence available at trial[68] and a case based largely on a questionable confession, the jury still convicted Washington of capital murder at his trial in 1984 and recommended that he be sentenced to death. It took a decade, in which Washington came within nine days of his execution, before he was cleared.

It is still unclear why Earl Washington would confess to a crime he did not commit. As a man of low intelligence, Washington was susceptible to pressure tactics in a police interrogation, and indeed, the case suggests that officers may have coached, if not directed, his statements. A civil suit in 2006 confirmed this conclusion when Washington won a verdict against the estate of the officer who led him to confess.[69] But because none of Washington's conversations with his interrogators was recorded, with the exception of the written confession that was prepared by the officers and only initialed by Washington, it is difficult to say exactly what transpired between Washington and the officers outside public view.

DAVID VASQUEZ

David Vasquez, too, is a man of low intelligence who was led to confess to a rape and murder by means of aggressive police questioning. Arlington officers originally went to Vasquez's workplace in Prince William County and, without telling him the reason for their request, asked him to come to the police station for an interview. At the Prince William County Police Station, the detectives questioned Vasquez for several hours and tape-recorded the interrogation. Police put off repeated requests by Vasquez to see his mother. Although he denied being in Arlington on the night of the murder, the police eventually told him, falsely, that his fingerprints were found inside the victim's home. Vasquez then told the police that he might have been present in the victim's home on the night of the murder, but he seemed confused about how he could have gotten there, since he does not drive and his mother was working that evening. At one point, Vasquez said: "It was my imagination that was there, [but] how my body would get there if I didn't . . ."

The police continued to question Vasquez, and his answers, although inculpatory, continued to be confused and became even less comprehensible. Vasquez eventually "admitted" to the police that he had sexual intercourse with the victim and, later, that he killed her, but he could not supply the details to the police. Instead, as the transcript shows, detectives provided the details to him:

> [*Detective 2*]: Whatcha use [to hang the victim]?
> *Vasquez*: The ropes?
> [*Detective 2*]: No, not the ropes. Whatcha use?
> *Vasquez*: Ah, my belt?
> [*Detective 2*]: No. Not your belt.
> [*Detective 1*]: Come on, David, think about what you used now!
> *Vasquez*: I just don't . . .
> [*Detective 1*]: Remember being out in the sun room, the room that sits out to the back of the house?
> *Vasquez*: Yeah, I know—
> [*Detective 1*]: The new addition, you remember being out there?
> *Vasquez*: I think so.
> [*Detective 1*]: And what did you cut down?
> *Vasquez*: A coat hanger?
> [*Detective 1*]: No, it wasn't a coat hanger, it was something like a coat hanger. What was it? By the window? . . . Think about the Venetian blinds, David. Remember cutting the Venetian blind cord?
> *Vasquez*: Ah, it was a thin rope.
> [*Detective 1*]: Yeah!

At the end of the interview, Vasquez seemed to be talking to himself in a confused manner, repeatedly saying that he knew he was not present, that he did not know how his fingerprints got in the home, and that he did not commit the crime.

The police asked Vasquez to accompany them to Arlington County, where they questioned him again. He repeated his request to see his mother and also to see his psychiatrist, all to no avail. The second interrogation followed much the same pattern as the first. At some point, however, one officer left the interrogation room with the tape recorder, and during his absence, Vasquez began recounting a "dream" statement describing the details of the murder. The detectives described the "dream statement," only a portion of which was recorded on audiotape, as "clear, certain. The vacancy was gone." The police arrested Vasquez after this statement and charged him with capital murder. After his arrest and processing, Vasquez repeated the "dream" statement again to the police.

Giving officers the benefit of the doubt, they may have thought they were dealing with a deranged killer. Police found a hair at the crime scene that an expert concluded was "consistent" with Vasquez's hair, and officers also uncovered a pornographic magazine in Vasquez's home depicting a woman bound, gagged, and with a rope around her neck. But Vasquez's blood type did not match the semen samples recovered from the victim, and his shoes did not match shoe prints found outside the point of entry at the home.

Why would the Commonwealth proceed with the prosecution when it was clear that Vasquez could not have committed the sexual assault to which he had confessed? The trial court later threw out two of Vasquez's confessions because officers had not read Vasquez his rights, but by then the mentally confused Vasquez had bought into his story and repeated it a third time. Faced with this admissible evidence and the prospect of conviction at trial for a capital offense, Vasquez's lawyers convinced him to plead guilty to a reduced charge, second-degree murder. Later, of course, the real murderer and rapist was caught, but not before more women were killed while Vasquez spent five years in prison under repeated attack.

CRAIG BELL

Although the Washington and Vasquez cases are among the clearest instances of damaging false confessions in Virginia, a third exoneree, Craig Bell, would have benefited from videotaped interrogations. Bell was convicted of murdering his fiancée in the middle of the night by stabbing her to death in their home. Although in at least four unrecorded statements to the police he consistently denied committing the crime,[70] the police claimed that Bell made inconsistent statements about important details of the crime to the police and to an emergency medical technician at the scene, and prosecutors used these inconsistencies to undermine Bell's credibility at trial. Police attempted to videotape at least one of their interrogations of Bell, but they discovered later that the audio portion of the recording failed to function. The missing recording made Bell's case all the harder, because to this day he claims that his statements were consistent and that one of the officers and the EMT lied.[71] Without the audiotape, however, jurors had to weigh the veracity of these competing claims.

Postconviction Remedies

Virginia's former "21-day rule" occupies an infamous place in American criminal justice. Fortunately, the rule has now been amended to permit defendants with evidence of their innocence to petition the Commonwealth's courts for a writ of actual innocence. But as commendable as the writ may be, Virginia's system of criminal justice—and, by extension, the justice processes of other states—requires further attention to ensure that the innocent do not languish in prison while the guilty remain free to prey on others when there is evidence that a conviction was erroneously entered.

As the American Bar Association's Committee on Innocence and the Integrity of the Criminal Justice System explained, "It is unlikely that any refinements in the police and prosecutor practices, improved rules at trial, or better defense representation will ever completely eliminate convictions of all who are factually innocent."[72] Yet since we know that wrongful convictions can and do occur in Virginia and other states and that the cost of wrongful convictions is high, it is essential that states have in place adequate postconviction remedies to ensure that errors can be corrected.

Crafting postconviction remedies requires a careful balance between the defendant's interest in proving his innocence and the state's interest in the finality of its criminal justice proceedings. As the U.S. Supreme Court stated in *Kuhlmann v. Wilson*,[73] "Even where, as here, the many judges who have reviewed the prisoner's claims . . . have determined that his trial was free from constitutional error, a prisoner retains a powerful and legitimate interest in obtaining his release from custody if he is innocent of the charge for which he was incarcerated." At the same time, as the Supreme Court explained,

the deterrent force of penal laws is diminished to the extent that persons contemplating criminal activity believe there is a possibility that
they will escape punishment through repetitive collateral attacks. . . .
Finality also serves the State's legitimate punitive interests. When a prisoner is freed on a successive petition, often many years after his crime,
the State may be unable successfully to retry him. This result is unacceptable if the State must forgo conviction of a guilty defendant through
the "erosion of memory" and "dispersion of witnesses" that occur with
the passage of time that invariably attends collateral attack.[74]

With its writ of actual innocence, Virginia now provides more vehicles than most states do for a defendant to contest his conviction in
court. Virginia offers three options: a petition for a writ of habeas corpus, a motion for a new trial, or a petition for a writ of innocence. But
because of the numerous substantive and procedural limitations on the
availability of these remedies, judicial findings of actual innocence are
extremely rare. Nine of the eleven Virginia exonerees whose cases the
ICVA reviewed were freed as a result of intervention by Virginia's governors or the parole board, not Virginia's courts. In two cases the courts
vacated convictions on grounds of innocence, but those proceedings
were not contested. In fact, none of the exonerations that the ICVA
studied resulted from contested proceedings in the Virginia courts. For
that matter, none of the exonerees whose cases the ICVA studied would
have been eligible for the new writ of actual innocence. Today, those
who are wrongfully convicted in Virginia remain largely dependent on
the good graces of the prosecutors who put them in jail, on the governor, or on the parole board to secure their release. Relief from the
parole board is increasingly rare because Virginia abolished parole in
1994, thereby making this option unavailable to prisoners who were
wrongfully convicted after that date.

Petition for a Writ of Habeas Corpus

How is it that existing law proves inadequate for considering postconviction relief? Under the law of Virginia (and of several other states),
an inmate may file a petition for a writ of habeas corpus to challenge
the legality of his conviction. The court will grant the petition if the
prisoner can show that he is being detained without lawful authority.[75]

The Virginia Supreme Court, however, has made clear that "an assertion of actual innocence is outside the scope of habeas corpus review, which concerns only the legality of the petitioner's detention."[76]

In order to secure a writ of habeas corpus, the prisoner must show that constitutional or other legal error occurred at trial. But we know that through honest human mistake, trials free from legal error still can result in wrongful convictions. For example, Julius Ruffin was not released until twenty-one years after his original arrest, when the governor issued him a pardon in March 2003. Even though the victim wrote Ruffin expressing her "sorrow and devastation" at his conviction, when he issued the pardon Governor Warner stated, "I find no fault with the verdict of the jury based upon the evidence available to it at the time of trial, nor with the actions of the attorneys for the Commonwealth or the court at trial."[77]

Five of the exonerees whose cases were examined by the ICVA filed petitions for writs of habeas corpus with the Virginia courts, but only one succeeded in obtaining release through that mechanism. Even in the one case in which a petition for a writ of habeas corpus was granted, the prisoner, Jeffrey Cox, was released only after the Commonwealth's attorney consented to an order vacating the original conviction. Because the habeas corpus process is focused on the existence of legal error and not on actual innocence and is subject to strict procedural rules such as statutes of limitations, it has not been an effective tool in securing the release of wrongfully convicted individuals.

Motion for a New Trial

Under Virginia Supreme Court Rule 1:1—the infamous "21-day rule"—a prisoner may file a motion for a new trial based on newly discovered evidence, but the motion must be filed no later than twenty-one days after the date of the order of conviction. After that time, the trial court loses jurisdiction and has no authority to act on a prisoner's motion.[78]

All the exonerations examined by the ICVA proceeded on the basis of evidence that became available significantly more than twenty-one days after the date of the original conviction. In the case of Russell Gray, another man confessed more than twenty-one days after the original conviction, meaning that a motion for a new trial could not be filed. Similarly, many of the cases relied on DNA testing techniques that did not become available until many years after the convictions were handed down.

A November 19, 2003, report by the "21-Day Rule Task Force" of the Virginia Crime Commission concluded that Virginia's 21-day rule was the most restrictive such rule in the nation. Whereas most states initially appeared to have a finite time limit in which to present newly discovered evidence, the Virginia Crime Commission concluded that court rules, case law, and other rules of procedure frequently provided exceptions. Based on conversations with assistant attorneys general in all fifty states and a legal analysis of statutes and rules, the Virginia Crime Commission concluded that thirty-eight states had no time limit, one state had a three-year time limit, seven states had a two-year time limit, and four states had a time limit of one year or less. No other state had a limit as restrictive as Virginia's.

Petition for a Writ of Actual Innocence

In 2002, Virginia took an important step to address the harsh results that can be produced by strict application of the 21-day rule. That fall, the Commonwealth created a new judicial remedy—the "writ of actual innocence"—for inmates convicted of a felony who could present newly discovered, exculpatory human biological evidence.[79] In 2004, the Commonwealth acted to expand availability of the writ to inmates who lacked human biological evidence to support their claims. In these cases, however, the writ is not available to defendants who pleaded guilty.[80]

These legislative developments are to be commended, but even with the new laws, some wrongfully convicted prisoners will remain ineligible for relief. For these individuals, clemency, with its attendant political pressures, will remain the only available option. Examples abound in the cases examined by the ICVA. Although the writ had not yet been established at the time David Vasquez was exonerated, he would not have been eligible for relief under it because he pleaded guilty in order to avoid a possible death sentence, and his claim of innocence was not based on human biological evidence. Conversely, the writ of innocence had been established at the time Marvin Anderson was exonerated, but he was not able to apply for relief because he was on parole and not incarcerated at the time human biological evidence of his innocence became available.

Craig Bell could not have demonstrated that the human biological evidence to support his claim of innocence was unknown or unavailable to him or his trial attorney at the time his conviction became final. Fingerprints, hair, and clothing found at the scene were tested before Bell's trial, and although they did not implicate him in the crime, Bell was convicted anyway. Only when those pieces of evidence were later linked to the true perpetrator who confessed to the crime was Bell exculpated. Jeffrey Cox also would have had difficulty proving that his "newly discovered" evidence of innocence—including evidence that prosecution witnesses lied about their criminal records and made prior statements inconsistent with their trial testimony—was unavailable to him or his attorney at the time his conviction became final. In short, in at least four of the eleven exonerations that the ICVA studied, the new laws, while certainly commendable, either would not have been applicable or might have been construed by a court to deny any possibility of relief.

Clemency

Like many states, the Virginia Constitution gives the governor the power to grant reprieves and pardons.[81] The governor's constitutional power to grant pardons and reprieves or to commute capital punishment also is authorized by statute.[82] A pardon is defined as an absolution of guilt and applies to both the punishment prescribed for the offense and the guilt of the offender. When the pardon is full, it relieves the punishment and blots out the guilt, so that in the eyes of the law the offender is as innocent as if he had never been convicted.

Clemency has many purposes: to ensure that justice is administered with mercy, to correct errors, and to allow the governor to assess the situation anew outside the rigid confines of the judicial decision-making process. A governor can look to the overall fairness of the situation and not be constrained by rules of procedure or evidence. He can make decisions based on factors beyond the law.

Clemency is a matter of the grace and discretion of the executive granting it. In Virginia, the governor is not required to review or accept for submission any clemency petition, even if the applicant presents compelling evidence of actual innocence.[83] If a petition for clemency is denied, there is no right of appeal. The governor's discretion for clemency decisions is high and usually unquestioned.[84]

Courts have stated that clemency proceedings are not an integral part of adjudicating the guilt or innocence of an accused.[85] Nevertheless, until recently, clemency was considered the only forum in which to pursue claims of actual innocence based on newly discovered evidence in Virginia, and it remains the exclusive option in many states.[86] In Virginia, clemency is the only forum for some defendants who pleaded guilty to crimes that they did not commit and to defendants whose evidence of actual innocence was not presented at trial because of ineffective assistance of counsel. Eight of the eleven exonerees whose claims were examined by the ICVA obtained relief through the clemency process and not through the courts.

Clemency is an imperfect tool for addressing claims of actual innocence, largely because of its discretionary nature and because it is perceived as presenting political risks to incumbent governors. Moreover, the clemency process is neither an evidentiary nor an adversarial proceeding. An inmate seeking clemency is not entitled to a hearing before the governor or the governor's designee. Although an inmate is permitted to submit a clemency petition and supporting documentation to the governor, the clemency process is not well suited to resolve contested claims of factual innocence. These claims typically involve credibility determinations that often cannot be decided on paper but instead require a hearing. These hearings are exactly the types of proceedings over which the courts are best suited to preside.

Postconviction Remedies in Other Jurisdictions

The ICVA reviewed information concerning 102 DNA exonerations nationwide that occurred between 1989 and 2004. Judicial remedies were provided in ninety cases (or approximately 88 percent of the time), and discretionary remedies (clemency, pardon, or parole) were provided in twelve cases (or approximately 12 percent of the time). Of the twelve cases in which discretionary procedures were used, seven (or approximately 58 percent) were from a single state, Virginia.[87]

The ICVA also investigated the extent to which postconviction remedies in other jurisdictions are made available to prisoners who entered pleas of guilty. In May 2003, the Virginia State Crime Commission conducted a fifty-state analysis of postconviction relief mechanisms. The ICVA started with the Virginia State Crime Commission's list of the postconviction relief mechanisms in each jurisdiction and conducted an independent review of those mechanisms to determine whether they were available to prisoners who entered pleas of guilt. The results, which appear in appendix 3, show that a majority of the states provide a mechanism for relief in the courts for prisoners who entered pleas of guilty. Only three states limit the availability of postconviction remedies to such prisoners.

Finally, the ICVA investigated the extent to which prisoners are permitted to file multiple petitions for postconviction relief. Again starting with the Virginia State Crime Commission's list of the postconviction relief mechanisms in each jurisdiction, the ICVA conducted an independent review of those mechanisms to determine whether prisoners were permitted to file multiple petitions for postconviction relief. As shown in appendix 4, these data indicate that only five states limit the number of petitions for postconviction relief that a prisoner can file.

Although praising Virginia for its progress in this area, the ICVA nonetheless recommended that the Commonwealth extend the availability of the writ of actual innocence to prisoners who entered a plea other than guilty. Under current Virginia law, the writ is unavailable to defendants who entered a plea other than not guilty and who rely on nonbiological evidence to support their claim of innocence.[88] This limitation presumably proceeds from an assumption that a person who is actually innocent would be unlikely to enter a plea of guilty. But as demonstrated by the exonerations studied by the ICVA and by other research, the facts are otherwise.

The states also should be concerned about the interplay between postconviction remedies and claims of ineffective assistance of counsel. Under Virginia law, for example, the writ of actual innocence is available only if the evidence that supports the prisoner's claim "was not known or available to the prisoner or his trial attorney of record at the time the conviction became final in the Circuit Court."[89] In addition, if the prisoner's claim is based on nonbiological evidence, the prisoner must show that the evidence could not, by the exercise of due diligence, have been discovered or obtained before expiration of the 21-day rule.[90] Thus, if evidence of actual innocence was available but was not presented at trial owing to the incompetence of trial counsel, the writ of innocence will not be issued.

Attorney error often plays a significant role in wrongful convictions (a point discussed later in this chapter). There does not seem to be any logical reason to deny postconviction relief to defendants who are innocent and, except for attorney error, would never have been convicted in the first place. Although theoretically such persons may be eligible for a writ of habeas corpus (based on the violation of their Sixth Amendment right to effective assistance of counsel), as a practical matter habeas corpus relief may be denied on procedural grounds, such as an inmate's failure to adhere to strict, statutory deadlines. Particularly at the federal level, complex procedural requirements have made the writ of habeas corpus increasingly difficult to obtain, especially for inmates who attempt to proceed pro se. In several cases reviewed by the ICVA, both Virginia and federal courts refused to overturn convictions on procedural grounds for ineffective assistance of counsel. Yet the ICVA's careful investigation showed that these errors played a significant role in the wrongful conviction of innocent persons. If attorney errors can lead to erroneous convictions, then postconviction remedies should take account of, and provide remedies for, ineffective assistance of counsel.

Criminal Defense

The ICVA did not devote the same amount of attention in its report to the problems of ineffective assistance of counsel. This was not an oversight by the commission but a recognition that the issue had already been studied quite carefully by at least two groups: the American Bar Association, in a report it commissioned from the highly respected Spangenberg Group, and the American Civil Liberties Union.

There can be little doubt that the system of appointed counsel for indigent defendants in Virginia is deficient and requires reform. Although the same is true for indigent defense in several other states, Virginia's system is especially defective. The failings of indigent defense are particularly troubling given the constitutional interests at stake. Under the Sixth and Fourteenth Amendments to the U.S. Constitution, defendants have a right to effective assistance of counsel when incarceration is threatened. In *Strickland v. Washington,*[91] the U.S. Supreme Court set the standard for this right, ruling that a criminal defendant must prove that the defense counsel's performance fell below an objective standard of reasonableness, as measured by the prevailing professional norms, and that the attorney's deficient representation prejudiced the defense in order to prevail on the claim.[92] Historically, the *Strickland* standard created a very high hurdle for defendants to surmount in order to prevail on claims of ineffective assistance of counsel. For example, the courts often presume that an attorney's decisions at trial were the result of "sound trial strategy" rather than incompetence.[93]

In addition to zealous representation, criminal defense attorneys also owe their clients a duty of loyalty. This is particularly important when an attorney represents a defendant whose interest may conflict with that of another client, whether past or present. In Virginia, if a lawyer reasonably believes that the representation of a client may be materially limited by his or her responsibilities to another client or another person, the lawyer may not represent the client unless the potential conflict of interest is disclosed to the client and the client consents to the representation.[94] In fact, the comments to the Virginia Rules of Professional Conduct clearly state that the potential conflict of interest in representing multiple defendants in a criminal case is "so grave that ordinarily a lawyer should decline to represent more than one co-defendant."[95] In a similar vein, in the context of a potential conflict between a lawyer's client and a witness represented by the lawyer, the Virginia Court of Appeals stated,

> If [a] witness's testimony is expected to incriminate the witness but exculpate the defendant, the attorney must either assert the witness's right to remain free from self-incrimination at the sacrifice of the defendant's best interest or allow the defendant to be exonerated at the risk of the witness incriminating himself. Again, a conflict of interest would exist.[96]

Virginia is far from alone in adhering to these standards. In many cases of exoneration, the courts have turned down claims of attorney conflict or ineffective assistance of counsel only to discover later that the defendant was innocent and that his conviction could have been prevented at trial by reasonable representation. Of the first seventy people exonerated by DNA evidence, the Innocence Project found that poor or ineffective defense counsel contributed to their clients' wrongful conviction twenty-three times.[97] A Columbia University study of capital case appeals, "A Broken System: Error Rates in Capital Cases, 1973–1995," found that ineffective lawyering was the biggest contributing factor to the wrongful conviction or death sentence for criminal defendants in capital cases during a twenty-three-year period.[98]

Five of the eleven cases of wrongful conviction studied by the ICVA involved defense lawyers who failed to disclose serious conflicts of interest, failed to appreciate the appearance of a conflict of interest, failed at trial to use clearly exculpatory information in their possession, or failed to vigorously challenge the government's evidence and/or missed crucial filing deadlines. On a broader level, the ICVA's survey research also found that some defense attorneys in Virginia failed to take advantage of certain prosecutors' open file discovery policies and therefore did not review all the information available to them when representing their clients.

A snapshot of the cases studied by the ICVA offers a glimpse of the scope of the problems.

Marvin Anderson

Marvin Anderson's trial lawyer had previously represented Otis Lincoln, the actual rapist, on an earlier attempted rape case. A police officer investigating the Anderson case told the attorney there was some evidence linking Lincoln to the Anderson case, and in fact, the lawyer admitted that he suspected Lincoln had committed the rape. Despite this terrible conflict, the lawyer failed to disclose his prior representation, his suspicions, or his conflict of interest to Anderson, all in apparent violation of Virginia's Rules of Professional Conduct.[99]

The lawyer made several other crucial errors. Before trial, he failed to ask the police to fingerprint the bicycle that Lincoln rode on the day of the rape, even though the bicycle was in police custody and might have had the perpetrator's fingerprints on it. He refused the requests by Anderson's mother to call Lincoln as a witness or to subpoena the two witnesses who had seen Lincoln accost two girls in the area of the rape shortly before it happened, who had heard Lincoln's threatening comments, and who had watched him ride toward the area of the rape immediately before it occurred. Later, at a hearing on Anderson's petition for habeas corpus, Lincoln testified and admitted that he had committed the rape for which Anderson had been convicted. None of this evidence was presented, much less suggested, to the jury at Anderson's five-hour trial.

Jeffrey Cox

Jeffrey Cox's lawyer took time out from the middle of a two-week federal trial to handle Cox's one-day trial in state court. Possibly because he was distracted and overworked by his other and larger ongoing case, the trial lawyer failed to thoroughly investigate the criminal backgrounds of the two eyewitnesses who identified Cox and failed to uncover the significant exculpatory evidence that could have undermined the witnesses' credibility. Cox's trial counsel also apparently failed to realize that the prosecution had never turned over the serology reports from the victim's autopsy, which later were discovered to contain important, exculpatory evidence.

The trial lawyer was not the only attorney to commit serious errors in Cox's case. After Cox's conviction, his parents asked an attorney to handle their son's appeal and learned that the attorney had previously represented Billy Madison, the initial and prime police suspect in the crime for which Cox was convicted. Assuring Cox's parents that the previous case had been an unrelated incident, the attorney persuaded them that he could effectively defend Cox. The attorney filed an appeal that was denied by the Virginia Court of Appeals but then failed to file a timely appeal before the Virginia Supreme Court. Realizing his error, the attorney filed a petition for a writ of habeas corpus on Cox's behalf, but he limited Cox's grounds for relief to the sole issue of the missed appeal.

When Cox learned he might be waiving all his other legal challenges in the habeas claim, he fired the appellate attorney and successfully petitioned the court on his own to withdraw the habeas petition. Later, after securing assistance from a different attorney, Cox was able to win exoneration and relief in a new habeas claim. He never would have had this opportunity if the first appellate lawyer had wasted his one and only opportunity for a habeas petition.

Edward Honaker

Part of Edward Honaker's defense at trial was that he could not have raped the victim because the crime laboratory serologist found spermatozoa on the slides taken from the vaginal swabs of the rape victim. Honaker testified at trial that he had had a vasectomy and therefore could not have been the source of spermatozoa in the rape. Yet Honaker's defense counsel never revealed to the Commonwealth's serologist that Honaker had had a vasectomy and could not produce sperm. The serologist later swore in an affidavit that had he been told by either the defense or the government about Honaker's vasectomy, he would have testified at trial that Honaker could not be the rapist. Nor did Honaker's trial lawyer present medical records or medical testimony at trial to corroborate Honaker's otherwise unsubstantiated claim that he had had a vasectomy before the rape occurred. These records did, in fact, exist and were presented to Governor George Allen as part of Honaker's clemency petition ten years later when DNA testing exonerated him.

Earl Washington Jr.

Throughout the Commonwealth's case against him, prosecutors contended that Earl Washington had raped and killed the victim on his own. It was no small matter, then, that Washington's trial attorney failed to present evidence to the jury that semen recovered from a blanket on the bed where the victim was raped came from a man with a blood type different from Washington's. Washington's lawyer also failed to introduce laboratory reports or expert testimony proving that Washington's fingerprints and palm prints did not match the prints found at the crime scene. How could Washington have committed this crime if the semen and prints at the crime scene did not match his? Perhaps prosecutors would have relied on a theory of an "unindicted co-ejaculator," but there was no evidence to suggest that the perpetrator had acted with a partner, nor did prosecutors make this argument at trial. When coupled with other strategic errors by Washington's trial counsel—including his failure to cross-examine the detective who took Washington's "confession" about the serious inconsistencies and mistakes in the story —it is not difficult to believe that jurors would have found reasonable doubt had they heard all the relevant and available evidence at trial.

Surprisingly, the courts did not see Washington's case in the same way. After his direct appeal was denied, his new pro bono lawyers filed a massive petition for habeas corpus relief, first in state court and later in federal court, claiming, among other reasons, that Washington had received ineffective assistance at trial. The Virginia state courts denied all of Washington's claims. Although the federal courts ultimately found that Washington's trial lawyer had provided ineffective assistance of counsel, they ruled that the lawyer's errors were not prejudicial and affirmed Washington's conviction and death sentence. In May 2006, Washington won a civil judgment in federal court against the detective who had, in Washington's view, intentionally pressured him into a false confession. The civil judgment should call into question just how harmless the failure to cross-examine this witness was at trial.

Troy Webb

Troy Webb's counsel seems to have gone out of his way to upset the jury without providing an affirmative defense or effectively cross-examine the prosecution's witnesses. After the trial, several jurors remarked that Webb came across as guilty because he did not present a "case for himself." This was the attorney's decision, which the courts might chalk up to a failed but acceptable trial strategy, yet the lawyer also made several insensitive comments about the victim and the jury during the trial. In addition to insulting the jurors' intelligence, he suggested that the victim was sexually promiscuous and may have been seeking sex at the time of the crime. Considering that this was a case of stranger rape and that the purpose of rape shield laws is to exclude the victim's sexual history from rape cases, the attorney's conduct reflected, at best, poor judgment.

While impugning the victim's character, Webb's attorney failed to ask her a crucial question—whether she had bathed or changed her underwear between her last sexual encounter with her boyfriend and the rape. This question was crucial, given that the perpetrator's blood type was A, the same as that of the victim's live-in boyfriend. Webb, by contrast, is a nonsecretor, meaning someone whose blood type cannot be identified from his semen samples. At trial, the Commonwealth's forensic technician testified that semen from someone with blood type A— the victim's boyfriend—could have masked a second person's semen from a nonsecretor—Webb. But if the victim had changed her underwear or bathed between her last sexual encounter with her boyfriend and the rape, the semen present could have come only from a different person with type A blood—presumably the actual perpetrator—and not from Webb. By failing to ask this simple question, Webb's attorney missed the opportunity to turn the serology reports into exculpatory evidence.

Recommendations

In recent years, a number of organizations with significant staff and resources have focused on the state of indigent defense delivery systems and the quality of indigent defense in both capital and noncapital cases nationwide.[100] These studies have specifically and thoroughly examined the provision of indigent defense services in Virginia as well.[101] Virginia's legislative and executive branches also have studied the Commonwealth's indigent defense system and its needs, and many of these studies have urgently proposed reforms to improve the quality of defense in the Commonwealth's courts.

By far the most comprehensive review of the indigent defense system in Virginia was the January 2004 Spangenberg Group report for the American Bar Association. At the conclusion of its review, which raised significant concerns about the quality of indigent defense services in the Commonwealth, the Spangenberg Group offered a series of recommendations to improve these services, among them,[102]

- The Virginia General Assembly should fund indigent defense services in cases requiring the appointment of counsel at a level that ensures that all indigent defendants receive effective and meaningful representation.
- The state should establish a professionally independent indigent defense commission to organize, supervise, and assume the overall responsibility of Virginia's indigent defense system.
- The newly created commission on indigent defense should have broad power and responsibility for delivering indigent defense services.
- The indigent defense commission should adopt performance and qualification standards for both private assigned counsel and public defenders. The standards should address workload limits, training requirements, professional independence, and other areas to ensure effective and meaningful representation.
- A comprehensive data collection system designed to provide an accurate picture of the provision of indigent criminal services in Virginia should be established and implemented by the statewide commission.

In 2004, the Virginia General Assembly responded to some of these concerns by creating the Indigent Defense Commission, responsible for overseeing the provision of legal counsel to indigent defendants in Virginia. The organization is charged with overseeing the training and certification of both private court-appointed attorneys and public defenders. But Virginia still does not have a statewide public defense system, which studies have shown is the most efficient and expert way to represent indigent defendants.[103] Nor, as of this writing, has the Commonwealth addressed the most serious problem in indigent defense: the abysmally low fee caps that prevent appointed attorneys from spending more than a few hours on a criminal case, unless it is a capital offense, and that severely limit the amount of resources available to appointed attorneys to investigate their clients' cases.

For this reason, the ICVA echoed the Spangenberg Group's call for more adequate funding of indigent defense in Virginia, as well as performance and qualification standards for both private assigned counsel and public defenders. Although Virginia deserves credit for its requirement that attorneys in death penalty cases be "capital qualified"—a standard ensuring that a death row defendant's trial attorney is relatively experienced—defendants in other crimes, even serious felonies, receive no such assurance that their attorneys have the skill, training, or time to mount a reasonable defense.

Of course, a capable and available attorney is no guarantee that an innocent defendant will be acquitted; nor is it impossible for a marginal lawyer to achieve an acquittal for his or her client. But it is axiomatic that an innocent defendant has a better chance of earning his deserved freedom if his attorney is, at a minimum, familiar with the facts of the case and attentive to their relevance at trial. The ICVA's recommendations, and those of several groups that came before it on this issue, were designed to improve an innocent defendant's chances of acquittal.

Scientific Evidence

As chapter 1 noted, DNA testing has revolutionized the investigation and prosecution of criminal cases as well as the postconviction exoneration of innocent defendants. Before DNA, investigators had to make do largely with hair and fiber analysis, fingerprinting, and blood typing, none of which is as accurate as DNA in connecting a suspect with a crime or clearing those who are innocent.

National studies of wrongful convictions have demonstrated that forensic evidence supposedly linking a defendant to a particular crime can be wrong.[104] In some of these cases, the scientific evidence was questionable or unreliable,[105] and at other times, experts offered slanted opinions, misstated conclusions, or even fabricated findings.[106] Often the scientific evidence was simply nonspecific, meaning that it placed the innocent defendants into a broader group within the population that could have provided the same physical evidence.[107] When added to other evidence in these cases, the scientific evidence was enough to convict the wrong people. Finally, in some cases the evidence was not properly preserved, creating significant barriers to later DNA testing that proved the defendant's innocence.

The ICVA's findings are consistent with the evidence in other jurisdictions in which nonspecific, faulty, or misused scientific evidence helped convict innocent people. In at least six of the eleven cases studied by the ICVA, forensic evidence purportedly linking exonerees to the crimes was a factor in their convictions. In at least four of the cases, the police or crime labs destroyed physical evidence that would have proved the inmates did not commit these crimes, and in one case, the samples were too degraded to be subjected to DNA testing only five years after the crime.

The Law and Practice of Forensic Evidence

Forensic evidence, sometimes called scientific evidence, can often demonstrate a strong link between a suspect and the crime he is charged with committing. In addition to admitting the evidence at trial, a prosecutor usually presents a scientific expert to explain the significance of the evidence to the judge or jury by describing whether and how it matches samples obtained from the suspect. This forensic expert frequently then offers an opinion about the likelihood that someone other than the defendant is the source of the physical evidence. The defense, too, may offer its own expert or forensic evidence to challenge the prosecution's case.

For much of the twentieth century, the predominant test used by federal courts to govern the admissibility of scientific evidence in the United States—known as the *Frye* rule—required scientific testimony to have gained general acceptance in the relevant scientific community before it could be admitted in court.[108] Then in 1993, the U.S. Supreme Court announced a new rule governing the admissibility of scientific evidence in the federal courts. The more flexible *Daubert* rule, as it has come to be known, requires the trial judge to consider, in a gatekeeping role, a variety of factors in determining whether expert scientific testimony rests on a reliable foundation and is relevant to the issue in the case.[109] Since the U.S. Supreme Court created it, more than half the states have adopted the *Daubert* standard.

The Virginia courts have never adopted either the *Frye* or *Daubert* standard to govern the admissibility of scientific testimony or evidence.[110] Instead, when scientific evidence is offered in Virginia, the trial judge must make

> a threshold finding of fact with respect to the reliability of the scientific method offered, unless it is of a kind so familiar and accepted as to require no foundation to establish the fundamental reliability of the system, such as fingerprint analysis, or unless it is so unreliable that the considerations requiring its exclusion have ripened into rules of law, such as "lie detector" tests, or unless its admission is regulated by statute, such as blood-alcohol test results.[111]

When prosecutors seek to use expert testimony about scientific evidence against a criminal defendant, it is vital that the defense have the opportunity to challenge or rebut the findings and conclusions of the government's experts. The ABA Standards for Criminal Justice state that in many cases, the availability of necessary expert services is essential to effective representation.[112] More important, the U.S. Supreme Court has long considered that separate defense experts, along with the opportunity to cross-examine government experts, are necessary to protect defendants' constitutional rights.[113]

In Virginia, however, the courts rarely authorize independent defense experts in indigent criminal cases.[114] Apparently, many court-appointed lawyers and public defenders do not even bother to request court permission to retain defense experts, because their experience shows that the courts are not likely to grant approval.[115] Thus in Virginia, it appears that criminal defendants must rely on court rulings concerning the admissibility of scientific evidence and the cross-examination by defense lawyers when challenging scientific evidence.

"Junk Science"

In recent years, some traditional forensic techniques have come under scrutiny, in part because of DNA exonerations proving that the evidence did not actually link the defendants to their supposed crimes. One example is the microscopic analysis of hair samples found at crime scenes and the comparison of the samples to known samples taken from suspects. Although hair comparison evidence has been admitted against criminal defendants for decades and the overwhelming majority of courts have found that it meets both the *Frye* and *Daubert* standards, recent studies raise serious questions about its reliability, questions that are only heightened given the numerous cases of wrongful conviction that included erroneous hair comparisons.[116]

For example, the Law Enforcement Assistance Administration Laboratory Proficiency Testing Program, involving more than 235 crime laboratories throughout the United States, found hair comparison analysis to be the weakest of all the forensic laboratory techniques tested, with error rates as high as 67 percent on individual samples and the majority of laboratories reaching incorrect results on four out of five hair samples analyzed.[117] Another study found that hair comparison error rates dropped from 30 to 4 percent when common hair comparison methods —which compare a questioned hair with a suspect's hair samples—were changed to a "lineup" method, in which examiners compare a hair sample from the crime scene with those from five potential suspects.[118] Just as errors and unconscious bias exist in eyewitness identification, they also are common in hair sample identification.

Although the traditional serology testing does not have the reliability problems associated with hair comparison analysis, it too has contributed to the wrongful conviction of innocent people.[119] Serology testing cannot identify a specific suspect but instead shows the likelihood that two people share the same blood type. Accordingly, it often substantially narrows the field of possibilities to include the suspect when his or her blood or other bodily fluids match the characteristics of those found at the crime scene.[120] As an expert explains:

> There is no question that the impact of statistical calculations on the probability of an innocent match in blood analysis has a great impact on the jury. If a serologist testifies that the blood sample taken from a defendant's clothing matches that of the victim's blood, and that the probability of these same characteristics occurring in the blood of human beings is only one in 20,000, then, in the mind of the fact finder, identity has been established with as much definitiveness as science can muster.

Yet exactly the opposite seems to be coming to light in the retesting, using DNA analysis, of the evidence in cases in which persons had been previously convicted on the basis of eyewitness testimony or traditional serology testimony. The mounting evidence is that the statistical inferences drawn from serological "identifications" of the defendant as the perpetrator appear to have been accepted as proof of a uniqueness that is simply not warranted.[121]

DNA testing has helped address the deficiencies of serology tests and hair comparison. Using biological evidence found at a crime scene, analysts can make exceedingly accurate estimates of the likely match between a suspect's DNA and that of the perpetrator. Such testing can be done at the time of the crime, comparing biological samples from the perpetrator and a known suspect. It can be done postconviction, when a defendant seeks to show a link between the perpetrator and a third person who, the defendant claims, is the correct suspect. Or it can be done as a general "fishing expedition" in which the perpetrator's DNA is run through a database of DNA collected from various other suspects or individuals. Matches made in this last way—also called "cold hits"—have popularized DNA testing among police and prosecutors because it can establish a link between a crime scene and a suspect whom officers might not otherwise have considered.

Important as DNA has become, it cannot resolve all the problems associated with scientific evidence. First, DNA evidence can degrade over time, meaning that the accuracy of a match (or exclusion) is much greater at the time a crime is committed. Second, testing can be quite expensive—more than $3,000 per test—especially if the defense must conduct the analysis because the state has decided not to test biological evidence found in connection with the crime. Even when the state requests DNA analysis, the backlog at many crime labs may be several months. Third, until recently many states, including Virginia, did not require biological evidence to be preserved, which made postconviction testing nearly impossible unless an analyst happened to retain a biological sample (and a chain of custody could be established), even in contravention of then-existing state policy. Fourth, some crimes are unlikely to render biological evidence. Unlike the crime of rape, in which semen or pubic hairs usually are available for testing, crimes like robbery do not readily present biological evidence.

In many crimes DNA testing can only link a suspect to a crime scene, not prove that he was the actual perpetrator. Hairs found outside an ATM could show, for example, who was present at a cash machine, but by themselves they cannot establish who mugged a patron.[122] Even in crimes in which the link is more obvious, like sexual assault, the DNA analysis of semen can establish who had sex with the victim, but the state still needs additional evidence to prove lack of consent. Finally, DNA analysis is only as accurate as the quality of the testing process and the care and skill of the technicians who conduct the analyses and testify to their results.

Scientific Evidence in the Cases of Virginia Exonerees

The ICVA found many of these problems in the cases it investigated. Even in some cases in which DNA testing was conducted, the experience raised questions about the past precision of Virginia's forensic process. In other cases, defendants were wrongly convicted in part because of the questionable scientific evidence or the mistaken or flawed testimony of forensic experts.

EARL WASHINGTON JR.

As Earl Washington's execution date neared, Governor Douglas Wilder ordered DNA testing in his case. DNA analysis was still a relatively new technology at the time, and it had not previously been used in the Washington case. Although DNA tests excluded Washington as the source of semen on a blue blanket recovered from the victim's apartment, the lab analyst who conducted the DNA tests said that he could not eliminate Washington as a potential source of semen from a separate vaginal swab from the victim. Based on these results, Governor Wilder commuted Washington's sentence to life in prison in January 1994, nine days before his scheduled execution, saying the test results raised a "substantial question" about Washington's guilt. Governor Wilder did not pardon Washington completely because he believed that the DNA tests did not erase all doubt about Washington's involvement in the crime.

Six years later, Governor James Gilmore ordered another series of even more sophisticated DNA tests on the evidence in Washington's case. As with the earlier test, the new DNA analysis was conducted by Jeffrey Ban, a DNA expert in the Virginia lab and a member of a panel of scientists that sets national DNA standards. This time, Ban declared that the semen stain on the blanket matched the genetic profile of Kenneth Tinsley, a convicted rapist whose DNA profile was contained in Virginia's DNA database. Governor Gilmore then ordered Washington's release.

However, Ban's results raised as many questions about the Virginia crime lab's analysis in the Washington case as they answered. As the *Chicago Tribune* explained in a series entitled "Forensic Science under the Microscope":

> Ban further reported that he was unable to obtain a genetic profile from a slide made from the vaginal swab—although at Washington's trial, a medical examiner had testified there was an abundance of sperm on the slide. Even more puzzling were the results of his tests on a second, similar slide. Not only did Ban exclude Washington, but he excluded Tinsley and, according to his report, turned up two additional unidentified genetic profiles.
>
> The exclusion of Washington was enough for Gilmore to grant him a pardon—just as Ban's earlier test was enough to prompt Wilder to commute his death sentence. After 17 years in prison, more than nine of them on Death Row, he was set free. That did not settle the matter, though. Tinsley's DNA was detected by the lab on the blanket. But because Ban said he did not find it on the slides, authorities did not prosecute Tinsley, leaving the case open. . . .
>
> Duplicate slides were sent to Dr. Ed Blake, a DNA expert, who was working for Washington's attorneys. His tests isolated only Tinsley's genetic profile, he said, and conclusively eliminated Washington. . . . Three other DNA experts, at the request of a Virginia newspaper, reviewed Ban's reports. They all agreed that his work was troubling and warranted further scrutiny. . . .
>
> In an interview with the *Tribune,* [Dr. Paul Ferrara, then director of the Virginia Division of Forensic Science] said it is possible for two scientists to come up with different test results because no two samples are alike—although Ban and Blake tested slides created from the same swab. "As far as we're concerned, there is no error at all except in the minds of [critics] . . . ," Ferrara said.[123]

Ferrara may now regret those remarks, since an investigation into the Washington case concluded that the state's crime lab made mistakes. As the next chapter details, many of those errors have now been corrected, but there is no doubt that more advanced testing and more careful protocols could have produced an earlier, accurate resolution in the Washington case.

EDWARD HONAKER

As noted earlier, the laboratory technician in Edward Honaker's case overstated the significance of the hair comparison he performed and consequently misled the jury. Based on his comparison of hairs found on the victim's shorts with Honaker's hair samples, the technician testified that in his opinion, it "is unlikely that the hair would match anyone other than the defendant, but it is possible." When DNA evidence later proved that Honaker was not the rapist, Dr. Ferrara provided an affidavit debunking the technician's inaccurate testimony. Moreover, when one of the world's leading experts on hair comparison later reexamined the hair analysis, he concluded that the hairs were not a match.[124] Honaker's lawyer did not retain an expert to refute the opinion of the Commonwealth's expert.

DAVID VASQUEZ

David Vasquez is an example of a defendant convicted despite forensic evidence that failed to link him to the crime scene. Vasquez's blood type did not match the blood type of the semen found in the victim or on her bathrobe. Moreover, none of the shoe impressions found outside her home matched any of Vasquez's shoes seized by the police. These inconsistencies notwithstanding, Vasquez's defense attorneys failed to retain a forensic expert's opinion because of Vasquez's "confession" in the case and the state lab's conclusion that the pubic hair samples taken from Vasquez were consistent with the hair recovered from the victim's body. If Vasquez had not been led to confess, his attorneys might very well have chosen to attack the forensic evidence rather than recommend that he plead guilty to second-degree murder.

CRAIG BELL

The jury convicted Craig Bell of murder despite forensic evidence that raised doubts about his involvement in the crime. A laboratory technician testified that hairs recovered from shorts left at the scene by the murderer matched neither Bell's pubic hair samples nor those of the victim. Semen stains on those shorts produced inconclusive results, neither implicating nor exonerating Bell. A partial palm print lifted from the window ledge where investigators found a screen knocked out—which later proved to be the real murderer's point of entry—did not match Bell, the victim, or any family members known to visit the couple. Blood evidence, however, could not exclude Bell as a suspect without the use of DNA technology. Type O blood belonging to the murderer was found at the crime scene, and a serologist testified at trial that 36 percent of the population, including Bell, has type O blood. Because this evidence was not controversial, Bell's lawyers did not retain an independent expert to review the government expert's analysis. Instead, they hired a private investigator and consulted with a forensic expert for an opinion about the blood splatter left in the apartment.

TROY WEBB

The serology evidence in Troy Webb's case was more complicated, but even so, the Commonwealth's expert identified Webb as a possible source of the semen from the rapist. Testing showed that Webb was a nonsecretor. The swabs from the victim's PERK showed blood type A. The victim's boyfriend happened to have blood type A as well, and the technician testified that semen from recent intercourse with the boyfriend could have masked the blood type from the semen of a nonsecretor like Troy Webb. While not conclusively identifying Webb as the rapist, the expert testified that Webb could not be ruled out as the perpetrator, which is true. But Webb's lawyers did not present a defense expert to analyze or refute the work of the Commonwealth's expert. The entire matter was resolved only when DNA testing became available, at which point Webb was cleared as a source of the semen. If Webb's case were tried today and DNA testing was conducted, it is highly unlikely that the Commonwealth would have prosecuted him, let alone that he would have been convicted.

Retention of Forensic Evidence

In four of the cases studied by the ICVA, the police destroyed critical biological evidence that would have—or, in one case, could have—proved the exonerees' innocence. Even though witnesses saw two kidnappers abduct the victim in Jeffrey Cox's case, the police inexplicably destroyed physical evidence three months after his conviction—before his appeal had even been heard and even though the second perpetrator had been neither identified nor arrested. The physical evidence destroyed by the police in the Cox case included the PERK recovered from the victim, which contained hairs foreign to the victim, swabs positive for saliva from her body, and fingernail scrapings.

In three of the cases—Marvin Anderson, Julius Ruffin, and Arthur Lee Whitfield—the Commonwealth's crime laboratory returned the swabs and samples from the PERKs to the police departments after testing the samples, and the police destroyed the kits once the exonerees were convicted. Had it not been for a fortuitous breach in policy by a state lab technician, all three would likely remain convicted, with two still incarcerated.[125] Mary Jane Burton performed the forensic testing in these cases for the Commonwealth. At the time, the Division of Forensic Science required that all physical evidence tested be returned to the respective law enforcement agencies, where the evidence was later destroyed. But Burton, who has since died, taped slides containing portions of the samples she tested to her personal files, which she retained in each case. Years later these slides were found and provided the basis for the DNA testing that cleared Anderson, Ruffin, and Whitfield.

Recommendations

At the time of the ICVA's report, Governor Mark Warner had ordered DNA testing in fewer than forty criminal cases from the 1970s and 1980s in which standard serology testing was used. These cases were culled from a review of approximately 10 percent of the cases on file in state archives.[126] The ICVA applauded this move, whose results exonerated two additional prisoners. (These cases and the results from more intensive forensic audits are discussed in the next chapter.) If advanced, accurate DNA testing is used to its full potential, then it is imperative to collect and preserve forensic evidence and to permit both the state and defense sufficient resources to test such evidence and consult experts to interpret the results.

Arthur Lee Whitfield's case illustrates the need for the first reform. It took more than three years after the General Assembly provided a statutory vehicle for testing biological evidence—and nearly twenty-two years after Whitfield was convicted—before authorities found the evidence that exonerated him. It thus is crucial to develop a protocol for cataloguing and preserving genetic evidence in crimes of this nature. As in Virginia, the other states should amend their current laws to require the preservation in all serious felony cases of human biological evidence that could be subjected to DNA testing.

DNA collection and testing require additional resources, which likely must come from either state or federal funds, given the more limited coffers of local jurisdictions. The advantages of such testing should now be obvious, as they essentially allow the state to place a suspect at, or exclude him or her from, a crime scene. The state's ability to more quickly—and accurately—close cases and secure convictions is a clear boon to the public, as is the growing opportunity for "cold hits" that identify likely perpetrators the state may not have suspected. Moreover, as the ICVA's research indicates, DNA testing can clear innocent suspects early in an investigation before they are erroneously convicted.

Prosecutors and defense attorneys also require enough funds to consult or retain experts to interpret the forensic testing. However, as stated earlier, the overwhelming majority of indigent defendants in Virginia are unable to retain the services of an expert. Part of this problem reflects the reticence of defense counsel to petition the court for support, but as research indicates, some of the intransigence reflects a calculation by trial counsel that the courts will reject their request.[127] Just as it is in Virginia, it is imperative that other state legislatures allocate enough resources to public defenders and court-appointed counsel for indigent defendants so that necessary defense experts can be retained in appropriate cases. It also is important that courts approve the appointment of independent expert witnesses when counsel for indigent defendants request them.

Virginia is one of only a few states that has not adopted either the *Frye* or the *Daubert* standards for evaluating scientific evidence. The current standard requires Virginia courts to make a threshold finding of the reliability of scientific evidence, but the Virginia Supreme Court has given trial courts great discretion to admit scientific evidence even when its reliability has been called into question. Indeed, this discretion is so great that trial court rulings are rarely overturned on appeal, even when the scientific techniques used in criminal cases are of at least questionable validity.

The prospect of these problems contributed to the U.S. Supreme Court's decision in *Daubert,* and those courts that have not yet adopted the *Daubert* rule would be wise to follow the High Court's lead. The

Daubert rule outlines several factors that trial and appellate courts should consider when determining the admissibility of scientific evidence, and at the same time, the rule makes none of the factors dispositive. Although the *Daubert* rule gives significant authority to the trial courts to serve as gatekeepers for scientific evidence, the rule also contemplates an important role for the appellate courts in reviewing the trial courts' decisions. Moreover, this standard leaves the courts receptive to improvements in scientific techniques that either offer new, more advanced methods or challenge past approaches that are no longer reliable. If the DNA exonerations show anything, it is that science and forensic methods continue to advance. The court should embrace these improvements within a structure that provides appropriate guidance and oversight for trial judges.

Open Files Discovery

The ICVA took some heat from prosecutors for its recommendation that Commonwealth's attorneys open their case files and share with defendants and their attorneys before trial all nonconfidential, nonprivileged material on pending criminal cases. This call went beyond the current, more limited rights to discovery in Virginia and was challenged as too permissive and potentially dangerous.

Although a fair argument can be made opposing the ICVA's recommendations, open files discovery need not put witnesses or others at risk in a case, nor should it overly burden prosecutors. Indeed, the greatest arguments in favor of open files discovery come from the prosecutors themselves, who report that open files discovery limits potential liability to police and prosecutors while spurring plea negotiations.

The Law of Discovery

As any beginning student of law or justice knows, the American criminal justice system is based on an adversarial model that places significant burdens on defendants to protect their own rights and interests and to uncover evidence in their cases on their own. In criminal matters, the evidence is normally gathered first by the police and the prosecution. This information is almost never shared with defendants before formal charges are sought, and often much of the evidence discovered by the police and prosecution is not shared even after charges have been filed. As the U.S. Supreme Court made clear in *Brady v. Maryland*,[128] criminal defendants have a constitutional right to obtain exculpatory evidence about their respective cases that is in the hands of prosecutors or the police. Unfortunately, sometimes police officers do not give this evidence to prosecutors in order to make it available to defendants, or prosecutors may not be aware that they have such information in their possession.

This does not vitiate the duty, however, for as the Court has said, the obligation to disclose "encompasses evidence 'known only to police investigators and not to the prosecutor.' In order to comply with *Brady*, therefore, 'the individual prosecutor has a duty to learn of any favorable evidence known to the others acting on the government's behalf in the case, including the police.' "[129] After all, in the American criminal justice system the prosecutor

> is "the representative not of an ordinary party to a controversy, but of a sovereignty whose obligation to govern impartially is as compelling as its obligation to govern at all; and whose interest, therefore, in a criminal prosecution is not that it shall win a case, but that justice shall be done."[130]

Apart from these "barebones" constitutional requirements, some states have discovery rules that go substantially beyond these standards and provide defendants with greater disclosure of the information known to the government. Virginia, however, is not among these states. Instead, Virginia law gives defendants the right to copy any written statements or confessions and the substance of any oral statements made by defendants to the police. These rules also entitle defendants to copy the written scientific reports of the Commonwealth's experts, but not the work notes or memoranda on which the reports were based.[131] The rules further provide that if defendants can show that physical evidence in possession of the Commonwealth—including papers, documents, or tangible objects—may be material to the preparation of their defense, the courts may order that defendants be permitted to inspect, copy, or photograph such evidence if the requests are reasonable.[132] Finally, under *Brady*, prosecutors in Virginia are obligated to provide to the defense any exculpatory evidence in their possession or in the possession of others acting on the Commonwealth's behalf, including the police.[133]

Defendants in Virginia are not legally entitled to, and often do not receive, other types of discovery that are generally provided to the accused in other jurisdictions. For example, Virginia defendants preparing for trial are not entitled to the names and addresses of eyewitnesses to a crime, nor can they insist that the Commonwealth provide the names of its trial witnesses until the trial begins.[134] They are not entitled to written or oral statements made by prospective Commonwealth's witnesses to police officers in connection with an investigation or prosecution, unless such statements are exculpatory,[135] or to copies of police investigative reports.[136] When Commonwealth witnesses at trial have given previous statements to the police, defendants are not permitted to obtain copies of those statements after the witnesses testify on direct examination in order to cross-examine the witnesses about inconsistencies in their statements.[137]

Virginia Practice

The ICVA surveyed Commonwealth's attorneys about their discovery practices in order to understand under what circumstances they do or would share information with the defense. As table 4.4 shows, half the offices that responded to the survey provide the minimum required by law. Perhaps a better way of stating this result is that half the responding Commonwealth's attorneys' offices provide *more* discovery than is required by law. About 40 percent of offices disclose investigative reports from police officers. A similar number provide witness statements. One-third of offices offer the names and addresses of the Commonwealth's witnesses who will testify at motion hearings or trial, and a quarter of prosecutors' offices provide summaries of reports from lab-

TABLE 4.4
Prosecutors' Disclosure Practices in Virginia

Disclosure Policy	Percentage of Responding Offices
Minimum required by law	50
Officers' investigative reports	42
Witnesses' statements	38
Names/addresses of witnesses	33
Summaries of labs	25
Officers' field notes	12
Bench or lab notes	4

Note: N = 26.

oratory technicians or forensic experts if written reports are not prepared. Finally, 12 percent of offices disclose officers' field notes, and just 4 percent provide bench or lab notes from forensic experts.

The ICVA's survey also included open-ended questions about discovery practices. When prosecutors were asked why they maintained an open files policy, their answers generally focused on issues of fairness and making sure that they complied with legal requirements to provide exculpatory evidence to the defense. As one office explained, the policy "avoids [the] failure to disclose exculpatory evidence" by forcing the "defendant to take responsibility for" investigating the case. Said another, "It is both fair and practical in day-to-day cases." Other offices said the policy helped make prosecutions more efficient, that open files policies help "better identify cases that require trial or not," lead to "better plea negotiations," and insulate the office from the failure to disclose evidence while having little practical effect on the success of prosecutions.

The ICVA's results—while admittedly based on a smaller sample than that of the report of the Spangenberg Group—paints a slightly better picture than the earlier research did. The Spangenberg Group found that in many criminal cases in which prosecutors do not have defendants' statements and obviously exculpatory information, defense counsel receive no discovery at all, not even the police reports forming the basis for the criminal accusations against the defendants. Furthermore, the Spangenberg Report noted that in a number of counties, including even those with purported open file discovery policies, discovery is dependent on an individual defense lawyer's relationship with the Commonwealth's attorney and that sometimes defense counsel receive more discovery if they choose not to file formal discovery requests with the court. Finally, that report found that even in counties in which the prosecutors have express "open files discovery," defense counsel sometimes believe that the prosecutors do not share everything with them.[138] Conversely, however, some Commonwealth's attorneys' offices surveyed by the ICVA reported that "some defense attorneys never look at the files."

The Need for Greater Discovery in Criminal Cases

In civil litigation the American legal system permits thorough and often exhaustive discovery of the evidence and information possessed by the opposing side. The parties can be required to share documents and to respond in writing to questions or "interrogatories" from the opponent, and either party may depose key witnesses under oath. In contrast, in criminal cases in which the defendants' liberty and sometimes their lives are at stake, the prosecutors' obligations to share information are drastically more limited.

More than thirty years ago, the Criminal Justice Section of the American Bar Association (ABA) created a comprehensive set of criminal justice standards addressing various facets of the criminal justice system, including the discovery process.[139] When the ABA issued the first seventeen volumes of standards in 1968, U.S. Supreme Court Chief Justice Warren Burger described the project as "the single most comprehensive and probably the most monumental undertaking in the field of criminal justice ever attempted by the American legal profession in our national history."[140]

The ABA's discovery standards are designed to promote the fair and expeditious resolution of criminal cases, to give defendants sufficient information to make informed plea decisions, to permit thorough preparation for trial and minimize surprise, to reduce trial interruptions and delays, to conserve judicial and professional resources, and to minimize burdens on victims and witnesses.[141] To this end, the second edition of the discovery standards states that prosecutors should disclose the following information to the defense within a reasonable time before trial and permit the defense to inspect, copy, test and photograph documents and tangible objects:[142]

- All written and all oral statements of the defendant or of any co-defendant that are within the possession or control of the prosecution and that relate to the subject matter of the offense charged, and any documents relating to the acquisition of such statements.
- The names and addresses of all persons known to the prosecution to have information concerning the offense charged, together with all written statements of any such person that are within the possession or control of the prosecution and that relate to the subject matter of the offense charged. The prosecution should also identify the persons it intends to call as witnesses at trial.
- The relationship, if any, between the prosecution and any witness it intends to call at trial, including the nature and circumstances of any agreement, understanding, or representation between the

prosecution and the witness that constitutes an inducement for the cooperation or testimony of the witness.

- Any reports or written statements of experts made in connection with the case, including results of physical or mental examinations and of scientific tests, experiments, or comparisons and of scientific tests, experiments, or comparisons. With respect to each expert whom the prosecution intends to call as a witness at trial, the prosecutor should also furnish to the defense a curriculum vitae and a written description of the substance of the proposed testimony of the expert, the expert's opinion, and the underlying basis of that opinion.

- Any tangible objects, including books, papers, documents, photographs, buildings, places, or any other objects, which pertain to the case or which were obtained for or belong to the defendant. The prosecution should also identify which of these tangible objects it intends to offer as evidence at trial.

- Any record of prior criminal convictions, pending charges, or probationary status of the defendant or of any co-defendant, and insofar as known to the prosecution, any record of convictions, pending charges, or probationary status that may be used to impeach any witness to be called by either party at trial.

- Any material, documents, or information relating to lineups, showups, and picture or voice identifications in relation to the case.

- Any material or information within the prosecutor's possession or control which tends to negate the guilt of the defendant as to the offense charged or which would tend to reduce the punishment of the defendant.

- If the prosecution intends to use character, reputation, or other acts as evidence, the prosecution should notify the defense of that intention and of the substance of the evidence to be used.

- If the defendant's conversations or premises have been subjected to electronic surveillance (including wiretapping) in connection with the investigation or prosecution of the case, the prosecution should inform the defense of that fact.

- If any tangible object which the prosecutor intends to offer at trial was obtained through a search and seizure, the prosecution should disclose to the defense any information, documents, or other material relating to the acquisition of such objects.

For criminal cases, many states adopted discovery rules modeled on the expansive policy urged by the ABA discovery standards. At least twenty-one states require prosecutors to provide to the defense most of the information called for by the ABA discovery standards,[143] and more than half the states require prosecutors to provide the majority of this information to defendants.[144] In contrast, only three states entitle defendants to as little discovery as prosecutors are obligated to provide to defendants in Virginia,[145] and no state allows prosecutors to provide less discovery than is permitted under Virginia law.[146]

Nearly half the Commonwealth's attorneys surveyed by the ICVA already go beyond these minimal standards. The challenge is to bring the rest of the state into conformity with the national trend, a move that would help the prosecution and defense alike. For these reasons the ICVA recommended that the Virginia General Assembly amend formal discovery rules to require that Commonwealth's attorneys share with the defense all the information that law enforcement and prosecutors have collected and have in their files, except for confidential and privileged information or any information that, if disclosed, could endanger witnesses or otherwise substantially threaten public safety. The ICVA recognized the need to limit sensitive information in the state's possession, although its proposal would place the burden on prosecutors to demonstrate the need to withhold this information.

Several of the cases investigated by the ICVA illustrate how open files discovery can help prevent erroneous convictions.

WALTER SNYDER

The police failed to disclose to Snyder the inconsistencies and hesitancy in the victim's reports. For example, they did not report that when the victim looked at a photo array of suspects, she indicated that four of them—but not Snyder—looked familiar. Indeed, although she stated that Snyder's eyebrows were memorable, she said she was not prepared to identify Snyder as the rapist. Rather than provide this information to the defense, the detective testified at trial that the victim positively identified Snyder as the rapist during this procedure. Finally, the victim told police that her attacker had smooth, soft hands and smelled like alcohol and body odor, but these facts were never disclosed to the defense. Instead, after learning that the police suspect, Snyder, worked with his hands as a heating and cooling repairman and lived in the basement of his parents' home, the victim testified at trial that the rapist smelled of alcohol, smoke, and "a musky-type odor . . . kind of a combination of oil and a basement." Without this information, the defense lacked an important opportunity to question the likely involvement of Snyder in the crime.

EDWARD HONAKER

In Edward Honaker's case, the rape victim and her male companion told a park police ranger that the rapist drove a yellow or light color truck. The victim also told the ranger that the attacker wore a very large crucifix, and she indicated that "she was not allowed to clearly see the individual during the entire sequence of events." All this information was contained in the park ranger's written report, which was never turned over to the defense. Instead, at trial both the victim and her companion identified Honaker's blue truck as the one driven by the rapist. The prosecution also introduced into evidence a small crucifix belonging to Honaker that was seized from his home, suggesting that this was the one identified by the victim.

Finally, and most important, the police and prosecution never revealed to the defense that four months after the crime, the rape victim and her boyfriend were hypnotized and that then, for the first time, identified Honaker's photograph as that of the rapist. Nor did the prosecution disclose that the two witnesses were together during the hypnosis while they were viewing photographs. Under Virginia law at the time, these witnesses' posthypnotic recollections, their out-of-court identification of Honaker's photograph, and their in-court identification of Honaker as the rapist would not have been admissible at trial.[147] If the defense had been aware of the hypnosis, Honaker's attorney presumably would have moved the court to exclude the witnesses' identification of Honaker.

JEFFREY COX

Jeffrey Cox's case turned largely on the testimony of two witnesses, whose prior felony convictions and pending charges were not known to the defense. Each of these facts would have undermined their credibility, a problem all the greater considering that the prosecution failed to correct the record at trial when one witness perjured himself about his criminal past. The other witness had criminal charges pending for failing to appear in court when she identified Cox at a pretrial hearing. Instead of sharing this information with the defense, the prosecutor vouched for the veracity of both witnesses in his closing argument.

The prosecution did not give the defense a forensic laboratory report indicating that two hairs found on the victim's body were very fine, white Caucasian hairs, which could not have matched Cox's brown hair. The police also did not turn over a second, exculpatory composite drawing that differed from one provided to the defense, nor did they disclose a "Crime Stoppers" report containing descriptions of the abductor derived from the government's two eyewitnesses that did not match Jeffrey Cox's physical description. Combined, these facts could have cast considerable doubts on Cox's involvement and guilt.

Concerns about Open Discovery

Some prosecutors have raised concerns about open files discovery practices, worried that full information would endanger state witnesses or give the defense an advantage at trial that it does not already have. The first is a fair claim, for in some cases witnesses are threatened or worse for agreeing to appear for the state. Building on past recommendations from the ABA and others, the ICVA's proposal took account of this possibility by exempting from disclosure any confidential or privileged material or any information that, if disclosed, could endanger others. The burden would be on the prosecution to establish this need, but if proven, the state could keep secret any information that would put others at risk.

Open files discovery gives the defense more information than it currently is entitled to receive, but that does not necessarily mean that the state will have greater difficulty convicting the guilty. The goal, of course, is to ensure that triers of fact have a more thorough and accurate picture of the facts of a case, but the duty is still on the defense to request and sift through the information provided by the prosecution. Open files discovery should not, and in the jurisdictions where it is practiced has not, turned the tables between prosecution and defense, making the former do the legwork for the latter. Rather, it ensures that no relevant information is inadvertently hidden. Indeed, many prosecutors who have adopted this practice report that they are able to secure guilty pleas more often and less contentiously once defendants and their attorneys have had an opportunity to review the prosecution's files.

One might say that open files discovery speeds up the criminal justice process for those cases in which the prosecution's evidence presents little doubt. It is in the other cases—those in which the facts are not as clear-cut—that the triers of fact should carefully examine the evidence and truly establish guilt rather than being led to a conviction without a deeper understanding of the case. Considering that many criminal defendants are indigent and are represented by underpaid attorneys who lack investigators, open files discovery would help them better balance the scales of justice when there is legitimate doubt about the state's case. For the state, open files discovery not only offers the prospect of swifter and easier pleas, but it also protects the state from later allegations of failure to disclose or other misconduct. Almost half the Commonwealth's attorneys' offices surveyed have successfully experimented with open files discovery. Other prosecutors have little to fear from this best practice.

Tunnel Vision

One of the most elusive problems identified by the ICVA's research, and certainly among the most difficult to remedy, is "tunnel vision," or the unwanted focus by police or prosecutors on a single suspect. [148] The ICVA's comprehensive examination revealed few instances of deliberate misconduct by those involved in the investigation and prosecution of criminal cases. But in some cases, detectives and prosecutors leaped too quickly to conclusions about suspects or failed to broaden their inquiry when the facts uncovered did not mesh with their theories of the case. Indeed, many cases of wrongful conviction involve high-profile and heinous crimes, which can create intense pressure on the police to solve the crimes and solve them quickly, which may lead to tunnel vision.

Although police officers do not deliberately or knowingly engage in tunnel vision, its existence leads officers to focus on, investigate, and gather evidence that supports their conclusion that the suspect is guilty and to disregard evidence that might lead to another suspect. As part of this process, the police may minimize or even sometimes ignore evidence suggesting that the suspect is innocent, that might undermine the evidence of guilt against the suspect, or that indicates another suspect may have committed the crime. Prosecutors and judges also can be susceptible to a form of tunnel vision. When prosecutors discount exculpatory evidence and when judges reject contrary evidence, the consequences are similar to those from police tunnel vision.

Tunnel vision afflicts many professions outside criminal justice. For example, its existence has been noted as a contributing factor in aviation accidents, such as when pilots limit their attention to a particular problem, like stuck landing gear, and fail to note that the aircraft is losing altitude.[149] One can imagine its influence in various errors and accidents, from mine explosions to medical malpractice, and as the ICVA's research indicates, it plays a role in erroneous convictions.

MARVIN ANDERSON

The only reason that Marvin Anderson, who had no criminal record, became a suspect was because the rape victim said that her attacker was a black man who claimed to have a white girlfriend, and Anderson was one of the few black men the investigating police officer knew who dated a white woman. But Marvin Anderson did not match the physical description of the assailant given by the rape victim; she described her attacker as five feet, four inches, to five feet, seven inches, in height with a thin moustache, and she told police that she scratched her assailant. Marvin Anderson was five feet, nine inches, tall, had a dark complexion, did not have a moustache, and had no scratches when he was interviewed by police shortly after the crime.

Moreover, soon after the rape occurred, rumors circulated in the community that Otis "Pop" Lincoln actually committed the crime. Lincoln had served jail time for a prior sexual attack and was awaiting trial on another sexual assault on a female college student at the time of this crime. Witnesses near the site of the rape saw Lincoln riding a bicycle shortly before the crime, heard him make sexually suggestive comments to young girls walking by, and listened as he professed his willingness to force sexual favors from women.

Nevertheless, the police apparently ruled out Lincoln as a suspect once the victim viewed a photograph of Anderson and identified him as her rapist. Anderson was promptly charged with the rape. Six years later, Lincoln testified in court during Anderson's habeas proceeding that he had robbed and raped the victim, but the prosecutors and the court rejected his confession. More than a decade later, DNA evidence proved that Lincoln committed the rape.

JULIUS RUFFIN

Julius Ruffin became a suspect because of a chance encounter that he had with the rape victim in an elevator. Like Marvin Anderson, Ruffin did not match the physical description given by the victim of the rapist in his case. Ruffin is six feet, one inch, tall, weighs 170 pounds, is a light-skinned black man, has prominent gold front teeth, and had facial hair at the time of the attack. By contrast, the victim described her attacker as a five-foot, six-inch-tall, 150-pound, dark-skinned black man, and did not mention gold teeth or facial hair. But once the victim had identified Ruffin as her attacker, both the police and prosecutors seemed to ignore the inconsistencies between her initial description and Ruffin's appearance.

DAVID VASQUEZ

In the David Vasquez case, two witnesses reported seeing Vasquez in the area around the time of the murder and described him as someone who had acted strangely in the past. The police appropriately considered Vasquez as a possible suspect or at least as someone detectives should interview. The police interrogated Vasquez and obtained a confession from him, but his confession contained many clues that should have led police to be wary of it. Even after confessing, Vasquez continued to express confusion about how he could have gotten from his home in a different county to the victim's home. Moreover, Vasquez's blood type did not match the perpetrator's semen. Even though the police apparently recognized that Vasquez had neither the physical ability nor the intellectual capacity to commit the crime by himself, the police clung to the idea that Vasquez was involved, even though no evidence linked him to the crime other than his confused confession obtained through a suggestive interrogation.

EARL WASHINGTON JR.

Earl Washington, as well, was charged with murder by the police based almost exclusively on his muddled confession a year after the crime occurred. Police very quickly eliminated Washington as a suspect in four other unrelated burglaries to which he confessed but persisted in their investigation of him for the murder. Washington's confession in the murder case was riddled with inconsistencies and glaring errors—such as getting the race of the victim wrong—but the police discounted those mistakes and proceeded to charge him with the murder.

RUSSELL GRAY

There certainly was reason to focus on Gray early in the investigation: an eyewitness identified him as the shooter in the murder, and another witness picked out his picture as someone she had seen in the area of the shooting. The police, however, interviewed only three of the many witnesses who had information about the crime and never spoke with witnesses later identified by the defense as having critical and exculpatory information. Moreover, persistent rumors circulated in the neighborhood that Michael Harvey, the actual shooter, committed the murder. These rumors became so serious that officers eventually interviewed Harvey and obtained a confession soon after Gray's conviction. The prosecutor who later helped exonerate Gray remarked that "there were a ton of people who could have testified that didn't" and that as a result, "we ended up trying a case with half the evidence and convicted the wrong man."[150]

CRAIG BELL

Craig Bell was accused and convicted of murdering his girlfriend principally on the basis of three pieces of information: Bell smoked the same type of cigarettes and had the same type of underwear as the actual murderer; his blood type matched that of the murderer; and he reportedly gave inconsistent unrecorded statements to the police. However, police and prosecutors discounted a number of facts suggesting that Bell had not murdered his girlfriend. First, the police found a window screen knocked out and a lamp hanging outside a downstairs window at the crime scene, which suggested someone had entered or fled the home through the window. A partial palm print on the window, which was later found to match the real killer, did not match Bell's or that of anyone else who lived or visited the home. Finally, community members reported seeing a naked black man running through the neighborhood the night that Bell's girlfriend was murdered. The real killer later told police that it was he who fled naked from Bell's home.

JEFFREY COX

Jeffrey Cox's photograph was included in photo arrays shown to the two eyewitnesses in his case because one of the original suspects, Steven

Hood, told police that Cox was known to spend time with the other prime suspect, Billy Madison. The police originally focused on Madison and Hood because they believed the abduction and murder were drug related; they knew that Madison had recently been beaten up by a drug dealer during a drug transaction; and they suspected that Madison and Hood were out for revenge in the neighborhood where the victim lived. But when two witnesses tentatively selected Cox's photograph in a photo array as resembling the knife-wielding kidnapper, the police ended their investigation of Madison and Hood and focused exclusively on Cox. Years later, an FBI agent who became convinced of Cox's innocence spearheaded an investigation that led not only to Cox's exoneration but also to Hood's arrest and conviction for the crime.

ARTHUR WHITFIELD

The police focused on Arthur Whitfield because he was a suspect in an attempted burglary that occurred on the same evening, around the same time, in a neighborhood close to where the rapes occurred, and both the burglar and rapist carried knives. Certainly, the police had strong reasons to suspect that Whitfield was the rapist.

But obvious evidence known by the police strongly suggested that Whitfield could not be the rapist of one, if not both, rapes. The second rape victim told the police that the rapist had no facial hair, a fact of which she was likely certain given that she said the rapist had repeatedly tried to kiss her. Whitfield, however, had a heavy moustache a week after the rapes when he appeared in a police lineup, and the police took photographs showing his moustache on that same day.

Recommendations

Tunnel vision has no simple "reform," for it plays against the natural tendency of any reasonable person to solve a heinous crime as quickly as possible. Once some facts are developed that seem to implicate a suspect, police and prosecutors are understandably hopeful that they can close the case and convict the perpetrator. Nevertheless, haste should not get in the way of accuracy, and for this reason it is important that police and prosecutors guard against the special dangers of tunnel vision.

One of the difficulties in addressing tunnel vision is the role orientation of some law enforcement officers and prosecutors, who find it difficult to believe that they would make serious errors or that a different approach on a case might have prevented a significant mistake. Law professor Daniel Medwed has written about this phenomenon in a related context, reporting that many prosecutors are resistant to postconviction claims of innocence.[151] But this should not be seen as a criticism of police officers or prosecutors specifically. It is, perhaps, human nature to believe that we are generally correct and to consider it unlikely that our unintended missteps would have serious or tragic consequences. That is the rub with tunnel vision—the errors least likely to be recognized may be the linchpin in a wrongful conviction.

Several recent studies of wrongful convictions have concluded that police training is the key to help officers avoid tunnel vision during their investigations.[152] These studies suggest that the police should be trained to pursue all reasonable investigatory leads, even those that point away from the suspect, and that they should be trained to document all exculpatory evidence indicating that a suspect may not be guilty of the crime being investigated and to include all this information in their official reports. Some commentators have recommended that case studies of wrongful convictions be used in order to highlight the dangers presented by tunnel vision.[153] The ICVA endorsed these recommendations.

Prosecutors, too, should be trained to evaluate their cases with a fresh eye, to ensure that all the facts add up to the defendant's guilt. Although it is understandably difficult for prosecutors to challenge police officers' investigations or to send a case back for further inquiry, they are, first, officers of the court, who are obligated to ensure that the cases they present are accurate. For this reason, new prosecutors should be trained to scan the files of contested cases going to trial for exculpatory as well as inculpatory evidence.[154] Refresher training, too, would benefit from the examination of wrongful convictions to underscore the potential perils of tunnel vision.

The Courts

One issue the ICVA did not tackle but that bears mentioning is the role of the courts in propelling a faulty case through to an erroneous conviction or failing to rectify the mistakes on appeal. Indeed, for all the attention in the ICVA's report to the mistakes of police, prosecutors, witnesses, and forensic scientists, it is important to note that *not one* of the eleven wrongful convictions identified by the ICVA was caught or corrected by the courts. In each case, a lone detective or prosecutor compiled the evidence necessary to set aside the verdict, or the defendant and his investigative team presented compelling justification to the governor or parole board to order further testing, release, or clemency. If wrongful convictions were to become a screenplay, the men and women of the bench might very well wear their traditional black robes and not white hats.

In the courts' defense, they see thousands of criminal cases each year, the vast majority of which present compelling evidence of the defendant's guilt. After all, as a chief trial judge once told me, if the police and prosecutors are doing their jobs, they will charge and pursue a prosecution when the evidence is strong and the likelihood of conviction is high. Judges might be excused, then, if they have grown accustomed to expecting that the defendants under indictment will be convicted.

This is not the same, however, as saying that judges should presume that charged suspects are guilty, nor should they give the benefit of the doubt to prosecutors. The central precept of the American criminal justice process—that a defendant is presumed innocent until proven guilty—is supposed to be followed. I have even heard of a trial judge who, during voir dire, asks members of the jury panel how many of them think the defendant is guilty. Anyone raising a hand is immediately excused because, as the judge reminds the rest of the panel, they are to start with the belief that the defendant is innocent until proven otherwise by the state.

It is difficult to know whether or how often judges waver from this belief. Certainly many defense attorneys (and prosecutors, too) can name trial judges in their areas who are "pro defendant" or "tend to credit the police." Such anecdotes contradict our eighth-grade civics view of the judiciary, but it has a place in reality. Trial judges, after all, are people, and many studies show judges have personal attitudes and policy preferences that find their way into their decisions.[155]

In actuality, these tendencies are likely to act at the margins, for no serious scholar of the courts believes that judges fail to root their decisions in case law or statutes. Erroneous convictions are most likely when unintentional or unconscious behavior or slapdash practices unfortunately propel cases forward to conviction. The courts share some of this responsibility, when, for example, trial judges fail to correct racial disparities in jury selection, when they deny motions to suppress for unreliable evidence or testimony, or when they fail to understand the power or limits of scientific evidence.[156]

The courts also may be too solicitous of the state on appeal, to the point that, critics say, the "courts seem more intent on preserving [a] conviction than doing justice."[157] In the Marvin Anderson and Russell Gray cases, judges heard postconviction testimony from the actual perpetrators admitting to the crimes, but in both instances the courts dismissed the confessions as lacking credibility. To be sure, postconviction proceedings are subject to legal standards that are different from those for the original trials. To win his freedom, a convicted defendant must show that no reasonable juror could have voted to convict, whereas at trial he must establish only reasonable doubt in order to escape conviction. Coupled with other evidence that might support a conviction and considering the number of guilty defendants behind bars who baldly claim they are innocent, one can understand why a judge hearing an appeal or a motion for reconsideration or new trial might be skeptical of defense witnesses.

Still, given how often the courts are willing to premise prosecutions and convictions on the self-interested testimony of so-called jailhouse snitches,[158] it is only fair for judges to consider postconviction witnesses with an open mind. In Virginia, the justice system is experimenting with a new writ of actual innocence, but there already is evidence that the court responsible for these cases, the Virginia Court of Appeals, will be highly skeptical of recantations or new confessions unless there is additional evidence to support the defendant's claim.

Perhaps the grandest failure of all is the courts' complicity in a system of indigent defense that ought to be found unconstitutional as a violation of defendants' Sixth Amendment rights. Virginia Chief Justice Leroy Hassell deserves credit for acknowledging the scope of the problem, having requested an additional $25 million from the General Assembly to pay for court-appointed lawyers. The legislators, however, provided only $8 million, which still places Virginia last in the country for compensating court-appointed lawyers. "That is just wrong, wrong, wrong,"[159] Hassell says, and yet his court and their brethren have permitted these systems of funding to continue—an approach that encourages indigent defendants to plead guilty or accept grossly inadequate representation.

The courts have been perfectly willing to step into other arenas where inadequate funding creates inequality. School funding most easily comes to mind, for which courts have found grossly disproportional state funding schemes to be unconstitutional.[160] Yet when the problem sits on their own doorstep, the courts seem to turn a blind eye, accepting a system of indigent defense that offers inadequate attorney and investigative time to many defendants who cannot provide for their own defense. Of course, there is no constitutional right to equal resources in criminal cases, nor should the state be required to provide the Cadillac of attorneys to defendants when a smooth-running Chevy will do. But in states like Virginia, indigent defendants don't even get a rusted-out Yugo. It is simply inconceivable that judges would permit "justice" to be rendered in their courtrooms when the defendants on trial before them are represented by attorneys who are not paid sufficiently to do more than read a case file and appear at trial. Funding systems like that in Virginia ought to be considered a violation of the Sixth Amendment.

Nor is it just the judges. A few years back I appeared at a conference on indigent defense in Virginia, where representatives of the bench, bar, and public-interest groups met to discuss the condition of Virginia's system of appointment and compensation. Everyone present agreed that Virginia's approach was unacceptable, but few seemed willing to take the ultimate step and reject it. The judges were unwilling to declare the system unconstitutional; the state bar was reluctant to issue an opinion declaring the fee caps a breach of professional duty; and private attorneys were loath to reject further court appointments as a sign of protest. Most of those present recognized that criminal adjudication could be ground to a halt if any of the participants were willing to translate words into action and refuse to cooperate with a system of indigent defense that they considered unconscionable. Nonetheless, they continued to support a flawed system.

Their reasons were many. Some were concerned about the effects on indigent defendants if defense attorneys refused to take new cases; others feared contempt citations by judges who would consider the protest a childish stunt. Many spoke about their fear of "throwing the baby out with the bathwater," preferring to "work for change within the system" rather than seeking to turn the criminal justice process on its head. Others, who grounded their views in "realpolitik," noted that many private attorneys, especially the young or inexperienced, needed the court appointments and were willing to accept substandard payments as a way of covering some of their costs while obtaining needed seasoning.

What went largely unsaid that day is that criminal justice reform has little to no constituency in the legislature or the general public unless it promises to reduce crime. Measures that "benefit" criminal defendants—even those that advance fairness and accuracy—are difficult to advance, especially if they have financial costs associated with them. If judges found Virginia's system of indigent defense to be unconstitutional and if lawyers essentially went on strike to protest their participation in a process that does not offer fair opportunity, there might be a great, and potentially more debilitating, backlash from the public and state legislators. Better to make marginal improvements by creating additional public defender offices or raising the fee caps slightly than to risk backsliding on an issue that has little public support. That seemed to be the consensus.

This is certainly an understandable sentiment, and it might even be laudable if there were not constitutional rights at stake. Even in a jurisprudential system that countenances balancing tests between government and citizen, there is little ground for a substandard system of indigent defense other than the desire to keep taxes down. Although we all share such interests—after all, who among us likes to pay taxes—we have obligations as a society to ensure that the least among us get a fair hearing before the power of the state punishes them. This is true when defendants are guilty but even more so when they are innocent. As I routinely ask my undergraduates, how many of us believe we could prove our innocence in a murder case if we were limited to twelve hours of attorney time?[161] The answer, by a show of hands in a lecture hall of more than two hundred students, is less than a dozen. Yet the defenders of our rights, the guardians of the criminal justice system—the courts— have permitted a practice of criminal defense that not only leaves the indigent unprotected but also reduces the accuracy of court proceedings. As the cases investigated by the ICVA indicate, errors can occur when neither side takes the time or, rather, has the time and resources to investigate cases to their logical conclusion.

Chapter 5 takes up these questions in greater depth, considering the trade-off among needed reforms and limited resources and political capital. Not all the recommendations made by the ICVA or presented in this book are of equal priority, nor are most of them likely to be adopted, even in jurisdictions promoting criminal justice reform. Instead, the goal of those who prize accuracy and fairness in the criminal justice process must be to identify which measures are most needed, to advance those that are feasible, and to keep pushing for those that deserve attention but are unlikely to be addressed in the near term. When I criticize the courts (and bar) for failing to stand up to fee caps and other inadequacies of indigent defense, it is not because I think they are wrong to weigh the political costs of dramatic action against potential success. It is because I think their calculus is off. Criminal justice reform must account for political pressures, for public opinion, for costs and interests that resonate outside "the usual suspects" in the reform community. That is why the failure to address many of the inadequacies identified by the ICVA and others is so tragic. People of goodwill from many perspectives can agree on many of the needed reforms.

5

Putting It All Together

The year 2009 will mark two decades since the first DNA exoneration. Over that time we seem to have reached the point at which virtually all the studies of wrongful convictions have come to similar conclusions. Among the most recent reports were those led by Professor Samuel Gross and the law firm of Dickstein, Shapiro, Morin & Oshinsky. Gross and a team of researchers published their findings in 2005, summarizing the sources of error in 328 wrongful convictions between 1989 and 2003.[1] Although most of the innocent people were convicted of minor crimes, the Gross team showed that the majority of exonerations have occurred in murder and rape cases. Nearly 80 percent of rape exonerations were the result of DNA testing, but because biological evidence is typically less often available in murder cases, only about a fifth of the murder exonerations were based on DNA. Interestingly, the study identified eyewitness misidentification—particularly in cross-racial identifications—as a leading cause of mistaken convictions in rape cases. Indeed, even though rapes of white women by black men comprise less than 10 percent of reported rapes, these cases accounted for half the total number of rape exonerations. In murder cases, the Gross study seemed to point at false confessions and perjury as the leading causes of wrongful convictions.

The findings by Gross's research team, though representing excellent research, do not suggest significantly new sources of wrongful convictions, as compared with prior studies. Nor does a 2006 report conducted by the law firm of Dickstein, Shapiro, under the supervision of Maryland's former U.S. senator, Joseph Tydings. Virginians for Alternatives to the Death Penalty (VADP) asked Tydings and his colleagues to compare Virginia's capital justice system with the recommendations of Illinois's Ryan Commission. Despite praising Virginia for "significant strides in some areas," the report concluded that the state had met only thirteen recommendations and had completely failed forty-eight of the Ryan Commission's eighty-five recommendations.[2]

Lest the reader misunderstand, I do not mean to criticize the Gross or VADP reports. Each is important and reflects the dedication of talented scholars and lawyers. But we have reached the point in the research on wrongful convictions in the United States where we have a pretty good idea of the sources of error. To be sure, as Richard Leo might argue, we cannot say why errors lead to conviction in some cases and not others,[3] but there is broad agreement on the deficiencies of the criminal justice system that lead to such serious and regrettable mistakes. With the exception of one source—the use of confidential informants, particularly "jailhouse snitches"—each of these was noted in the ICVA's report, as well as in most other studies of wrongful conviction. They include

- Errors in eyewitness identification.
- High-pressure interrogations, particularly of suspects with mental deficiencies.
- Antiquated forensic testing.
- Inadequate, if not ineffective, assistance of defense counsel.
- Tunnel vision by law enforcement officers or prosecutors, including inadvertent errors and misconduct.
- Failures to disclose exculpatory evidence.
- Testimony by questionable informants.
- The lack of adequate postconviction remedies to address wrongful convictions.

Perhaps we can reexamine the sources of error after more states enact recommended reforms, but we are arguably at the point where we should stop concentrating so many resources on researching the nature of wrongful convictions and instead vigorously address their reform. It's as if we're stuck in Richard Leo's "familiar plot" of wrongful convictions,[4] convinced that if we keep telling the story of innocent men who were erroneously convicted, the recommendations we offer will be enacted by policymakers who recognize the wisdom of our prescriptions. Neither I nor the ICVA is immune from this criticism. Much has been accomplished over the last twenty years to prevent potential wrongful convictions, but the plethora of reports that describe similar findings should be a sign that what we have uncovered goes beyond a single jurisdiction or state. These are systemic deficiencies in the American criminal justice process, weaknesses that warrant a coordinated and strategic effort to address.

Even the recommendations offered by earlier reports are beginning to coalesce around many of the same measures. In 1932 when Yale law professor Edwin Borchard first probed wrongful convictions, he offered two proposals that presaged future measures: courts should not introduce a defendant's confession at trial until it is given before a magistrate and in the presence of witnesses, and independent investigative bodies should review wrongful convictions.[5]

A half century later, Michael Radelet, Hugo Bedau, and Constance Putnam were less optimistic that Borchard's recommendations would prevent wrongful convictions. In their estimation, most erroneous convictions were the result of mistaken eyewitness testimony, unreliable polygraph evidence, sloppy and corrupt police work, and false confessions—problems that were endemic to the criminal justice system and could not be changed without "drastic revision of the rules [of criminal procedure that would] be impossible to enact."[6] As the authors concluded, "Miscarriages of justice in capital (and non-capital) cases will continue. We deceive ourselves if we think otherwise."[7]

Radelet, Bedau, and Putnam seem to be a minority among scholars and advocates who have examined wrongful convictions, for virtually every other individual or group that has examined the issue has offered a litany of recommendations that it believes will prevent mistaken convictions. These include domestic efforts as well as the work of government commissions in the United Kingdom and Canada. Britain's Royal Commission on Criminal Justice has now returned more than "352 recommendations covering a range of activities, including police investigations, safeguards for suspects, the prosecution process, pretrial procedures, the trial process, forensic science, and other expert evidence and the appeals process."[8] Canada's 2001 Manitoba Commission of Inquiry into the case of Thomas Sophonow recommended many of the same measures as did the ICVA, including the electronic recording of both custodial interrogation and eyewitness identification. Interestingly, both the Canadian and British commissions singled out tunnel vision as a serious problem, recommending mandatory entry-level and refresher courses for law enforcement officers.[9]

Closer to home, Barry Scheck and Peter Neufeld, the godfathers of innocence projects, outlined several proposals for reform in their 2001 book (written with Jim Dwyer), most of them echoing the ICVA's conclusions. Among these were postconviction DNA testing, improved practices for eyewitness identification, and the elimination of "junk science," such as hair comparisons, as courtroom evidence.[10]

The Ryan Commission

The most thorough set of recommendations came from Illinois's "Ryan Commission," which in 2002 released a report with eighty-five proposals to reform the system of capital investigations and prosecutions and thus to prevent wrongful convictions. By 2004, the Illinois General Assembly had acted on many of these recommendations, which one of the Ryan Commission's cochairs, Thomas Sullivan, outlined in a separate publication.[11] According to Sullivan, the General Assembly:

- Passed a statute based on the commission's recommendation to require the electronic recording of interrogations of in-custody suspects in homicide cases.
- Adopted the commission's recommendations to improve eyewitness lineup and photo-spread procedures. Witnesses must now be told that the suspect may not be in the array, that they are not obligated to make an identification, and that they should not assume that the administrator of the procedure knows who the suspect is. Law enforcement officers must electronically record lineups and photo spreads when practicable. Without requiring statewide, sequential double-blind procedures, the General Assembly funded a one-year pilot program in three police departments to test the best format for eyewitness identification procedures.
- Endorsed the commission's recommendation that in felony cases, police officers be required to turn over all investigative materials from their files to prosecutors.
- Enacted the commission's proposal that the prosecution be required to disclose to the defense before a capital trial any inducements or promises it made to state witnesses.
- Created a pretrial hearing in capital cases to determine the reliability of any "snitch testimony" offered by the state. As the commission recommended, the burden is on the state to prove the

reliability of the witness's testimony. In addition, the General Assembly precluded capital punishment in cases in which the only evidence of guilt is the uncorroborated evidence of a single witness.

- Passed two of the commission's proposals concerning DNA and other forensic testing. Before trial, courts are now authorized to order a database search comparing the defendant's DNA with the genetic profile of any biological evidence found in the case. Illinois also allows postconviction forensic testing. In cases in which identity was an issue at trial, a court

> may order forensic testing, including DNA comparisons, upon a showing by the defense that the evidence was not subject to testing at the time of trial, has not been altered, and the results have the potential to produce relevant new evidence, even though the results may not completely exonerate the defendant.[12]

Of course, the news is not completely good from Illinois, for the General Assembly and the Illinois Supreme Court have either failed to act or rejected some of the Ryan Commission's recommendations, among which are the following:[13]

- The Illinois Supreme Court did not name the type of exculpatory evidence that prosecutors must disclose to defendants before trial.
- The General Assembly did not establish an independent forensic lab, with civilian personnel, to replace the crime lab operated by the state police.
- The General Assembly did not create pattern jury instructions on the questionable reliability of snitch testimony or the difficulties of cross-racial identifications.
- Illinois requires judges who preside over capital cases to attend a capital litigation seminar once every two years, but the Illinois Supreme Court did not follow the commission's recommendation to establish additional training and certification standards.
- Although the commission's recommendations were directed primarily toward capital cases, the commissioners also encouraged Illinois policymakers to "broaden the application of many of the recommendations" to felony cases as a whole. But "with very few exceptions, this crucial proposal has not been implemented by the Illinois General Assembly, the Illinois Supreme Court or lower

courts, the Administrative Office of the Illinois Courts, or Illinois law enforcement agencies."[14]

In December 2004, the Justice Management Institute, in collaboration with a number of nonprofit organizations and with funding from the Open Society Institute, convened a workshop in Chapel Hill, North Carolina, entitled "Ensuring a Reliable and Effective Criminal Justice System." In a novel twist, the workshop hosted teams of judges, prosecutors, defense attorneys, law enforcement officials, and academicians from several states to brainstorm and create "action plans" to advance criminal justice reform in their respective states. I was fortunate to attend this workshop and commend the organizers for casting a wide net when creating state teams and envisioning the necessary participants in reform efforts. Interestingly, many of the solutions that flowed from the workshop echoed recommendations made by earlier groups, generally falling into one of the following five categories:

- Address mistaken eyewitness identification by electronically recording identification procedures, using double-blind methods, following the sequential technique, recording the witness's confidence, and avoiding any suggestions about suspects in a lineup.
- Replace "junk" or sloppy forensic techniques, such as hair comparison, with independent DNA testing conducted both promptly after a crime and also after conviction when there are reasonable questions about a defendant's innocence.
- Use open files discovery, electronically record custodial interrogation, and provide additional training to reduce misconduct or inadvertent mistakes by police or prosecutors.
- Limit the admissibility of testimony by jailhouse snitches.
- Mitigate poor defense lawyering with smaller caseloads, better funding, greater availability of investigators, additional training, and higher performance standards.

The American Bar Association (ABA)

The American Bar Association has made these issues a priority as well. Over a three-year period, the ABA's House of Delegates adopted several resolutions endorsing many of the same measures recommended by the

Ryan Commission, the ICVA, and other individuals and organizations involved in criminal justice reform. Indeed, the ABA has been one of the nation's leaders in urging better resources and performance standards for indigent defense. In addition to urging jurisdictions to "identify and attempt to eliminate the causes of wrongful conviction," the ABA—under the leadership of its Criminal Justice Section's Ad Hoc Innocence Committee—has called attention and sought solutions to eight problems identified in the criminal justice system:[15]

- False confessions
- Eyewitness identification procedures
- Shoddy forensic evidence
- Jailhouse informants
- Inadequate defense counsel
- Misconduct by investigative personnel
- Prosecutorial discretion
- Compensation for the wrongly convicted

The first six issues—and the ensuing recommendations—should be familiar to anyone who has reviewed the reports of the Ryan Commission or the ICVA, or who has read the several journal articles and books on wrongful convictions. The last two are mentioned in this literature, but perhaps not as often as the other sources are. In singling out prosecutors, the ABA has sought reasonable workloads and additional training for prosecutors while also urging prosecutors to remind law enforcement officers to turn over all available evidence to the state's lawyers. In turn, the ABA has called for the preservation of evidence by prosecutors for a reasonable time after conviction. Like the Ryan Commission, the ABA has recommended that prosecutors' offices create internal procedures to review cases based on eyewitness testimony, confessions, or confidential informants, to ensure that the evidence presented at a trial is reasonably reliable.

In addressing compensation for the wrongly convicted, the ABA has moved from simply preventing error to addressing the consequences of those tragic mistakes for the innocent who have been exonerated. Other groups have taken up this call to help with "life after exoneration." Indeed, there now exists an organization called the Life after Exoneration Program, which is advised by many of the same individuals involved with the Innocence Project.[16] In his 2004 State of the Union address,

President George W. Bush touched on the issue of prisoner reentry, proposing a "four-year, $300 million initiative to reduce recidivism and the societal costs of reincarceration by helping inmates find work when they return to their communities."[17] If assisting the convicted to reenter society is a national priority, then aiding the innocent must be even more important. Unfortunately, however, the issue did not generate much interest until the last few years. In fact, as of 2006, thirty-one states did not have compensation statutes to reimburse the exonerated and atone for the time that they were forced to spend in prison.[18]

Consensus of Top Recommendations

With so many reports centered on similar recommendations, it may be difficult to decide where to begin in enacting reform. In general, two issues have received the greatest emphasis. Perhaps the most popular has been electronically recording custodial interrogations, a top priority of Northwestern University's Center on Wrongful Convictions[19] and an issue ably championed by the cochair of the Ryan Commission, Thomas Sullivan. In a 2005 issue of the *Journal of Criminal Law and Criminology*, Sullivan reported on research by his colleagues at the law firm of Jenner and Block, which found that more than three hundred police and sheriff's departments in forty-three states, along with all the departments in Alaska and Minnesota, record full custodial interviews in various kinds of felonies, and most important, they all "enthusiastically support this practice."[20]

For Sullivan, the crucial issue is how a state institutes electronic recording. His preference is statewide legislation, because it is "more comprehensive."[21] But there is a risk that law enforcement officers and prosecutors may believe the practice is being "rammed down [their] throats,"[22] even if they ultimately conclude that electronic recording is useful. As discussed later in this chapter, a more acceptable and incremental approach may be to convince individual police departments to adopt electronic recording as a "best practice." In April 2006, for example, the Detroit Police Department agreed to videotape interrogations of all suspects in crimes punishable by life in prison without parole. The decision was part of a settlement in a civil suit brought by the family of a mentally ill man who spent seventeen years in prison after confessing to a rape and murder he did not commit. Detroit's police chief cited electronic recording as a mechanism to help reform a department that was already operating under two consent decrees with the U.S. Justice Department for other abuses.[23]

If electronic recording has the most enthusiastic supporters, eyewitness identification reforms have seen the most print, including, not inconsequentially, a report from the North Carolina Actual Innocence Commission, which focused its initial attention on the likely causes and best practices to prevent mistaken eyewitness identification.[24] At least four improvements generate universal agreement from reformers:[25]

- Double-blind procedures.
- Instructing witnesses that the actual perpetrator may or may not be present in the lineup or array.
- Selecting fillers who closely match the suspect.
- Gauging the witness's confidence immediately after an identification and before later feedback clouds the person's memory.

When the National Institute of Justice released its training manual for eyewitness evidence in 1999, the agency concluded that there was "not a consensus" to recommend sequential over simultaneous lineups.[26] Since that time, the debate has continued. Although the majority of research on eyewitness identification and most of the reports on wrongful convictions recommend sequential procedures, there is a

> dissenting view among some well-respected social scientists that the research has not proceeded far enough to determine under what conditions, if any, a sequential line up is to be preferred to a simultaneous line up. . . . These dissenters do not argue that simultaneous line ups are the preferred method, and some seem to believe that sequential line ups will eventually be proven superior in many circumstances. Nevertheless, their current view, if accepted, suggests that the scientific evidence is insufficient to choose one method over another; therefore, either might do.[27]

The debate has only intensified with the release of new reports on the experience of differing identification methods. In 2006, a study from the Chicago Police Department concluded that sequential identification procedures had a higher error rate and led to fewer identifications as a whole than did simultaneous lineups. The Chicago report was presented at a conference at Loyola Law School and cast "a cloud over the

sequential system."[28] Subsequent analysis of the study protocol, however, revealed that it was not double-blind (because officers who knew
the "correct" suspect were in the room for simultaneous but not sequential lineups) and thus had not properly controlled for the possibility that officers administering the identification procedures might have
influenced the witnesses' recognition.[29] Nonetheless, the report's very
existence may "retard the [sequential] system throughout the country
until this gets sorted out."[30]

Sequential identification procedures got a boost more recently when
Hennepin County, Minnesota, released the results of its own experience
with identification procedures. Hennepin County, of course, includes
Minneapolis and has a distinguished history of evaluative research of
its criminal justice system. Hennepin's study confirmed what earlier research had suggested—that double-blind sequential identification procedures lead to fewer errors than do simultaneous methods.[31]

The ICVA recommended double-blind sequential identification methods, and this book does as well. Nevertheless, this may be one area in
which reformers do not have a sufficiently broad consensus to justify
expending their political capital pushing one approach over the other.
Instead, as some have suggested, reform might focus on those improvements that have broad agreement and support, "reducing pressure on
witnesses by advising them that they do not have to pick someone;
making sure that 'fillers' strongly resemble the suspect; and recording
what the witness says upon choosing a suspect, so juries can hear how
certain they were about a pick."[32] Relying on simultaneous methods
may be, in a sense, a "cop-out"—permitting officers to avoid change
under the pretense that the research for sequential procedures is not yet
sufficient—but if reform depends on broad-based support, then the
switch to sequential methods may need to wait until other improvements are enacted first.

Subsequent Developments in Virginia

Virginia has continued to make progress since the release of the ICVA's
report, although it has been far from a straight line forward. In 2005, as
the ICVA was finishing its deliberations, the Virginia State Crime Commission (VSCC) issued a report on mistaken eyewitness identification.
The VSCC's report was based on a combination of literature review,

legal research, training materials, surveys of law enforcement agencies, and site visits. All in all, it was a thorough report, with the VSCC making four central recommendations:[33]

- Amend the Code of Virginia to require local police and sheriff's departments to have a written policy for conducting in-person and photographic lineups.
- Request the Department of Criminal Justice Services (DCJS) and the Virginia State Crime Commission to establish a work group to develop a model policy for conducting in-person and photographic lineups.
- Request the DCJS to amend the entry-level and in-service criminal justice academy requirements to train only for the sequential method in lineups. Include this standard as part of the accreditation process for law enforcement agencies, and present this information to annual meetings of the Virginia Sheriffs' Association and the Virginia Chiefs of Police Association.
- Amend the Code of Virginia to designate the Virginia State Police, through the Central Criminal Records Exchange, as a repository for all mug shots and queries for photographic lineups.

In July 2005, the DCJS issued a sample order on suspect lineup procedures for police departments and sheriff's offices in Virginia. [34] The sample order, which appears in appendix 3, incorporates many of the recommendations found in the National Institute of Justice's 1999 report, *Eyewitness Evidence: A Guide for Law Enforcement*,[35] and, in fact, goes beyond those measures by recommending sequential over simultaneous procedures. However, the DCJS's sample order does not explicitly call for double-blind procedures, which the Chicago Police Department's study shows are imperative if eyewitness identification procedures are to be accurate. Moreover, the sample order, albeit a significant step forward, is only a model measure and has not been required by the General Assembly.

21-Day Rule

On May 21, 2004, Governor Mark Warner signed an amendment to Virginia's "21-day Rule," making the writ of actual innocence available to inmates who have both biological and nonbiological evidence of innocence.[36] But as of late 2006, no one had yet won a new trial or freedom based on the writ. The most promising case appeared to be that of Aleck Carpitcher, who in 1999 was convicted of molesting an eleven-year-old girl solely on the basis of her testimony. Nine months later the girl recanted, explaining that she had been jealous because Carpitcher spent so much time with her mother.

Carpitcher filed a writ of actual innocence with the Virginia Court of Appeals, but in January 2006 the court rejected his claim, concluding that recanted testimony is "insufficient to reverse his conviction." Although a Roanoke County judge already had deemed the girl "no longer credible," the court of appeals ruled that there "must be clear and convincing proof that the witness testified falsely at trial, and not merely proof that by reason of conflicting statements [the] testimony is unworthy of belief." [37]

The court's ruling helped clarify the extent of the writ of actual innocence. Although recanted testimony is acceptable evidence under the writ, some legislators argued that it should not be admitted. "Post-trial changes in testimony are dubious, they said, because witnesses are often influenced to recant by those loyal to the defendant or by their own feelings of guilt." This reasoning was accepted by the court of appeals, which viewed recanted testimony "with suspicion" because of the "obvious . . . opportunity and temptation for fraud."[38]

The appellate court's decision was upheld by the Supreme Court of Virginia in March 2007, which ruled that recanted testimony is not sufficient evidence to establish the writ of actual innocence. As a result, Carpitcher, who was convicted "based on a witness who has recanted her testimony," is going to spend most of his life in prison. As law professor Darryl Brown explained, "The bottom line is [that this case] shuts down exonerations for defendants in Virginia who don't have DNA evidence." If the writ of actual innocence will have any teeth, its power will be limited to those few cases in which a defendant has new biological evidence that establishes his innocence.[39]

The Case of Roger Coleman

Aleck Carpitcher's case is one of two from Virginia that disappointed reformers, although in the second case, activists received the cooperation they sought from the Commonwealth only to be surprised by the forensic results. With the state abuzz over the number of DNA exonerations in the last decade, death penalty foes had petitioned Governor Mark Warner to retest the biological evidence in the case of a man already executed in Virginia. The convicted defendant, Roger Coleman, had gone to his death uttering a seemingly immortal warning: "An innocent man is going to be murdered tonight."[40]

Coleman had received legal assistance from Centurion Ministries, a nonprofit group dedicated to "vindicat[ing] and free[ing] from prison those who are completely innocent of the crimes for which they have been unjustly convicted and imprisoned for life or death."[41] Jim McCloskey, the Centurion Ministries' executive director, had promised Coleman that he would continue fighting to clear the condemned man's name. Finally, in the waning days of his administration, Mark Warner became the first governor nationwide to order postexecution DNA testing. An earlier test in 1990 had placed Coleman "within two percent of the population that could have committed" the rape and murder of his sister-in-law,[42] but newer technology would be able to pinpoint Coleman's connection to the crime, or, as many of his supporters expected, exonerate Coleman posthumously.

On January 12, 2006, the test came back confirming Coleman's guilt. In a report by the Canadian Centre of Forensic Sciences, laboratory officials estimated "the odds that someone other than Coleman could have left the DNA 'fingerprint' [at the crime scene] to be 1 in 19 million."[43] To his credit, Jim McCloskey did not shrink from the conclusions. In a media release, McCloskey acknowledged that "Roger Coleman is the killer of [his sister-in-law]. We now know that Roger's proclamations of innocence, even as he sat strapped in the electric chair moments before his death, were false." McCloskey continued:

> Those of us who seek the truth in criminal justice cases must never be afraid of finding it. If there is a means to discover the truth, we must never shrink or shy away from using it in our search. We must never stop the hard effort to touch the factual bottom of any case. The Truth can be very elusive, and even illusory. Our search for facts can delude us into thinking that what we have found is gold, only to discover that it is in fact fool's gold. But once the gold of absolute truth is revealed, we must embrace it, and be thankful that we have finally uncovered it.[44]

The Case of Robin Lovitt

If the Coleman case disappointed or even embarrassed death penalty foes, the case of Robin Lovitt helped forge an unusual coalition of advocates to commute the death sentence of a Virginian convicted of murder. In 1998, Robin Lovitt was convicted of stabbing to death the manager of a pool hall in Arlington. Lovitt admitted that he had stolen from the pool hall's cash register, but he denied killing the victim. But Lovitt lost the chance to prove his innocence when a court clerk erroneously destroyed most of the evidence in his case, including the murder weapon—a pair of scissors—that Lovitt had hoped to test with advanced forensic technology.[45]

Lovitt's case drew a wide assortment of supporters, including former solicitor general Ken Starr, who served as Lovitt's pro bono appellate counsel; the former Virginia attorney general Mark Early, a pro-death-penalty Republican who lost to Governor Warner in 2001 and now directs the Prison Fellowship; as well as many groups that oppose the death penalty. Although the coalition was unsuccessful in winning Lovitt relief in court, on November 28, 2005, Governor Warner commuted Lovitt's sentence to life without parole. Warner, who acted on the eve of Lovitt's scheduled execution, declared that the "Commonwealth must ensure that every time this ultimate sanction is carried out, it is done fairly." Early concurred with his former political opponent, saying, "To have executed [Lovitt] would have undermined the death penalty in Virginia."[46]

Earl Washington Jr.'s Civil Suit

The Warner administration advanced another step when in Earl Washington's civil suit for erroneous conviction and imprisonment, the defense stipulated that Washington was factually innocent. Although the defendant, a deceased police officer, had been sued in his individual capacity, the Commonwealth helped secure counsel for his estate and paid for the representation. It was no small matter, then, for the defense to declare what others had believed for years but that some justice officials had refused to acknowledge—that Washington had been wrongly convicted. Years earlier, additional DNA testing had cleared Washington of the rape of the young mother and had even identified a different inmate, Kenneth Tinsley, as the likely perpetrator, but some high-ranking officials in Culpeper County (where the case was tried) "still believe Washington was involved."[47] In fact, in a 2004 interview, the husband of the slain woman says he has "learned the most . . . from Washington's lawyer," claiming that Culpeper authorities have stonewalled him.[48] To date, Virginia authorities have yet to charge Tinsley with the rape or murder, even though state officials "reopened the investigation" in 2000.[49]

Washington ultimately prevailed in the civil suit when a federal jury in May 2006 determined that the state police officer who recorded Washington's false confession "deliberately fabricated" evidence against him that led to the wrongful conviction.[50] The jury of eight whites and one black awarded Washington $2.25 million in damages for his time on death row, the largest civil rights verdict in Virginia's history.[51]

Ironically, the *Virginian-Pilot* observed, "Virginia could have saved itself a bundle of grief if lawmakers had granted Washington's initial request for $1 million in compensation in 2003. His attorneys filed the civil suit after a legislative panel gave him nothing, in part because his attack on an elderly neighbor set events in motion." The newspaper's editorial board urged the Commonwealth to "give up" an appeal in Washington's civil suit to avoid "more embarrassment and more wasted dollars" in a case that showed the need for further reform in Virginia's criminal justice system.[52] The Commonwealth eventually took that advice, agreeing in March 2007 to settle Washington's case for $1.9 million and formally acknowledge what many had known for years—that serious errors had been made in this case.[53]

Arthur Lee Whitfield Case

At the same time, the Commonwealth has found itself on the opposite side of a victim who continues to claim that Arthur Lee Whitfield raped her in 1981, despite forensic evidence suggesting that a different man, Aaron Doxie III, was the perpetrator. The victim contends that the state lab commingled and misidentified evidence from her case with that of Whitfield's other victim. In 2005, she sent a fifteen-page letter to Governor Warner opposing Whitfield's application for a full pardon, declaring that she is certain she correctly identified Whitfield.

In response, Dr. Paul Ferrara of VDFS said the mix-up has been "checked and double-checked' and discounted."[54] John R. Doyle III, the Commonwealth's attorney who recommended Whitfield's release after DNA testing cleared him and pointed to Doxie, also stands by his decision. "My heart goes out to" the victim, says Doyle. "She is 1,000 percent sincere in what she's said then and now. . . . [However, b]ased on the evidence before me, the case would not now come to trial."[55] The victim remains resolute in part because she recalls her attacker as having green or hazel eyes, as Whitfield has, whereas Doxie has brown eyes. Both she and the other victim say their perpetrator was not circumcised—and Whitfield is not—whereas Doxie is circumcised.[56]

Governor Warner failed to act on Whitfield's pardon application before his term expired, leaving the matter for Governor Tim Kaine to consider. Kaine has not yet decided on Whitfield's case, but in an interesting twist, the matter rests on Kaine's desk because of an unusual decision by the Virginia Supreme Court that limits the court's jurisdiction over claims of actual innocence. In October 2005, the high court ruled against Whitfield's application for a writ of actual innocence, concluding that its authority to declare actual innocence based on biological evidence applies only to cases in which the petitioner is incarcerated. Since Whitfield had already been released from prison on parole, the court said that it could not rule on his petition and dismissed his case.[57] The court's decision represents a "catch-22" for some exonerated defendants and, in the words of two dissenting justices, "subverts the legislative intent of the statute and renders the provisions as applied absurd."[58] Although Whitfield has been on parole since DNA testing cleared him in 2004, his only means of restoring his name and full legal rights is a gubernatorial pardon.

Audit of the State Crime Lab

The combined effect of the Whitfield and Washington cases has set into motion a number of reforms involving forensic evidence. In September 2004, following several exonerations based on biological evidence kept by serologist Mary Jane Burton, Governor Warner ordered the Virginia Department of Forensic Science (VDFS)—the state's crime lab—to test 10 percent of the old case files that contained biological evidence. Thirty-one cases were tested, resulting in the exoneration of two additional men who had since completed their sentences for rape. Warner pardoned both of them, Willie Davidson, who had been convicted in Norfolk, and Phillip Thurman, wrongly convicted in Alexandria.

The two additional exonerations prompted Warner to order lab officials to review all remaining old case files and, "where appropriate," to test any biological evidence found that had not been previously subjected to DNA examination. According to Dr. Paul Ferrara, director of VDFS, the lab "holds 660 boxes containing about 165,000 such files from 1974 to 1988." From these there could be more than 300 cases for testing.[59] As of the writing of this book, the testing has been ongoing, and results should be forthcoming.

At the same time that he directed retesting of biological evidence, Governor Warner also ordered a broad review of the VDFS after a separate audit "found crucial mistakes in the lab's work in the [Earl] Washington case."[60] The earlier investigation was conducted by the American Society of Crime Laboratory Directors Laboratory Accreditation Board (ASCLD), which in addition to scolding the VDFS's analyst, Jeffrey Ban, for inaccurate findings also criticized "pressures from outside the laboratory and excessive managerial influence from within the laboratory" that may have influenced the inaccurate reports.[61]

As a check on the lab's quality management, the ASCLD recommended a "thorough examination of a minimum of 50 cases in the Virginia system dealing with low level DNA . . . to determine whether process errors occurred and whether conclusions are scientifically supported."[62] Governor Warner appointed Virginia appellate judge Robert Humphreys as the "special master" to lead that inquiry, which was conducted by five DNA experts. The team reviewed 123 cases, concluding that the "testing methods employed by [the VDFS] contain no endemic deficiencies" and that the VDFS had "consistently conducted its low-level DNA testing within the boundaries of established and scientifically accepted practice."[63] Although the team disagreed with "an interpretive conclusion with respect to one of the items analyzed" in a capital case, the outside reviewers did not believe it "substantially affected the integrity of the" scientific conclusion in the matter or the defendant's guilt.[64]

According to Governor Warner, the results of the several audits reaffirmed the reputation and integrity of the VDFS, which "has an international reputation in fighting crime."[65] Others, however, saw the situation as mixed. All five experts assigned to the review came from other

crime labs rather than reflecting a mix of academicians and practitioners; moreover, they spent three months examining more than one hundred cases, whereas the earlier ASCLD review of the Washington case
lasted seven months. Perhaps most confusing is that the five-person
panel issued a series of recommendations to improve quality management at the VDFS lab when its report did not seem to mention such
problems.

In any case, the Virginia Department of Forensic Science has undergone one of the most intensive reviews of a state crime lab that was
not accused of intentional error. Before he left office, Governor Warner
appointed thirteen scientists to a permanent scientific advisory committee created by the General Assembly to oversee the VDFS. The team
includes "a cross-section of academics as well as crime lab officials
from other states, federal agencies, and the military" and has been
praised by observers as including qualified "people without an [ideolog-
ical] agenda."[66] Although there remains some confusion on the advisory
board about the extent of the members' mandate—whether they are to
advise the lab's director or serve as watchdogs—Virginia has nonetheless been on the forefront of reform, making it only the second state in
the country after New York to create a scientific review panel for the
crime lab.[67]

The Indigent Defense Commission

As explained in chapter 1, the Virginia General Assembly created the
Indigent Defense Commission (VAIDC) in 2004 to provide oversight
and certification of attorneys who represent indigent defendants in the
Commonwealth. Beginning on July 1, 2005, all attorneys who wish to
represent Virginia defendants through court appointments must be certified and included on the VAIDC's list of qualified attorneys. The certification process takes account of a lawyer's background, experience,
and training.[68] For example, felony counsel must complete six hours of
continuing legal education developed by the VAIDC and demonstrate
that they have been either the lead or a co-counsel in four earlier felony
cases. Capital counsel must demonstrate even higher qualifications, including experience as a co-counsel on the defense of at least two capital
cases over the past seven years.[69]

As useful as these measures undoubtedly are, the VAIDC and Virginia's indigent defense system continue to receive serious criticism. In 2004, the Virginia State Bar adopted the American Bar Association's ten principles for a public defense delivery system,[70] which demand lower caseloads for public defenders, parity in resources and salaries between prosecutors and public defenders, and the abolishment of fee caps on the private bar.[71] Change has been slow. As Joanmarie Davoli, a former public defender for Fairfax County—one of Virginia's largest and most prosperous communities—has said, accepting "cases on a court appointed basis . . . in Virginia is tantamount to providing pro bono services."[72] Nor does the VAIDC fare better in her eyes, as she called the organization "a bloated bureaucracy" that "grossly underpay[s] current employees and under-staff[s] existing offices."[73] Even Robert Humphreys, a former Commonwealth's attorney for Virginia Beach and now a judge on the Virginia Court of Appeals, admitted that it is "imperative that . . . at some point both an enlightened governor and General Assembly . . . recognize and honor their moral and constitutional responsibility [to raise the fee caps], or the criminal justice system in Virginia will grind to a halt from a dearth of lawyers willing to take court appointments."[74] As this book was going to press, there were signs that the Virginia General Assembly was prepared to raise rates for indigent attorneys and even give judges the authority to waive fee caps in particular cases. If these changes come to pass, it will be a welcome and needed step forward for Virginia's criminal justice system. As others, most notably Virginia State Senator Ken Stolle, have said for years, the fee caps are "an embarrassment to Virginia."[75]

Subsequent Developments Elsewhere

Next to Virginia, California and Wisconsin have seen the greatest amount of activity surrounding wrongful convictions and legal reform.

California

In 2004, the leader of the California senate, John Burton, succeeded in establishing the California Commission on the Fair Administration of Justice (CCFAJ). Concerned that "a number of people have been exonerated and released from prison after serving several years in prison" and recognizing that California statute now "allows convicted persons to obtain DNA testing after their conviction," the California General Assembly established the CCFAJ to examine whether California's criminal justice "process has failed in the past, resulting in wrongful executions or the wrongful conviction of innocent persons." The CCFAJ's organizing statute gives the commission until December 2007 to "make any recommendations and proposals designed to further ensure that the application and administration of criminal justice in California is just, fair, and accurate."[76]

California's Senate Committee on Rules has appointed twenty-four members to the CCAJ, including district attorneys, police chiefs, judges, professors, and the attorney general of California. Perhaps aware that the December 2007 deadline is approaching, the CCAJ has been quite active, investigating problems identified in existing practices of eyewitness identification and interrogation and subsequently intending to address "jailhouse informant testimony, forensic evidence, prosecutorial misconduct, defense lawyer incompetence, and the administration of the death penalty."[77] The CCAJ's initial recommendations drew a favorable response from the state legislature. In September 2006, the General Assembly approved the CCAJ's proposals to require audiotaping during custodial interrogations of suspects in violent felonies and to set new guidelines for eyewitness identification procedures.[78]

Unfortunately, these measures were vetoed by California Governor Arnold Schwarzenegger and not overridden by the General Assembly. Whether they will eventually be passed remains in doubt at this writing. In refusing to sign the electronic recording bill, Schwarzenegger noted that the legislation defined "custodial interrogations" differently than does the U.S. Supreme Court for the issuance of "Miranda warnings."[79] He also worried that the bill did not appropriately define when an individual was "suspected" of a crime. But it was Schwarzenegger's reasoning that was suspect, for as CCAJ Chairman John Van de Kamp noted, the "only difference between 'custodial interrogation' as defined in" the legislation and the *Miranda* case "was that [the bill] was limited to interrogation 'conducted at a place of detention,' thus narrowing the applicability of the bill."[80]

Schwarzenegger's veto message regarding eyewitness identification was even more curious. The CCAJ considered but rejected an earlier proposal that would have set binding rules for police agencies. Instead, the CCAJ's proposal—and the General Assembly's bill—would have called on the attorney general to form a task force to draft statewide police guidelines for eyewitness identification procedures, taking into account the CCAJ's findings. Governor Schwarzenegger's veto, however, was premised on the fact that the bill "circumvent[ed] the legislative process" by permitting executive agencies to set "statewide policy that could have a life-altering impact on an individual participating in our justice system."[81] Presumably, then, Schwarzenegger would have been comfortable with the CCAJ's original proposal. Only time will tell whether the CCAJ's recommendations are again raised, let alone adopted, in California.

As the CCAJ was in high gear, one of the state's most respected newspapers, the *San Jose Mercury News,* went public with the results of a three-year investigation into Santa Clara County's criminal justice system. Dubbed by some an "exposé," the newspaper's multipart series painted a worrisome portrait of criminal justice in one of the state's wealthiest jurisdictions. Reporters from the *Mercury News* reviewed the records of 727 criminal jury trial appeals decided by California's Sixth District Court of Appeal. The paper also uncovered about two hundred cases of "questionable conduct" that were not part of the study period but that reporters had learned about when reviewing files and interviewing lawyers.[82] From this research the paper reached several shocking conclusions:

- In more than one in every three cases, trials were marred by "questionable conduct that worked against the defendant," but in only 5 percent of the cases did the defendant receive a new trial or a reduced sentence from the appellate court.
- In one hundred of the 727 cases, prosecutors withheld evidence that could have helped defendants. Some prosecutors defied judge's orders, while others misled jurors during closing arguments.
- In 100 of the 727 cases, defense attorneys were deficient. In nearly fifty cases, the attorneys failed at the most basic functions, from properly investigating a case to presenting it adequately.
- In more than 150 cases, judges made questionable rulings that favored the prosecution or failed to properly instruct jurors on the law.
- In more than one hundred cases, the appellate court concluded there was error but refused to overturn the verdict. In fifty of these cases, outside experts engaged by the newspaper said that the court had misstated facts or used questionable reasoning.[83]

As scandalous as the *Mercury News*'s findings may appear, there are reasons to question the extent of the problems identified in the series. At times the paper seemed to conflate conformity to existing legal doctrine that the reporters found lacking (for example, the "harmless error" standard) with deliberate judicial malfeasance. Nor is it clear why readers should trust the reporters' or their experts' legal judgment—on admittedly fluid questions—over that of the county's judges. Finally, Santa Clara County is hardly the worst among California's prosecutors' offices and court systems in handling criminal cases. But that may well be the point of the *Mercury News*'s series. Even the criminal justice system of one of California's most prosperous and respected counties has serious deficiencies. Certainly, the CCAJ's work and findings suggest that more needs to be done to improve California's criminal justice process.

Wisconsin

California (and the nation) might well take a lesson from Wisconsin, which has made considerable progress in improving its criminal justice system. The state was initially shocked in 2003 when DNA evidence exonerated Steven Avery, a man who had served eighteen years in prison for a rape conviction based on the testimony of a single eyewitness and microscopic hair comparison. In response, Representative Mark Gundrum, the Republican chair of the Wisconsin Assembly Judiciary Committee, created the "Avery task force," inviting twenty individuals, including legislators, judges, law enforcement officers, prosecutors, defense attorneys, and a victim's advocate, to participate in an informal body to consider reforms to prevent wrongful convictions.[84]

The task force's work came as the Wisconsin Supreme Court issued a landmark decision requiring that interrogations of juveniles in detention facilities be electronically recorded.[85] The timing of the court's ruling, combined with revelations from Avery's exoneration, helped spur reform, and in 2005 the Wisconsin General Assembly adopted many of the proposals issued by the Avery task force and introduced as legislation by Representative Gundrum. Gundrum's bill had four notable features. First, it codified the Wisconsin Supreme Court's holding on juvenile interrogations and also made electronic recording for adults a statewide policy.[86] Second, it required each law enforcement agency in the state to adopt written policies to reduce the risk of eyewitness error, a requirement underscored by the state attorney general's promulgation in March 2005 of a model policy and procedure for eyewitness identification.[87] Third, the legislation offered new procedures for retaining DNA evidence. Finally, it prioritized DNA testing in postconviction cases and provided additional funding so that labs could meet this requirement.[88]

The success of the Avery task force persuaded four notable legal entities in the state to create the Wisconsin Criminal Justice Study Commission (WCJSC). In August 2005, the University of Wisconsin Law School joined Marquette University Law School, the State Bar of Wisconsin, and the Wisconsin Attorney General's Office to establish the WCJSC. Recognizing that "the Commission's sponsors are responsible for educating criminal justice professionals," the four institutions assembled a body of twenty-seven persons from across the justice community to explore "issues raised by wrongful convictions."[89] The WCJSC's charter statement envisioned three to five meetings per year over a three-year period. As of late 2006, the WCJSC had already met five times, and its members were considering a proposal to limit the admissibility of interrogations obtained by deception. Future meetings are likely to take up such issues as "junk science" and jailhouse snitch testimony, although it is unclear whether the WCJSC will push to enact new legislation and policy or will be content to raise issues for consideration, as study commissions do. For that matter, Wisconsin's attorney general, who had been a prime sponsor of the WCJSC, was defeated in the 2006 election, and it is too early to say how her successor will approach the study commission.

North Carolina

In the fall of 2006, North Carolina made news by creating the Innocence Inquiry Commission (NCIIC). Signed into law by the Democratic governor, Mike Easley, the eight-member panel will be "made up of a judge, a prosecutor, a defense lawyer, a sheriff, a crime victim advocate, and others." [90] The NCIIC pulls a page from the United Kingdom's Criminal Cases Review Commission, which has the ability "to review suspected miscarriages of justice and decide if they should be referred to an appeal court."[91] Similarly, the NCIIC will have "legal authority to recommend that the courts review specific cases" for wrongful convictions.[92] This power makes the NCIIC a first in the United States. Unlike other state innocence bodies, which generally "recommend changes in laws or procedures . . . to prevent future wrongful convictions," the NCIIC will "look into claims of actual innocence" and, if convinced "that a convicted offender has produced new and sufficient evidence of actual innocence," will forward the case to North Carolina's chief justice.[93] The chief will then appoint a three-judge panel to reconsider the matter, the judges empowered to "overturn the conviction if [they] unanimously find clear and convincing evidence that the defendant is innocent of the charges."[94]

The NCIIC is designed to start slowly, as a statute limits the commission's jurisdiction in its first two years to cases in which the defendant pleaded not guilty. After that, the NCIIC may hear cases from defendants who pleaded guilty or *nolo contendere.* If the North Carolina legislature does not reauthorize the NCIIC, it will disband after four years.[95]

The North Carolina Innocence Inquiry Commission is a significant step forward in the systemic consideration and reversal of wrongful convictions, in much the same way as Virginia adopted a writ of actual innocence. Presuming that the North Carolina Actual Innocence Commission (NCAIC) continues as well, North Carolina will have a two-pronged strategy to prevent wrongful convictions through the NCAIC while correcting any erroneous convictions with the NCIIC. Once again, credit goes to former North Carolina chief justice I. Beverly Lake Jr., whose efforts in creating the NCAIC also led to the NCIIC. Governor Easley, too, deserves praise for recognizing North Carolinians' collective interests in preventing and reversing wrongful convictions. "As a state prosecutor for more than 15 years, I know law enforcement's greatest nightmare is to have an innocent person in jail or death row," the governor explained when signing the legislation. "We should continue to ensure that we have the ultimate fairness in the review of our cases . . . [to] ensure that the people in our prisons in fact belong there."[96]

The Federal Level

Although most of the progress in reform has taken place in the states, Congress stepped up to the plate in 2004 when it passed the "Justice for All Act." After considerable lobbying and involvement by outside groups,[97] legislators passed a large package that responded to the calls of both victims and advocates for the wrongly convicted. The statute gives new rights to victims, including the opportunity to be heard at sentencing and release hearings, and a companion section, entitled the "Innocence Protection Act" (IPA), establishes mechanisms and funding for postconviction DNA testing.[98] These latter provisions are extraordinary, recognizing that federal defendants can be, and are, convicted of crimes they did not commit. Under the IPA, a federal inmate may apply for postconviction DNA testing under the following terms:

- He must assert in an affidavit that he is innocent.
- The evidence to be tested may not have been previously tested, although testing using newer and more reliable methods may be requested.
- Testing must be likely to produce new evidence that raises a reasonable probability that the defendant did not commit the offense.
- The inmate must file an application for testing within three years of conviction unless he can show good cause for failing to apply earlier.

The IPA permits the courts to appoint counsel for indigent defendants seeking postconviction testing, and in fact, Congress authorized $25 million over five years to help the states cover the cost of DNA testing. Grants may be made to states under the IPA to improve capital prosecution and defense services, and $755 million has been set aside to help crime labs reduce the backlog in DNA testing. Finally, the IPA increases the amount of compensation to the wrongly convicted. Whereas federal defendants used to receive a flat fee of $5,000 for each year of wrongful imprisonment, that figure has risen to $50,000 a year for noncapital and $100,000 a year for capital erroneous convictions.[99]

Looking to the Future: A Different Agenda for Reform

Remarkably, the IPA was a bipartisan effort to reform and improve the federal and state criminal justice systems. The legislation was jointly sponsored by Representatives James Sensenbrenner (R-WI) and William Delahunt (D-MA), respectively chairman and a member of the House Judiciary Committee, and was passed through the joint efforts of Senators Oren Hatch (R-UT) and Patrick Leahy (D-VT), then chairman and ranking member of the Senate Judiciary Committee. President George W. Bush signed the IPA into law on October 30, 2004.[100]

It may seem odd that political conservatives would join to pass legislation that gives more rights to convicted defendants. To be sure, the path of the IPA to passage was not easy, and the adoption of some of its components may be explained by its coupling with other elements of the Justice for All Act that advance victims' rights. Still, it is not inconceivable that the IPA found a bipartisan audience, for few if any reasonable people would want to keep the innocent behind bars. President Bush made this point when, in his 2005 State of the Union address, he stated:

> Because one of the main sources of our national unity is our belief in equal justice, we need to make sure Americans of all races and backgrounds have confidence in the system that provides justice. In America we must make doubly sure no person is held to account for a crime he or she did not commit—so we are dramatically expanding the use of DNA evidence to prevent wrongful conviction. Soon I will send to Congress a proposal to fund special training for defense counsel in capital cases, because people on trial for their lives must have competent lawyers by their side.[101]

Of course, Bush's 2005 statement may be seen as at odds with his record as governor of Texas, where he "presided over 152 executions, more than any governor in any state in modern U.S. history." Nor had Bush previously harbored public doubts about the criminal justice system, once declaring his confidence that "we have not put to death [in Texas] anyone who has been innocent."[102]

The last word in Mr. Bush's statement—innocence—figures prominently in the success of the IPA and other enacted measures to reform the criminal justice system. Just as DNA testing provided unequivocal proof that many individuals were serving time for crimes they did not commit, the causes of erroneous convictions received greater attention. When the innocent also were situated on death row, and in states like Illinois where they numbered more than just a handful, it became virtually impossible for policymakers to ignore the problem. If it had not been for DNA testing, several states stood ready to execute a number of innocent men. Even today, their names and faces come easily to mind. Earl Washington Jr., the mentally challenged Virginian who was led to confess to a rape and murder he did not commit; Charles Irvin Fain, an Idahoan convicted largely on the basis of snitch testimony; and Rolando Cruz and Alejandro Hernandez, delinquents whose tale of exoneration in Illinois included indictments for several of the sheriff's deputies and prosecutors who helped convict them. More than one hundred other innocent persons convicted of serious crimes they did not commit were released from imprisonment and, in several cases, from death row only with the assistance of dedicated attorneys, investigators, and journalists. The tales of their wrongful convictions, and especially their ordeals for exoneration, made compelling news stories.

The Process of Reform

The result of these exonerations was to create a climate for reform or, as John Kingdon might say, a window of opportunity for policy change. Considering that entrenched policies, particularly those concerning criminal justice, change "only slowly, and not usually by large amounts even over long periods,"[103] advocates for change had to strike fast when media reports of serious, indeed tragic, erroneous convictions reached the public's consciousness.

Political scientists Frank Baumgartner and Bryan Jones term this process "positive political feedback," in which "small inputs can cascade into major effects as they work their ways through a complex system."[104] They distinguish positive feedback from negative feedback, in which "the investment of more and more political resources into the political fray achieves" incremental policy reform. Positive feedback encapsulates such experiences as "bandwagons, slippery slopes, and waves," in which political ideas and proposals "take shape, gain momentum . . . become popular quickly and diffuse throughout larger areas of the political system."[105]

In the case of wrongful convictions, the reports of exonerations created a groundswell of support to "do something" to prevent these errors. No longer could defenders of the criminal justice process unflinchingly claim that "the system works." To be sure, the system works much more often than it does not, but public confidence in the criminal justice process was at risk as people became accustomed to reading more and more stories about exonerated defendants. That change was coming seemed almost inevitable. The question was how extensive reform would be and who would be responsible for leading the charge.

In this respect, the Kingdon and Baumgartner and Jones models of policy change presaged a potential competition for control of the policy debate. With the window of opportunity opening, who would step forward with proposals for reform, and whose initiatives would win out? Would self-styled "reformers," activists largely associated with the criminal defense bar, be able to seize the mantle of change and push through extensive measures? Did the death row exonerations, for example, portend the end of capital punishment in some states? Conversely, would the "law and order" crowd enter the debate, offering more modest proposals to fine-tune but not overhaul the American criminal justice system? Were the exonerations, as one district attorney labeled them, "episodic, not epidemic"?[106] Did the eventual clearing of innocent men prove that "the system worked" and that additional reform was unnecessary?

For students of politics, the ensuing policy debate was anticipated in the same way that one looks forward to a political campaign. In a sense, each side was competing over the "policy image" of the exonerations, or as Baumgartner and Jones would say, the "image or . . . understanding that links the problem with a possible governmental solution."[107] On one side were the reformers, arguing that the system had convicted and almost executed innocent people. Serious change was necessary, they claimed, to prevent future, and potentially even worse, tragedies. On another side stood some prosecutors and law enforcement officials, reminding the public that the innocent had, in fact, been freed and that in any event we should remember the criminal justice system makes relatively few errors in protecting the public from dangerous criminals. Additional attention might be warranted, they acknowledged, but wholesale "reform" was both unnecessary and a potential risk to public safety.

Considering that politics is the art of the compromise, it is hardly surprising that the initial reform has fallen somewhere between these poles. The Innocence Protection Act contains provisions for postconviction DNA testing, even while the reach of the federal death penalty has been expanded over the years. California's Commission on the Fair Administration of Justice achieved a consensus package of reforms, only to find that it must continue to negotiate with Governor Schwarzenegger over the terms of those measures. And in Virginia we have seen new model lineup procedures without any requirement that the standards actually be adopted. Even in Illinois, where the governor emptied death row and the General Assembly responded with a significant package of legislative reforms, several recommendations from the Ryan Commission remain unaddressed.

It is difficult to say whose approach to wrongful convictions has been most successful. Indeed, it may be indecorous, perhaps even crude, to assess criminal justice reform in the same way that we evaluate political contests, asking which side has "won" the policy debate. On one hand, the status quo has been changed, with several states and the federal government enacting measures to improve eyewitness identification procedures, record custodial interrogations, fund DNA testing, and permit postconviction review. No longer can the criminal justice system hide behind the fiction of infallibility, its defenders sloughing off pointed attention with the claim that reform endangers public safety. At the same time, many of the systemic inequities in American criminal justice continue. In many jurisdictions, defense attorneys and prosecutors lack sufficient resources to provide effective advocacy; law enforcement agencies are denied the latest technologies to improve investigations and minimize error; and perhaps most troubling, many states lack a judicial vehicle to consider new evidence of innocence.

The Importance of Resourceful Policy Advocates

If there is one lesson from these policy debates, it is that reform is most feasible when advanced by actors with resources, although these resources are not necessarily financial. The most successful change agents were those considered to be "insiders" in the criminal justice system, particularly people who were networked with others in the legal or political communities, who commanded a high professional reputation, and who often were perceived as being conservative. Such actors were taken more seriously by observers and often could forestall opposition to reform because they were considered to be both powerful and protective of the interests of law enforcement officers, prosecutors, and judges. If these leaders were so concerned that they would propose reform, then other policymakers sat up and took note, for the former were not known to be rash or radical. Indeed, the professional and personal networks of change agents only heightened their legitimacy and resources.

Another way to think of these reform actors is as "spark plugs" who responded to the window of opportunity by pushing reform proposals. Some of their initiatives were more ambitious than others, but in each case reform was pushed by at least one actor who had a measure to advance. As such, their activities fit well with Kingdon's model of policy-making, in which actors, proposals, and windows of opportunity converge. Reform did not percolate up gently or get the attention of policy-makers and politicians in the usual course of business. Rather, it took a perceived "crisis," one that here generated considerable media attention, to put the issue of criminal reform on the policy agenda. At that point, dedicated actors arose to advance proposals for reform.

One need look no further than the experience in North Carolina, Wisconsin, or even in Congress to find these actors. Christine Mumma, the executive director of the North Carolina Actual Innocence Commission, was a leading force in advancing innocence review and eyewitness identification reform in her state. Mumma is a moderately conservative, former businesswoman, a Catholic Republican who could not countenance the state's convicting innocent individuals. She also happened to be a law clerk to North Carolina's chief justice, I. Beverly Lake, and, in his words, was the "guiding light and driving force behind the Actual Innocence Commission. She called some of the North Carolina cases to my attention and brought it all into focus, along with the national picture. She got me centered on it," the chief justice said.[108]

Mumma's connection to Justice Lake and her reputation as a serious and clearheaded thinker helped stir action in North Carolina, for her interest in the subject could not easily be ignored. She was not a wild-eyed radical who might have scared off policymakers or been easily dismissed. Rather, she was a relatively conservative insider with a strong connection to one of the pillars of North Carolina's legal community. That she had the energy, drive, and interest to tackle wrongful convictions meant that reform had a strong chance in the state. As Bill Kenergly, the Republican district attorney in Salisbury, North Carolina, and a member of the North Carolina Actual Innocence Commission, explained, most issues of legal reform "require a 'spark plug. . . . We certainly have one in Chris Mumma.'"[109] That North Carolina also created the Innocence Inquiry Commission is, in large part, credited to Chris Mumma's efforts.

Wisconsin, too, has seen successful reform at the hands of several re-spected "insiders" who were drawn to the issue of wrongful convic-tions. University of Wisconsin law professor Keith Findley and Wiscon-sin state representative Mark Gundrum teamed up to create and staff the "Avery task force" that led not only to a series of legislative reforms that passed the Wisconsin General Assembly in 2005 but also the cre-ation of the Wisconsin Criminal Justice Study Commission. That Gun-drum, the conservative Republican chair of the State Assembly's Judi-ciary Committee, and Findley, a former public defender "animated by liberal social justice values,"[110] found common ground meant that the push for reform would be difficult to defeat along partisan lines.

Bipartisan coalitions, especially among animated insiders, often pro-duce successful legislative change, a phenomenon also seen in the pas-sage of the Innocence Protection Act. The IPA was initially championed by Senator Patrick Leahy and Congressman William Delahunt, even though both were Democrats in a Congress controlled by Republicans. Under these circumstances, the IPA might very well have been attacked as providing more resources for inmates—albeit those innocent of their convictions—rather than devoting federal attention and dollars to crime control. Leahy and Delahunt, their staffs, and outside supporters of the IPA all recognized this conundrum and deftly sought allies across the aisle to marry the IPA with additional rights for crime victims to pro-duce a larger, politically successful package of reforms in the Justice for All Act.

If there is one area in which the Innocence Commission for Virginia could have been more successful, it is in reaching out to political insid-ers on both sides of the aisle. To be sure, the ICVA was careful to main-tain "balance," ensuring that the members of its advisory board were associated with both Republican and Democratic causes and sympa-thetic to both law enforcement and defense communities. But one of the ICVA's strongest assets—its independence from state functionaries —meant that its research and results did not have an immediate politi-cal constituency to act on the ICVA's recommendations. No state official had commissioned the ICVA's work, and neither the State Crime Com-mission nor the General Assembly were awaiting the ICVA's report to consider additional reform measures.

The ICVA addressed this potential liability by seeking to shore up the legitimacy of the commission's existence and investigation. We high-lighted the respectability of the law firms and advisory board members involved in the ICVA, and the thoroughness of our research earned us kudos in the press. But in retrospect, we should have had a more definitive outreach strategy to involve key legislators, judges, and other justice leaders in the ICVA's findings and to recruit potential policy advocates to advance reforms consistent with the ICVA's recommendations. Although Virginia has certainly enacted a great deal of justice reform over the last half decade, it might very well have done more.

The Future of "Innocence"

Keith Findley reminds us that the "window of opportunity" for justice reform "will not remain open forever. As DNA is used increasingly before conviction, the body of wrongful convictions that can be exposed through postconviction DNA testing will diminish, and ultimately disappear."[111] This is not to say that wrongful convictions will vanish—although we can certainly hope that DNA analysis will clear more innocent suspects before trial—but there are likely to be fewer uncontested postconviction exonerations. This scenario presents a mixed bag. On one hand, we should applaud a justice system that applies the latest available technology to identify the guilty and clear the innocent as early in the criminal justice process as possible. Even recognizing that many crimes lack human biological evidence and that DNA testing is sometimes limited to placing a suspect at a crime scene without proving that he actually committed the crime, DNA analysis is nonetheless a significant step forward in criminal investigations that we all should welcome.

On the other hand, DNA exonerations have been the "hook" to attract press attention to wrongful convictions and the various deficiencies in the criminal justice system that unfortunately, and most often unwittingly, convict the innocent. As innocent men have walked out of prison upon the finding of exculpatory DNA evidence, reporters have been there to chronicle the problem of wrongful convictions and the deep pain and suffering left in their wake. Without such press attention, reformers would have had little or no window through which to press their proposals, for few observers would have perceived there to be a problem in the criminal justice system to address.

Yet, what exactly is "the problem" that would justify policy reform? Even a short perusal of the criminal justice literature would find many such possibilities, from criticisms that the justice system is biased against the poor[112] to concerns that victims have little say in sentencing.[113] Many of these concerns are valid, but what attracted the public's attention—and what undoubtedly has driven recent reform of the criminal justice system—is undeniable proof that innocent people have been convicted. Nor does innocence alone explain the groundswell for reform. It is the prospect of executing an innocent man, a possibility that no longer seems so remote, that has largely captured the press's attention and captured the public's concern.

California provides an excellent example. According to *San Francisco Magazine,* the state has freed two hundred wrongly convicted defendants in the last fifteen years, nearly twice the number of known exonerations in Illinois and Texas combined. However, because only a handful were death row inmates, the story received "surprisingly little fanfare. . . . California's innocence problem, it turns out, is primarily a matter of life, not death. . . . In short, an innocent Californian convicted of murder is almost better off being sentenced to death than to life in prison—at least the case will get a long, hard look."[114]

If justice reform has largely turned on innocence, what will happen to other worthy issues of reform in the criminal justice system if the number of DNA exonerations declines? Some people in the reform community say that it is time to abandon innocence as a organizing principle. Not only are clear claims of innocence past their zenith, they maintain, but concentrating on innocent suspects deflects needed attention from the greater swath of defendants who, although perhaps guilty, have been caught, prosecuted, and convicted by methods that subvert the Constitution.[115] For that matter, some advocates say, the term *innocence commission* or similar such titles conveys a prodefense bias toward reform activities.[116]

These reformers have it half right. There is little doubt that the criminal justice system suffers from a number of shortcomings, weaknesses that go beyond the factors that have convicted innocent people. The work of the ICVA and countless other study commissions has uncovered many issues, from failures to record custodial interrogations, to problematic identification procedures, to inadequate defense counsel. Of course, these problems are much more serious when they lead to the wrongful conviction of an innocent person, but they represent failings in their own right when they sidetrack investigations, slow the justice process, or deny individuals the true measure of rights promised in the Constitution.

The central question, then, is not whether further reforms are needed apart from those necessary to protect the innocent from wrongful conviction. That is elementary. The more difficult, strategic question is how to pursue such an agenda even if innocence "sells" but clear claims of innocence are likely to decline. Americans will not miraculously "see the light" of justice reform simply because certain practices do not match the promised ideals of the criminal justice system. For the most part, the public is content to trust criminal justice professionals to carry out these responsibilities, convinced that the system will work most of the time and that in any event, they themselves are unlikely ever to be on the receiving end of criminal punishment. "It doesn't take a rocket scientist to understand that indigent criminal defendants don't have much of a political constituency," says Virginia appellate judge Robert Humphreys,[117] a stark reminder that recent criminal justice reform relied heavily on the issue of innocence. If not for the shocking revelations that innocent men had been convicted and that some of them would otherwise have been executed, the public's veil of trust might never have been pierced.

For that matter, Americans are reluctant to press for reforms that would largely benefit the guilty. Fundamentally, the public wants protection from crime, not necessarily assurances that the rights of defendants, and especially guilty ones at that, will be protected. Consider an editorial from the *Virginian-Pilot,* a newspaper that has supported the ICVA and that more than most has pressed strongly for justice reform. Writing shortly after DNA testing confirmed the guilt of Roger Coleman, the editorial board sought to "remind . . . those who trusted for many years in Coleman's innocence . . . that vicious killers are also, at times, adept liars."[118]

If the paper's admonition was a slight rap to the reform community's knuckles, other commentators have delivered a hard blow to the head. Kerry Dougherty, a columnist for the *Virginian-Pilot,* whipsawed reformers when writing about her "respect [for] those who oppose capital punishment on moral grounds" before condemning the "callous indifference these folks frequently display toward the victims of crimes and their willingness to believe the drivel about innocence that echoes along death row."[119] Even Roy Malpass, a professor at the University of Texas at El Paso and a past participant in the research group on eyewitness identification for the National Institute of Justice, publicly took issue with the claim that "it's better to let 10 guilty persons free to protect against one innocent person being wrongfully convicted. . . . 'I'm fine with that when we're dealing with juvenile shoplifters,'" Malpass observed. "I'm not fine with that for terrorists."[120]

As unpleasant as some activists may find it, reform must appeal to a realpolitik. There is nothing unusual about this, for the last several decades of political science research reveals that most voters and politicians act on the basis of self-interest.[121] In practice, this means that innocence will continue to generate interest in reform as long as there remain indisputable, serious cases of wrongful conviction. Although innocence does not touch the public directly, it does go to the core of what it means to trust the criminal justice system and delegate its operation to others. None of us wish to believe that we accept a criminal justice process that could convict and irrevocably punish innocent individuals. But if as predicted, cases of factual exoneration are likely to wane, reformers must consider a different strategy.

The future of innocence-based reform may be even worse if Baumgartner and Jones are correct about policy change. According to them, policy diffusion looks like a logistic S-shaped curve. "Policy adoption is slow at first, then very rapid, then slow again as the saturation point is reached." Change tends to happen quickly, returning to long periods of equilibrium as the "attention of governmental elites" wanes and "the apathy of those not keenly interested in the particular issue" allows problems to recede from the policy agenda.[122]

To combat these natural tendencies, the reform community needs to change the terms of the debate and the locus of reform. Reformers must appeal to the public's self-interest, advancing policy proposals on their ability to better protect the community and save tax dollars. These are not specious arguments. Many of the measures advanced by the ICVA and other study commissions can help law enforcement better identify the correct perpetrators, encourage guilty pleas, and lock up dangerous criminals without fear that a conviction will later be overturned because police had the wrong suspect. Even measures generally associated with "defendants' rights"—like adequately compensated trial counsel—can save taxpayers money because appeals will be shorter and retrials less likely. It costs more than $20,000 per year to incarcerate a person.[123] It goes without saying that these funds should not be wasted.

If this seems like a conservative agenda for reform, it is, but in many ways, that is the point. Reform will go nowhere if actors simply wait for "enlightened [officials to] recognize and honor their moral and constitutional responsibilit[ies]."[124] None of the recommendations advanced by the various state study commissions will be enacted simply by appealing to civil liberties or a call to the higher good. Perhaps this is a weakness of the American political process; maybe it represents a failure of public action to realize the principles of our nation's founders. In any case, there is a political reality that we face and a choice that we must make. No one ever was elected in this country by appearing "soft on crime," which unfortunately is how criminal justice reform looks to many politicians and voters. We can curse this phenomenon, futilely seek to "educate" the public, or we can use arguments and imagery that are politically palatable. The policy proposals have not changed; only the supporting rhetoric has.

Encouraging Professionalism

These are key lessons from the ICVA's work in Virginia, which offer a guide to the ICVA and others that seek to advance or implement the recommendations for reform already offered. There is another important reminder as well. The reform and law and order communities have more in common than they sometimes acknowledge. We all seek protection from crime. We all want wise and efficient stewardship of public monies. If this book has been largely sympathetic to criminal justice reform, it also adds a warning not to confuse reform with antipathy to the officials who serve in the criminal justice system and permit it to function. Experience tells me that the vast majority of law enforcement officers, prosecutors, judges, and corrections officers are dedicated professionals in the service of justice. Although I understand the argument of defense attorneys that there is nobility in attending to the needs of society's worst-off—its indigent criminal defendants—there also is honor in protecting our communities from crime and helping society mete out justice. Reform must recognize and respect these principles, not oppose them.

Perhaps the best way to maintain momentum for reform is to inculcate these values into the practices of criminal justice officials. Until now, most reform efforts have been directed to legislatures and judges, seeking to codify into law the various "lessons learned" from postconviction exonerations. But if innocence cases are harder to find, and if the political process is generally unsympathetic to criminal justice reform (or at least to measures that will not directly reduce crime), then policy actors need a different outlet. Baumgartner and Jones classify this challenge as "venue shopping," or moving an "issue from the realm of parallel processing to the realm of serial processing by reallocating attention."[125] Put another way, if a policy avenue is unlikely to be successful, advocates need to redefine the locus of reform.

The most promising venue for criminal justice reform is in the local police departments, sheriff's offices, and district attorneys' offices that form the front line of America's criminal justice system. This initially may seem odd to some observers, since law enforcement officers and prosecutors are not usually considered top advocates for criminal suspects. But the same reforms that may be envisioned as prodefendant can also be advanced under the aegis of greater professionalism and best practices for criminal justicians. Many police officers would like equipment to videotape interrogations, their colleagues in other jurisdictions reporting a rise in guilty pleas when suspect statements are recorded and can be shown at trial.[126] Prosecutors, too, believe that their jobs are often easier when defendants are well represented; in these cases, state's attorneys need not perform both their responsibilities and those of the defense in order to stave off a later claim of ineffective assistance of counsel.[127] Police and prosecutors also require in-service training for their employees, which might provide a fine opportunity to review the risks and nature of "tunnel vision" that unfortunately can sidetrack investigations and prosecutions.

Reforms like these allow for collaboration across the many spectra of the criminal justice system, rather than perpetuating the antagonistic culture that has some in the defense bar pointing fingers at police and prosecutors as unwilling to evolve and the latter refusing to acknowledge weaknesses in their practices that could be improved. The American criminal justice system lags embarrassingly behind its brethren in medicine, who are now winning plaudits for openly addressing problems that occur during medical procedures. A prime example is Brigham and Women's Hospital, one of Harvard Medical School's teaching hospitals, which has been recognized as "a leader in patient safety," in part for its "openness when things go wrong. 'It's a culture that says, yes, we have a problem, let's shine a light on it and fix it rather than trying to cover it up,' says chief medical officer Dr. Andy Whittemore."[128]

If there is any profession that might have feared liability for openly acknowledging its errors, it is medicine, which has to deal with attorneys and ensuing malpractice suits. But if doctors can admit their errors and work to remedy and prevent them, then law enforcement officers and lawyers should be willing to do the same. It should not have to take additional exonerations—including the dreaded possibility that an executed defendant will later be proven innocent—to convince policymakers and justice officials to do for our criminal justice system what doctors and hospital administrators have done for medicine. The stakes are high in both vocations, and as trained professionals, criminal justicians should demonstrate their ability to learn from and address problems that may occur in their field, not just circle the wagons.

A Challenge: Decoupling Reform from the Death Penalty

Virginia State Senator Ken Stolle, chair of the state crime commission and a supporter of capital punishment, has said, "It is only a matter of time before Virginia and other states ban the death penalty." Although Stolle has worked hard to improve safeguards against wrongful executions, he believes that "inevitably, someone who is innocent will be executed." When that happens, Stolle foresees the end of capital punishment.[129]

Senator Stolle may ultimately be correct, but in the near term, few cases under investigation will likely provide clear, irrefutable evidence that an innocent person has been executed. To be sure, Radelet and Bedau purport to have uncovered such evidence in the past, but their findings, albeit impressive, have not proved to be incontrovertible. Barring such findings, then, we may be moving to a point where the reform community faces a schism regarding the death penalty. Until now, both pro- and antideath penalty activists have been able to unite under the banner of innocence review because the cause serves both interests. Supporters of the death penalty seek to prevent erroneous convictions, in part to perfect a penal system that countenances taking human life. Opponents, by contrast, have seen exonerations as proof that errors naturally abound in the criminal justice process and that the threat is too great to permit executions.

As more states pursue innocence review and consequently adopt reforms, the likelihood of further errors—or at least the kind that would convict and sentence an innocent person to death—will likely drop. We do not know by how much, but it will become harder for abolitionists to argue that the threat of error in capital punishment is extremely high. In response, abolitionists may shirk from reforms, concerned that improvements to the criminal justice process pave the way for additional executions. For their part, death penalty proponents may become exasperated with their abolitionist colleagues, seeing the reform movement as a smokescreen to eliminate capital punishment. If so, they too may abandon the partnership.

We have already seen schisms among potential reformers around the death penalty. Describing the North Carolina Actual Innocence Commission, Chris Mumma explained that members agreed not to "represent their personal viewpoints on [capital punishment] as being shared by other Commission members or the Commission as a whole."[130] The situation became so heated at one point that some members threatened to quit out of concern that legislators were associating the commission's work with a moratorium on capital punishment.

It is time to separate criminal justice reform from the death penalty. To be sure, capital punishment has given reform "legs" because the stakes are so high, but the problems uncovered in wrongful convictions are not limited to capital cases, and the reforms proposed will help improve many aspects of the criminal justice process. In fact, the *real* problem is that many cases below capital prosecutions do not get the attention they deserve to prevent and rectify error.

I recognize the likely result is a series of reforms implying the justice system can be perfected or at least improved enough to give us confidence that the right people are being convicted and acquitted. And this may, indeed, provide enough cover to allow death penalty proponents to continue capital punishment. It is a risk we must bear, for as concerned as I am about the death penalty,[131] we should not hold other reforms hostage to the abolitionists' fear that additional reforms will weaken the barrier against an expanded death penalty. Abolitionists cannot have it both ways. They cannot say, as David Dow suggested, that we should stop focusing on claims of innocence because they avoid the more prevalent and "appalling violations of legal principle" in cases of the guilty[132] and then complain when a focus on innocence leads to reforms that make it possible to more fairly convict and sentence the guilty to death.[133]

The death penalty needs to be addressed directly: Is it legitimate? This is a deep and important question and one that may well turn on how accurate the criminal justice process can become. However, even Justice Antonin Scalia acknowledges, "The criminal justice system is made up of human beings, and fallible beings make mistakes."[134] To support capital punishment, then, proponents must be willing to accept the possibility—as does Scalia—that at some point "we are going to execute innocent people."[135] Perhaps the advantages gained by capital punishment make up for the loss of innocent life at the hands of the state; maybe society is obligated to take a strong moral stand against premeditated killing by imposing the "ultimate punishment" on extreme wrongdoers. In any event, just as capital punishment may not be explained away by presupposing that the process will be free of errors, opponents should not stand in the way of additional reforms that do, in fact, lower the risk of wrongful executions. As Larry Marshall argues, civilized societies do not kill their citizens.[136] By the same token, they do not slow reforms to protect the innocent because those measures may make the case against executing the guilty more difficult.

A More Perfect System

The preamble to the United States Constitution explains that the framers of our government sought "to form a more perfect union."[137] More than two hundred years later, critics claim that those who seek to reform the American criminal justice system "are demanding an impossibility—a perfect system."[138] With due respect, such criticisms misunderstand and mischaracterize the case for reform. Regardless of whether the errors of the criminal justice system are episodic or epidemic, they still warrant review and reform, not because reform will lead to an error-free process, but because the participants in the system deserve our attention and efforts. Victims should not have to relive a crime through multiple trials or, more tragically, be attacked by a felon who could have been caught earlier. Police officers and attorneys should have the latest technology available to them to close cases and screen out the uninvolved. And of course, the innocent should not be subject to erroneous charges or wrongful convictions.

None of these concerns should make us unsupportive of, or unsympathetic to, the dedicated men and women who staff our law enforcement agencies, prosecutors' offices, and judicial benches. Rather, these concerns demand the best from the state's penal power. Criminal justice is now a profession. The least we can expect from criminal justice policymakers is the same level of professionalism as is practiced by aircraft operators and doctors, who are willing to examine and correct systemic errors. To reject postexoneration review, to keep pointing fingers at reformers rather than confronting the errors uncovered through research, is to make others wonder why, in a Shakespearian vein, the opponents of reform "doth protest so much."[139]

Appendix 1
*Instructions for Volunteer
ICVA Investigators*

Thank you for agreeing to assist the Innocence Commission for Virginia (ICVA). The Commission is a joint project of the Innocence Project of the National Capital Region, the Administration of Justice Program at George Mason University, and the Constitution Project.

ICVA's mission is three-fold: to identify common errors in cases in which innocent people have been wrongly convicted of serious cases, to propose policy reforms to help prevent wrongful convictions from occurring in the future, and to offer a series of best practices to improve the investigation and prosecution of serious criminal cases in Virginia. ICVA's work depends on the contributions of volunteers like yourself who have agreed to investigate the circumstances of particular cases.

By now you should have received the name of a Virginia case in which a defendant has been exonerated of a serious crime or there exist compelling reasons to doubt the defendant's conviction. We ask that you now immerse yourself in the facts and procedural history of the case in order to chronicle what went wrong in the investigation and prosecution of the case and explain the process by which the conviction was eventually challenged.

On the next page we have provided a series of suggested data to collect when investigating the case and drafting your report, but we are more concerned that you provide a thorough account than that you answer each item posed. If you have any questions, please feel free to consult Don Salzman or Julia Sullivan of ICVA, who will be happy to talk to you about the case.

As you begin to consider a research strategy, we offer the following advice:

1. Remember that you are conducting factual research to understand what happened in a case, not researching law books to determine a legal answer. So, think like a reporter, asking the five "W" questions: Who, What, Where, When, and Why. Be creative and thorough in your work and in the sources you consult.

2. A good place to start is Lexis/Nexis or other news coverage available on the Internet. We will provide you with some preliminary materials on the cases. Many of the cases have been covered by the news media, and you may wish to use these reports if you believe them to be credible. The reporters who wrote these stories are also excellent sources, often familiar with a case and willing to share their knowledge and impressions.

3. Other good sources include the pleadings from the case, any reported (or unreported) judicial decisions, or even the case record. It may be necessary to seek such documents from the courts involved.

4. Please try to contact the various individuals involved in your case, including the defendant and his attorney(s) as well as the prosecutors and law enforcement officials who handled the matter. It is important to contact both sides involved in the case to get a balanced view, but keep in mind that some people will not want to talk with you and may resent your inquiries. Try not to take this personally. It is helpful to convey that you are simply trying to find out what happened. Remember always to be polite, measured, professional, and persistent, but also to respect a person's wish not to speak with you.

5. Do not contact the judges involved in the case, nor should you seek to uncover the identity of jurors who heard the matter.

6. When contacting individuals, please say that you are acting on behalf of the Innocence Commission for Virginia, and feel free to forward them the ICVA's mission statement. But you should not intimate that you are acting in an official or government capacity. The Innocence Commission is an important project, and it serves crucial public purposes, but the ICVA is not acting for or under the direction of any governmental body.

7. If you have any questions about your assignment, please contact the individuals mentioned above, or Misty Thomas.

Innocence Commission for Virginia

Case Reports

The Innocence Commission of Virginia (ICVA) will rely your report to understand how and why erroneous convictions occur in Virginia. It is imperative, then, that your research and report be thorough. It is likely that some of your work will be included in the Commission's final report, educating the public and policymakers about problems in Virginia's criminal justice system.

We ask you to focus on two central questions: How is it that the defendant in the assigned case was convicted, and what factors later raised compelling doubts about the conviction? Rather than requiring that you follow a particular format for the report, we leave the presentation to your best judgment. That said, we encourage you to consider the questions raised below. Not all of these facts will pertain to each case, but they are a good place to begin in explaining the facts of the case and exoneration. As always, if you have any questions, please contact the ICVA.

Issues During Case Investigation

Defendant's Name
Defendant's Demographics (age, race/ethnicity, gender, IQ, mental illnesses, socioeconomic status)
What type of crime(s) was involved? What happened and where?
Who was the victim? What were his/her demographics? What happened to him/her? (Was it a cross racial crime?)
How did the defendant become a suspect?
How much press attention did the crime receive at the time?
Were there eyewitnesses to the crime? How many? What did they claim to see?
Was there any pretrial identification procedure done, such as a show-up at the scene, a photo array (or simply one photo shown to a witness or witnesses), or an in-person line-up? How was it conducted? Who did the participants claim to identify, and how certain was any identification?
Was there forensic or scientific evidence involved in the case? What type? Was it tested, and how?

Which law enforcement agency investigated the case? Which officers or detectives were involved?

How was the defendant linked to the crime?

Were there co-defendants? If so, who were they and what happened to them? Did any of the co-defendants cooperate with the police or prosecutors against the defendant?

Were there other known suspects at the time? If so, why was the defendant singled out? Why were the other suspects excluded or eliminated as suspects?

Did the defendant have and report an alibi?

Was any evidence lost or mishandled during the investigation?

False confessions, snitch testimony, bad forensic science?

Issues at Trial

Which office prosecuted the defendant?

How soon after the crime did the trial occur?

Which prosecutors handled the case?

In which court, and before which judge, did the case occur?

Was the defendant represented by counsel? Who was the lawyer(s), in what office does s/he work, and what is his/her legal background and training?

Were there any co-defendants who were also tried? If so, were they tried jointly or in a separate trial?

How long was the trial?

Was it a bench or jury trial, or did the defendant plead guilty?

Which evidence or witnesses did the prosecution present?

Which evidence or witnesses did the defense present?

Was any expert or forensic testimony presented at trial? If so, what kind of evidence was it and how did purportedly link the defendant to the crime?

Did the defense file any pretrial motions? What were the grounds for the motions? Were the pretrial motions argued by the defense and decided by the trial judge? If so, what were the trial judge's rulings on the motions?

On what charges were the defendant and any co-defendants convicted/acquitted?

What was the sentence?

Issues Postconviction

Did the defendant file any appeals? In what courts and on what counts? What were the results of those appeals?

Was the defendant represented by counsel on any of his/her appeals? Who was the lawyer(s), in what office does s/he work, and what is his/her legal background and training?

What factors raised doubts about the conviction—new witnesses or evidence, recantations or changes to witnesses' testimony, a more thorough investigation or better representation by subsequent counsel, or other developments?

Did the defendant seek to introduce new exculpatory evidence postconviction? How long after trial was this attempt made?

Were new forensic tests conducted? What type, and what were the results?

What issues were raised on appeal?

Has the defendant been officially cleared of the crime? By whom —a court, a prosecutor's office, or the Governor? When did this occur, and what convinced them?

If the defendant has not yet been cleared, what are the prospects?

If the defendant was released from prison, how long did s/he serve? Was the defendant released because he served his sentence, was paroled, or was released early because he was exonerated, received clemency, or the prosecutor decided not to re-try?

Who was the exonerating attorney?

Where is the defendant now?

Appendix 2
The ICVA's Surveys of Law Enforcement Agencies and Commonwealth's Attorneys

As part of the investigation, the ICVA's researchers surveyed law enforcement agencies and prosecutors' offices in Virginia to learn more about their practices pertaining to eyewitness identification, custodial interrogation, and discovery. The survey focused on three questions: How often and under what circumstances do law enforcement agencies conduct eyewitness identifications? How often do such agencies perform custodial interrogations and under what circumstances? To what extent do prosecutors share information from their investigations with defendants and defense counsel?

Law Enforcement Agencies

The ICVA contacted 276 law enforcement agencies in Virginia to participate in a survey, which was submitted to them by electronic and traditional mail and by facsimile. An accompanying letter asked the head of each agency to choose a "supervisor or other individual with knowledge of these subjects" to complete and return the survey. One hundred twenty-seven agencies participated in the survey, representing a 46 percent response rate, which was higher than the percentage of agencies that responded to a similar survey conducted by the Virginia State Crime Commission in 2004. The survey was sent to police departments and sheriff's offices, recognizing that some sheriff's offices are primarily responsible for law enforcement in their jurisdictions, that some share such duties with police departments, and that others are primarily responsible for corrections and court security. Of the responding agencies, 85 percent have law enforcement duties.

The survey asked whether the agencies were involved in taking or obtaining the confessions of criminal suspects. The respondents answering this question in the affirmative were then asked which methods they used to record the custodial interrogation of suspects, as well as their reasons for using these methods. Law enforcement agencies also were asked about the practices they use for eyewitness identification, including "showups" (or field identifications), lineups, photo arrays, single photos, and their reasons for using particular techniques.

The survey reads as follows:

Survey of Law Enforcement Best Practices

This short survey will help the Innocence Commission for Virginia to understand the best practices used by law enforcement agencies in the Commonwealth. It is being asked of all police departments and sheriff's agencies in Virginia to determine a) which organizations have law enforcement responsibilities and b) the procedures they use in obtaining suspects' confessions or identifications. *Responses are purely for research purposes and will remain anonymous. No agency or jurisdiction will be identified in the results.*

The survey should take less than 15 minutes to complete. Please have a supervisor or other individual with knowledge of these subjects complete the survey. When finished please fax the survey to the Commission at 202-785-7555. You may also mail the survey to our address, P.O. Box 10240 Arlington, VA 22210. Because the Commission is operating on a short deadline, we ask that you respond by February 13 if possible. If you have any questions—or if you would prefer to respond more informally—please call Commission Chair Jon Gould at 703-993-8481 or email him at innocencecommission@yahoo.com. Thank you for your assistance on this important project.

Please circle or fill-in all responses as appropriate:

1. How is your agency best described?
   a. Police department
   b. Sheriff's office
   c. Other (please describe)
2. Does your agency have law enforcement responsibilities?
   a. Yes
   b. No

If no, please stop the survey and return it. Thank you for your assistance.
If yes, please continue to the next question.

3. How is your jurisdiction best described?
   a. City or municipality
   b. County
   c. City/municipality *and* County
   d. Other (please describe)

4. How would you describe the surrounding area you serve? (Please circle all that apply)
   a. City
   b. Suburb
   c. Rural

5. Approximately how many sworn officers does your agency employ?

   _____

The following five questions pertain to criminal confessions:

6. Is your agency involved in taking or obtaining the confessions of criminal suspects?
   a. Yes
   b. No

If no, please skip ahead to question 11.
If yes, please continue with question 7.

7. Which methods do you use to record the custodial interrogation of suspects? (Please circle all that apply.)
   a. Have the suspect write out a statement
   b. Have an officer record the statement in writing
   c. Audiotape the statement
   d. Videotape the statement
   e. Other (please describe)

8. How often do you use videotape to record the custodial interrogation of suspects?
   a. Never
   b. Rarely
   c. Occasionally
   d. Mostly
   e. Always

9. If you use videotape to record the custodial interrogation of suspects, in what types of cases do you employ the technology?
   a. All kinds of cases
   b. Felonies only
   c. Serious felonies only
   d. Capital cases only
   e. Other (please explain)
   f. Not Applicable (don't use videotape)

10. If you do not use videotape to record the custodial interrogation of suspects, what is the reason? (Please circle all that apply.)
    a. Expense of videotaping interrogations
    b. Difficult to operate/requires additional technical staff
    c. Hinders or interferes with interrogation process or officers' rapport with suspect
    d. Had not considered videotape before
    e. Other (please explain)
    f. Not Applicable (already use videotape)

The following seven questions pertain to eyewitness identification:

11. Which out-of-court identification methods do you use with eyewitnesses? (Please circle all that apply.)
    a. Show-up in the field
    b. In-person line-up
    c. Photographic array or photographic spread
    d. Presentation of a single photograph to a witness

12. If you use a photographic array or photographic spread, how do you show eyewitnesses the photographs?
    a. In a group of photographs that the eyewitness can view simultaneously
    b. One photograph at a time
    c. Either method A or B at the investigating officer's discretion
    d. Not Applicable (don't use photographic arrays or photographic spreads)

13. If you use an in-person line-up, how are the suspects shown to the eyewitnesses?
    a. In a group so that the witnesses can view the line-up participants simultaneously
    b. One line-up participant at a time

    c. Either method A or B at the investigating officer's discretion

    d. Not Applicable (don't use in-person line-ups)

14. If you use a show-up, line-up or photo array, are eyewitnesses told that a suspect is likely among those to be viewed?

    a. Never

    b. Rarely

    c. Occasionally

    d. Mostly

    e. Always

    f. Not Applicable (don't use any of these procedures)

15. If you use a show-up, line-up or photo array, are eyewitnesses told that they do not have to identify anyone during the procedure if they do not see the suspect?

    a. Never

    b. Rarely

    c. Occasionally

    d. Mostly

    e. Always

    f. Not Applicable (don't use any of these procedures)

16. If you use a show-up, line-up or photo array, do you videotape the eyewitness identification procedures and the comments of the eyewitnesses?

    a. Never

    b. Rarely

    c. Occasionally

    d. Mostly

    e. Always

    f. Not Applicable (don't use any of these procedures)

17. If you use a show-up, line-up or photo array, does the officer interacting with the witness know who the likely suspect is?

    a. Never

    b. Rarely

    c. Occasionally

    d. Mostly

    e. Always

    f. Not Applicable (don't use any of these procedures)

The following question is your opportunity to elaborate:

18. Is there anything else we have not asked about these subjects that we should know? (Please explain below.)

When completed, please fax the survey to the Commission at 202-785-7555. You may also mail the survey to our address, P.O. Box 10240 Arlington, VA 22210. All responses are anonymous and will remain confidential. If you have any questions, please phone Commission Chair Jon Gould at 703-993-8481 or email him at innocencecommission@yahoo.com.

Thank you for your assistance. We very much appreciate your time.

Commonwealth's Attorneys

The ICVA contacted 120 Commonwealth's attorneys' offices in Virginia to participate in the survey, of which 26 responded. The response rate, approximately 22 percent, may seem low at first, but it tracks the response rates from other voluntary surveys of criminal justice officers. Although we would have preferred a higher rate, the findings are nonetheless instructive. (Interestingly, smaller offices were more likely to respond than larger offices were. Despite these patterns, the data discussed in this section are statistically significant.)

The survey queried prosecutors about their discovery practices, to understand under what circumstances they shared information from a criminal case with the defendant and/or defense counsel. The survey was particularly interested in partial-open-files and open-files policies and probed the prosecutors' reasons for their approaches. Like the surveys of law enforcement agencies, our questions used a mix of structured and open-ended responses.

The survey was as follows: ·

Survey of Discovery Practices

This short survey will help the Innocence Commission for Virginia to understand the best practices used by prosecutors in the Commonwealth. It is being asked of all Commonwealth's Attorney's Offices in Virginia to determine the methods and procedures they use for discovery in criminal cases. *Responses are purely for research purposes and will remain anonymous. No agency or jurisdiction will be identified in the results.*

The survey should take less than 15 minutes to complete. Please have a supervisor or other individual with knowledge of these subjects complete the survey. When finished, please fax the survey to the Commission at 202-785-7555. You may also mail the survey to our address, P.O. Box 10240 Arlington, VA 22210. Because the Commission is operating on a short deadline, we ask that you respond by February 13 if possible. If you have any questions—or if you would prefer to respond more informally—please call Commission Chair Jon Gould at 703-993-8481 or email him at innocencecommission@yahoo.com. Thank you for your assistance on this important project.

Please circle or fill-in all responses as appropriate:

1. What is the best description of your office's jurisdiction?
   a. City or municipality
   b. County
   c. City/municipality *and* County
   d. Other (please describe)

2. How would you describe the surrounding area you serve? (*Please circle all that apply.*)
   a. City
   b. Suburb
   c. Rural

3. Approximately how many attorneys does your office employ?
   _____

4. How many of these attorneys handle criminal trials? _____

5. What is the average annual caseload for trial attorneys in your office? _____

The following questions concern discovery practices in criminal cases:

6. What is your office's practice for providing investigative materials to the defense in criminal cases? (*Please circle all that apply.*)
   a. Provide only the discovery required by the Rules of the Supreme Court of Virginia and the obligations under the relevant case law to provide exculpatory evidence to the defense.

b. Provide investigative reports prepared by law enforcement officers.

c. Provide summaries of opinions and conclusions of laboratory or forensic experts or specialists if no written reports are prepared.

d. Provide written statements taken by law enforcement officers from witnesses, copies of audio or videotaped witness statements, or summaries of witness oral statements made by law enforcement officers.

e. Provide field notes made by law enforcement officers concerning their overall investigation and notes of their interrogation or questioning of the defendant.

f. Provide bench notes or laboratory notes of any laboratory or forensic experts or specialists.

g. Identify the names and addresses of Commonwealth witnesses who will testify at motions hearings or at trial.

h. Provide copies of photographs, charts or other demonstrative evidence and permit the review of physical evidence that will be introduced at trial.

i. Permit the defense to review but not copy all non-privileged material in law enforcement or Commonwealth's Attorney files. (Partial "open files" discovery policy.)

j. Permit the defense to copy all non-privileged material in the law enforcement files or Commonwealth's Attorney file. ("Open files" discovery policy.)

If you did not circle "i" or "j" in question 6, please skip ahead to question 9.

If you did circle "i" or "j" in question 6, please continue with questions 7 and 8.

7. Are there any cases in which you do not permit the defense to review and copy nonprivileged material in the case file? Who makes these decisions? Please explain.

8. What is your office's reason for an "open files" practice? What are its advantages and disadvantages? Please explain.

The last question is for all respondents.

9. Is there anything else we have not asked about these subjects that we should know? Please explain below or on the back.

When completed, please fax the survey to the Commission at 202-785-7555. You may also mail the survey to our address, P.O. Box 10240 Arlington, VA 22210. All responses are anonymous and will remain confidential. If you have any questions, please phone Commission Chair Jon Gould at 703-993-8481 or email him at innocencecommission@yahoo.com.

Thank you for your assistance. We very much appreciate your time.

Appendix 3

Postconviction Relief for the Introduction of New Evidence: Pleas, New Evidence, and Statutes of Limitations

State	State Statute or Court Rule	Postconviction Relief for Pleas? (Yes or No)	New Evidence?	Time Limit	Relevant Case / Case References
Alabama	Rule 32.2 of AL Rules of Criminal Procedure	Yes, but only with exceptions. Paragraph (b) states that challenges to guilty-plea proceedings are subject to the same limitations as postconviction relief proceedings; they are prohibited unless they meet certain key requirements for new evidence.	Paragraph (b)(2) asserts that as long as petitioner can present new evidence that was not known/could not have been known at the time of the original trial/guilty plea and that failure to consider such evidence would constitute a miscarriage of justice, then relief can be considered.	There is generally a one-year time limit: it is one year past either the date judgment is handed down or (if no appeal) the date for filing an appeal lapses.	

State	State Statute or Court Rule	Postconviction Relief for Pleas? (Yes or No)	New Evidence?	Time Limit	Relevant Case Case References
Alaska	AK Stat. §12.72.020	Yes, but only with exceptions. Doesn't especially preclude relief in the aftermath of a guilty plea. Paragraph (a) limits the circumstances under which a petitioner can seek such relief. Defendants are normally given only one chance for postconviction relief.	Paragraphs (b)(2) and (b)(2)(A) state that if an applicant can establish due diligence regarding new evidence and that the evidence was not known within two years of the guilty sentencing and/or that it can show the innocence of the petitioner, a claim can be heard by the courts.	Paragraph (a)(3) says if the petitioner claims that the sentence was illegal, there is no time limit.	
Arizona	AZ Rev. Stat. Ann. §§13-4234 and 17 A.R.S. AZ Rules of Criminal Procedure Rule 32 of AZ Rules of Criminal Procedure	Yes. Doesn't especially preclude relief in the aftermath of a guilty plea. However, does specify that anyone who pleads guilty or no-contest and has a probation violation is entitled to postconviction relief; thus relief seems to be ensured.	Under the heading "Scope of Remedy," the statutes state that a petitioner has grounds for relief as long as material facts exist and they meet specific requirements. Paragraph (e)(1–3) states that the facts must be found only in the aftermath of the trial, that due diligence was exercised, and that the new material is not cumulative or for the sole impeachment of testimony. The exception	No specific time limits found.	

is for material that would impeach testimony or evidence that had a determining factor in the outcome of the trial.

Arkansas	Rule 37.2 of AR Rules of Criminal Procedure	Yes with extreme limitations, and specific mention of guilty-pleas. Paragraph 37.2(c) states that if a conviction was obtained through a plea of guilty, a petition claiming relief may be filed within 90 days of the handing down of the judgment.	Yes, see time limit column. In *Smothers v. State* (1981), the court ruled that a postconviction petition filed after the three-year mark was invalid due to the lack of evidence supporting the petitioner's argument that the conviction was void.	Paragraph 37.2(c) leaves some ambiguity regarding whether a petitioner has 3 years or 90 days. There is a 3-year window within which all postconviction petitions must be filed (see citation next column). As ruled in *Gass v. State* (1989)—regarding rule 37.2 (c)—this three-year limitation starts on the date judgment is handed down. In *Williams v. State* (1987), the courts ruled that only when there is sufficient proof of evidence to void the original judgment will a petition filed after the three-year period be recognized.	28 U.S.C.A § 2254; Ark.Rules Crim.Proc., Rule 37.1 et seq. *Williams v. Lockhart*, 1989, 873 F2d 1129, rehearing denied, certiorari denied 110 S.Ct. 344 493 U.S. 942, 107 L.Ed2d 333. *Gass v. State*, 1989, 298 Ark. 548, 769 S.W.2d 24. *Williams v. State*, 1987, 293 Ark. 73, 732 S.W. 2d 456.

State	State Statute or Court Rule	Postconviction Relief for Pleas? (Yes or No)	New Evidence?	Time Limit	Relevant Case / Case References
California	CA Penal Code §1473 Writ of Corum Nobis	Yes. In recent case law, the courts have laid out provisions under which relief may be considered (see far right column). In light of specific evidence that might have altered the outcome of a trial (had it been known), a petition for relief will considered. Though not specifically mentioned, it would seem this would extend to guilty pleas and pleas of no contest as well. The case law lays out clear specifications regarding what the nature of material fact and evidence must be in order for relief to be granted/considered.	In *People v. Espinoza*, the court ruled that newly discovered evidence is a basis for relief but that it is not sufficient if the evidence merely weakens the prosecution's case. Only if it undermines the entire case, and not necessarily specific testimony or evidence, can relief be considered. In *People v. Kasim*, the court also ruled that failure by the prosecution to disclose evidence favorable to the defense is a due process violation (thus relief could be considered), regardless of whether the failure was intentional. In *In re Pratt*, the Court ruled that false evidence is material only if by the nature of its fallaciousness it	In *In re Sanders*, the court makes it clear that even if it is untimely, a petition will be accepted if it fits one of three specifications: (i) demonstrates that an error of constitutional magnitude is responsible at trial and absent the error, the petitioner would not have been convicted; (ii) the petitioner is innocent of the crimes he committed, (iii) the death penalty was issued and imposed in light of facts that, if otherwise false, would have not brought the death penalty; and/or (iv) the sentence was implemented under an invalid statute.	*In Re Robert Hackett*, 223 Cal.App.3d 1488 (1990). *People v Espinoza* (App. 6 Dist. 2002) 116 Cal.Rprtr.2d 700, 95 Cal.App. 4th 1287, review denied. *People v. Kasim* (App. 4 Dist. 1997) 66 Cal.Rprtr.2d 494, 56 Cal.App. 4th 1360, rehearing denied. *In re Pratt* (app. 2 Dist. 1999) 82 Cal.Rprtr.2d 260, 69 Cal. App.App. 4th 1294. *In re Sanders* (1999) 87 Cal. Rprtr.2d 1038.

| Colorado | Rule 33 of CO Rules of Criminal Procedure | Yes, but with exceptions. In recent case law, the courts have laid out provisions under which possible relief may be considered (see columns to the right).

In *People v. Rosales*, the court specified that motions for a new trial based on newly discovered evidence are disfavored unless there has been a gross abuse of discretion. | could reasonably be said to have determined the outcome of the trial.

In *People v. Young*, the court set forth the following test for a motion for a new trial (because of new evidence) to succeed: (1) the evidence was discovered posttrial, (2) defendant made all possible efforts to uncover evidence prior to and during trial phase, (3) evidence is not cumulative or impeaching in nature, (4) if/when presented, the evidence in question would bring about an acquittal in a retrial.

In *DeLuzio v. People*, the court ruled that false or mistaken testimony that could have influenced the verdict and/or another trial result in a different outcome is valid grounds for the granting of a new trial. | Paragraph (c) states that a motion for a new trial should be filed as soon as possible after the issuing of judgment and as soon as the (new) facts become known to the defendant. For motions regarding grounds outside the discovery of new evidence, a fifteen-day window exists (post-judgment). | *People v. Schneider,* 25 P.3d 755 (2001).

People v. Young, App. 1999, 987 P.2d 889, modified on denial of rehearing, certiorari denied.

People v. Estep, App. 1990, 799 P.2d 405, certiorari denied.

People v. Rosales, App. 1995, 911 P.2d 644, rehearing denied, certiorari denied.

People v. Graham, App. 1994, 876 P.2d 68, certiorari denied.

People v. Williams, App. 1992, 827 P.2d 612.

DeLuzio v. People, 1972, 494 P.2d 589, 177 Colo. 389. |

State	State Statute or Court Rule	Postconviction Relief for Pleas? (Yes or No)	New Evidence?	Time Limit	Relevant Case Case References
Connecticut	CT Gen. Stat. §52-270 CT Gen. Stat. §52-470 CT Gen. Stat. §52-582	??? Paragraph (a) states that the superior court has the power to grant a new trial regarding any motion that comes before it.	In *Summerville v. Warden, State Prison*, the court set forth the test specifying that new evidence would be allowed to generate a new trial as long there was significant support that such evidence could/would change the outcome of the trial and verdict.	None found.	*Summerville v. Warden, State Prison* (1994) 641 A.2d Conn. 397. *Asherman v. State* (1987) 521 A.2d 578, 202 Conn. 389.
Delaware	DE Code Ann. Tit. 11 §4504 Rules 33 and 61 of DE Criminal Rules Governing the Court of Common Pleas	??? Paragraph (a) states that the courts may allow DNA testing as a means to illustrate innocence. The paragraph lays out distinct provisions regulating the granting of said relief. Paragraph (b) states that if DNA evidence is not available but other evidence is and that it was either not known or not presented at trial, it can be grounds for relief as well.	Paragraph (a) lays out the following conditions: (1) testing must be performed on evidence relating to the trial/conviction; (2) the evidence was not previously tested because the technology did not exist yet; (3) identity was an issue in the trial; (4) the evidence has not been altered or tampered with; (5) the testing will/may produce new evidence relevant to the claim of innocence;	Paragraph (a) instructs that a person has a 3-year window to file a petition for relief, postconviction.	

| Florida | Rule 3.851 of FL Rules of Criminal Procedure Yes. Paragraph (a) states that anyone who has been sentenced or convicted and can make the following claims is entitled to relief: (1) conviction is in violation of the Constitution of the United States or the state; (2) the court was without jurisdiction to implement sentence; (3) sentence exceeds the maximum or is otherwise erroneous; (4) material facts, not yet presented at trial that (if heard) would vacate the sentence; (5) sentence has expired; (6) sentence is erroneous. | In *Padron v. State* (2000), the court ruled that new evidence must adhere to the following: the evidence was discovered posttrial, defendant made all possible efforts to uncover evidence prior to and during trial phase, if/when presented, the evidence in question would bring about an acquittal in a retrial. | (6) the scientific testing method is one accepted within the scientific community.

Paragraph (b) states that unless a motion can meet certain restrictions, it must be filed within two years of the final judgment, and one year after a death penalty verdict. The exceptions are (1) facts on which the motion was based were not known to the defendant or not ascertained through due diligence before and during the trial; (2) incompetent counsel; (3) constitutional rights or laws were not applicable to the case during trial. | *Padron v. State*, App. 2 Dist., 769 So.2d 432 (2000). *Lamar v. State*, App. 2 Dist., 768 So.2d 500 (2000). |

State	State Statute or Court Rule	Postconviction Relief for Pleas? (Yes or No)	New Evidence?	Time Limit	Relevant Case Case References
Georgia	GA Code Ann. §5-5-40	Probably yes (?) It seems the courts have ruled that discretion lies with the courts themselves.		Two years	*Harris v. State*, 2004 Ga.
Hawaii	Rule 40 of HI Rules of Penal Procedure	Yes. In Rule 40(a)(1), the statute lays out guidelines for seeking relief. The guidelines require that a motion for relief be filed only after the handing down of the sentence, for an argument for postconviction relief to be accepted.	The guidelines from 40(a)(1) are (i) judgment or sentence was obtained in violation of the Constitution or state law; (ii) court was without jurisdiction; (iii) the sentence is illegal; (iv) newly discovered evidence; (v) anything else that is grounds for attacking the judgment.		

Idaho	Rule 34 of ID Criminal Rules Rule 33 (c)	Yes. Rule 34 states that the courts (in the interest of justice) may grant a new trial and if there was no jury, the court may also vacate the judgment. Rule 33 (c) permits the withdrawal of a guilty plea at any time for manifest injustice.	Rule 34 states that petitioners have 2 years after the final judgment to file a petition for postconviction relief based upon the discovery of new evidence.	*State v. Gardner*, 126 Id. 428 (1994).
Illinois	725 IL Comp. Stat. 5/116-1	Yes. In paragraph (b), the statute states that the courts are given the power to grant a new trial following the finding/verdict of guilt.	In *People v. Williams*, the Court upheld a ruling that set forth a standard by which new evidence could merit postconviction relief: the evidence had to have been (1) discovered posttrial/sentencing, (2) it could have not been discovered prior to or during trial, (3) it is material and not just cumulative, (4) it is of such weight that it could alter the outcome of the trial, including the verdict.	*People v. Williams*, App. 1 Distr. 1998, 229 Ill. Dec. 734 295 Ill. App. 3d 456, 692 N.E. 2d 723, appeal denied 232 Ill. Dec. 852, 178 Ill. 2d 595, 699 N.E. 2d 1037.

State	State Statute or Court Rule	Postconviction Relief for Pleas? (Yes or No)	New Evidence?	Time Limit	Relevant Case Case References
Indiana	Rule 1 of IN Procedure for Postconviction Remedies	Yes. Section 1(a) states that anyone whose appeal for relief meets specific conditions can reasonably expect to have his petition considered.	The conditions laid out in Section 1(a) are (1) conviction is in violation of the Constitution of the United States or the state; (2) the court was without jurisdiction to implement sentence; (3) sentence exceeds the maximum or is otherwise erroneous; (4) material facts not yet presented at trial that (if heard) would vacate the sentence; (5) sentence has expired; (6) sentence is erroneous.	Section 1(a) also notes that a motion for relief that meets any of the conditions it lays out can be filed at any time for the purposes of securing relief. In *Holland v. State* (1993), the court ruled that even a petition filed 12 years past was valid, since evidence was justified and the prosecution had not shown any reason why the petitioner would have known about the problems with his conviction at or immediately after trial.	*Holland v. State*, 1993 N.E. 2d 429.

Iowa	IA R. Crim. P. 2.24 No. In *State v. Alexander* (1990), the court ruled that a "defendant who entered [a] guilty plea to charges of willful injury was not entitled to [a] new trial on grounds of newly discovered evidence; [a] new trial was available as a remedy only to defendants who had already been to trial." The rulings do not preclude those who had a trial from seeking relief.			*State v. Alexander,* 1990, 463 N.W. 2d 421.
Kansas	KS Stat. Ann. §22-3501	Probably yes. Paragraph(1) states that the courts (in the interest of justice) may grant a new trial and if there was no jury, the court may also vacate the judgment.	In *State v. Hemminger,* the court ruled that criminal cases dating beyond July 1, 1970, are not restricted to two years' postconviction to file new a motion for relief based on new evidence.	Paragraph (1) states that a motion for a new trial may be made within 2 years after final judgment if it regards/is based on the finding of new evidence.	*State v. Humdinger,* 207 K. 172, 177, 483 P.2d 1096.

State	State Statute or Court Rule	Postconviction Relief for Pleas? (Yes or No)	New Evidence?	Time Limit	Relevant Case Case References
Kentucky	Rule 60.02 of KY Rules of Civil Procedure	Probably yes. Rule 60.02 states that it is at the court's discretion to accept a petition for postconviction relief. 60.02(b) states that newly discovered evidence not discovered in time to move for a new trial is grounds for the granting of such relief.	In *Barnett v. Com.* (1998), the court upheld this statute. In *Stacey v. Com.* (2004), the court ruled that in the matter of a guilty plea, in which a defendant was not capable due to mental incompetence, he was also not able to necessarily agree to a guilty plea and thus this presented an acceptable argument for postconviction relief.		*State v. Walton*, 256 Kan. 484, 489 (1994). *State v. Bey*, 270 Kan. 544 (2001). *Barnett v. Com.* (Ky. 1998) 979 S.W. 2d 98. *Stacey v. Com.* (Ky. App. 2004) 2004 W.L 691760.

Louisiana	LA Code Crim. Proc. Ann. Art. 853	No. A court will consider a motion for postconviction relief if it shows good cause and is filed within the prescribed time. In *State v. Montz*, the court ruled that trial courts lack the jurisdiction to hear a motion for new trial based on newly discovered evidence, where motion was filed after order of appeal from conviction had been entered.		*State v. Montz*, App. 4 Cir.1994, 632 So.2d 822, 1992-2073 (La.App 4 Cir. 2/11/94), writ denied 637 So.2d 499, 1994-0605 (La. 6/3/94).
Maine	Rule 33 of ME Rules of Criminal Procedure Tit.15 §2121–2132 postconviction relief	Probably no. The courts will consider relief if in the interest of justice. If the original court conducted the trial without a jury, the new court can abandon the former judgment, take new testimony, and form a new judgment.	The discovery of new evidence provides the grounds for a new trial.	A motion for a new trial based on newly discovered evidence can be made only before, or within 2 years after, entry of the judgment in the criminal docket.

State	State Statute or Court Rule	Postconviction Relief for Pleas? (Yes or No)	New Evidence?	Time Limit	Relevant Case/ Case References
Maryland	Rule 4-331 of MD Rules, Criminal Causes	??? Paragraphs (a) and (b) state that the court may order a new trial in the interest of justice. In addition, the court has revising power and control over the judgment in the case of fraud, mistake, or irregularity.	In *Newman v. State*, the court ruled that newly discovered evidence is a basis for relief, but (1) the new evidence could not have been discovered by due diligence in time to move for a new trial within 10 days after the entered verdict, and (2) the evidence may well have produced a different result.	(c) (1)A motion for a new trial based on newly discovered evidence should be filed within one year after the date the court imposed sentence or the date it received a mandate issued by the Court of Appeals or the Court of Special Appeals, whichever is later. (c) (2) A motion for a new trial can be filed at any time if a sentence of death was imposed and the newly discovered evidence can prove the innocence of defendant. (c) (3) A motion for a new trial can be filed at any time if the motion is based on DNA identification testing or other generally accepted scientific techniques that would show the innocence of the defendant.	*Newman v. State*, 2003, 2003 WL 22939055. *Skok v. State*, 361 Md. 52 (2000).

| Massachusetts | Rule 30 of MA Criminal Procedure | Yes. If the liberty of a defendant is restrained pursuant to a conviction, the defendant can file a motion for postconviction relief from the trial judge presiding at the initial trial. | In *Commonwealth v. Solomonsen*, the court ruled that to succeed on a motion for new trial on the basis of newly discovered evidence, the defendant must demonstrate that the evidence was newly discovered and that it was credible, material, and cast real doubt on the justice of the conviction.

In *Commonwealth v. Pike*, the court ruled that a defendant must also show that the evidence was unknown to the defendant or defendant's counsel and not discoverable through reasonable pretrial diligence at the time of trial. | Paragraph (a) states that any person who is imprisoned or whose liberty is restrained pursuant to a criminal conviction may, at any time, file a written motion requesting the trial judge to release him or her to correct the current sentence. | *Commonwealth v. Solomonsen* (2000) 735 N.E.2d 411, 50 Mass.App.Ct. 122, review denied.

Commonwealth v. Pike, 431 Mass. 218 (2000). |

State	State Statute or Court Rule	Postconviction Relief for Pleas? (Yes or No)	New Evidence?	Time Limit	Relevant Case / Case References
Michigan	MI Comp. Laws. Ann. §770.2	Yes.		A motion for a new trial must be made within 60 days after entry of the judgment or within any further time allowed by the trial court during the 60-day period. In *People v. Johnson*, the court ruled that while there is no final time limitation by existing rule, the court does not look favorably on a long delayed motion for a new trial.	*People v. Hernandez*, 443 Mich. 1 (1993). *People v. Johnson* (1971) 192 N.W.2d 482, 386 Mich. 305, two judges concurring and two judges concurring in result.
Minnesota	MN Stat. Ann. §590.01	Yes. The defendant can file a motion for relief if the conviction violates the person's rights. In *State v. Williams*, the court ruled that the Supreme Court will apply the same standard of review to a conviction based on plea of guilty as applied to a conviction based on a jury verdict.	In *Sutherlin v. State*, the court found that newly discovered evidence will only be used to grant postconviction relief if four elements are met: (1) evidence was not known to petitioner or counsel at time of trial; (2) evidence could not have been discovered through due diligence before	In *Sykes v. State*, the court found that timeliness is not required by the postconviction statute, although it is a factor to be considered when determining whether relief should be granted.	*State v. Williams*, 1969, 282 Minn. 240, 163 N.W.2d 868. *Sutherlin v. State*, 1998, 574 N.W.2d 428, rehearing denied, certiorari denied 118 S.Ct. 2351, 524 U.S. 942, 141 L.Ed.2d 721. *Hodgson v. State*, 1995, 540 N.W.2d 515.

trial; (3) evidence is not cumulative, impeaching, or doubtful; and (4) evidence probably would produce an acquittal or a more favorable result.

Mississippi	MS Code Ann. §99-39-5	Yes, but with exceptions. The defendant can file a motion for relief if the conviction or sentence is in violation of the U.S. Constitution or the Constitution or laws of Mississippi. However, limitations for relief begin when the three-year time limit for appeals expires.	In *Meeks v. State*, the court found that in order to warrant the granting of a new trial on the ground of newly discovered evidence, it must appear that the evidence is such as will probably change the result if a new trial is granted, that it has been discovered since the trial, that it could not have been discovered before the trial by the exercise of due diligence, that it is material to the issue, and this it is not merely cumulative or impeaching.	A motion for relief must be filed within 3 years after the time in which the prisoner's direct appeal is ruled upon by the Supreme Court of Mississippi, or if no appeal was taken, within 3 years after the time for taking an appeal from the judgment of conviction or sentence has expired, or in case of a guilty plea, within 3 years after entry of the judgment of conviction. An exception to this ruling is evidence, not reasonably discoverable at the time of trial, which would have conclusively caused a different result in the conviction or sentence.	*Martin v. State*, 1980, 295 N.W.2d 76. *Sykes v. State*, App. 1998, 578 N.W.2d 807, review denied, certiorari denied 119 S.Ct. 619, 525 U.S. 1055, 142 L.Ed2d 558. *Meeks v. State* (Miss. 2001) 781 So.2d 109, rehearing denied.

State	State Statute or Court Rule	Postconviction Relief for Pleas? (Yes or No)	New Evidence?	Time Limit	Relevant Case Case References
Missouri	Rule 91 Writ of Habeas Corpus	Yes, but with extreme limitations. In *State v. Garner* (1998), the court ruled that the courts have a wide body of discretion in hearing a postconviction motion on the basis of new evidence and that it does not give much favor to such requests. In *Burton v. Dormire* (2002), the court ruled: "Under Missouri law there are no means for a criminal defendant to present claims of newly discovered evidence to the judiciary after the time to file a motion for new trial has expired; narrow exceptions permit consideration of newly discovered evidence that completely exonerates a defendant." In *State v. Garner* (1998), the court ruled: "Missouri pro-	In *State v. Flemming* (1993), the court ruled that newly discovered evidence as a basis for postconviction relief must be material, probably influence the outcome of the trial, not be cumulative or impeaching, and previously not found even with proper due diligence and discovery methods. *State v. Stone* (1994) reaffirmed the burden of proof on the defendant and emphasized that evidence must be such that it would alter the outcome of the trial.		*State v. Young*, 943 S.W.2d 794 (App. W.D. 1997). *Wilson v. State*, 813 S.W.2d 833 (1991). *State v. Stone* (App. W.D. 1994) 869 S.W. 2d. *Burton v. Dormire*, C.A.8 (Mo) 2002, 295 F.3d 839, rehearing and rehearing en banc denied, certiorari denied 123 S.Ct. 1904, 538 U.S. 1002, 155 L.Ed2d 831. *State v. Garner* (App. W.D. 1998) 976 S.W.2d 57, denial of postconviction relief reversed 62 S.W.3d 716. *State v. Flemming* (App. S.D. 1993) 855 S.W.2d 517.

	cedures do not provide a means for a criminal defendant to present claims of newly discovered evidence to the judiciary after the time to file a motion for new trial has expired; the only formally authorized means . . . is by application to the governor for executive clemency or pardon."			
Montana	MT Code Ann. §46-21-102	Yes.	See next column.	Section 46-21-102(2) states that in light of newly discovered evidence that would establish the innocence of the petitioner, a postconviction petition may be filed within one year of the date of the conviction or when the petitioner discovers the existence of the evidence in question, whichever is later. For all other instances, petitioners have one full year, starting at the date of the conviction.

State	State Statute or Court Rule	Postconviction Relief for Pleas? (Yes or No)	New Evidence?	Time Limit	Relevant Case/Case References
Nebraska	NE Rev. Stat. §29-2103	Yes, but severe limitations. Court rulings and state law make it clear that postconviction relief is held in little regard, although it is available. In *State v. Russell* (1992), the court ruled that a judge is not required to grant a hearing for postconviction relief if it merely alleges conclusions of law or fact and/or contains sufficient facts regarding the unconstitutionality of a judgment against the defendant and that such a denial will not result in a voiding of the sentence. In *State v. Otey* (1989), the courts ruled that issues known to the defendant which could have been addressed on direct appeal are	Very little said. However, in *State v. Otey* (1991), the courts ruled that a defendant is entitled to a relief hearing if the grounds relied on in the first trial did not exist at the time of the first motion.		*State v. Russell*, 239 Neb. 979, 479 N.W. 2d 798 (1992). *State v. Kerr*, 232 Neb. 799, 442 N.W. 2d 381 (1989). *State v. Cole* 207 Neb. 318, 298 N.W. 2d 776 (1980). *State v. Otey*, 236 Neb. 915, 464 N.W. 2d 352 (1991). *State v. Hochstein*, 216 Neb. 515, 344 N.W. 2d 469 (1984). *State v. Sheldon*, 181 Neb. 360 148 N.W. 2d 301 (1967).

		not sufficient grounds for relief.
		The courts also ruled that a mere constitutional issue is not sufficient but that the issues must involve grounds for the setting aside of a sentence (*State v. Cole*, 1980).
Nevada	NV Rev. Stat. Ann. 176.515	???
New Hampshire	NH Rev. Stat. Ann. §526.4	???
New Jersey	Rule 3:22-12 of NJ Rules Governing Criminal Practice	???
New Mexico	Rule 5-802 of NM Rules of Criminal Procedure for the District Courts	Probably no. On appeal in *U.S. Sisneros* (1979), the court ruled that upon accepting/making a plea of guilty with the knowledge that no lighter sentence was being provided, the defendant could not then make a motion for postconviction relief.

State	State Statute or Court Rule	Postconviction Relief for Pleas? (Yes or No)	New Evidence?	Time Limit	Relevant Case Case References
New York	N.Y.C.P.L.R 440.10	???			
North Carolina	NC Gen. Stat. §15a-1415	Yes.	In *State v. Stukes* (2002), the court laid out conditions for new evidence to be considered material and a valid reason for consideration for relief: (1) witnesses give new evidence, (2) the evidence is reasonably considered true, (3) material and relevant, (4) the evidence was not known despite thorough due diligence and proper procurement, (5) not cumulative, (6) does not impeach or discredit a witness, and (7) combined with a new trial, a new verdict and outcome would likely be reached. In *State v. McDowell* (1984), the court ruled that evidence that would have had a bearing on the outcome of the trial and	Paragraph (a) states that a noncapital defendant may seek relief at any time after the verdict is handed down. For capital defendants, relief must be filed within 120 days of a specific list of events. Paragraph (b) states that a defendant may file a motion for relief past 10 days only with specific exceptions. Paragraph (c), however, allows for a defendant to file a motion for relief at any point on the grounds of newly discovered evidence as long as the evidence is/will be influential in determining the defendant's status as guilty or innocent.	*State v Stukes*, 2002 153 N.C. App. 770, 571 S.E.2d 241. *State v. McDowell*, 1984, 310 S.E. 2d 301, 310 N.C. 61

North Dakota	ND Cent. Code §29-32.1-03	???	the verdict and that was withheld by the prosecution (and unknown to the defense) is material and grounds for the granting of relief.	This paragraph requires that the motion be as timely as possible upon the discovery of such evidence.
Ohio	Rule 33 of OH Rules of Criminal Procedure	???	In *U.S. v. Garland* (1993), the court affirmed rules that newly discovered evidence must satisfy to be accepted as grounds to hear a motion for posttrial relief: the defendant needs to show that the facts were not previously known nor were able to be known through due diligence to him or his counsel; the information is not merely cumulative nor impeaching; and the evidence would bring about an acquittal if the case were reheard.	*U.S. v. Garland* (C.A. (Ohio) 1993) 991 F.2d 328.

State	State Statute or Court Rule	Postconviction Relief for Pleas? (Yes or No)	New Evidence?	Time Limit	Relevant Case Case References
Oklahoma	OK Stat. Ann. Tit. 22 §1080	Yes. Tit. 22 §1080 states that anyone who has been sentenced or convicted and can make the following claims is entitled to relief: (1) conviction is in violation of the Constitution of the United States or the state; (2) the court was without jurisdiction to implement sentence; (3) sentence exceeds the maximum or is otherwise erroneous; (4) material facts, not yet presented at trial, that (if heard) would vacate the sentence; (5) sentence has expired; (6) sentence is erroneous. In *Brecheen v. Reynolds* (1994), the court makes a clear statement that it considers postconviction relief to be reserved for only rare circumstances not everyday appeals.	In *Romano, v. State* (1996), the court emphasizes the need for the evidence to have been undiscoverable (such as DNA, when there was not a means to collect DNA) even with good due diligence.		*Romano v. State*, Okla.Crim.App., 917 P.2d 12 (1996).

| Oregon | OR Rev. Stat. §136.535 OR Rev. Stat. §138.530 | ??? ORCP 64 B(4) states certain restrictions for the filing of relief. | Not stated. | In recent cases (see right) the applications for new trial based on newly discovered evidence are not favored. To warrant granting of a motion for new trial, newly discovered evidence must be such as will probably change the result if a new case is granted; been discovered since trial; could not have been discovered before trial; be material to the issue; not be merely cumulative of former evidence; and not be merely impeaching or contradictory of former evidence. | *State v. Disorbo*, 1981, 54 Or.App. 877, 636 P.2d 986. *Oberg v. Honda Motor Co., Ltd.*, 1993, 316 Or. 263, 851 P.ed 1084. |

State	State Statute or Court Rule	Postconviction Relief for Pleas? (Yes or No)	New Evidence?	Time Limit	Relevant Case Case References
Pennsylvania	42 PA Cons. Stat. §9541	Yes. Paragraph (a)(2) states that to be eligible for postconviction relief, a petitioner must be seeking relief from conviction because of one of the following: (i) judgment or sentence was obtained in violation of the Constitution or state law, (ii) ineffective assistance of counsel, (iii) plea of guilty due to circumstances, when the petitioner is actually innocent, (iv) improper obstruction by government officials of the right to appeal, (v) the existence of material facts not known nor presented in previous trials, which require vacating the conviction for the sake of justice, (vi) sentence is greater than the maximum allowed, (vii) court was without jurisdiction.	In *Com. v. Fiore* (2001), the court upheld the specific instructions on the nature of newly discovered evidence. The court specified that such evidence must: (1) have been discovered after the trial, (2) not be cumulative, (3) not solely impeach credibility, (4) likely lead to a change in the verdict.		*Com. v. Casner*, 461 A.2d 324, 315 Pa.Super.12, Super. 1983. *Com. Martinez*, 539 A.2d 399, 372 Pa.Super. 202, Super.1988

In *Com v. Martinez*, the courts ruled that after the acceptance of a guilty plea, a defendant only later can challenge the validity of the plea and the legality of the sentence.

In *Com v. Casner*, the court stated the same and added that a challenge to the guilty plea would not be entertained either unless there had also been a motion made to withdraw the plea during trial.

In *Com. v. McCauley*, the courts ruled that if a defendant had agreed to a plea bargain, then he was not entitled to postconviction relief.

State	State Statute or Court Rule	Postconviction Relief for Pleas? (Yes or No)	New Evidence?	Time Limit	Relevant Case Case References
Rhode Island	RI Gen. Laws §10-9.1	Yes. Paragraph (a) states that anyone who has been sentenced or convicted and can make the following claims is entitled to relief: (1) conviction is in violation of the Constitution of the United States or the state; (2) the court was without jurisdiction to implement sentence; (3) sentence exceeds the maximum or is otherwise erroneous; (4) material facts, not yet presented at trial that (if heard) would vacate the sentence; (5) sentence has expired; (6) sentence is erroneous.		In *State v. Bishop* (1981), the court ruled that even when the time limit for filing a motion has expired, a petitioner is not necessarily precluded from filing a motion if it is based on the discovery of new evidence.	*State v. Bishop*, 439 A.2d 255 (I.I. 1982) 28 October 8, 2004, 1:55 P.M.

South Carolina	SC Code Ann. §17-27-10	Yes.	See next column.	Paragraph (c) states that petitioners who seek postconviction relief on the grounds of newly discovered evidence, have one year to file a motion upon the discovery of such evidence.	None.
South Dakota	SD Codified Laws §21-27-1	No. 15-6-60 (b) states certain restrictions for the filing of relief.	Paragraph 15-6-59 (b) states that newly discovered evidence, which by due diligence could not have been discovered in time to move for a new trial, allows for relief to be considered.	There is a one-year time limit after the judgment, order, or preceding was entered or taken.	*Boyles v. Webster*, 677 N.W.2d 531 (2004). *Haggar v. Olfert*, 1986, 387 N.W. 2d 45.
Tennessee	Rule 14 of TN Rules of Appellate Procedure	???			

State	State Statute or Court Rule	Postconviction Relief for Pleas? (Yes or No)	New Evidence?	Time Limit	Relevant Case Case References
Texas	TX Crim. Proc. Code Ann. §40.001	Yes. Article 40.001 merely states that "a new trial shall be granted an accused where material evidence favorable to the accused has been discovered since trial."	In *Wortham v. State*, the court ruled that a court can deny a motion for relief unless the petition can show that new evidence was unknown and/or unavailable to petitioner at time of trial, that such lack of knowledge was not due to lack of due diligence, and that evidence is not merely impeaching and can change the verdict. This was followed up with a similar ruling in *State v. Weiss* (1999).		*State v. Gonzalez*, 855 S.W.2d 692 (1993). *Wortham v. State* (App. 9 Dist. 1995) 903 S.W 2d 897, petition for discretionary review refused. *State v. Weiss* (App. 9 Dist.1999) 8 S.W. 3d 342, rehearing denied.
United States (Federal Law)	Federal Rules of Criminal Procedure. Rule 33 Federal habeas corpus	Yes.	Paragraph (1): "Any motion for a new trial grounded on newly discovered evidence must be filed within 3 years after the verdict or finding of guilty. If an appeal is pending, the court may not grant a motion for a new trial until the appellate court remands the case."		*Schlup v. Delo*, 513 U.S. 298 (1995). *Bousley v. U.S.*, 523 U.S 614 (1998).

| Utah | UT Code Ann. §78-35a-107 | ??? Utah allows for post-conviction relief. | Paragraph (1)(e) specifies that a motion for postconviction relief can/will address new evidence. | Paragraph (1) states that a petitioner is entitled to relief as long as the petition is filed within one year of: (a) the last day to file an appeal, (b) entry of the judgment by the court of appeals, (c) last day of filing before the Utah Supreme Court or the U.S. Supreme Court, (d) date of decision made on writ of certiorari, (e) date on which the petitioner became aware or was aware of the evidentiary facts on which the petition is based.

However, paragraph (3) leaves it to the court to make the final decision and allows for the court to waive such a time limit if it feels that such a waiver is indeed merited (e.g., is in the best interests of the pursuit of justice). |

State	State Statute or Court Rule	Postconviction Relief for Pleas? (Yes or No)	New Evidence?	Time Limit	Relevant Case/Case References
Vermont	Rule 33 of VT Rules of Criminal Procedure	Probably no.			
Washington	WA Rev. Code §10-73-100 Rule 16.4 of WA Rules of Appellate Procedure	Yes. In Rule 16.4(c), the statute lays out guidelines for seeking relief. In order for relief to be considered, certain provisions apply: (i) the court was without jurisdiction; (ii) the judgment or sentence was obtained in violation of the Constitution or state law; (iii) material facts were not known or presented in previous trials, which require the reversal of the conviction for the sake of justice; (iv) changes in laws are material to the conviction and are sufficient reason to be applied retroactively.	In *In re Greening* (2000), the court ruled that though motions for postconviction relief are accepted, grounds raised in a postconviction motion that were available but not relied on in a prior petition may result in the dismissal of the motion. In *In re Brown* (2001), the court ruled that the rules for postconviction relief for capital punishment based on newly discovered evidence are the same as those applied for postconviction relief in general (see left column). In particular, the material must not be solely impeaching or cumulative.	In *State v. Brand* (1992), the court ruled that the defendant need only to have acted "with reasonable diligence in discovering evidence and seeking relief" and that the one year time limit is superseded by this.	*In re Greening* (2000) 141 Wash. 2d 687, 9 P.3d 206. *In re Brown* (2001) 143 Wash. 2d 431, 21 P.3d 687. *State v. Brand* (1992) 65 Wash. App. 166, 828 P.2d 1, review granted 119 Wash. 2d 1013, 833 P.2d 1390, reversed on other grounds 120 Wash.2d 365, 842 P.2d 470 reconsideration denied.

| Washington, D.C. | DC ST § 23-110 of the District of Columbia Criminal Law and Procedures and Prisoners

D.C. Innocence Protection Act | Yes. Paragraph (a) states that a petitioner is entitled to make a motion to vacate a sentence if his sentence meets the following obligations: (1) judgment or sentence was obtained in violation of the Constitution or state law, (2) court was without jurisdiction, (3) sentence is greater than the maximum allowed, (4) otherwise subject to attack. Paragraph (c) states that if the conditions are met, then the court has the power to vacate the provisions, correct the sentence or grant a new trial. | In *Porter v. U.S.* (2003), the court laid out guidelines for using newly discovered evidence as valid grounds for postsentencing relief. The evidence must (1) have been discovered after the trial, (2) not be cumulative, (3) not solely impeach credibility, (4) likely lead to a change in the verdict. | On the one hand, the provisions of paragraph (b) state that if a motion meets the conditions laid out in paragraph (a), then a motion can be granted at any point. However, in *Washington v. U.S.* (2003), the court ruled that a defendant was not entitled to a new trial because a 13-year delay was too much even with new evidence to accurately try the case.

The court also stated that even though harsh, it has no power to consider an untimely appeal for relief, since time periods for filings are jurisdictional. It made a similar ruling in *Taylor v. U.S.* (2000). | *Washington v. U.S.,* 2003 834 A.2d 899.
Porter v. U.S., 2003 826 A.2d 398.
Taylor v. U.S., 2000, 759 A.2d 604. |

State	State Statute or Court Rule	Postconviction Relief for Pleas? (Yes or No)	New Evidence?	Time Limit	Relevant Case Case References
West Virginia	Rule 33 of WV Rules of Criminal Procedure	???			
Wisconsin	WI Stat. Ann. §974.06	???			
Wyoming	Rule 33 of WY Rules of Criminal Procedure	???			

SOURCE: Innocence Commission for Virginia, 2005.

Appendix 4

Postconviction Relief for the Introduction of New Evidence: Times Available

State	State Statute or Court Rule	Explicit Number of Limitations?	Relevant Case References
Alabama	Rule 32.2 of AL Rules of Criminal Procedure	No	
Alaska	AK Stat. §12.72.020	Yes, according to paragraph (a)(6) of the statute and commentary in the "Notes to Decisions" section, defendants are generally entitled to only one petition for postconviction relief.	*Hertz v. State*, 8 P.3d 1144 (Alaska Ct. App. 2000). *Linton v. State*, 27 P.3d 782 (Alaska Ct. App. 2001).
Arizona	AZ Rev. Stat. Ann. §13-4234 Rule 32 of AZ Rules of Criminal Procedure	No	
Arkansas	Rule 37.2 of AR Rules of Criminal Procedure	Yes, according to commentary under the heading "Successive petitions" in the "Notes to Decisions" section, second petitions are not considered unless the first petition for relief was specifically denied without prejudice to filing a subsequent petition.	
California	CA Penal Code §1473	No	
Colorado	Rule 33 of CO Rules of Criminal Procedure	No	
Connecticut	CT Gen. Stat. §52-270 CT Gen. Stat. §52-470 CT Gen. Stat. §52-582	No	

State	State Statute or Court Rule	Explicit Number of Limitations?	Relevant Case References
Delaware	DE Code Ann. Tit. 11 §4504 Rules 33 and 61 of DE Criminal Rules Governing the Court of Common Pleas	No	
Florida	Rule 3.851 of FL Rules of Criminal Procedure	No	
Georgia	GA Code Ann. §5-5-40	No	
Hawaii	Rule 40 of HI Rules of Penal Procedure	No	
Idaho	Rule 34 of ID Criminal Rules	No	
Illinois	725 IL Comp. Stat. 5/116-1	No	
Indiana	Rule 1 of IN Procedure for Postconviction Remedies	No	
Iowa	IA R. Crim. P. 2.24	No	
Kansas	KS Stat. Ann. §22-3501	No	
Kentucky	Rule 60.02 of KY Rules of Civil Procedure	No	
Louisiana	LA Code Crim. Proc. Ann. Art. 853	Maybe. One of the entries under the heading "Amended and supplemental motions" in the "Notes to Decisions" section reads "Accused was entitled as matter of right to only one motion for new trial, and was not entitled after appeal to a second motion based on newly discovered evidence."	*State v. Smith*, Sup.1924, 156 La. 818, 101 So. 209.
Maine	Rule 33 of ME Rules of Criminal Procedure	No	
Maryland	Rule 4-331 of MD Rules, Criminal Causes	No	
Massachusetts	Rule 30 of MA Criminal Procedure	No	

State	State Statute or Court Rule	Explicit Number of Limitations?	Relevant Case References
Michigan	MI Comp. Laws. Ann. §770.2	No	
Minnesota	MN Stat. Ann. §590.01	No	
Mississippi	MS Code Ann. §99-39-5	No	
Missouri	Rule 29.11 of MO Supreme Court Rules, Rules of Criminal Procedure	No	
Montana	MT Code Ann. §46-21-102	No	
Nebraska	NE Rev. Stat. §29-2103	No	
Nevada	NV Rev. Stat. Ann. 176.515	No	
New Hampshire	NH Rev. Stat. Ann. §526.4	No	
New Jersey	Rule 3:22-12 of NJ Rules Governing Criminal Practice	No	
New Mexico	Rule 5-802 of NM Rules of Criminal Procedure for the District Courts	No	
New York	N.Y.C.P.L.R 440.10	No	
North Carolina	NC Gen. Stat. §15a-1415	No	
North Dakota	ND Cent. Code §29-32.1-03	No	
Ohio	Rule 33 of OH Rules of Criminal Procedure	No	
Oklahoma	OK Stat. Ann. Tit. 22 §1080	No	
Oregon	OR Rev. Stat. §136.535 OR Rev. Stat. §138.530	No	
Pennsylvania	42 PA Cons. Stat. §9541	No	
Rhode Island	RI Gen. Laws §10-9.1	No	
South Carolina	SC Code Ann. §17-27-10	No	
South Dakota	SD Codified Laws §21-27-1	No	
Tennessee	Rule 14 of TN Rules of Appellate Procedure	No	

State	State Statute or Court Rule	Explicit Number of Limitations?	Relevant Case References
Texas	TX Crim. Proc. Code Ann. §40.001	No	
Utah	UT Code Ann. §78-35a-107	No	
Virginia		Yes	
Vermont	Rule 33 of VT Rules of Criminal Procedure	No	
Washington	WA Rev. Code §10-73-100 Rule 16.4 of WA Rules of Appellate Procedure	Yes, Paragraph (d) of Rule 16.4 states that with respect to personal restraint petitions, "no more than one petition for similar relief on behalf of the same petitioner will be entertained without good cause shown."	
West Virginia	Rule 33 of WV Rules of Criminal Procedure	No	
Wisconsin	WI Stat. Ann. §974.06	No	
Wyoming	Rule 33 of WY Rules of Criminal Procedure	No	

SOURCE: Innocence Commission for Virginia, 2005.

Appendix 5
Virginia DCJS Model Lineup Procedures

Police / Sheriff's Department   General Orders
Subject: Suspect Lineup Procedure   Number: 2-39
Effective Date: July 1, 2005   Review Date: (annually)
Amends / Supersedes: New   Approved: _____ Chief of Police/Sheriff
VLEPSC Standards:

NOTE: This order is for internal use only and does not enlarge an officer's civil or criminal liability in any way. It should not be construed as the creation of a higher standard of safety or care in an evidentiary sense, with respect to third-party claims. Violations of this directive, if proven, can only form the basis of a complaint by this department, and then only in a non-judicial setting.

Index Words

Eyewitness Evidence: A Guide for Law Enforcement
eyewitness identification
fillers (nonsuspects)
lineup
lineup Identification Form
lineup identification number
mugshots
photo lineup
right to counsel
sequential lineup

Policy

The Department attaches the highest priority to the protection of the citizens that we serve. Recognizing that innocent persons may occasionally get caught up in the criminal investigative process and be wrongly implicated in criminal matters, we attach equal importance to clearing innocent persons as that attached to arresting the guilty.

According to a 1999 National Institute of Justice report, over 75,000 people a year become criminal defendants based on eyewitness identification. Research of cases in which DNA evidence has been used to exonerate individuals previously convicted of crimes, leads many experts to conclude that improved, more reliable methods of handling eyewitness identifications may promote higher standards of justice. For example, of the 151 DNA exoneration cases studied, nationally, in 61 of the first 70, mistaken eyewitness identification was a factor leading to the conviction; and, in 45 of the first 82 DNA exoneration cases, a photographic line up was the type of pre-trial identification procedure used.

Recognizing that the traditional system for conducting eyewitness identification procedures is not infallible and that the procedures did not incorporate the growing body of psychological study of eyewitness memory and behavior, the United States Department of Justice (DOJ) developed guidelines for conducting these procedures. The purpose of the guidelines is to prevent eyewitness error rather than correcting errors after they have occurred. The guidelines take the basic elements of police investigations and suggest workable changes in order to achieve more consistent eyewitness results.

The following procedures incorporate the recommendations issued by the United States Department of Justice in its *Eyewitness Evidence: A Guide for Law Enforcement.* An identification obtained through a line up composed in this manner should minimize the risk of misidentification and have stronger evidentiary value than one obtained without these procedures. Specifically, use of these procedures should maximize the reliability of identifications, minimize unjust accusations of innocent persons and establish evidence that is reliable and conforms with established legal procedure.

Purpose

To establish a policy for the preparation and presentation of photographic and in-person line ups.

Definitions

Lineup: A *lineup* is any procedure in which a witness to a crime or other incident is asked to identify one or more suspects from among a group of persons in order to determine or confirm the identity of the suspect(s). Such procedures involve either actually viewing of persons or viewing of photographs.

Photo lineup: A photo line up is any line up procedure in which photographs are used instead of live persons. These procedures are often used when a suspect has not been identified or when such person has not been located or arrested.

Sequential lineup: A sequential line up is a particular method of conducting a suspect line up in which persons or photographs are presented to the witness one at a time, rather than in any sort of grouping.

Procedures: General Responsibilities

1. Department personnel shall strictly adhere to established procedures for conducting suspect line ups in order to avoid the possibility of error or of undue suggestiveness to witnesses.

2. Department personnel shall be trained in line up procedures to establish uniformity and consistency of such procedures and to establish a high level of competence in carrying out this important aspect of a criminal investigation.

3. Department personnel shall report any known errors, flaws or non-conformance with established procedures in the conduct of a suspect line up that they may observe or become aware of to their supervisor in order that corrective actions may be taken and safeguards established to protect the innocent.

4. The Department will confer with the Office of the Commonwealth's Attorney in establishing line up procedures in order to assure the best use of this type of evidence and to assure that procedures established are compatible with the prosecution of criminal cases. Likewise, instructions given to witnesses during a line up procedure will be those established and approved in consultation with the Commonwealth's Attorney.

Procedures: Composing the Lineup

1. The investigator in charge should select an individual who does not know which member of the line up is the "true" suspect to conduct any line ups in order to avoid inadvertent signs or body language that may lead or cause a witness to make an incorrect identification. The officer/investigator selected should be thoroughly familiar with this procedure.

2. Assure that law enforcement and/or prosecutorial personnel present and involved in the case are knowledgeable about the procedure so that they will not interfere or influence any witness during the process. Unnecessary personnel should be removed from the location where the process is being conducted.

3. Ensure that the line up is comprised in such a manner that the suspect does not unduly stand out. However, complete uniformity of features is not required.

4. Avoid mixing color and black and white photos. Photos should be either all black and white or all color.

5. Cover any portions of mugshots or other photographs that provide identifying information. Ensure that no writings or information concerning previous arrest(s) will be visible to the witness. If it is necessary to block-out or cover a notation, such as a name on one photo, then similar blocking-out or covering marks should be placed on all photos so that they will appear alike.

6. Use photos of the same size and basic composition, and never mix mugshots with other snapshots or include more than one photo of the same suspect.

7. Include only one suspect in each identification procedure.

8. Select fillers (non suspects) who generally fit the witnesses' description of the offender. When there is a limited or inadequate description of the offender provided by the witness, or when the description of the offender differs significantly from the appearance of the suspect, fillers should resemble the suspect in significant features.

9. Select a photo that resembles the suspect's description or appearance at the time of the incident, if multiple photos of the suspect are reasonably available to the investigator.

10. Ensure that the photos are reasonably contemporary.

11. Include a minimum of five fillers (non-suspects) per identification procedure.

12. Create a consistent appearance between the suspect and fillers so that the photos depict individuals who are reasonably similar in age, height, weight and general appearance, and are of the same sex and race. However, avoid using fillers who so closely resemble the suspect that a person familiar with the suspect might find it difficult to distinguish the suspect from the fillers.

13. Create a consistent appearance between the suspect and the fillers with respect to any unique or unusual feature—such as a scar or tattoo - used to describe the perpetrator by artificially adding or concealing that feature.

14. Place the suspect in different positions in each line up when conducting more than one line up for a case with multiple witnesses or suspects.

15. Avoid reusing fillers in line ups shown to the same witness when showing a new suspect.

16. Review the array, once completed, to ensure that the suspect does not unduly stand out.

17. Assign each photo/person a line up identification number. Record the identification number on the back of each photo. Refer to that photo/person only by that number. The nature of the identification number should be purposely complex to the witness, so that any inadvertent glance should not significantly hinder the identification process or alert the witness as to the identity of the actual suspect. [Note: Some departments use the assigned case number and simply add a series of numbers and or letters at the beginning, end or in the middle of the case number. For example, with a case number such as 2005—12345, one could create ID numbers like A 2005—12345, or 2005—12345 B, or 2005—C—12345.]

18. After each photo/person has been assigned an identification number, record the number along with all other pertinent information on the Line up Identification Form.

19. Record the presentation order of each line up and ensure that a complete written record of the proceeding is made and retained. In addition, the photos themselves should be preserved in their original condition. For live line ups, a group photo should be taken of all persons in the line up together to illustrate size differences among the line up participants. This photo must not be shown to the witness, but will be included with the completed case file.

20. Remember that a defendant who has been charged with a crime

has a constitutional right to counsel for all proceedings that involve the defendant personally which follow that status.

21. Photo line ups need not consider right to counsel issues as they do
not involve the defendant personally.

22. Advise the accused that he may take any position in the live line
up that he prefers and may change positions prior to summoning a
new witness.

23. Ensure that witnesses are not permitted to see nor are they shown
any photographs of the accused immediately prior to the line up.

24. Ensure that not more than one witness views each line up at a
time and that they are not permitted to speak with one another
during line up proceedings.

Procedures: Conducting the Identification Procedure

1. The identification procedure should be conducted in a manner
that promotes the accuracy, reliability, fairness and objectivity of
the witness' identification. These steps are designed to ensure the
accuracy of identification or non-identification decisions.

2. Assure that all law enforcement and/or prosecutorial personnel
present and involved in the case are knowledgeable about the procedure so that they will not interfere or influence any witness during the process. Unnecessary personnel should be removed from
the location where the process is being conducted.

3. When presenting the line up, the person administering the line up
should use the approved standard instructions for witnesses prior
to the line up that the offender might or might not be among those
in the photo array or live line up, and therefore, the witness
should not feel compelled to make an identification.

4. Assure the witness prior to the line up that regardless of whether
an identification is made, the police will continue to investigate the
incident.

5. Instruct the witness that if the offender is seen in the line up, he/
she might not appear exactly the same as on the date of the incident because features such as clothing, head or facial hair can
change. Additionally, photos do not always depict the true complexion of a person, which might be lighter or darker than shown

in the photo. Be careful not to imply or lead the witness to believe that the suspect's appearance has actually changed in any way.

[Note: For example, saying to a witness that "The suspect's appearance could be different, for example if he has since gotten a tattoo," may imply to the witness that the police know the suspect got a tattoo. If uncertain about identity, this could lead the witness to pick out someone in the line-up with a tattoo simply for that reason.]

6. Provide the following additional viewing instructions to the witness:

   a. Individual photos/persons will be viewed one at a time.

   b. Photos/persons are in random order.

   c. Take as much time as needed in making a decision about each photo/person.

   d. All photos will be shown, even if an identification is made prior to viewing all photos.

   e. Confirm that the witness understands the nature of the sequential procedure.

   f. Instruct the witness that the procedure requires the investigator to ask the witness to state, in his/her own words, how certain he/she is of any identification.

   g. Present each photo to the witness separately, in a previously determined order, as documented on the line up worksheet, removing those previously shown.

   h. Care should be taken to avoid the witness turning over the photo and reading the identification number recorded on the back.

   i. Avoid saying anything to the witness that may influence the witness' selection.

   j. If an identification is made, avoid reporting or confirming to the witness any information regarding the individual he or she has selected, until the entire process (including all required signatures and paperwork) has been completed.

   k. If the witness requests to view the photo/person sequence again, (or specific photos/persons again), they may be shown a second time, but must be shown again in the same sequence in its entirety even if the witness makes an identification during this second showing.

l. Instruct the witness not to discuss the identification procedure or its results with other witnesses involved in the case and discourage contact with the media.

Procedures: Recording Identification Results

1. When conducting an identification procedure, the person administering the line up shall preserve the outcome of the procedure by documenting any identification or non-identification results obtained from the witness. A complete and accurate record of the outcome of the identification procedure is crucial. This record can be a critical document in the investigation and any subsequent court proceedings.
2. When documenting the identification procedure, the person administering the line up should record both identification and non-identification results, including the witness' own words.
3. Document in writing the photo line up procedures, including identification information and sources of all photos used, names of all persons present at the line up, and date and time of the identification procedure.
4. Ensure that the results are signed and dated by the witness and the person administering the line up.
5. Ensure that no materials indicating previous identification results are visible to the witness.
6. Ensure that the witness does not write on or mark any materials that will be used in other identification procedures.

Notes

NOTES TO THE ACKNOWLEDGMENTS

1. Jon B. Gould, "Florida Moves North: Electoral Reform in Virginia Post-2000," a Century Foundation Report (New York: Century Foundation, 2002). Available online at http://www.tcf.org/Publications/ElectionReform/va-gould.pdf (last accessed January 22, 2007).

2. Jon B. Gould, "It's Not Just for Law School Anymore: Clinical Education on the Death Penalty for Undergraduates," 53 *Journal of Legal Education* (2003): 615–634.

3. Jon B. Gould, "After Further Review: A New Wave of Innocence Commissions," 88 *Judicature* (2004): 126–131.

NOTES TO THE INTRODUCTION

1. See http://www.thefutoncritic.com/showatch.aspx?id=in_justice (last accessed November 2, 2006).

2. Ibid.

3. Tom Shales, "With 'In Justice,' ABC Is Guilty of Petty Theft," *Washington Post,* December 31, 2005, C1.

4. See theFutoncritic.com.

5. Samuel R. Gross, Kristen Jacoby, Daniel J. Matheson, Nicholas Montgomery, and Sujata Patil, "Exonerations in the United States 1989 through 2003," 95 *Journal of Criminal Law and Criminology* (2005): 523–560.

6. Thomas P. Sullivan. "Repair or Repeal: The Report of the Illinois Governor's Commission on Capital Punishment," *Champion* 26 (2002): 10.

7. Steve Weinberg, "A Short History of Exposing Misconduct," Center for Public Integrity. Available online at http://www.publicintegrity.org/pm/default.aspx?act=sidebarsb&aid=37 (last accessed June 13, 2006).

8. Thomas P. Sullivan, "Preventing Wrongful Convictions—A Current Report from Illinois," 52 *Drake Law Review* (2004): 606.

9. Joshua Marquis, "The Myth of Innocence," 95 *Journal of Criminal Law and Criminology* (2005): 501–521.

10. Margaret Edds, *An Expendable Man: The Near-Execution of Earl Washington, Jr.* (New York: New York University Press, 2003).

11. Editorial, "Delayed Justice for Earl Washington," *Virginian-Pilot,* May 10, 2006, B8.

12. At the time of this book's publication, that judgment was under appeal.

13. Barry C. Scheck and Peter J. Neufeld, "Toward the Formation of 'Innocence Commissions,'" 86 *Judicature* (2002): 98–105.

14. Arizona, Connecticut, Indiana, Maryland, Massachusetts, Nevada, and Pennsylvania.

15. Innocence Commission for Virginia, *A Vision for Justice: Report and Recommendations Regarding Wrongful Convictions in Virginia* (2005), xvii. Available online at http://www.icva.us (last accessed December 1, 2006).

16. According to a report by the New Jersey Supreme Court Special Committee on the Recordation of Custodial Interrogations, installing a covert audiovisual recording system in an interrogation room costs between $1,500 and $7,000. Available online at http://www.judiciary.state.nj.us/notices/reports/cook report.pdf (last accessed December 7, 2006). As with all electronic devices, these costs are likely to fall as the prices for the component parts drop.

17. Thomas P. Sullivan, "Electronic Recording of Custodial Interrogations: Everybody Wins," 95 *Journal of Criminal Law and Criminology* (2005): 1128.

18. Sharon Prather, "Lights, Camera, Confession," *St. Paul Pioneer Press,* July 17, 2006. Available online at http://www.nacdl.org/sl_docs.nsf/freeform/mandatory:018 (last accessed November 30, 2006).

19. Sullivan, "Electronic Recording of Custodial Interrogations," 1128.

NOTES TO CHAPTER 1

1. Richard A. Leo, "Rethinking the Study of Miscarriages of Justice: Developing a Criminology of Wrongful Conviction," 21 *Journal of Contemporary Criminal Justice* (2005): 202. Available online at http://www.deathpenaltyinfo .org/article.php?did=209&scid=23 (last accessed June 21, 2006).

2. Bruce P. Smith, "The History of Wrongful Execution," 56 *Hastings Law Journal* (2005): 1188–1189.

3. Ibid., 1189.

4. Steve Weinberg, "A Short History of Exposing Misconduct," Center for Public Integrity. Available online at http://www.publicintegrity.org/pm/default .aspx?act=sidebarsb&aid=37 (last accessed June 13, 2006).

5. Smith, "The History of Wrongful Execution," 1216.

6. Leo, "Rethinking the Study of Miscarriages of Justice," 203.

7. Ibid.

8. Weinberg, "A Short History of Exposing Misconduct."

9. Ibid.

10. Ibid.

11. David Margolick, "25 Wrongly Executed in the U.S., Study Finds," *New York Times,* November 14, 1985, A19.

12. Hugo Adam Bedau and Michael L. Radelet, "Miscarriages of Justice in Potentially Capital Cases," 40 *Stanford Law Review* (1987): 21.

13. See http://www.afsc.org/pwork/0499/049906.htm (last accessed June 9, 2006).

14. Ibid.

15. Stephen J. Markman and Paul G. Cassell, "Protecting the Innocent: A Response to the Bedau–Radelet Study," 41 *Stanford Law Review* (1988): 121.

16. Hugo Adam Bedau and Michael L. Radelet, "The Myth of Infallibility: A Reply to Markman and Cassell," 41 *Stanford Law Review* (1988): 161.

17. Michael L. Radelet, Hugo Adam Bedau, and Constance E. Putnam, *In Spite of Innocence: Erroneous Convictions in Capital Cases* (Boston: Northeastern University Press, 1992).

18. See http://www.afsc.org/pwork/0499/049906.htm (last accessed June 9, 2006).

19. Radelet, Bedau, and Putnam, *In Spite of Innocence,* 17.

20. C. Ronald Huff, Arye Rattner, and Edward Sagarin, *Convicted but Innocent: Wrongful Conviction and Public Policy* (Thousand Oaks, Calif.: Sage, 1996).

21. Richard A. Leo and Richard J. Ofshe, "The Consequences of False Confessions: Deprivations of Liberty and Miscarriages of Justice in the Age of Psychological Interrogation," 88 *Journal of Criminal Law and Criminology* (1998): 429.

22. Martin Yant, *Presumed Guilty: When Innocent People Are Wrongly Convicted* (Buffalo, N.Y.: Prometheus Books, 1991).

23. Leo, "Rethinking the Study of Miscarriages of Justice," 204.

24. For more information on DNA and DNA testing, consult http://www.innocenceproject.org/docs/IPDNA_WEB.pdf (last accessed June 21, 2006).

25. Ibid.

26. See http://www.cellsalive.com/cells/mitochon.htm (last accessed June 21, 2006).

27. See http://www.innocenceproject.org/docs/IPDNA_WEB.pdf (last accessed June 21, 2006).

28. See http://www.innocenceproject.org/docs/DNAExonerationFacts_WEB.pdf (last accessed June 21, 2006).

29. For a chart on state laws concerning DNA evidence, consult http://www.genelex.com/paternitytesting/paternitybook_appen.html (last accessed June 21, 2006).

30. See http://www.fbi.gov/hq/lab/codis/program.htm (last accessed June 21, 2006).

31. Ibid.

32. See http://www.law.northwestern.edu/depts/clinic/wrongful/exonerations/ Dotson.htm (last accessed June 21, 2006).

33. Edward Connors, Thomas Lundgrean, Neal Miller, and Tom McEwen, *Convicted by Juries, Exonerated by Science: Case Studies in the Use of DNA Evidence to Establish Innocence after Trial* (Washington, D.C.: U.S. Department of Justice, 1996).

34. Peter Neufeld and Barry Scheck, "Commentary." In Connors et al., *Convicted by Juries, Exonerated by Science,* xxviii.

35. See http://www.innocenceproject.org/about/ (last accessed June 21, 2006).

36. See http://www.innocenceproject.org/docs/DNAExonerationFacts_WEB .pdf (last accessed June 9, 2006).

37. Samuel R. Gross, Kristen Jacoby, Daniel J. Matheson, Nicholas Montgomery, and Sujata Patil, "Exonerations in the United States 1989 through 2003," 95 *Journal of Criminal Law and Criminology* (2005): 523–560.

38. *Kansas v. Marsh,* 165 L.Ed. 429 (2006), J. Scalia concurring, at 456.

39. Joshua Marquis, "The Innocent and the Shammed," *New York Times,* January 26, 2006, A23.

40. Dan Simon. "Are Wrongful Convictions Episodic or Epidemic?" Paper presented at the annual meeting of the Law and Society Association, July 2006.

41. Ibid.

42. Ibid.

43. For further discussion of this phenomenon, consult http://www.psychology .iastate.edu/faculty/gwells/The_pleading_effect.pdf (last accessed July 27, 2006).

44. According to Marquis, there were 15 million felony convictions between 1989 and 2003, or approximately 1 million per year. Two percent of this figure is 20,000 erroneous convictions.

45. Michael Welch, "Race and Social Class in the Examination of Punishment," in *Justice with Prejudice: Race and Criminal Justice in America,* edited by Michael J. Lynch and E. Britt Paterson (Guilderland, N.Y.: Harrow and Heston, 1996), 159.

46. Samuel Walker, Cassia Spohn, and Miriam DeLone, *The Color of Justice: Race, Ethnicity, and Crime in America* (Belmont, Calif.: Wadsworth, 2000).

47. John Lamberth, "Driving While Black: A Statistician Proves That Prejudice Still Rules the Road," *Washington Post,* August 16, 1998, C1.

48. *New Jersey v. Soto,* 734 A.2d 250, 360 (NJ Super. Ct. Law Div. (1996)).

49. Brigid Schulte, "Maryland Settles Lawsuit over Racial Profiling," *Washington Post,* April 3, 2003, B1.

50. See http://www.deathpenaltyinfo.org/article.php?did=1725 (last accessed June 21, 2006).

51. See http://www.deathpenaltyinfo.org/article.php?did=209&scid=23 (last accessed June 21, 2006).

52. Smith, "The History of Wrongful Execution," 1218.

53. The first of the exonerations chronicled by the ICVA took place in 1987, when Craig Bell was cleared of the murder of his fiancée. As described later in this chapter, it took until 2000 and the case of Earl Washington before wrongful convictions became a potent political issue in Virginia.

54. Much of this section comes from a report I wrote for the Century Foundation: Jon B. Gould, "Florida Moves North: Electoral Reform in Virginia Post-2000," a Century Foundation Report (2002). Available online at http://www.tcf.org/Publications/ElectionReform/va-gould.pdf (last accessed January 22, 2007).

55. Ibid.

56. Ibid.

57. See http://www.lva.lib.va.us/whoweare/exhibits/political/twentieth.htm (last accessed July 30, 2006).

58. Paul W. Keve, *The History of Corrections in Virginia* (Charlottesville: University of Virginia Press, 1986).

59. Alexander W. Pisciotta, review of *The History of Corrections in Virginia*, by Paul W. Keve, 33 *American Journal of Legal History* (1989): 165.

60. Ibid.

61. American Bar Association, Standing Committee on Legal Aid and Indigent Defendants, *A Comprehensive Review of Indigent Defense in Virginia* (2004). Available online at http://www.abanet.org/legalservices/downloads/sclaid/indigentdefense/va-report2004.pdf (last accessed July 10, 2006).

62. Ibid.

63. Each of the quotations in this paragraph is from Joe Jackson and June Arney, "Sentenced to Die without Fair Trials," *Virginian-Pilot,* June 26, 1994. Available online at http://scholar.lib.vt.edu/VA-news/VA-Pilot/issues/1994/940626/06270296.htm (last accessed June 9, 2006).

64. Ibid.

65. Ibid.

66. Ibid.

67. *Furman v. Georgia,* 408 U.S. 238 (1972).

68. *Gregg v. Georgia,* 428 U.S. 153 (1976).

69. See http://www.deathpenaltyinfo.org/article.php?scid=8&did=1110 (last accessed June 9, 2006).

70. Jackson and Arney, "Sentenced to Die without Fair Trials."

71. See http://www.insideout.org/documentaries/dna/thestories3.asp (last accessed June 9, 2006).

72. *Herrera v. Collins,* 506 U.S. 390 (1993).

73. Jackson and Arney, "Sentenced to Die without Fair Trials."

74. Ibid.

75. Samuel Walker, *Popular Justice: A History of American Criminal Justice* (New York: Oxford University Press, 1998).

76. Jeffrey Reinman, *The Rich Get Richer and the Poor Get Prison* (Needham Heights, Mass.: Allyn & Bacon, 2001), 1.

77. Katherine Beckett, *Making Crime Pay: Law and Order in Contemporary American Politics* (New York: Oxford University Press, 1997), 106.

78. Steven J. Rosenthal, review of *Making Crime Pay,* by Katherine Beckett, *Contemporary Sociology* 27 (1998): 307–308.

79. Sara Sun Beale, "Rethinking Federal Criminal Law: What's Law Got to Do with It? The Political, Social, Psychological and Other Non-Legal Factors Influencing the Development of (Federal) Criminal Law," 1 *Buffalo Criminal Law Review* (1997): 64.

80. Ibid., 24.

81. Ibid., 64–65.

82. Walker, *Popular Justice.*

83. *Mapp v. Ohio,* 367 U.S. 643 (1961).

84. *Miranda v. Arizona,* 384 U.S. 436 (1966).

85. *Gideon v. Wainwright,* 372 U.S. 335 (1963).

86. Indeed, the Kerner Commission, which was asked to investigate urban riots of African Americans between 1964 and 1968, concluded that "our nation is moving towards two societies, one black, one white—separate and unequal." Available online at http://historymatters.gmu.edu/d/6545/ (last accessed January 22, 2007).

87. Ted Gest, *Crime & Politics* (New York: Oxford University Press, 2001).

88. Walker, *Popular Justice.*

89. Robert H. Langworthy and John T. Whitehead, "Liberalism and Fear as Explanations of Punitiveness," 24 *Criminology* (1986): 575–591.

90. Steven F. Cohn, Steven E. Barkan, and William A. Halteman, "Punitive Attitudes toward Criminals: Racial Consensus or Racial Conflict?" *Social Problems* 38 (1991): 287.

91. Under a referendum passed by California voters, a defendant convicted of three felonies is subject to a mandatory, and severe, prison sentence.

92. Tom R. Tyler and Robert J. Boeckmann, "Three Strikes and You Are Out, but Why? The Psychology of Public Support for Punishing Rule Breakers," 31 *Law and Society Review* (1997): 237.

93. Walker, *Popular Justice,* 213.

94. Beckett, *Making Crime Pay,* 106.

95. Indeed, Samuel Walker has gone as far as to call this period an "imprisonment orgy." Walker, *Popular Justice,* 222.

96. Consider George H. W. Bush's 1988 campaign against Michael Dukakis, in which the victor pummeled Dukakis as being "soft on crime" for permitting prison furloughs. By 1996 it was the Democrat, Bill Clinton, who emphasized his passage of a crime bill that tightened sentences.

97. *Habeas corpus* is a separate legal claim that may be filed after exhaust-

ing all appeals in which an inmate challenges the constitutionality of his imprisonment. As such, habeas corpus tests only whether the petitioner has been accorded due process, not whether he is innocent. Since Washington's case, Virginia law has changed to provide for the appointment of counsel for indigent defendants in state habeas corpus proceedings. See Virginia Code Annotated § 19.2–163.7 (2003).

98. Jackson and Arney, "Sentenced to Die without Fair Trials."

99. Margaret Edds, *An Expendable Man: The Near-Execution of Earl Washington, Jr.* (New York: New York University Press, 2003), 196–197.

100. Tim McGlone, "Virginia High Court Proposes Dropping '21-Day Rule,'" *Virginian-Pilot,* October 14, 2000, B1.

101. See http://leg1.state.va.us/cgi-bin/legp504.exe?011+ful+CHAP0787 (last accessed June 15, 2006).

102. Christina Nuckols, "Gilmore Signs Bill Opening DNA Window," *Virginian-Pilot,* May 3, 2001, A1.

103. See http://www2.sbe.state.va.us/web_docs/election/results/2002/nov/ (last accessed June 15, 2006).

104. Rex Springston, "Evidence Proposal Relaxes Law," *Richmond Times-Dispatch,* November 16, 2000, A1.

105. Maria Sanminiatelli, "State Senator Will Propose Legislation to Bypass 21-Day Rule," *Associated Press,* November 15, 2000.

106. Laurence Hammack, "Death Penalty a Live Issue for General Assembly," *Roanoke Times,* February 4, 2001, A15.

107. Alan Cooper, "21-Day Rule May Be Eliminated," *Richmond Times-Dispatch,* November 5, 2002, A1.

108. See http://www.ppionline.org/ndol/ndol_ci.cfm?kaid=106&subid=122&contentid=251143 (last accessed June 15, 2006).

109. See http://dls.state.va.us/pubs/hilights/2004/welcome.htm#conam (last accessed June 15, 2006).

110. *Williams v. Taylor,* 529 U.S. 362 (2000).

111. *Atkins v. Smith,* 536 U.S. 304 (2002).

112. See http://www.deathpenaltyinfo.org/article.php?scid=9&did=188#state (last accessed June 9, 2006).

113. American Bar Association, *A Comprehensive Review of Indigent Defense in Virginia.*

114. See http://www.indigentdefense.virginia.gov/aboutus.htm (last accessed July 19, 2006). The Virginia Indigent Defense Commission is discussed at greater length in chapter 5.

115. Consider Donna Coker, "Addressing the Real World of Racial Injustice in the Criminal Justice System," 93 *Journal of Criminal Law and Criminology* (2003): 827–879.

116. In Georgia, the race of the victim was a predictor for death sentences.

In Philadelphia, the race of the defendant proved predictive as well. See David C. Baldus, George Woodworth, and Charles A. Pulaski, *Equal Justice and the Death Penalty: A Legal and Empirical Analysis* (Boston: Northeastern University Press, 1990); David C. Baldus, George Woodworth, David Zuckerman, Neil Alan Weiner, and Barbara Broffitt, "Racial Discrimination and the Death Penalty in the Post-Furman Era: An Empirical and Legal Overview, with Recent Findings from Philadelphia," 83 *Cornell Law Review* (1998): 1638–1770.

117. Samuel R. Gross and Robert Mauro, "Patterns of Death: An Analysis of Racial Disparities in Capital Sentencing and Homicide Victimization," 37 *Stanford Law Review* (1984): 27.

118. See the 2005 report of the Government Performance Project, which concluded, "There is little that Virginia does not do well in government management." Available online at http://results.gpponline.org/StateOverview.aspx?id=138 (last accessed July 24, 2006).

119. See http://www.ccrc.gov.uk/about/about_27.htm (last accessed June 13, 2006).

120. David Kyle, "Correcting Miscarriages of Justice: The Role of the Criminal Cases Review Commission," 52 *Drake Law Review* (2004): 657.

121. Ibid., 660.

122. See http://www.ccrc.gov.uk/about/about_27.htm.

123. Kyle, "Correcting Miscarriages of Justice," 666.

124. Barry C. Scheck and Peter J. Neufeld, "Toward the Formation of 'Innocence Commissions,'" 86 *Judicature* (2002): 100; Watson Sellar, "A Century of Commissions of Inquiry," 25 *Canadian Bar Review* (1947): 1.

125. Scheck and Neufeld, "Toward the Formation of 'Innocence Commissions,'" 100.

126. Richard J. Wolson and Aaron M. London, "The Structure, Operation, and Impact of Wrongful Conviction Inquiries: The Sophonow Inquiry as an Example of the Canadian Experience," 52 *Drake Law Review* (2004): 678.

127. Yant, *Presumed Guilty.*

128. David Horan, "The Innocence Commission: An Independent Review Board for Wrongful Convictions," 20 *Northern Illinois University Law Review* (2000): 95.

129. Ibid., 96–97.

130. Lissa Griffin, "The Correction of Wrongful Convictions: A Comparative Perspective," 16 *American University International Law Review* (2001): 1301.

131. Barry Scheck, Peter Neufeld, and Jim Dwyer, *Actual Innocence: When Justice Goes Wrong and How to Make It Right* (New York: Signet, 2001).

132. Scheck and Neufeld, "Toward the Formation of 'Innocence Commissions.'"

133. See http://www.ntsb.gov/Abt_NTSB/history.htm (last accessed June 15, 2006).

134. 49 USC 1112.

135. See http://www.ntsb.gov/Abt_NTSB/history.htm.

136. Linda T. Kohn, Janet M. Corrigan, and Molla S. Donaldson, eds., *To Err Is Human: Building a Safer Health System* (Washington, D.C.: National Academies Press, 2000), 269.

137. Ibid.

138. Ibid.

139. Samuel P. Harbison and Glenn Regehr, "Faculty and Resident Opinions Regarding the Role of Morbidity and Mortality Conference," *American Journal of Surgery* 177 (1999): 136–139. An easily accessible version of the results is David G. Jacobs, "Been There . . . Done That . . ." paper presented at the 2002 Congress of the American College of Surgeons. Available online at http://www.facs.org/education/congress2002/gs04jacobs.pdf (last accessed June 15, 2006).

140. The number of such errors made by the criminal justice system is highly controversial. Even taking the largest estimate offered by Bedau and Radelet, the number of innocent people arguably put to death is easily dwarfed by a single crash of a transatlantic jet.

141. More than eleven states have instituted committees or commissioned studies to evaluate the fairness of their criminal justice processes, particularly those that govern capital cases. In addition to Illinois and North Carolina, Arizona, California, Connecticut, Indiana, Maryland, Massachusetts, Nevada, Pennsylvania, and Wisconsin all had undertaken some form of inquiry.

142. Thomas P. Sullivan, "Repair or Repeal: The Report of the Illinois Governor's Commission on Capital Punishment" *Champion* 26 (2002): 10.

143. Weinberg, "A Short History of Exposing Misconduct."

144. Cable News Network, "Illinois Suspends Death Penalty," January 31, 2000. Available online at http://archives.cnn.com/2000/US/01/31/illinois.executions.02/ (last accessed July 18, 2006).

145. Thomas P. Sullivan, "Preventing Wrongful Convictions—A Current Report from Illinois," 52 *Drake Law Review* (2004): 606.

146. Paul Meincke, "Governor Ryan Grants Blanket Clemency for Death Row Inmates," WLS-TV, Chicago, January 11, 2003. Available online at http://abclocal.go.com/wls/story?section=News&id=160295 (last accessed July 18, 2006).

147. Christine C. Mumma, "The North Carolina Actual Innocence Commission: Uncommon Perspectives Joined by a Common Cause," 52 *Drake Law Review* (2004): 647–656. For additional information, consult http://www.innocenceproject.org/docs/NC_Innocence_Commission_Mission.html (last accessed June 13, 2006).

148. Mumma, "The North Carolina Actual Innocence Commission," 649–650.

149. According to Christine Mumma, the executive director of the North Carolina Actual Innocence Commission, the commission had seven original objectives: (1) to identify the most common causes of conviction of the innocent, both nationally and in North Carolina; (2) to educate members regarding each type of causation; (3) to provide a forum for an open and productive dialogue among commission members regarding each type of causation; (4) to identify current North Carolina procedures implicated by each type of causation; (5) to identify, through research, experts, and discussion, potential solutions in the form of procedural or process changes or educational opportunities for elimination of each type of causation; (6) to consider potential implantation plans, cost implications, and the impact on conviction of the guilty for each potential solution; and (7) to issue interim reports recommending solutions for each causation issue identified, including recommended implementation plans, cost implications, and potential impact on the conviction of the guilty. See Mumma, "The North Carolina Actual Innocence Commission."

150. Mumma, "The North Carolina Actual Innocence Commission," 653.

151. See http://www.law.duke.edu/innocencecenter/causes_and_remedies.html (last accessed July 18, 2006).

NOTES TO CHAPTER 2

1. *Burdine v. Johnson,* 231 F.3d 950 (5th Cir. 2000), *rev'd en banc,* 262 F.3d 336 (5th Cir. 2001), *cert. denied, Cockrell v. Burdine,* 2002 U.S. LEXIS 4179 (U.S. June 3, 2002).

2. Daniel J. Foley, "The Tennessee Court of Appeals: How Often It Corrects the Trial Courts—And Why," 68 *Tennessee Law Review* (2001): 557.

3. See http://www.innocenceproject.org/ (last accessed January 22, 2007).

4. Ray Long and Steve Mills, "Ryan to Review Death Row Cases," *Chicago Tribune,* March 3, 2002, A1. Professor Marshall is now on the faculty of Stanford University Law School.

5. The Death Penalty Information Center (DPIC) reported that, as of January 22, 2007, 1,060 defendants had been executed nationwide since reinstitution of the death penalty in 1976. See http://www.deathpenaltyinfo.org/article.php?scid=8&did=146 (last accessed January 22, 2007). During the same time period, 123 people were released from death row with evidence of their innocence. See http://www.deathpenaltyinfo.org/article.php?did=412&scid=6 (last accessed January 22, 2007).

6. ACLU Death Penalty Campaign. Available online at http://www.aclu.org/death-penalty/toolkit_pt3.html (last accessed August 19, 2002).

7. Probono.net, "About the Death Penalty." Available online at http://www

.probono.net/areas/about.cfm?Area_ID=7&geographic_area=NY (last accessed August 19, 2002).

8. ACLU Death Penalty Campaign.

9. Stephen B. Bright, "Neither Equal nor Just: The Rationing and Denial of Legal Services to the Poor When Life and Liberty Are at Stake," 1997 *Annual Survey of American Law* (1997): 834.

10. Christopher W. Carmichael, "An Argument on the Merits for More De-Paul Graduates in Federal Court Clerkships," 50 *DePaul Law Review* (2001): 1073.

11. University of Georgia School of Law Legal Aid & Defender Clinic. Information available online at http://www.uga.edu/legalaid/ (last accessed January 22, 2007).

12. See, for example, http://www.wcl.american.edu/clinical/criminal.cfm and http://www.law.georgetown.edu/clinics/cjc/index.html (last accessed May 30, 2006).

13. Indeed, as fine as the course, P416-Capital Punishment, may be at Indiana University, its syllabus says that students will "discuss the facts surrounding capital punishment, including its history, current practices, and the role of juries." See Indiana University, Department of Criminal Justice, http://www.indiana.edu/~crimjust/descriptions/P416.htm (last accessed August 19, 2002).

14. The report is available online at http://adj.gmu.edu/news/reporttitle_000.html and http://adj.gmu.edu/news/reporttotal.html (last accessed May 30, 2006).

15. For more information on Mr. Amolsch's practice, please consult http://www.dnadefense.com/ (last accessed May 30, 2006).

16. See http://www.wcl.american.edu/innocenceproject/ (last accessed May 30, 2006).

17. Ann Springer, "A History of NARAL," unpublished manuscript, Northwestern University School of Law, 2004.

18. John D. McCarthy and Mayer N. Zald, "Resource Mobilization Theory," in *Social Movements in an Organizational Society,* edited by Mayer N. Zald and John D. McCarthy (New Brunswick, N.J.: Transaction Books, 1987).

19. John W. Kingdon, *Agendas, Alternatives, and Public Policies* (New York: HarperCollins, 1995).

20. See http://www.greenmediatoolshed.org/training/IsYourGroupCommunicating/TheMediaDebate.adp (last accessed May 30, 2006).

21. Mancur Olson, *The Logic of Collective Action: Public Goods and the Theory of Groups* (Cambridge, Mass.: Harvard University Press, 1971).

22. See http://www.deathpenaltyinfo.org/article.php?did=209&scid=23 (last accessed June 21, 2006).

23. *Brown v. Board of Education,* 347 U.S. 483 (1954).

24. Barry C. Scheck and Peter J. Neufeld, "Toward the Formation of 'Innocence Commissions,'" 86 *Judicature* (2002): 98–105.

25. Marvin Zalman, "Cautionary Notes on Commission Recommendations: A Public Policy Approach to Wrongful Convictions," 41 *Criminal Law Bulletin* (2005): 169–194.

26. Keith A. Findley, "Learning from Our Mistakes: A Criminal Justice Commission to Study Wrongful Convictions," 38 *California Western Law Review* (2002): 339, 353.

27. Ibid., 353.

28. See http://www.wcl.american.edu/innocenceproject/ICVA/files/Beverly%20Monroe.pdf?rd=1 (last accessed June 5, 2006).

29. See http://www.truthinjustice.org/beverly-no-retrial.htm (last accessed June 5, 2006).

30. Under *Brady v. Maryland,* 373 U.S. 83 (1963), the courts will overturn a conviction if the prosecution fails to disclose exculpatory evidence to the defense.

31. We were further torn by the fact that Beverly Monroe's daughter, Katie, had recently been hired by the Constitution Project, one of the ICVA's sponsors. Katie, quite understandably, was convinced of her mother's innocence, as were many others in the steering committee. But we could not allow this connection to supersede the criteria we had established for the ICVA's cases. Although we assigned the case for investigation, the findings from the Monroe case did not become the basis for the ICVA's conclusions and recommendations.

32. Michelle Washington, "Hearing Could Re-implicate Man Freed by DNA," *Virginian-Pilot,* February 16, 2005, B2.

33. Virginia holds its elections for state offices in "odd" years, in this case 2005. By contrast, elections for federal representatives from Virginia are held in even years.

34. These and other news stories are available on the ICVA's website, http://www.icva.us.

NOTES TO CHAPTER 3

1. Richard A. Leo, "Rethinking the Study of Miscarriages of Justice: Developing a Criminology of Wrongful Conviction," 21 *Journal of Contemporary Criminal Justice* (2005): 207.

2. In truth, I'm a lawyer too, although I prefer to think of myself as a "recovering lawyer."

3. David R. Dow, "The End of Innocence," *New York Times,* June 16, 2006, A27.

4. American Lung Association, available online at http://www.lungusa.org/site/pp.asp?c=dvLUK9O0E&b=39853 (last accessed August 14, 2006).

5. Ontario Lung Association, available online at http://www.on.lung.ca/your lungs/lungcancer.html (last accessed August 14, 2006).

6. Unless otherwise noted, the material presented comes from the ICVA's investigation reports. Additional information is available on the ICVA's website at http://www.icva.us (last accessed March 6, 2006).

7. Margaret Edds, *An Expendable Man: The Near-Execution of Earl Washington, Jr.* (New York: New York University Press, 2003).

8. *Habeas corpus* is a separate legal claim that may be filed after exhausting all appeals in which an inmate challenges the constitutionality of his imprisonment. As such, habeas corpus tests only whether the petitioner has been accorded due process, not whether he or she is innocent. Since Washington's case, Virginia law has changed to provide for the appointment of counsel for indigent defendants in state habeas corpus proceedings. See Virginia Code Annotated § 19.2–163.7 (2003).

9. For the text of Governor Wilder's offer, see the PBS show *Frontline*, available online at http://www.pbs.org/wgbh/pages/frontline/shows/case/cases/washingtonclem.html (last accessed February 14, 2006).

10. The term is used half in jest at times by judicial observers, who have no other term to describe similar cases.

11. *Frontline.*

12. Since the time of the Washington case, the Virginia Division of Forensic Science has been elevated to department status and is now called the Virginia Department of Forensic Science.

13. Brooke Masters, "Missteps on Road to Injustice," *Washington Post*, November 30, 2000, A1.

14. See http://www.thejusticeproject.org/press/news-updates/compensation-awarded-to-earl.html (last accessed August 8, 2006); Maria Glod, "Former Death-Row Inmate Would Get $1.9 Million," *Washington Post*, March 28, 2007, B2.

15. See http://www.pbs.org/wgbh/pages/frontline/shows/burden/innocents/ (last accessed February 9, 2006).

16. Phone interview with Craig Bell, February 2006.

17. Ibid.

18. Sara L. Bensley, "A Report on the Case of Jeffrey David Cox" (2005): 5–6. Available online at http://www.icva.us (last accessed March 10, 2006).

19. Ibid., 7–8.

20. Ibid., 9.

21. Ibid., 11.

22. Ibid., 35.

23. Ibid., 33.

24. Ibid., 34, emphasis added.

25. Ibid., 36.

26. Ibid., 42.

27. Ibid., 43.

28. Brooke A. Masters, "New Evidence Overturns Virginia Murder Conviction," *Washington Post,* November 14, 2001, B1.

29. Robert E. Jordan III, Jamie B. Beaber, and Frank Cush Jr., "A Report on the Case of Russell Leroy Gray Prepared for the Innocence Commission for Virginia" (2005): 14. Available online at http://www.icva.us (last accessed March 6, 2006).

30. Joseph Williams, "City Man Pardoned after Three Years," *Richmond Times-Dispatch,* April 12, 1990, A16.

31. See http://www.dna.gov/case_studies/convicted_exonerated/honaker (last accessed March 6, 2006).

32. See http://www.criminaljustice.org/PUBLIC/INJUST/true0001.htm (last accessed March 6, 2006).

33. Ibid.

34. *Batson v. Kentucky,* 476 U.S. 79 (1986).

35. Seth A. Tucker, Matthew J. Watkins, and Stephen W. Rodger, "A Report on the Case of David Vasquez: Prepared for the Innocence Commission for Virginia" (2005): 3. Available online at http://www.icva.us (last accessed March 6, 2006).

36. Ibid., 4–5.

37. Ibid., 5–7.

38. Ibid., 9.

39. Ibid., 10.

40. Ibid., 13.

41. *North Carolina v. Alford,* 400 U.S. 25 (1970).

42. Tucker, Watkins, and Rodger, "A Report on the Case of David Vasquez," 20.

43. Ibid.

44. Ibid., 52.

45. Jane Luxton, Anne Ortmans, Melissa Shultz, Emily Sweet, and Melissa Brennan, "A Report on the Case of Troy Webb: Prepared for the Innocence Commission for Virginia" (2005): 3. Available online at http://www.icva.us (last accessed August 17, 2006).

46. Michelle J. Anderson, "Understanding Rape Shield Laws." Available online at http://www.vawnet.org/SexualViolence/PublicPolicy/RapeShield.pdf (last accessed August 16, 2006).

47. Michelle Washington, "State Court Dismisses Man's Request for Ruling of Innocence," *Virginian-Pilot,* November 3, 2005, B1.

48. Michelle Washington, "In Letter to Governor, Victim Opposes Pardon for Man Convicted, Exonerated," *Virginian-Pilot,* December 23, 2005, B5.

49. Michelle Washington, "Hearing Could Re-implicate Man Freed by DNA," *Virginian-Pilot,* February 16, 2005, B2.

50. Washington, "In Letter to Governor."

51. Ibid.

52. Consider some of the cases uncovered by the Ryan Commission in which officers of the Chicago Police Department are alleged to have beaten suspects into confessing. Available online at http://www.idoc.state.il.us/ccp/ccp/reports/commission_report/summary_recommendations.pdf (last accessed January 22, 2007).

53. As late as 1994, tobacco executives were testifying to this effect at congressional hearings. See http://stic.neu.edu/Nyc/nyc-complaint.htm (last accessed October 17, 2006).

54. See http://www.cdc.gov/TOBACCO/sgr/sgr_2004/consumerpiece/page2.htm (last accessed October 17, 2006).

55. *McCleskey v. Kemp*, 481 U.S. 279 (1987).

56. Ibid., 308, 312.

57. A law clerk from that term, Edward Lazarus, lambastes the justices in his book, *Closed Chambers: The First Eyewitness Account of the Epic Struggles inside the Supreme Court* (New York: Penguin Books, 1999). According to Lazarus, Baldus's findings left little explanation for the disparity in capital sentencing other than racial animus on the part of jurors or prosecutors.

58. For ease of presentation, the identification methods were shortened.

59. Of course, certainty is on a continuum, but for these purposes it is presented as a bivariate concept.

60. Leo, "Rethinking the Study of Miscarriages of Justice," 18.

61. Ibid., 13.

NOTES TO CHAPTER 4

1. Gary L. Wells and Elizabeth A. Olson, "Eyewitness Testimony," 54 *Annual Review of Psychology* (2003): 277–278.

2. *Neil v. Biggers*, 409 U.S. 188, 197 (1972), quoting *Simmons v. U.S.*, 390 U.S. 377, 384 (1968)).

3. *McCary v. Commonwealth*, 228 Va. 219 (1984).

4. *McCary v. Commonwealth*.

5. *Hairston v. Commonwealth*, 1995 Va. App. 173 (1995); *Chambers v. Commonwealth*, 1995 Va. App. Lexis 761 (1995).

6. *Curtis v. Commonwealth*, 396 S.E.2d 386 (Va. App. 1990).

7. *Rodríguez v. Commonwealth*, 20 Va. App. 122, 128 (1995).

8. *Wise v. Commonwealth*, 6 Va. App. 178, 189 (1988); *see also Graham v. Commonwealth*, 250 Va. 79 (Va. App. 1995).

9. Daniel Yarmey, "Eyewitness Identification: Guidelines and Recommendations for Identification Procedures in the United States and Canada," 44 *Cana-*

dian Psychology (2003): 181; Brian L. Cutler and Steven D. Penrod, *Mistaken Identification: The Eyewitness, Psychology, and the Law* (Cambridge: Cambridge University Press 1995).

10. Gary L. Wells and Donna M. Murray, "What Can Psychology Say about the *Neil vs. Biggers* Criteria for Judging Eyewitness Identification Accuracy?" *Journal of Applied Psychology* 68 (1983): 347.

11. Richard E. Nisbett and Timothy D. Wilson, "Telling More Than We Can Know: Verbal Reports on Mental Processes, *Psychology Review* 84 (1977): 231.

12. Wells and Murray, "What Can Psychology Say."

13. Ibid.

14. Ibid.

15. Wells and Murray, "What Can Psychology Say"; Gary L. Wells, "Verbal Descriptions of Faces from Memory: Are They Diagnostic of Identification Accuracy?" *Journal of Applied Psychology* 70 (1985): 619.

16. Wells and Murray, "What Can Psychology Say."

17. Gary L. Wells and Amy L. Bradfield, "Good, You Identified the Suspect: Feedback to Eyewitnesses Distorts Their Reports of the Witnessing Experience," *Journal of Applied Psychology* 83 (1998): 360; Gary L. Wells and Amy L. Bradfield, "Distortions in Eyewitnesses' Recollections: Can the Postidentification-Feedback Effect Be Moderated?" *Psychological Science* 10 (1999): 138.

18. Wells and Bradfield, "Good, You Identified the Suspect," 363.

19. Ibid., 366–367.

20. Ibid., 367.

21. Wells and Murray, "What Can Psychology Say."

22. Wells and Bradfield, "Distortions in Eyewitnesses' Recollections," 366–367.

23. Wells and Murray, "What Can Psychology Say."

24. Wells and Bradfield, "Distortions in Eyewitnesses' Recollections," 363.

25. Gary L. Wells, Mark Small, Steven Penrod, Roy S. Malpass, Solomon M. Fulero, and C. A. E. Brimacombe, "Eyewitness Identification Procedures: Recommendations for Lineups and Photospreads," 22 *Law and Human Behavior* (1998): 1; Gary L. Wells, "The Psychology of Line Up Identifications," *Journal of Applied Psychology* 14 (1984): 89.

26. Wells et al., "Eyewitness Identification Procedures."

27. Nancy M. Steblay et al., "Eyewitness Accuracy Rates in Sequential and Simultaneous Line Up Presentations: A Meta-Analytical Comparison," 25 *Law and Human Behavior* (2001): 459.

28. Virginia State Crime Commission, "Mistaken Eyewitness Identification: A Report to the Governor and General Assembly of Virginia," House Document no. 40 (Richmond: Virginia State Crime Commission, 2005).

29. Roy S. Malpass and Patricia G. Devine, "Eyewitness Identification: Line Up Instructions and the Absence of the Offender," *Journal of Applied Psychology* 66 (1981): 482–489; Nancy M. Steblay, "Social Influence in Eyewitness Recall: A Meta-Analytic Review of Line up Instruction Effects," 21 *Law and Human Behavior* (1977): 283.

30. National Institute of Justice, *Eyewitness Evidence: A Guide for Law Enforcement* (Washington, D.C.: U.S. Department of Justice,1999).

31. Expert testimony is admissible if the area of expertise to which the expert will testify is not within the range of the common experience of the jury. See *Coppola v. Commonwealth*, 220 Va. 243, 252 (1979), *cert. denied*, 444 U.S. 1103 (1980).

32. Barry Scheck, Peter Neufeld, and Jim Dwyer, *Actual Innocence: Five Days to Execution and Other Dispatches from the Wrongly Convicted* (New York: Doubleday, 2000); Samuel R. Gross, Kristen Jacoby, Daniel J. Matheson, Nicholas Montgomery, and Sujata Patil. "Exonerations in the United States 1989 through 2003," 95 *Journal of Criminal Law and Criminology* (2005): 523–560.

33. Gross et al., "Exonerations in the United States 1989 through 2003," 7–8. In regard to rape exonerations, 106 of 120 involved misidentifications.

34. C. A. Meissner and J.C. Brigham, "Thirty Years of Investigating Own-Race Bias in Memory for Faces: A Meta-Analysis," 7 *Psychology, Public Policy and Law* (2001): 3.

35. These studies of miscarriage of justice examined cases in which people were exonerated both before trial and after they were convicted.

36. Hugo Adams Bedau and Michael L. Radelet, "Miscarriages of Justice in Potentially Capital Cases," 40 *Stanford Law Review* (1987): 21–179; Edward Connors et al., *Convicted by Juries, Exonerated by Science: Case Studies in the Use of DNA Evidence to Establish Innocence after Trial*, research report for the U.S. Department of Justice (Washington, D.C.: U.S. Department of Justice, 1996); Scheck, Neufeld, and Dwyer, *Actual Innocence*, 262; Innocence Project, Case Profiles, available online at http://www.innocenceproject.org/case (last accessed February 7, 2005).

37. See *Washington Post* series "False Confessions," available online at http://www.washingtonpost.com/wp-dyn/metro/md/princegeorges/government/police/confess (last accessed February 7, 2005).

38. Wanda J. DeMarzo and Daniel de Vise, "Spotlight on False Confessions," *Miami Herald*, December 22, 2002. Available online at http://www.law-forensic.com/miami_herald_fc1.htm (last accessed January 19, 2007).

39. Saul Kassin and Katherine Neumann, "On the Power of Confession Evidence: An Experimental Test of the Fundamental Difference Hypothesis," 21 *Law and Human Behavior* (1997): 482.

40. *Miranda v. Arizona,* 384 U.S. 436 (1966).

41. *Brown v. Mississippi,* 297 U.S. 278 (1936).

42. *Miranda v. Arizona.*

43. *R.I. v. Innis,* 446 U.S. 291, 298 (1980).

44. *R.I. v. Innis,* 300.

45. Consider the factors cited in *Withrow v. Williams,* 507 U.S. 680, 693–94 (1993).

46. Ibid.

47. *Stephan v. State,* 711 P.2d. 1156, 1159 n.6 (Alaska 1985), quoting *Harris v. State,* 678 P.2d 397, 414 (Alaska App. 1984); *Davis v. State,* 438 P.2d 185, 194 (Wash. 1968); *Ashcraft v. Tennessee,* 322 U.S. 143, 152–53 (1944).

48. *Jackson v. Commonwealth,* 266 Va. 423, 438 (2003).

49. Stephen A. Drizin and Richard A. Leo, "The Problem of False Confessions in the Post-DNA World," 82 *North Carolina Law Review* (2004): 907–909.

50. Cathy Young, "Miranda Moras," *Reason* (April 2000). Available online at http://reason.com/0004/fe.cy.miranda.shtml (last accessed January 19, 2007).

51. Drizin and Leo, "The Problem of False Confessions in the Post-DNA World," 917–918.

52. Drizin and Leo, "The Problem of False Confessions in the Post-DNA World," citing Nathan Gordon and William Fleisher, *Effective Interviewing and Interrogation Techniques* (San Diego: Academic Press, 2001); Fred E. Inbau, John E. Reid, Joseph P. Buckley, and Brian C. Jayne, *Criminal Interrogation and Confession* (Gaithersburg, Md.: Aspen Publishers, 2001): 209–347; Richard J. Ofshe and Richard A. Leo, "Decision to Confess Falsely: Rational Choice and Irrational Action," 74 *University of Denver Law Review* (1997): 1002–1006 (1997).

53. Ofshe and Leo, "Decision to Confess Falsely," 985–986 (footnote omitted).

54. Gisli H. Gudjonsson, *The Psychology of Interrogations and Confessions: A Handbook* (Hoboken, N.J.: Wiley, 2003): 285; Paul Hourihan, "Earl Washington's Confession: Mental Retardation and the Law of Confessions," 81 *Virginia Law Review* (1995): 1491–1494.

55. Gudjonsson, *The Psychology of Interrogations and Confessions,* 57–74.

56. "Interrogation still takes place in privacy. Privacy results in secrecy and this in turn results in a gap in our knowledge as to what in fact goes on in the interrogation room." *Miranda v. Arizona,* 384 U.S. 436, 448 (1966).

57. Drizin and Leo, "The Problem of False Confessions in the Post-DNA World"; Inbau et al., *Criminal Interrogation and Confession*; Ofshe and Leo, "Decision to Confess Falsely."

58. Videotaping refers to either analogue or digital video technologies.

59. A defendant caught on camera legitimately confessing has fewer avenues

to challenge the case against him than if he can go to trial to try to undermine the confession.

60. Va. Code Ann. § 19.2–62.

61. Wanda J. DeMarzo and Daniel de Vise, "Experts Tape Police Interrogations," *Miami Herald,* December 24, 2002, A1.

62. These examples are based on the American Law Institute's Model Code of Pre-Arraignment Procedure.

63. For those law enforcement agencies that currently do not have videotape capabilities, identical sanctions should apply when police fail to audiotape custodial interrogations.

64. *Stephan v. State,* at 1162; *State v. Schroeder,* 560 N.W.2d 739, 740–41 (Minn. Ct. App. 1997); *State v. Miller,* 573 N.W.2d 661, 674–75 (Minn. 1998); *George v. State,* 836 P.2d 960, 962 (Alaska Ct. App. 1992); *Bodnar v. Anchorage,* No. A-7763, 2001 WL 1477922, at 2 (Alaska Ct. App. Nov. 21, 2001).

65. For more information, consult http://www.innocenceproject.org/causes (last accessed January 19, 2007).

66. Gross et al., "Exonerations in the United States 1989 through 2003."

67. Editorial, "Delayed Justice for Earl Washington," *Virginian-Pilot,* May 10, 2006, B8.

68. The police claimed that Washington admitted leaving a shirt behind at the crime scene, and the police found a shirt in the victim's home. But the jury never learned that police showed Washington the shirt during the interrogation and held it up while he "described" the shirt that he left at the scene.

69. Editorial, "Delayed Justice for Earl Washington."

70. The police apparently attempted to videotape one of these interrogations, but the equipment malfunctioned, and no audio of the questioning was recorded.

71. Telephone interview with Craig Bell, February 2006.

72. American Bar Association, "Report of the Post Conviction and Systematic Issues Subcommittee of the ABA Criminal Justice Section's Innocence Committee to Ensure the Integrity of the Criminal Justice Process," draft, 2003, 1–2.

73. *Kuhlmann v. Wilson,* 477 U.S. 436, 452 (1986).

74. *Kuhlmann v. Wilson,* 452–453 (footnotes and citations omitted).

75. Virginia Code Annotated, § 8.01–654.

76. *Lovitt v. Warden,* 585 S.E.2d 801, 827 (Va. 2003).

77. Moreover, a petition for a writ of habeas corpus must be filed with the Virginia courts within one year of the date the conviction became final. See Virginia Code Annotated, § 8.01–543(A)(2). Often, through no fault of the prisoner, the evidence of innocence does not become available for more than a year. In most of the cases that the ICVA reviewed, biological evidence of innocence became available more than a decade after the original conviction became final. In David Vasquez's case, several years elapsed between the date of his convic-

tion and the date that the actual perpetrator committed a similar crime that investigators were able to link to the crime for which Mr. Vasquez was imprisoned. In the four cases the ICVA investigated—Craig Bell, Jeffrey Cox, Russell Gray, and David Vasquez—that did not contain biological evidence of innocence, only in Bell's case was evidence of his innocence discovered within one year after his conviction became final.

78. In Craig Bell's case, the trial court vacated the conviction, even though it arguably had no jurisdiction to do so under Virginia Supreme Court Rule 1:1. In *In re Department of Corrections*, 222 Va. 454 (1981), the court held that a trial court had no jurisdiction to vacate a sentence more than twenty-one days after the date of the original order and that the Commonwealth's acquiescence could not reconfer jurisdiction.

79. Virginia Code Annotated, § 19.2–327.3.

80. Virginia Code Annotated, § 19.2–327.10.

81. Virginia Constitution, Article V § 12.

82. Virginia Code Annotated, § 53.1–229.

83. *Cherrix v. Braxton*, 131 F. Supp. 2d 756, 768 (E.D. Va. 2001).

84. *Ohio Adult Parole Auth. v. Woodard*, 523 U.S. 272, 275 (1998).

85. *Ohio v. Woodard*, 285.

86. *Royal v. Taylor*, 188 F.3d 239, 243 (4th Cir. 1999); *Cherrix v. Braxton*, 131 F. Supp. 2d 756, 767 (E.D. Va. 2001); *Michie's Jurisprudence of Virginia and West Virginia*, Pardon, Probation, and Parole, § 2.

87. For another investigation of clemency procedures nationwide, consider Michael Heise, "Mercy by the Numbers: An Empirical Analysis of Clemency and its Structure," 89 *Virginia Law Review* (2003): 239–310.

88. In some circumstances, the writ of innocence also is not available to prisoners who entered a plea of guilty and who rely on biological evidence. Virginia Code Annotated, § 19.2–327.1.

89. Virginia Code Annotated, § 19.2–327.3.

90. Virginia Code Annotated, § 19.2–327.10.

91. *Strickland v. Washington*, 466 U.S. 668 (1984).

92. *Strickland v. Washington*; *Lovitt v. Warden*, 266 Va. 216 (2003).

93. *Lovitt v. Warden*, 249 (citing *Strickland v. Washington*, 689).

94. Rule 1.7. Conflict of Interest, Virginia Rules of Professional Conduct, Supreme Court Rule, part 6, section II, 1.7 (2004).

95. Ibid., 7.

96. *Dowell v. Commonwealth*, 3 Va. App. 555, 560 (1987) (decided under Former Disciplinary Rule 5–105).

97. Data available online at http://www.innocenceproject.org/causes/index.php (last accessed January 20, 2007).

98. James S. Liebman, Jeffrey Fagan, and Valerie West, "A Broken System: Error Rates in Capital Cases, 1973–1995," Columbia Law School, Public Law

Research Paper no. 15 (June 12, 2000). Available online at http://www2.law .columbia.edu/instructionalservices/liebman (last accessed February 7, 2005).

99. Rule 1.7 states: "A lawyer shall not represent a client if the representation of that client may be materially limited by the lawyer's responsibilities to another client or to a third person . . . unless . . . the client consents after consultation."

100. American Bar Association, Standing Committee on Legal Aid and Indigent Defendants, "Principles of a Public Defense Delivery System" (Chicago: American Bar Association, February 2002); The Constitution Project, "Mandatory Justice: Eighteen Reforms to the Death Penalty" (Washington, D.C.: The Constitution Project, 2001).

101. ACLU of Virginia, "Broken Justice: The Death Penalty in Virginia" (Richmond: ACLU of Virginia, November 2003): 31–36 (focusing on quality of counsel issues in capital cases).

102. Spangenberg Group, "A Comprehensive Report of Indigent Defense in Virginia" (Chicago: American Bar Association, Standing Committee on Legal Aid and Indigent Defendants, June 2004).

103. West Virginia Indigent Defense Task Force Report (2000). Available online at http://www.wvpds.org (last accessed October 29, 2004). FY02 North Carolina Office of the Appellate Defender and Private Counsel Cost-Benefit Analysis (2003). Available online at http://www.aoc.state.nc.us/www/ids (last accessed October 29, 2004). Judicial Branch of Georgia, "Indigent Defense." Available online at http://www.georgiacourts.org/aoc/press/idc/idc.html (last accessed January 20, 2007).

104. Connors et al., *Convicted by Juries, Exonerated by Science*; consider also http://www.innocenceproject.org/causes/index.php (last accessed January 20, 2007).

105. Connors et al., *Convicted by Juries, Exonerated by Science*, 25.

106. Ibid., 15, 18.

107. Ibid., 15.

108. *Frye v. United States*, 293 F. 1013 (D.C. Cir. 1923). Originally governing evidence in federal courts, the *Frye* standard also became the controlling rule in forty-five states. See "Note," 40 *Ohio State Law Journal* (1979): 757, 769.

109. *Daubert v. Merrell Dow Pharmacies, Inc.*, 509 U.S. 579 (1993).

110. *O'Dell v. Commonwealth*, 234 Va. 672, 695–97 (1988) (declining to adopt *Frye* standard); *John v. Im*, 263 Va. 315 (2002) (leaving question of whether to apply *Daubert* analysis to future consideration).

111. *Spencer v. Commonwealth*, 240 Va. 78 (1990).

112. ABA Standards for Criminal Justice, *Providing Defense Services*, 3rd ed. (Washington, D.C.: American Bar Association, Criminal Justice Standards Committee, 1992).

113. *United States v. Wade,* 388 U.S. 218, 227–28 (1967); *Barefoot v. Estelle,* 463 U.S. 880, 898–99 (1983).

114. Spangenberg Group, "A Comprehensive Report of Indigent Defense in Virginia," 62 (nonmental health defense experts were authorized by the courts in less than 1 percent of the felony cases in fiscal year 2002). No data exist on the use of defense experts in privately retained cases in Virginia.

115. Spangenberg Group, "A Comprehensive Report of Indigent Defense in Virginia," 64.

116. L. S. Miller, "Procedural Bias in Forensic Science Examinations of Human Hair," 11 *Law and Human Behavior* (1987):157–158; E. Imwinkelried, "Forensic Hair Analysis: The Case against the Underemployment of Scientific Evidence," 39 *Washington and Lee Law Review* (1982): 41–44.

117. J. Peterson et al., *Crime Laboratory Proficiency Testing Research Program* (Washington, D.C.: U.S. Government Printing Office, 1978); Imwinkelried, "Forensic Hair Analysis," 44 (incorrect results involved those in which the wrong result was reached and those in which technicians provided incorrect analysis or explanations).

118. Miller, "Procedural Bias in Forensic Science Examinations of Human Hair," 160–161.

119. Connors et al., *Convicted by Juries, Exonerated by Science,* 15.

120. Ibid.

121. Andre A. Moenssens, "Symposium on Scientific Evidence: Foreword: Novel Scientific Evidence in Criminal Cases: Some Words of Caution," 84 *Journal of Criminal Law and Criminology* (1993): 13–14.

122. Among other reasons, the DNA testing could not establish when a person had been at the ATM.

123. Maurice Possley, Steve Mills, and Flynn McRoberts, "Scandal Touches Even Elite Labs," *Chicago Tribune,* October 21, 2004, A1. Virginia is not an exception. Consider the problems uncovered in the Houston Police Department's crime lab: "Hot Topic: HPD Crime Lab," *Houston Chronicle,* available online at http://www.chron.com/content/chronicle/special/03/crimelab/index.html (last accessed January 18, 2007).

124. John C. Tucker, *May God Have Mercy: A True Story of Crime and Punishment* (New York: Norton, 1997), 345.

125. Marvin Anderson was paroled but still continued to fight to clear his name. DNA testing helped him prove his innocence and receive a gubernatorial pardon.

126. Maria Glod and Michael D. Shear, "Testing Ordered on Old Va. Cases: DNA Work Affects Dozens of Inmates," *Washington Post,* October 1, 2004, B1.

127. Charlie Burnham, "Availability of Investigators to Court-Appointed Counsel in Virginia." Unpublished paper, George Mason University, 2006.

128. *Brady v. Maryland,* 373 U.S. 83 (1963).

129. *Strickler v. Greene,* 527 U.S. 263, 280–281 (1999), quoting *Kyles v. Whitley,* 514 U.S. 419, 433–434 (1995).

130. *Strickler v. Greene,* 281, quoting *Berger v. U.S.* 295 U.S. 78, 88 (1935).

131. *Spencer v. Commonwealth,* 385 S.E.2d 850 (Va. 1989), *cert. denied,* 493 U.S. 1093 (1990).

132. Rule 3A:11(b), Rules of the Virginia Supreme Court.

133. *Stover v. Commonwealth,* 211 Va. 789, 795 (1971), citing *Brady v. Maryland,* 373 U.S. 83 (1963); *Harrison v. Commonwealth,* 405 S.E.2d 854, 857 (Va. App. 1991).

134. *Watkins v. Commonwealth,* 331 S.E.2d 422 (Va. 1985), *cert. denied,* 475 U.S. 1099 (1986), *Lowe v. Commonwealth,* 239 S.E.2d 112 (Va. 1977), *cert. denied,* 435 U.S. 930 (1978). However, the Virginia rules require prosecutors to file witness subpoenas in the court file but do not provide sanctions for their failure to do so. Virginia Code Annotated § 19.2–267.

135. *Currie v. Commonwealth,* 391 S.E.2d 79 (1990); *Spencer v. Commonwealth,* No. 2207-0102, 2002 Va. App. LEXIS 604 (Va. App. Oct. 8, 2002) (accused not entitled to reports, interview documentation and internal documents of Child Protective Services in cases in which the defendant was alleged to have sexually abused a minor).

136. *Commonwealth v. Sellers,* 11 Va. Cir. 113, 1987 Va. Cir. LEXIS 171 (Oct. 20, 1987).

137. *Bellfield v. Commonwealth,* 208 S.E.2d 771, 774 (Va. 1974).

138. *Bellfield v. Commonwealth,* 771.

139. American Bar Association, Criminal Justice Section, "Criminal Justice Standards" (Chicago: American Bar Association, 1968).

140. Ibid.

141. The second edition of the standards can be found at http://www.abanet.org/crimjust/standards (last accessed February 7, 2005).

142. Ibid.

143. Alaska, Arizona, Connecticut, Hawaii, Idaho, Illinois, Maryland, Michigan, Minnesota, Missouri, New Hampshire, New Jersey, New Mexico, Ohio, Oklahoma, Oregon, Oklahoma, Pennsylvania, Rhode Island, Vermont, and Washington. See the ICVA Discovery Practices Chart online at http://www.icva.us (last accessed June 30, 2006).

144. In addition to the states listed in previous footnote, see also California, Florida, Maine, Montana, North Dakota, and Wisconsin.

145. Kansas, Kentucky, and Texas.

146. See the ICVA Discovery Practices Chart online at http://www.icva.us (last accessed June 30, 2006).

147. *Hall v. Commonwealth,* 403 S.E.2d. 362 (1991).

148. Social scientists refer to this concept as confirmatory bias, which is the tendency of researchers to "seek out or selectively pay attention to information that confirms what they already know or believe to be the case while ignoring or dismissing information that contradicts their theory." Randy Borum et. al., "Improving Clinical Judgment and Decision Making in Forensic Evaluation," 21 *Journal of Psychiatry and Law* (1993): 47–48.

149. Consider the crash of Eastern Airlines flight 401 on December 29, 1972. A summary of the NTSB's report can be found at http://www.ntsb.gov/ntsb/brief.asp?ev_id=66756&key=0 (last accessed August 16, 2006).

150. Joseph Williams, "Wrong Man behind Bars, Wilder Told," *Richmond Times-Dispatch,* April 11, 1990, A-6.

151. Daniel Medwed, "The Zeal Deal: Prosecutorial Resistant to Post-Conviction Claims of Innocence," 84 *Boston University Law Review* (2004): 125–183.

152. "The Inquiry Regarding Thomas Sophonow," Report and website produced by the Province of Manitoba, Canada. Available online at http://www.gov.mb.ca/justice/sophonow (last accessed January 22, 2007); Fred Kaufman, "The Commission on Proceedings Involving Guy Paul Morin," Ontario Ministry of the Attorney General (1998). Available online at http://www.attorneygeneral.jus.gov.on.ca/english/about/pubs/morin (last accessed January 22, 2007); Governor's Commission on Capital Punishment, "Report of the Governor's Commission on Capital Punishment," April 15, 2002; available online at http://www.idoc.state.il.us/ccp/ccp/reports/commission_report/summary_recommendations.pdf (last accessed January 22, 2007).

153. Kent Roach, "Wrongful Convictions and Criminal Procedure," 42 *Brandeis Law Journal* (Winter 2003/4): 349–369.

154. Voluntary pleas arguably do not present as grave a risk, although at least one of the eleven cases investigated by the ICVA presented the scenario of tunnel vision exacerbating a mistaken plea.

155. Jeffrey A. Segal and Harold J. Spaeth, *The Supreme Court and the Attitudinal Model Revisited* (Cambridge: Cambridge University Press, 2002).

156. Consider the case of Julius Ruffin, in which two integrated juries hung on his conviction but a third all-white jury quickly convicted him.

157. Interview with commentator on the Jeffrey Cox case. The commentator's identity is being kept confidential at this person's request.

158. Thomas P. Sullivan, "Preventing Wrongful Convictions—A Current Report from Illinois," 52 *Drake Law Review* (2004): 605–617.

159. Maggie Thornton, "Virginia Supreme Court Chief Justice Speaks at University," *Cavalier Daily,* April 27, 2006; available online at http://www.cavalierdaily.com/CVArticle.asp?ID=27035&pid=1443 (last accessed July 24, 2006).

160. Consider http://www.schoolfunding.info/states/state_by_state.php3 (last accessed August 11, 2006).

161. A fee cap for such a charge of $1,096, divided by the state's maximum hourly rate of $90, leaves a little more than twelve hours of attorney time.

NOTES TO CHAPTER 5

1. Samuel R. Gross, Kristen Jacoby, Daniel J. Matheson, Nicholas Montgomery, and Sujata Patil, "Exonerations in the United States 1989 through 2003," 95 *Journal of Criminal Law and Criminology* (2005): 523–560.

2. Virginians for Alternatives to the Death Penalty, *Equal Justice and Fair Play: An Assessment of the Capital Justice System in Virginia* (2006). Available online at http://vadp.org/reports/reports/equal-justice-and-fair-play.html (last accessed January 25, 2007).

3. Richard A. Leo, "Rethinking the Study of Miscarriages of Justice: Developing a Criminology of Wrongful Conviction," 21 *Journal of Contemporary Criminal Justice* (2005): 201–223.

4. Ibid., 207.

5. Michael L. Radelet, Hugo Adam Bedau, and Constance E. Putnam, *In Spite of Innocence* (Boston: Northeastern University Press, 1992), 278.

6. Ibid., 279.

7. Ibid.

8. David Kyle, "Correcting Miscarriages of Justice: The Role of the Criminal Cases Review Commission," 52 *Drake Law Review* (2004): 657.

9. Ibid.

10. The three called for postconviction DNA testing if there is a reasonable probability of exoneration; the adoption of NIJ's 1999 guidelines for eyewitness identifications; the vetting of "snitch" testimony by experienced prosecutors; the insulation of forensic labs from pressure by law enforcement officers; the replacement of "junk science," like hair comparison, with DNA testing; the creation of disciplinary committees to supervise and penalize wayward police officers and prosecutors; a rise in the fees for appointed defense attorneys; and the formation of state and federal innocence commissions like the CCRC in England, Wales, and Northern Ireland. See Barry Scheck, Peter Neufeld, and Jim Dwyer, *Actual Innocence: When Justice Goes Wrong and How to Make It Right* (New York: Signet, 2002), 351–357.

11. Thomas P. Sullivan, "Preventing Wrongful Convictions—A Current Report from Illinois," 52 *Drake Law Review* (2004): 605–617.

12. Ibid., 613.

13. Ibid., 605–617.

14. Ibid., 617.

15. American Bar Association, Criminal Justice Section, Ad Hoc Innocence Committee, *Achieving Justice: Freeing the Innocent, Convicting the Guilty* (Washington, D.C.: American Bar Association, 2006), xv–xxix.

16. See http://www.exonerated.org/index.php (last accessed August 3, 2006).

17. See http://www.whitehouse.gov/news/releases/2004/01/20040123-4.html (last accessed August 3, 2006).

18. See http://www.exonerated.org/compensation.php (last accessed August 3, 2006).

19. Steven A. Drizin and Marissa J. Reich, "Heeding the Lessons of History: The Need for Mandatory Recording of Police Interrogations to Accurately Assess the Reliability and Voluntariness of Confessions," 52 *Drake Law Review* (2004): 619.

20. Thomas P. Sullivan, "Electronic Recording of Custodial Interrogations: Everybody Wins," 95 *Journal of Criminal Law and Criminology* (2005): 1128–1130. Among the reasons that Sullivan cites, voluntary admissions and confessions become indisputable when recorded; unwarranted allegations of abusive conduct drop off; officers can focus more on a suspect's demeanor and nonverbal cues during interrogations, since they don't have to take notes; covert recording often captures a suspect's incriminating statements when officers are out of the room; officers can review the tape and follow up on leads; recordings prove useful in training new officers; and electronic recording improves public confidence in the criminal justice process.

21. Ibid., 1131.

22. Ibid., 1127.

23. Jeremy W. Peters, "Wrongful Conviction Prompts Detroit Police to Videotape Certain Interrogations," *New York Times*, April 11, 2006, A14.

24. The commission's report is available online at http://www.innocence project.org/docs/NC_Innocence_Commission_Identification.html (last accessed June 13, 2006).

25. Timothy S. Eckley, "Law versus Science and the Problem of Eyewitness Identification," 89 *Judicature* (2006): 230–232.

26. See http://www.ojp.usdoj.gov/nij/pubs-sum/188678.htm (last accessed August 3, 2006).

27. American Bar Association, *Achieving Justice*, 35.

28. Kate Zernike, "Questions Raised over New Trend in Police Line Ups," *New York Times*, April 19, 2006, A1.

29. David Feige, "Witnessing Guilt, Ignoring Innocence?" *New York Times*, June 6, 2006, A21.

30. Zernike, "Questions Raised."

31. Amy Klbuchar, Nancy K. Mehrkens Steblay, and Hilary Lindell Caligiuri, "Improving Eyewitness Identifications: Hennepin County's Blind Sequential Line Up Pilot Project," 4 *Cardozo Public Law, Policy and Ethics Journal* (2006): 381–413.

32. Zernike, "Questions Raised."

33. Virginia State Crime Commission, "Mistaken Eyewitness Identification:

A Report to the Governor and General Assembly of Virginia," House Document no. 40 (Richmond: Virginia State Crime Commission, 2005).

34. See http://www.dcjs.virginia.gov/cple/sampleDirectives/manual/rtf/2-39.rtf (last accessed July 20, 2006).

35. National Institute of Justice, *Eyewitness Evidence: A Guide for Law Enforcement* (1999). Available online at http://www.ncjrs.gov/pdffiles1/nij/178240.pdf (last accessed June 17, 2006).

36. See http://dls.state.va.us/pubs/hilights/2004/welcome.htm#conam (last accessed June 15, 2006).

37. Laurence Hammock, "State Appellate Court Rejects Carpitcher's Innocence Claim," *Roanoke Times,* January 25, 2006, A1.

38. Ibid.

39. Laurence Hammack, "Recanted Testimony Not Enough to Free Man," *Roanoke Times,* March 3, 2007, B6.

40. Frank Green, "DNA Test for Executed Man," *Richmond Times-Dispatch,* January 6, 2000, A1.

41. See http://www.centurionministries.org/ (last accessed July 28, 2006).

42. Green, "DNA Test for Executed Man."

43. Frank Green, "DNA Tests Prove Coleman's Guilt," *Richmond Times-Dispatch,* January 13, 2006, A1.

44. See http://www.centurionministries.org/cases.html (last accessed July 28, 2006).

45. Christina Nuckols, "Warner Commutes Killer's Death Sentence," *Virginian-Pilot,* November 30, 2005, A13.

46. Ibid.

47. Brooke Masters, "Missteps on Road to Injustice," *Washington Post,* November 30, 2000, A1.

48. Frank Green, "Justice Undone in 1982 Killing," *Richmond Times-Dispatch,* March 31, 2004, B1.

49. Masters, "Missteps on Road to Injustice."

50. Editorial, "Delayed Justice for Earl Washington," *Virginian-Pilot,* May 10, 2006, B8.

51. See http://www.thejusticeproject.org/press/news-updates/compensation-awarded-to-earl.html (last accessed August 8, 2006).

52. Editorial, "Delayed Justice for Earl Washington."

53. Maria Glod, "Former Death-Row Inmate Would Get $1.9 Million," *Washington Post,* March 28, 2007, B2.

54. Michelle Washington, "In Letter to Governor, Victim Opposes Pardon for Man Convicted, Exonerated," *Virginian-Pilot,* December 23, 2005, B5.

55. Ibid.

56. Michelle Washington, "Hearing Could Re-implicate Man Freed by DNA," *Virginian-Pilot,* February 15, 2005, B2.

57. Michelle Washington, "State Court Dismisses Man's Request for Ruling of Innocence," *Virginian-Pilot,* November 3, 2005, B1.

58. Ibid.

59. Michelle Washington, "DNA Testing Clears 2 More; Governor Wants Full Review," *Virginian-Pilot,* December 15, 2005, A1.

60. Editorial, "An Encouraging Report on State Lab," *Virginian-Pilot,* September 22, 2005, B8.

61. Innocence Project press release, "Historic Audit of Virginia Crime Lab Errors in Earl Washington, Jr.'s Capital Case" (2005). Available online at http://www.innocenceproject.org/docs/VA_Lab_Audit_Press.pdf (last accessed July 31, 2006).

62. Transmittal letter from Judge Robert J. Humphreys to Governor Mark Warner, summarizing DNA External Review Report. Available from the Virginia Department of Forensic Science online at http://www.dfs.virginia.gov/services/forensicBiology/externalReviewReport.pdf (last accessed July 31, 2006).

63. Ibid.

64. Ibid.

65. Christina Nuckols, "DNA Lab Review Finds Only One Major Error," *Virginian-Pilot,* September 17, 2005, B3.

66. Christina Nuckols, "Governor Appoints Panel to Oversee Virginia's Crime Lab," *Virginian-Pilot,* August 9, 2005, B3.

67. Ibid.

68. Virginia Indigent Defense Commission, http://www.indigentdefense.virgina.gov/requirements.htm (last accessed July 24, 2006).

69. Ibid.

70. See http://www.abanet.org/legalservices/sclaid/defender/brokenpromise/downloads/va.pdf (last accessed August 8, 2006).

71. American Bar Association, "Ten Principles of a Public Defense Delivery System" (2002). Available online at http://www.abanet.org/legalservices/downloads/sclaid/indigentdefense/tenprinciplesbooklet.pdf (last accessed August 8, 2006).

72. Joanmarie Ilaria Davoli, "The Soul of the Public Defender," 18 *Journal of the Virginia Trial Lawyers Association* (2006): 11.

73. Ibid., 17.

74. Robert J. Humphreys, "The State of Indigent Defense in Virginia," 18 *Journal of the Virginia Trial Lawyers Association* (2006): 8.

75. Tom Jackman, "Lawyers for Indigent Up for Pay Increase," *Washington Post,* March 4, 2007, C6.

76. California Commission on the Fair Administration of Justice, http://www.ccfaj.org/charge.html (last accessed September 25, 2006).

77. "California Legislature Adopts Measures Recommended by California Commission on the Fair Administration of Justice to Prevent Wrongful Convic-

tions," press release of the California Commission on the Fair Administration of Justice, September 1, 2006.

78. Bob Egelko, "California Legislature Approves Bills on Wrongful Convictions," *San Francisco Chronicle,* September 8, 2006, B3.

79. Office of the Governor of California, Veto message for SB 171, September 30, 2006. Available online at http://gov.ca.gov/pdf/press/sb_171_veto.pdf (last accessed October 3, 2006).

80. "Commission chair John Van de Kamp Response to Governor Arnold Schwarzenegger's Vetoes of Measures Recommended by California Commission on the Fair Administration of Justice to Prevent Wrongful Convictions," press release of the California Commission on the Fair Administration of Justice, October 2, 2006.

81. Office of the Governor of California, Veto message for SB 1544, September 30, 2006. Available online at http://gov.ca.gov/pdf/press/sb_1544_veto.pdf (last accessed October 3, 2006).

82. Fredric N. Tulsky, "Review of More Than 700 Appeals Finds Problems throughout the Justice System," *San Jose Mercury News,* January 22, 2006, A1.

83. Ibid.

84. See http://www.law.wisc.edu/facstaff/download.php?iID=211 (last accessed October 3, 2006).

85. See http://www.wislawjournal.com/archive/2005/0831/avery.html (last accessed October 3, 2006).

86. "If law enforcement authorities fail to record adult interrogations when recording is feasible, juries will be instructed that electronic recording is statewide policy and that they can consider the failure to record in evaluating the evidence." See http://www.law.wisc.edu/fjr/innocence/avery_taskforce.htm (last accessed October 3, 2006).

87. See http://www.doj.state.wi.us/dles/tns/EyewitnessPublic.pdf (last accessed October 3, 2006).

88. Ibid.

89. See www.law.wisc.edu/webshare/0210/commission_charter_statement.pdf (last accessed October 3, 2006).

90. "North Carolina Establishes Innocence Inquiry Commission," *Criminal Justice Newsletter,* October 1, 2006, 3.

91. See http://www.ccrc.gov.uk/about/about_27.htm (last accessed June 13, 2006).

92. "North Carolina Establishes Innocence Inquiry Commission,"

93. Ibid.

94. Ibid.

95. Ibid.

96. Ibid.

97. Although a number of groups deserve credit, special mention should go

to the Justice Project. See http://www.thejusticeproject.org/ (last accessed September 27, 2006).

98. See http://www.ojp.usdoj.gov/ovc/publications/factshts/justforall/welcome.html (last accessed September 27, 2006).

99. Death Penalty Information Center, "Summary: The Innocence Protection Act of 2004." Available online at http://www.deathpenaltyinfo.org/article.php?scid=40&did=1234 (last accessed July 24, 2006).

100. See http://www.thejusticeproject.org/national/ipa/ (last accessed September 27, 2006).

101. See http://www.whitehouse.gov/news/releases/2005/02/20050202-11.html (last accessed June 17, 2006).

102. Peter Baker, "Behind Bush's Bid to Save the Innocent," *Washington Post,* February 4, 2005, A9.

103. Frank R. Baumgartner and Bryan D. Jones, *Agendas and Instability in American Politics* (Chicago: University of Chicago Press, 1993), 16.

104. Ibid., 17.

105. Ibid.

106. Joshua Marquis, "The Myth of Innocence," 95 *Journal of Criminal Law and Criminology* (2005): 501–521.

107. Baumgartner and Jones, *Agendas and Instability in American Politics,* 26–27.

108. Matthew Eisley, "Lawyer Boosts Confidence in Convictions," *Raleigh News and Observer,* March 26, 2003, B1.

109. Ibid.

110. Katherine R. Kruse, "Instituting Innocence Reform: Wisconsin's New Governance Experiment," *Wisconsin Law Review* (2006):645–737, 713.

111. Keith A. Findley, "Learning from Our Mistakes: A Criminal Justice Commission to Study Wrongful Convictions," 38 *California Western Law Review* (2002): 337.

112. Jeffrey Reinman, *The Rich Get Richer and the Poor Get Prison* (Needham Heights, Mass.: Allyn & Bacon, 2001).

113. See http://www.jfa.net/ (last accessed October 10, 2006).

114. Nina Martin, "Innocence Lost," *San Francisco Magazine,* November 2004, 84–86.

115. David R. Dow, "The End of Innocence," *New York Times,* June 16, 2006, A27.

116. Findley, "Learning from Our Mistakes."

117. Ibid.

118. Editorial, "Final Verdict in on Roger Coleman," *Virginian-Pilot,* January 14, 2006, B8.

119. Kerry Dougherty, "Supporters of Dead Killer Can Eat Crow at DNA Result," *Virginian-Pilot,* January 14, 2006, B1.

120. Zernike, "Questions Raised over New Trend in Police Line Ups."

121. Consider Bryan Caplan, "Libertarianism against Economism: How Economists Misunderstand Voters, and Why Libertarians Should Care," unpublished paper, George Mason University, 2000. Available online at http://www.gmu.edu/departments/economics/bcaplan/selfir.doc (last accessed October 17, 2006).

122. Baumgartner and Jones, *Agendas and Instability in American Politics,* 18.

123. See http://www.nadcp.org/whatis/costoftreatment.html (last accessed October 11, 2006).

124. Humphreys, "The State of Indigent Defense in Virginia," 8.

125. Baumgartner and Jones, *Agendas and Instability in American Politics,* 20.

126. Sullivan, "Electronic Recording of Custodial Interrogations."

127. Interview with Judge Robert Humphreys, September 6, 2006.

128. Claudia Kalb, "Fixing America's Hospitals," *Newsweek,* October 16, 2006. Available online at http://www.msnbc.msn.com/id/15175919/site/newsweek/ (last accessed October 16, 2006).

129. Christina Nuckols, "The Death Penalty Is Hottest Topic," *Virginian-Pilot,* October 30, 2005, A1.

130. Christine C. Mumma, "The North Carolina Actual Innocence Commission: Uncommon Perspectives Joined by a Common Cause," 52 *Drake Law Review* (2004): 655.

131. I am largely persuaded that theoretically, capital punishment is acceptable for certain heinous crimes, but I remain deeply concerned about the uneven and imperfect application of this ultimate punishment.

132. Dow, "The End of Innocence."

133. Dow does not make this second point.

134. Marquis, "The Myth of Innocence."

135. Ibid.

136. Larry Marshall is a professor at Stanford Law School and former legal director for the Center on Wrongful Convictions at Northwestern University. He has made this argument to many audiences.

137. United States Constitution; see http://www.law.cornell.edu/constitution/constitution.preamble.html (last accessed October 12, 2006).

138. Marquis, "The Myth of Innocence."

139. William Shakespeare, *Hamlet,* act 3. Quotation available online at http://www.enotes.com/shakespeare-quotes/lady-doth-protest-too-much-methinks (last accessed January 24, 2007).

Index

About the Author

Jon B. Gould is an associate professor at George Mason University, where he is director of the Center for Justice, Law & Society. He is a former U.S. Supreme Court fellow and is the chair of the Innocence Commission for Virginia, a nonprofit, nonpartisan organization helping prevent wrongful convictions in Virginia.